CONFRONTING TERRORISM

NIJHOFF LAW SPECIALS

VOLUME 56

Netherlands Institute of International Relations 'Clingendael'

Confronting Terrorism
European Experiences, Threat Perceptions and Policies

Edited by

Marianne van Leeuwen

KLUWER LAW INTERNATIONAL
THE HAGUE / LONDON / NEW YORK

A C.I.P. Catalogue record for this book is available from the Library of Congress.

ISBN 90-411-1960-4

Published by Kluwer Law International,
P.O. Box 85889, 2508 CN The Hague, The Netherlands.
sales@kluwerlaw.com
http://www.kluwerlaw.com

Rebecca Solheim, Linguistic Editing
Kitty l'Ami, Lay-out

Printed on acid-free paper

Preface

Marianne van Leeuwen

This book is the product of a project on terrorism and counter-terrorism in Europe that was initiated by the Netherlands Institute of International Relations 'Clingendael' in The Hague in the early spring of 2001.

Twelve specialists have written for this book in a period when, even more than usual, claims were being made on their time, their attention and intellectual skills. I am truly grateful to them all for their willingness to participate and for sharing their knowledge and insights. Working with them has been a learning experience for me.

As editor, I am responsible for the overall concept of the work. Responsibility for opinions and interpretations presented in the individual chapters, however, rests with the authors.

The Netherlands Ministry of Foreign Affairs has very generously supported the Clingendael project financially. I have, moreover, benefited from the continuous encouragement and suggestions given by a number of the Ministry's staff members.

The Hague, Autumn 2002

Contents

1 Confronting Terrorism

Marianne van Leeuwen

The idea for this book was born in early spring 2001, when the Twin Towers of the World Trade Center in New York were still standing tall. At that time, terrorism was considered to be a major issue in only a few European countries, for the obvious reason that most countries, even those like Germany and Italy that had been shaken by repeated terrorist outrages in the 1970s and 1980s, had been spared terrorist attacks for quite some time. Only in Spain had the ETA become active again after a period of self-imposed rest, while in the United Kingdom, the threat of attacks by extremist splinter groups continued even as the difficult 'peace process' with the IRA was beginning to bear fruit. Perhaps as a consequence, relatively few European scholars felt inspired to write about terrorism. Veterans in the field had turned to different subjects, such as the study of juvenile crime in major cities.

In the United States, by contrast, concern about terrorism and political violence had risen during the 1990s, again for an obvious reason. Major attacks had been launched against American citizens, both on US soil (the first attack on New York's World Trade Center in 1993; the attack by Timothy McVeigh on the Murrah Federal Building in Oklahoma City in 1995) and abroad (attacks against US military personnel in Saudi Arabia in 1995 and 1996; attacks against the US embassies in Nairobi and Dar es Salaam in 1998; attack against the USS *Cole* in 2000). The Clinton administration had therefore placed the fight against terrorism prominently on its security agenda. After the attack in March 1995 by members of the Japanese AUM sect on the Tokyo metro, the administration took the threat of terrorist use of 'unconventional' (biological, chemical, nuclear and radiological) weapons particularly seriously and initiated studies to analyse terrorist threats, scan existing counter-terrorist policies, and propose countermeasures in case of 'catastrophic' attacks. Such initiatives were given bipartisan support in Congress. Substantial funds were allocated to programmes to improve the management of terrorist crises. American scholars also showed intense interest in issues of terrorism and counter-

M. van Leeuwen (ed.): *Confronting Terrorism*, pp. 1-9
© 2003 Kluwer Law International. Printed in the Netherlands.

terrorist policies, and particularly in catastrophic threats. As a consequence, literature on terrorism during the 1990s was dominated by American studies.

The original idea for this book was to provide more input of European expertise in the international public debate on terrorism by making a comparative study of a number of European countries, covering their recent experiences with terrorism (of a national and/or international nature), their threat perceptions, and the counter-terrorist policies that they were pursuing, as well as the causal links (or lack of them) between these three elements. Chapters were also planned on threat perceptions and policy-making in the European Union, and on European contributions to policy-making at the level of the United Nations.

Then came 11 September 2001. Arguably, the terrorist outrages of that day made most European experiences of the past ten years look pale. For a while at least, the attacks functioned as a great equalizer within Europe as far as threat perceptions were concerned. Public awareness of the pernicious potential of terrorism increased sharply, dramatically so in countries that had not had truly traumatic problems with terrorism on their own soil for some time. The attacks also triggered a re-evaluation by governments, parliaments and specialized organizations of threat perceptions and legislative, judicial and investigative policies to fight terrorism in many European countries as well as in the European Union. In New York, terrorist issues rose to urgent prominence on the agenda of the United Nations. EU member states actively participated in the decision-making processes in the UN.

In the light of these events, the outline of the book needed adjusting. In particular, the authors of the country studies were asked to analyse the effects of the attacks on two main issues raised in all the chapters: the evolution of threat perceptions; and changes in policy-making. The authors of the chapters dealing with the European Union and the United Nations also included relevant '11 September effects' in their chapters.

A Few Notes on Defining Terrorism: An Elusive Concept

It is standard procedure for studies on terrorism to start with the issue of definitions. Some readers may consider this issue tedious, but the tediousness does not detract from its relevance. I should like to stress that the following notes reflect my personal views. The authors in this book do not necessarily share my arguments, although I believe that many of them agree with most of my assumptions. They have not been asked to work with one 'consensus' definition, as that would have detracted from the authenticity of their arguments and complicated their analyses of the positions of various governmental positions. Readers are not left in the dark, however. Authors have commented on definitional matters in their chapters when they considered this necessary or useful.

I shall not try to add a definition of my own to the impressive collections already existing. I shall merely discuss a number of common and important difficulties in coming to grips with the concept of terrorism, partly by presenting some suggestions to discriminate between 'terrorism' on the one hand and various different forms of violence on the other.[1]

I argue here, first of all, that the concept of terrorism is essentially value ridden. It cannot be completely neutral. If this thesis is correct, then it is impossible to capture 'terrorism' in universally accepted laws and rules. Valiant attempts at breaking down the problem of definition into important components of the terrorist phenomenon have led, and may further lead, to impressive and much needed results, but sooner or later interpretative differences are bound to (re-)emerge. Thus, it will not be possible to define a universally accepted distinction between terrorists and freedom fighters trying to implement their right of self-determination. In the absence of universal consensus on the concept of 'terrorism', implementing a prohibition of membership of or support for a 'terrorist' organization will become subject to interpretative arguments. The debate within the EU on the status of the Kurdistan Workers Party is a point in case.

Motivations and Aims

Terrorists go into action because they want to change the political and/or social order. Radical religious aims are also to be categorized under this heading. Three major motivational trends may be discerned: nationalistic/ethnic, extreme left- or right-wing ideologies, and religious extremism. These trends may intertwine.

Terrorists are unable to realize their ambitions by peaceful means either because they are confronting a repressive enemy with superior power (a state) or because they are essentially unpopular, that is, not able to gather enough public support to win by democratic means through an electoral process. The two factors may go together.

There are some risks of 'definition pollution' in connection with terrorist aims. For example, terrorists may engage in ordinary criminal activities (robbery, drugs trade, arms trade, smuggling, extortion, etc.) in order to finance their 'political work', but their focus is on political ends, not on material gain. When material gain becomes their prime or even sole goal, terrorists turn into common criminals. Similarly, in cases when terrorists become so infatuated with violence that they terrorize for violence's sake rather than for a political or ideological purpose, they cease to be terrorists: they have become psychopaths. It should be noted that it can be quite difficult to decide whether certain terrorists have crossed the border and become ordinary criminals or psychopaths. The motivations to join a terrorist organization may differ from individual to individual even within one group, and may be quite complex – a mix of material, ideological and psychological elements. On the other hand, they may be unexpectedly trivial. Thus, in some parts of the world where employ is hard to obtain (such as in Sudan, Pakistan, Afghanistan and Egypt), joining a terrorist organization may mean an opportunity to get a reasonably paid 'regular' job.

---

1   Literature on the subject abounds. For brevity's sake, I mention two books that I have used in preparing for this chapter: Peter Waldmann, *Terrorismus: Provokation der Macht* (Munich: Gerling Akademie Verlag, 1998); and the somewhat older Alex P. Schmidt and Albert J. Jongman *et al.*, *Political Terrorism: A New Guide to Actors, Authors, Concepts, Data Bases, Theories and Literature* (Amsterdam, Oxford and New York: North-Holland Publishing Company, 1988).

Working Methods

Generally speaking, terrorists have an asymmetrical relationship with their enemy. That terrorists are capable of terrible bloodshed should not obscure the fact that terrorism essentially springs from weakness, not from strength. Terrorists are not able to raise armed forces to defeat the enemy in a regular or even guerrilla war. They usually go into action in an urban setting. They are unable to conquer territory, even for limited periods of time. Their strategy is to defeat the enemy through demoralization because military victories or conquest are outside their reach. This means they need a two-track multiplier effect. Their attacks must scare the enemy into demoralization and retreat, mainly by frightening civilians and undermining peoples' trust in the authorities, and at the same time stimulate public sympathy and support for their cause. Their attacks are essentially meant as a strategy of communication rather than an instrumental strategy. Terrorists do not kill because they want to eliminate a particular victim, but because they want their act of murder to send a message to two larger groups: their enemies (in order to demoralize them), and their potential sympathizers (in order to stimulate their active support). Therefore, terrorists have traditionally tried to have their views and ambitions publicized. They have been careful to be threatening but not to be overly violent in practice. Catastrophic attacks (see below) imply a breach of this rule, unless the chosen setting of the attack is clearly confined to enemy ground ('long distance terrorism'). This may be true of al-Qaeda tactics: they may wish to frighten 'the West', and to gain sympathy in 'the Islamic world' at the same time. Certain groups may practice both terrorist and guerrilla tactics, alternating these tactics in place or time. The al-Qaeda network has shown itself capable both of perpetrating terrorism (in Africa, in the United States, and elsewhere in the world) and of engaging simultaneously in irregular warfare (in Afghanistan, together with the Taliban).

Organizational Aspects

Terrorists are organized at sub-state level. They may cooperate with congenial groups elsewhere, and in that sense may be part of (an) international terrorist network(s). Modern means of communication (such as the internet and mobile telephones) have already facilitated international coordination in terrorist circles, stimulating the formation of geographically widespread and very decentralized all-channel networks. Terrorists may receive financial and logistical support from states with which they share common enemies, but they are not under their sponsors' control. In exceptional cases, patron-client roles may even be reversed. Terrorists may sponsor a state, put it on their payroll as it were, in exchange for a safe haven, training opportunities and so on. This was, for instance, reportedly the case in the relationship between al-Qaeda and the Sudanese government during the early 1990s.

There is another organizational aspect especially worth noting: some terrorist organizations have worked (or still work) closely together with charities and political parties. This has in particular been the case for groups with a nationalistic/ethnic agenda. Examples of such controversial twins abound, famous ones in Europe being the IRA and Sinn Fein, or the ETA and Batasuna (formerly Herri Batasuna).

Major interpretative differences have emerged in connection with the organizational aspects of terrorism:

(1) Probably the most contentious issue is the question of whether states can be categorized as terrorist. This issue has, for instance, bedevilled political debate in the United Nations, where some members have persistently argued that there are states deserving to be branded as 'terrorist' and have introduced the concept of 'state terrorism'. According to others, states that terrorize their own population, their neighbours or perhaps even people and governments at the other end of the globe, should not be categorized as terrorist, even if their deeds are particularly abhorrent, because it would overstretch any definition of terrorism and make it meaningless. If at all possible, the regimes in question should be forced to change their ways and preferably brought to justice. Justification for action against them (military, economic or legal) should be found in them having committed crimes against humanity, or war crimes, or genocide, or perhaps even in their being *sponsors* of terrorism (see below), but not under the heading of terrorism. According to this interpretation, hit men employed by a state to kill enemies or stimulate subversion should not be categorized as terrorists. They are, rather, to be seen as hired murderers or civil servants or soldiers – of a kind.

(2) One contentious issue highlighted after 11 September 2001 is whether 'regular' political parties or charities with terrorist affiliations should be placed on international lists of terrorist organizations, with all the legal consequences that this might entail. After all, the non-violent partner organizations may themselves function within the law of the land. Moreover, they may provide governments seeking diplomatic solutions for a terrorist problem with a conduit to their terrorist counterparts. It may be argued that governments engaged in the fight against terrorism work against their own best interests if, under a formal or informal prohibition of their own making, they cannot make use of these conduits. On the other hand: these 'regulars' frequently do provide terrorist organizations with essential financial or public relations support and thus act as sponsors.

State Sponsorship

State sponsorship of terrorism has become a particularly controversial issue after the 11 September attacks. Just after those fatal occurrences, the US president rhetorically divided the world into states that fight terrorism and states that do not, suggesting that the latter category consists of sponsors of terrorism. On several occasions, he directed very dire threats to a handful of countries that he dubbed the Axis of Evil. But the president put many other countries on warning as well. The relationship between terrorists and states, however, cannot always be painted so attractively simple in black and white.

Terrorists cannot work in a material or geographic vacuum. Consequently, there will always be *some kind of* relationship between states and terrorists. State authorities targeted by terrorists will try to put a stop to this threat, by prevention, repression or diplomacy. That much seems clear (white). States that are not targeted themselves may still try actively to counter terrorism, for instance by sharing relevant information with allies or by international diplomatic initiatives or by participating in military activity jointly with allies who have been hit by terrorists. But then the shades of grey appear. States may shelter terrorists unwittingly. Authorities of 'failed' states may be aware of terrorist presence but lack the means to put a stop to it. Governments may be aware of the presence of terrorists on their territory and physically capable of doing something about it but still decide not to do so. They may feel some sympathy for the terrorists' cause, or they may have no legal instruments to tackle their unwanted guests because these do nothing illegal during their stay, or they may fear adverse effects from aggressive counter-terrorist policies. The situation only becomes clear (black, in this case) again if a state actively supports a terrorist group or terrorist groups, by providing them with funds, weapons, training, housing, a safe haven and a base.

Putting a stop to state sponsorship of terrorism is an important element in a comprehensive counter-terrorist strategy, yet even the rough sketch of the range of state-terrorist relationships drawn above suggests that approaches will have to be tailor-made and flexible.

Catastrophic Terrorism

As this particular brand of terrorism has become an overwhelming theme in international debate and, more particularly, a major justification for the use of military means against terrorists, I briefly present its relevant elements.

First of all, catastrophic attacks are extremely murderous in intention. It is a matter of debate whether mass murder is the main purpose, or whether, more traditionally, the killings are a (particularly horrible) means to bring a message across. There is no doubt that terrorists leading catastrophic attacks know beforehand that they are going to kill numerous human beings. In addition, they may deliberately kill themselves in the process. In the case of terrorists with an apocalyptic agenda, committing indiscriminate mass murder fits the ideology. In other cases, including that of al-Qaeda, a motive to kill as many people as possible deliberately and indiscriminately is not so plausible, while the more traditional explanation – multiplying the impact of the intended message – does seem to make more sense. Yet another explanation may be that the terrorists consider themselves engaged in total war and aim to harm their enemy as painfully as possible.

Secondly, catastrophic attacks are commonly described as indiscriminate. Perpetrators indeed do not seem to care that they kill and even whom they kill, but until now their material targets have always had a clear symbolic meaning. Most – although not all – of the time, symbols of American military or economic power have been attacked. The list of attacks against American targets given earlier in the introduction clearly illustrates this. Until now, with the exception of Lockerbie in 1988, European countries have been spared catastrophic attacks – although it may be argued that the attacks on the Paris Metro of 1995 came close, at least in intention.

Thirdly, catastrophic terrorists seldom claim their deeds directly or make concrete demands of their opponents in direct connection with their attacks. They consider their enemy to be of fathomless immorality and in fact beneath contempt. This is not an enemy to negotiate with; he should be unconditionally defeated and possibly annihilated. It should be noted that the putative incarnation of this brand of terrorism, Osama bin Laden, has publicly explained his world view quite frequently, on Arabic and American television and on the internet. He has even suggested that he masterminded the 11

September attacks. It is quite likely that his messages have been aimed at Islamic listeners and viewers at least as much as at a western public.

Fourthly, concerns about terrorist use of nuclear, chemical, biological or radiological weapons are focused on catastrophic perpetrators. Incidents of terrorist use of unconventional weapons have until now been extremely small in number, but many American analysts in particular fear that catastrophic perpetrators will in the near future start to use unconventional weapons because of the massive lethal effects and because they are extremely 'scary'. Moreover, it is argued that access to such weapons has become easier over time. While al-Qaeda's interest in obtaining them has been documented, it should be noted that, on the one hand, mass destruction can be achieved by very simple conventional means (Stanley knives and aeroplanes are the terrifying example); and on the other hand, that it is incorrect indiscriminately to ascribe massively destructive effects to all unconventional weapons. Some may have a disruptive rather than destructive impact (which, of course, can be quite serious enough). Terrorists may indeed aim to use unconventional devices to cause massive disruption rather than massive destruction.

Policy-makers and Defining Terrorism

Aiming at clarity, scholars may agree on a working definition of terrorism. For practitioners of politics and security and intelligence services, on the other hand, the concept of terrorism may swell or shrink in scope and detail according to the political, bureaucratic or practical preferences of authorities and organizations as they defend their ideals and interests in policy-making forums or vie for public attention and support. Even within the governmental circles and specialized agencies of one country, definitions may vary. Important differences in outlook exist in concepts used by the security services of friendly states. This may hamper effective cooperation in the struggle against terrorism. On an international level, too, agreement has been difficult to reach. The United Nations have been striving for decades to produce internationally applicable legal instruments in the fight against international terrorism without being able to reach a comprehensive consensus definition of the evil they want to defeat. It will be especially important to see how the September 2001 attacks have influenced political debate on defining terrorism, since the outcome of those debates will be a decisive factor in policy-making. In many of this book's contributions, authors have shed their light on precisely these issues.

The Outline

As indicated above, the purpose of this book is to add to the volume of European expertise in the international public debate on terrorism, by making a comparative study of a number of countries in Europe, covering (1) their recent experiences with terrorism, (2) their threat perceptions and (3) the counter-terrorist policies that they have been pursuing, and the causal links (or lack of these) between these three elements. Authors were asked to deal with a set of identical questions in their chapters in order to optimize comparability. Specifically, the authors of the country studies were asked to present:

a) A very concise characterization of terrorist activity (both of national and international origin) per country, concentrating on the past ten years and indicating motivations, relevant organizational data, typology of attacks, 'seriousness' and persistence, and international ramifications, as a background to:

b) An analysis of present-day threat perceptions in government, the media and (if data are available) the general public,

c) An outline of the legal basis and organization of counter-terrorism per country. To what political bodies are security services and (special) police forces accountable?,

d) An outline per country of positions on international counter-terrorist cooperation,

e) General conclusions: author's suggestions for the improvement of counter-terrorist policies per country.

The countries selected were France, Germany, Greece, Ireland, Italy, the Netherlands, Spain, Sweden and the United Kingdom. The sequence in which the country chapters are presented in this book is not based on alphabetical order. It rather follows the combined criterion of severity and topicality of terrorist threats and experiences, starting with the most 'serious' cases. Thus, the United Kingdom and Spain come first, while the Netherlands and Sweden come last.

More countries could have been added, especially from the eastern part of the continent. This would certainly have made the survey more complete but also far more complex. It was felt that the variety in experiences, threat perceptions and policy solutions that would come out of a comparative analysis of the nine selected countries, all member states of the European Union, would be quite rich enough for one book. Limiting the study to EU countries had the additional advantage of facilitating a logically demarcated comparison of international counter-terrorist cooperation. On the issue of international cooperation, two overarching chapters were also included, one on threat perceptions and decision-making in the European Union and one on European input into the decision-making process in the United Nations. These two organizations were also selected out of a larger number of possible choices, including NATO and the OSCE. As the chosen focus was on legislative, judicial and investigative approaches rather than on military ones, the selection was considered justifiable. The authors of the chapters on the European Union and the United Nations were asked to focus on attempts within the EU and the UN to harmonize counter-terrorist policies in order to make them more effective. In this context, they have analysed how the organizations have struggled with the issue of defining terrorism.

As the authors had not yet started working on their contributions by 11 September 2001, there was time to adjust the project's outline to include the attacks' impact on threat perceptions and policy-making in Europe. The analysis of European policy-making in the country chapters and the chapter on the European Union had become if anything even more relevant than in the original outline. The urgency to find adequate, harmonized answers to terrorist threats was sharply felt in Brussels and would lead to new policy directives. While the American concern with catastrophic attacks had been vindicated in a horrible fashion, it was also true that European governments were now facing the important and politically sensitive task of considering whether, and if so, how, to adjust their standing anti-terrorism policies and perhaps even their constitutional rules to the new situation. They also had to decide how to deal with demands made by the United

States in the course of their efforts to build an international coalition against terrorism. Similar considerations became visible within the United Nations. In the world organization, the urgency was felt to find effective ways to fight terrorism while maintaining high standards of respect for human rights.

Undoubtedly, military actions against al-Qaeda terrorists and their Taliban sponsors in Afghanistan have been the most striking developments in counter-terrorist policies since 11 September 2001. Still, it was decided not to include an analysis of European contributions to the military actions against the Taliban and the decision-making preceding such contributions, as such an analysis would divert from the project's central objective. Authors were asked to focus on equally important, although perhaps less spectacular, issues such as changes in threat perceptions, issues of anti-terrorism legislation (its effectiveness and its relation to constitutional rights), the effectiveness of security services and the call for better cooperation between them on a national and international scale, and diplomacy and coalition building.

Throughout spring and early summer 2002, when the authors were finalizing their manuscripts, many new developments occurred concerning the issues discussed on the following pages. In order to protect authors and the editor from their natural inclination to update continuously, the arbitrary time limit of 1 August 2002 has been imposed on all chapters.

2 Policy Options and Priorities: British Perspectives

Clive Walker

Introduction

The Terrorism Act 2000 marked an important new phase in the laws against political violence within the United Kingdom. The Act established a more unified regime and brought about important modifications, with a greater emphasis upon international terrorism. In addition to the Terrorism Act, one of the official responses to the attacks of 11 September 2001 has been the Anti-terrorism, Crime and Security Act 2001, which allows for detention without trial as well as a host of policing and criminal law reforms. The laws against terrorism in the United Kingdom have been both extensive and, at times, extreme, to an extent that has triggered derogations from rights under the European Convention. This chapter will provide an analysis of the legal measures and will analyse their political backgrounds and practical implementation.

Terrorist Experience, Threat Perception and Policy-making

Experiences and Perceptions

The United Kingdom can claim with some assurance to have encountered more con-figurations and episodes of political violence than any other polity in the world. This thrasonical statement is founded upon two elements.

The first is historical and relates to the bygone days of the British Empire. Leaving aside the case of Ireland, which is detailed elsewhere in this book, notable anti-colonial campaigns of political violence were experienced in Palestine, Kenya, Malaysia, Cyprus

M. van Leeuwen (ed.): *Confronting Terrorism*, pp. 11-35
© 2003 Kluwer Law International. Printed in the Netherlands.

and Aden. The cumulative experience has shaped a significant part of British anti-terrorist policy-making in areas such as special powers and police/military relations.[1] In regard to special powers, the use of 'deep interrogation' (no longer an officially sanctioned technique)[2] and broad policing powers represent the progeny of those days.

The second element of experience of political violence arises from the persistent campaigns in Ireland against its incorporation within a predominantly British state over a period of more than three centuries. The severance of the Irish Free State (now the Irish Republic) in 1922 eventually focused the conflict upon Northern Ireland. The inventory of laws responding to this political violence is correspondingly substantial and prolonged. The current catalogue reacts primarily to the campaign of the Provisional Irish Republican Army from 1970 onwards. In the early days of the campaign in Northern Ireland, there was a distinctly militaristic approach that was shaped by previous colonial conflicts. Nevertheless, the emphasis upon a military strategy became at best distasteful and at worst shameful in the light of the internment without trial and torture of detainees and lethal confrontations such as Bloody Sunday in 1972. Therefore, in line with the assumption of responsibility by the UK government pursuant to 'Direct Rule' after March 1972, a review was quickly undertaken by Lord Diplock.[3] His report formed the basis for the wide-ranging Northern Ireland (Emergency Provisions) Acts 1973-98, which included special criminal processes (including non-jury trials), a host of special policing powers and the possibility (not in fact implemented since 1975) of internment without trial.[4] However, it was not until 1975 that the Royal Ulster Constabulary (RUC), after a lengthy process of reform and reinforcement, was able to resume primacy in security affairs.

Given that between 1966 and 1999 3,636 deaths occurred in Northern Ireland related to political violence[5] and that the Provisional IRA is widely considered to be the most proficient exponent of political violence in western Europe, some kind of legislative response is not surprising. Even in Great Britain, where the equivalent figure for fatalities is 121,[6] there has been a Prevention of Terrorism (Temporary Provisions) Act in continuous use from 1974 until 2000, while its predecessor, the Prevention of Violence Act 1939, endured until 1954.[7] The first version of the Prevention of Terrorism Act (the last was issued in 1989) was a swift response to the deaths in the Birmingham pub bombings carried out by the Provisional IRA in November 1974. The Criminal Justice (Terrorism and Conspiracy) Act 1998 likewise was the rejoinder to the outrage of those Republican dissidents (entitled the Real IRA) who perpetrated the Omagh bombing in August 1998.

---

1   See F. Kitson, *Low-Intensity Operations* (London: Faber and Faber, 1971).
2   *Ireland* v. *UK*, App. no. 5310/71, Ser. A No. 25; 2 E.H.R.R. 25.
3   *Report of the Commission to consider Legal Procedures to Deal with Terrorist Activities in Northern Ireland*, Cmnd. 5185 (London: 1972).
4   See G. Hogan and C. Walker, *Political Violence and the Law in Ireland* (Manchester: Manchester University Press, 1989); and L.K. Donoghue, *Counter-Terrorism Law* (Dublin: Irish Academic Press, 2001).
5   D. McKittrick, S. Kelters, B. Feeney and C. Thornton, *Lost Lives* (Edinburgh: Mainstream, 1999).
6   Home Office and Northern Ireland Office, *Legislation against Terrorism*, Cm.4178 (London: 1998), para. 2.2.
7   See C.P. Walker, *The Prevention of Terrorism in British Law* (Manchester: Manchester University Press, 1992).

These anti-terrorist codes had taken on an air of permanence by the end of the 1990s, not only because of the longevity of Irish irredentism but also because, during the 1980s, the Prevention of Terrorism Acts were extended following a report by Lord Jellicoe in 1983 to encompass terrorism from international (foreign) sources.[8] The targeting of foreign terrorism arose partly in response to overt incidents (such as attacks on Israeli targets by Palestinian groups and by Sikh groups on Indian targets) and also partly out of the concern that Britain was becoming a base for fund-raising and laundering and for organizational and propaganda activities, to the annoyance of several foreign governments, notably Egypt and Saudi Arabia.

The interplay between experience, threat perception and policy-making became relatively settled by the mid-1990s after 25 years of campaigning by the Provisional IRA. However, two factors have since triggered a major reorientation. The first was the calling of a ceasefire by the Provisional IRA, later replicated by most other Irish terrorist groups. The ceasefire was first called in 1994, broke down in 1996 but has been reasserted since 20 July 1997. One of the implications for counter-terrorism laws was to call into question the derogation under Article 15 of the European Convention issued in December 1988 concerning powers of police detention.[9] There was also a political impetus towards an inspection of the legislation, as 'demilitarization' was a demand on both sides. It was a condition of the 'Peace Process' in Northern Ireland pursuant to the Belfast Agreement signed on Good Friday 1998[10] that security matters should be reviewed, and a review was also a crucial part of the arrangements for the decommissioning of terrorist weapons.[11] However, Irish terrorism is considered to remain a substantial threat, even if the 'hot' political terrorism has been replaced by a 'colder' version in which paramilitary punishment attacks, logistical preparations and pervasive racketeering and extortion remain to the fore.[12] The Provisional IRA's 'sincere apologies and condolences' for the deaths of 'non-combatants',[13] such as were killed in the 'Bloody Friday' attacks in 1972, represent a rather bounded degree of repentance and contain no promise as to the termination of paramilitary activities.

As a result of these developments, a general review of counter-terrorism laws was produced in 1996 by Lord Lloyd assisted by Mr Justice Kerr (both senior judicial figures).[14] The government's broadly supportive response[15] appeared in 1998. The impetus towards reform was given further impetus by the passage of the Human Rights Act 1998, incorporating large parts of the articles of the European Convention on Human

---

8   *Report of the Operation of the Prevention of Terrorism (Temporary Provisions) Act 1976*, Cmnd. 8803 (London: 1983); see C.P. Walker, 'The Jellicoe Report on the Prevention of Terrorism (Temporary Provisions) Act 1976', *Modern Law Review*, 46, 1983, p. 484; C.P. Walker, 'Prevention of Terrorism (Temporary Provisions) Act 1984', *Modern Law Review*, 47, 1984, p. 704; B. Dickson, 'The Prevention of Terrorism (Temporary Provisions) Act 1989', *Northern Ireland Legal Quarterly*, 40, 1989, p. 592.

9   *Brogan v. UK*, Application nos. 11209, 11234, 11266/84, 11386/85, Ser. A. No. 145-B (1989) 11 E.H.R.R. 539; *Brannigan & McBride v. UK*, App. nos. 14553/89, 14554/89, Ser. A vol. 258-B (1994) 17 E.H.R.R. 539.

10 British-Irish Agreement reached in the multi-party negotiations, Cm. 3883 (London: 1998).

11 *Report of the International Body on Decommissioning*, http://www.britainUSA.com/nireland/law&order.asp (London: 1996), para. 53.

12 Northern Ireland Select Committee, *The Financing of Terrorism in Northern Ireland* (2001-02 HC 978).

13 *The Times*, 17 July 2002, p. 1.

14 *Inquiry into Legislation against Terrorism*, Cm. 3420 (London: 1996).

15 *Legislation Against Terrorism*, Cm. 4178 (London: 1998).

Rights and Fundamental Freedoms into UK law. However, aside from the amendment of the measures that necessitated the derogation under Article 15, no other radical changes can be attributed to this influence.[16]

Drawing to a conclusion the reform process resulting from this first phase was the Terrorism Act 2000, which came into force in February 2001 and allowed the removal of the derogation notice.[17] The Act provides a substantial code of measures for Britain and Northern Ireland and therefore deals with both Irish and foreign terrorism. Two features are noteworthy. One is that it is permanent legislation (with the exception of a subset of special powers for Northern Ireland under Part VII; the view has been taken that it will be a very slow haul to eradicate paramilitarism in Northern Ireland). Equally, the causes of international terrorism are manifold and the UK state cannot alone hope either to eradicate them or to be immune from their emanations. The second notable feature is that the legislation has been extended to all forms of terrorism, which means that 'domestic' terrorism – terrorism arising from causes within Great Britain – has become the subject of legislation for the first time. This advance should be seen as largely precautionary, for no such terrorism – whether Scottish or Welsh nationalism or single-issue movements relating to animal rights, abortion, globalization, immigration or otherwise – has made a major impact.[18]

The new definition of 'terrorism' which allows this extended purview is set out in section 1 of the Terrorism Act:

'(1) In this Act "terrorism" means the use or threat of action where
(a) the action falls within subsection (2),
(b) the use or threat is designed to influence the government or to intimidate the public or a section of the public, and
(c) the use or threat is made for the purpose of advancing a political, religious or ideological cause.
(2) Action falls within this subsection if it
(a) involves serious violence against a person,
(b) involves serious damage to property,
(c) endangers a person's life, other than that of the person committing the action,
(d) creates a serious risk to the health or safety of the public or a section of the public, or
(e) is designed seriously to interfere with or seriously to disrupt an electronic system.
(3) The use or threat of action falling within subsection (2) which involves the use of firearms or explosives is terrorism whether or not subsection (1)(b) is satisfied.
(4) In this section
(a) "action" includes action outside the United Kingdom,
(b) a reference to any person or to property is a reference to any person, or to property, wherever situated,

---

16   See C. Gearty, 'Terrorism and Human Rights', *Legal Studies*, 19, 1999, at p. 379.
17   See J.J. Rowe, 'The Terrorism Act 2000', *Criminal Law Review*, 2000, p. 527; C. Walker, *Blackstone's Guide to the Anti-Terrorism Legislation* (Oxford: Oxford University Press, 2002).
18   See *Inquiry into Legislation against Terrorism*, Cm. 3420 (London: 1996), para. 1.24; Home Office and Northern Ireland Office, *Legislation against Terrorism*, Cm.4178 (London: 1998), para. 3.10; M. Taylor and J. Horgan, 'Future Developments of Political Terrorism in Europe', *Terrorism and Political Violence*, 11(4), 1999, p. 83; and R. Monagahan, 'Terrorism in the Name of Animal Rights', *Terrorism and Political Violence*, 11(4), 1999, p. 159.

(c) a reference to the public includes a reference to the public of a country other than the United Kingdom, and

(d) "the government" means the government of the United Kingdom, of a Part of the United Kingdom or of a country other than the United Kingdom.

(5) In this Act a reference to action taken for the purposes of terrorism includes a reference to action taken for the benefit of a proscribed organization.'

The essence is in section 1(1), which contains three conjunctive legs, all of which must normally be satisfied (subject to section 1(3), as described below). In part, the definition is intentionally broad, as it serves as the platform for investigative police powers where there must be some margin of error. It is conversely not a term on which a criminal offence is based.[19] Overall, it is submitted that the changes in the terms of the *definition* are not, with one exception, tremendously significant. That exception relates to the inclusion of section 1(2)(e), which is designed to take account of cyber-terrorism.[20] Rather, it is the circumstance of how it is then applied later in the Terrorism Act – the *remit* – which is remarkable. The remit has been uncoupled from its historical grounding in the Irish conflict and so raises the possibility of the disproportionate use of draconian provisions in circumstances where ordinary policing and laws could cope with isolated or incompetent terrorists. Neither aspect is very satisfactory. In terms of *definition*, relevant measures should instead be designed around a combination of the types of seriously threatening and destabilizing offences being perpetrated; and, in terms of *remit*, the nature of the collectives that carry them out and that render less capable normal criminal justice processes. In this way, the emphasis should be upon severe and collective political violence, rather than terrorism per se. Consequently, if the legislation is too disestablished from its Irish grounding in this way, then one ought to seek further qualifications to ensure that special powers really are a necessary and proportionate response.

The second ingredient in the recent reorientation of the UK's anti-terrorism laws concerns the events of 11 September 2001. The catastrophic attacks and mass deaths that occurred in New York, Washington DC and Pennsylvania undoubtedly shook to their core the political classes of the United States and resulted in terrified and blundering denials of constitutional rights, unmatched since the eras of the World Wars. Yet it is more surprising that there should have been so strong a reaction in the United Kingdom. After all, the attacks were not perpetrated against UK targets as such, although it is estimated that around 67 British citizens died in New York. It is also the case that the United Kingdom already had newly formulated laws against international terrorism as well as a formidable security apparatus honed by Irish campaigns. But counteraction there has been, and it is explained by three motivations.

---

19   House of Commons Debates, vol. 346, col. 410, 15 March 2000, Charles Clarke.

20   See R.E. Stephens, 'Cyber-biotech Terrorism', in H.W. Kushner, *The Future of Terrorism* (Thousand Oaks: Sage, 1998); D.E. Denning, *Information Warfare and Security* (New York: ACM Press, Addison-Wesley, 1999); L. Valeri and M. Knights, 'Affecting Trust: Terrorism, Internet and Offensive Information Warfare', *Terrorism and Political Violence*, 12(1), 2000, p. 15; J.M. Post, K.G. Ruby and E.D. Shaw, 'From Car Bombs to Logic Bombs', *Terrorism and Political Violence*, 12(2), 2000, p. 97; V. Mitliaga, 'Cyberterrorism', *Legal Executive*, February 2002, p. 4;
and Infowar.com, http://www.infowar.com/class_3/class_3.shtml.

The first is that there was a growing analysis that the nature of terrorism was changing and that even recent reviews had failed to capture adequately some of the trends. The nature and scale of the attacks on 11 September 2001 conduced to an explication that terrorism had developed a 'Third Millennium' format, characterized by a multifaceted threat, unbounded by instrument, organization or location, and motivated by religious and cultural ideals rather than rooted in national self-determination or a particular political ideology.[21] That change was personified by the al-Qaeda group, functioning as part of the 'network of networks' that is the World Islamic Front, of which al-Qaeda is the most prominent component.

It was realized in the United Kingdom even before 11 September 2001 that a new threat was emerging,[22] and so al-Qaeda was legally proscribed (banned) in February 2001. Nevertheless, this legal ban betrays a second motivation for further action – the realization that al-Qaeda activities (and other parts of the network, including such proscribed groups as Egyptian Islamic Jihad) had been occurring within the United Kingdom for some years. In particular, out of the nineteen hijackers, eleven had links with the United Kingdom.[23]

The third motivation for action was a more generalized concern to increase security and to reassure the public. The trend next represents part of a fundamental switch away from reactive policing of incidents to proactive policing and management of risk.[24] Thus, the Anti-terrorism, Crime and Security Act 2001 became a receptacle for a diverse range of measures, several of which could only very tenuously be related to al-Qaeda or even terrorism in any shape or form, a point which is half-admitted in the title of the legislation. The changes are perhaps best explained by the development of a 'risk society' – in the words of Ulrich Beck, 'an epoch in which the dark sides of progress increasingly come to dominate social debate'.[25] The inherent destabilization involved in the process of 'reflexive modernization'[26] heightens the demand for security, although such a demand cannot be met entirely by state resources and requires multi-tiered responses (not least through private or semi-private insurance).[27]

Policy Strands

Having set out some of the perceptions and experiences of terrorism in the United Kingdom over the past three decades, and especially the influences during the past decade, this chapter will now reflect more upon policy strands.

---

21 See X. Raufer, 'New World Disorder and New Terrorism', *Terrorism and Political Violence*, 11(4), 1999, p. 30.
22 See UK Defence Select Committee, *The Threat from Terrorism* (2001-02 HC 348-I), para. 24.
23 See *The Times*, 15 September 2001, p. 1.
24 See HM Inspector of Constabulary, *Policing with Intelligence* (London: 1997/98); JUSTICE, *Under Surveillance* (London: 1998); and R.V. Ericson and K.D. Haggerty, *Policing the Risk Society* (Oxford: Clarendon Press, 1997).
25 U. Beck, *Ecological Enlightenment* (New Jersey: Humanities Press, 1995), p. 2.
26 U. Beck, *Risk Society* (London: Sage, 1992), p. 87.
27 See C. Walker and M. McGuinness, 'Risk, Political Violence and Policing the City of London', in A. Crawford (ed.), *Crime, Insecurity, Safety and the New Governance* (Cullompton: Willan Publishing, 2002).

One emergent area of policy-making has just been outlined, namely, the perspective of risk management, which recognizes the fragmentation and globalization of threat and seeks to respond by pre-emptively managing risk rather than responding to events in the traditional criminal justice mode.

A more persistent policy strand adverts to the delicate conflict of objectives and values inherent in counter-terrorism legislation. These were outlined by the UK's Home Secretary Jack Straw when introducing the Terrorism Bill:[28]

> 'Although all crime to some degree plainly threatens the stability of the social and political order, terrorism differs from crime motivated solely by greed in that it is directed at undermining the foundations of government. It poses special difficulties for those of us who live in liberal democracies. Our sense of outrage is all the greater because in such democracies the overwhelming majority of the population believe that there are adequate non-violent means for expressing opposition and dissent. However, we will have handed the terrorists the victory that they seek if, in combating their threats and violence, we descend to their level and undermine the essential freedoms and rule of law that are the bedrock of our democracy.'

One can detect that the primary values underlying the speech relate to liberalism and democracy, and these are also evident in the values put forward by the reviewers whose recommendations influenced the current laws. Lord Lloyd in his review of the legislation in 1996 set four principles for the legislation to meet, and it is against these that it should be judged:[29]

> '(i) Legislation against terrorism should approximate as closely as possible to the ordinary criminal law and procedure;
> (ii) Additional statutory offences and powers may be justified, but only if they are necessary to meet the anticipated threat. They must then strike the right balance between the needs of security and the rights and liberties of the individual;
> (iii) The need for additional safeguards should be considered alongside any additional powers;
> (iv) The law should comply with the UK's obligations in international law.'

Yet the counter-terrorism legislation in force today falls short in a number of ways, in particular that there is no requirement for proof at any time of (i) and that (iii) has also not been observed. One might also suggest that Lord Lloyd's tests themselves are insufficiently demanding. Full constitutional governance requires on a continuous basis:[30]

- a 'rights audit', which means that the rights of individuals are respected according to traditions of the domestic jurisdictions and the demands of international law. The latter will include the periodic review of the very existence of any emergency or special measures;
- 'democratic accountability', which includes attributes such as information, open and independent debate and an ability to participate in decision-making;

---

28   House of Commons Debates, vol. 341, col. 152, 14 December 1999.
29   *Inquiry into Legislation against Terrorism*, Cm. 3420 (London: 1996) para. 3.1.
30   C.P. Walker, 'Constitutional Governance and Special Powers against Terrorism', *Columbia Journal of Transnational Law*, 35, 1997, p. 1.

- and 'constitutionalism' – the subjection of government to norms, whether legal or extra legal (such as codes). More specific requirements in the field of special powers include the public articulation of reasons in support of particular actions taken for the public welfare, assurances through effective mechanisms that the crisis cannot be ended by normal means and that powers will not be used arbitrarily, and adherence to the overall purpose of the restoration of fundamental features of constitutional life. It also requires at a more individual level that excesses can be challenged, including through the courts.

Has the UK state lived up to these ideals? Some would claim that, especially in the context of Northern Ireland, there has been an unwholesome 'dirty war' equivalent to any Latin American experience.[31] In particular, the Terrorism Act does not provide for the kind of structure that ensures the future democratic accountability for the operation of this type of law. There is no formal, periodic review conducted by Parliament and no clear criteria set by which to judge necessity, proportionality or success. The government has conceded the appointment of a reviewer (Lord Carlisle) on an extra-statutory basis, but the reviewer is not formally linked to Parliament and has no special powers or resources.[32] These criticisms notwithstanding, a slow process of scrutiny and reform has produced not only the most extensive counter-terrorist code in western Europe but also a diminished rate of abuse and complaint, which has not entirely prejudiced or obviated the peace process being conducted at the same time. In addition, the Anti-terrorism, Crime and Security Act 2001 does ensure a full and independent review (by section 122) of its contents.

Turning to the liberal strand of the policy, the demand to take rights seriously is an easy mantra to express but more complex to execute. According to Lord Hope in *R.* v. *Director of Public Prosecutions, ex p. Kebilene*:[33]

'Then there is the nature of the threat which terrorism poses to a free and democratic society. It seeks to achieve its ends by violence and intimidation. It is often indiscriminate in its effects, and sophisticated methods are used to avoid detection both before and after the event. Society has a strong interest in preventing acts of terrorism before they are perpetrated – to spare the lives of innocent people and to avoid the massive damage and dislocation to ordinary life which may follow from explosions which destroy or damage property.'

This passage suggests that there are rights issues on both sides and that counter-terrorism legislation is not inherently antithetical to rights, and a claim to a need for distinct anti-terrorist laws can be made at three levels.

The first level concerns the powers and duties of states. In principle, it is justifiable for liberal democracies to defend their existence and their values, even if this defence involves some limitation of rights. This point is also reflected in Article 17 of the European Convention of Human Rights. It is also very much the point of the power of derogation from the Convention in time of emergency under Article 15. Aside from the power to take action, there is a state's responsibility to act against political or para-

---

31 See M. Dillon, *The Dirty War* (London: Hutchinson, 1990).
32 See http://www.homeoffice.gov.uk/oicd/carlirep.pdf.
33 *R.* v. *Director of Public Prosecutors, ex p. Kebilene*, 1999, 3 WLR 972, at p. 1000.

military violence and to safeguard the right to life of its citizens (as under Article 2 of the European Convention). In addition, states should more generally ensure the enjoyment of rights and democracy (under Article 1) and under United Nations instruments must also not harbour or condone terrorism.[34]

The second level of justification is more morally grounded. This argument points to the illegitimacy of terrorism as a form of political expression – the fact that many of its emanations are almost certainly common crimes, crimes of war or crimes against humanity, even if the political cause of the terrorist is deemed legitimate.

Thirdly, there is the observation that terrorism is a specialized form of criminality that presents peculiar difficulties in terms of policing and criminal process – such as its remote organization, capacity to intimidate and sophistication. It therefore demands a specialist response to overcome the difficulties posed for normal detection methods and processes within criminal justice. Criminal laws and criminal procedures (including policing powers) are not monolithic. Just as variations have been adopted against, for example, rapists, serious fraudsters and drug traffickers,[35] so terrorists may warrant different treatment because of their atypical methods and targets. In the case of terrorists, aside from their methods and impacts, the special attributes that hinder the re-establishment of public safety and democratic processes relate essentially to two features: the sophistication of the paramilitary groups in terms of organization and training; and the transnational scale of their activities in some cases. In Northern Ireland, one might add the difficulty of obtaining assistance from paramilitary-affected communities, either through intimidation or popularity or through the observance of counter-intelligence precautions.

These arguments, either singularly or cumulatively, have for many decades been convincing to the rulings elites within the United Kingdom.[36] The belief in counter-terrorism laws extends to key members of the present UK government. Speaking in 1994, Tony Blair stated: '... it is not in dispute, and never has been, that we need anti-terrorist legislation'.[37] There is an important proviso. Since it is the aim of terrorism to achieve political gains through violence, the prime point of counter-strategy for states to consider is whether there can be a response to those political gains that are sought. Can there be political dialogue of some kind that averts the need for violence? Liberal democracies have the capacity to be responsive to political demands, especially of minorities and even of the unsavoury representatives of terrorism. This is demonstrated in Northern Ireland, where the peace process has reduced the rate of political violence, albeit not to zero.

Applying these human rights ideals to the Terrorism Act, one might, in the light of the foregoing discussion, concede that legislation along these lines is justifiable, although its invocation must be tested rigorously. Going further, the UK government claimed, pursuant to section 19 of the Human Rights Act 1998, that the legislation is compatible with European Convention rights. On paper, one might assess that compliance has largely been achieved, especially as the House of Lords has already indicated that in 'reading

---

34   See, for example, United Nations General Assembly Resolutions 40/61 of 9 December 1985; and 49/60 of 9 December 1994.

35   See Sexual Offences (Amendment) Act 1976; Drug Trafficking Offences Act 1994; Criminal Justice Act 1987.

36   B. Porter, *The Origins of the Vigilant State* (London: Weidenfeld & Nicolson, 1978) p. 192.

37   House of Commons Debates, vol. 239, col. 300, 2 March 1994.

down' statutory provisions in order to comply with the Convention, account must be taken of the special threat posed by terrorism.[38]

A liberal audit of the Anti-terrorism, Crime and Security Act 2001 suggests a more worrying picture. Partial success might be claimed. Even in the face of the 11 September 2001 attacks, the new legislation did not strike out in all the new and alarming directions pursued in the United States, such as military tribunals.[39] Conversely, the government conceded that a derogation under Article 15 was unavoidable and one was duly lodged[40] concerning the extended power to detain a foreign national under Part III of the Act. In such cases, detention that lasts for more than a short period may be incompatible with Article 5(1)(f) (which permits the lawful arrest or detention of a person to prevent his effecting an unauthorized entry into the country or of a person against whom action is being taken with a view to deportation or extradition). It may even be doubtful whether the purpose of detention in those circumstances, where deportation is not a lawful option, remains within Article 5(1)(f). The ground for the derogation is cited as the fact that 'There exists a terrorist threat to the United Kingdom from persons suspected of involvement in international terrorism'.

This derogation was registered by the Council of Europe's Secretariat on the 18 December 2001. By way of further justification, the Minister of State (Beverley Hughes), pointed to 'the events of 11 September; the two UN Security Council resolutions[41] that pointed to the threat to international security and gave permission, as it were, for states to take measures to protect themselves; engagement in conflict in Afghanistan as a close ally of the United States; the presence of suspected terrorists here; further threats by Osama bin Laden and his supporters; and their preparedness to use nuclear, chemical and biological weapons; and the material found during the conflict in Kabul'.[42] Further, in response to the criticism that no other Council of Europe member state has reacted in the same way,[43] the Home Secretary claimed that the evidence did point to the United Kingdom as being acutely at risk:[44]

> 'We are adjudged internationally to be more at risk than the Danes or other smaller European countries, we know that we are, and the steps we have taken since 11 September, in terms of civil contingencies and security protection, have reflected that heightened concern. Our position internationally and our support for the United States have increased that danger. Also, as the Germans and French are often pointing out, we have a larger host community of those who the Germans and French allege are organizing for international terror.'

---

38 See, likewise, the view of the European Court of Human Rights: *Klass* v. *Germany*, App. no. 5029/71, Ser. A 28, paras. 48-49, 59; *Brogan* v. *UK*, App. nos. 11209, 11234, 11266/84, 11386/85, Ser. A. no. 145-B, (1989), 11 E.H.R.R. 539, para. 48; *Fox, Campbell and Hartley* v. *UK*, App. nos. 12244, 12245, 12383/86, Ser. A 182 (1990), 13 EHRR 157, para. 44.

39 See US Presidential Order, *Detention, Treatment, and Trial of Certain Non-Citizens in the War Against Terrorism*, of the 13 November 2001 (66 Federal Register 57831), section 4.

40 See http://conventions.coe.int/Treaty/EN/CadreListeTraites.htm; Human Rights Act 1998 (Designated Derogation) Order 2001 (SI no. 3644).

41 See Security Council Resolution 1368 (S/RES/1368); General Assembly Resolution 1373 (A/RES/56/1).

42 House of Commons Debates, vol. 375, col. 146, 19 November 2001.

43 See J. Wadham and S. Chakrabarti, 'Indefinite Detention Without Trial', *New Law Journal*, 151, 2001, p. 1564.

44 Joint Committee on Human Rights, *Reports on the Anti-terrorism, Crime and Security Bill* (2001-02 HL 51, HC 420).

By contrast, the Parliamentary Joint Committee on Human Rights (in its Report on the Anti-terrorism, Crime and Security Bill) expressed severe qualms about the legitimacy of the derogation:[45]

> 'We have concluded that, on the evidence available to us, the balance between freedom and security in the Bill before us has not always been struck in the right place. In particular, although we recognize the dilemma from which the Home Secretary sought to free himself by recourse to the derogation from Article 5, we are not persuaded that the circumstances of the present emergency or the exigencies of the current situation meet the tests set out in Article 15 of the ECHR.'

On the other hand, the House of Commons Defence Select Committee found that 'The position continues to be that there remains no intelligence of any specific threat to the UK at present', but it accepted that there is a continuing threat.[46]

The fundamental question is whether there is a sufficient degree of public emergency within the meaning of Article 15. It is true that devastating attacks have occurred in the United States, resulting in British deaths. It is also true that there have for some years been present in the United Kingdom persons suspected of involvement in terrorism abroad, including alleged members of the organizations deemed responsible for the attacks. Recent examples include Khalid al Fawwaz, Ibrahim Eidarou and Adel Abdel Bary, who are awaiting extradition,[47] Zacarias Moussaoui[48] and Richard Reid,[49] both under arrest in the US for links to hijackings, and the approximately two dozen British citizens detained in Afghanistan or Guantanamo Bay, Cuba.[50] But does this evidence of wayward citizens abroad justify a derogation at home? It must be noted that relevant organizations such as al-Qaeda have never carried out attacks in the United Kingdom and have branches elsewhere in other European countries, none of which has taken comparable action. It must be borne in mind that, with the full panoply of the Terrorism Act in force, including the proscription of al-Qaeda, extensive measures dealing with terrorist finances and offences and conspiracy and incitement to commit offences abroad, the United Kingdom was already the most legally fortified country in Europe. Next, the number of arrests since 11 September 2001 has been very modest, with many resulting in quiet releases without charge. There have been just nine detentions without trial (two of whom have been allowed to leave the jurisdiction and presumably now represent an even greater threat to security since they are at large and out of reach).[51] Can such a small cohort of people create an emergency sufficient to destabilize the rights regime of a powerful country like the United Kingdom? There are problems arising from the selective nature of the detention power – it applies only to deportable, non-citizens, with the result

---

45   Joint Committee on Human Rights, *Reports on the Anti-terrorism, Crime and Security Bill* (2001-02 HL 51, HC 420), para. 78.
46   UK House of Commons Defence Select Committee, *The Threat from Terrorism* (2001-02 HC 348-I), paras. 43, 50.
47   *Al Fawwaz* v. *Governor of Brixton Prison*, 2001, 1 WLR 1234, 2 WLR 101.
48   *The Times*, 12 December 2001, p. 3.
49   *The Times*, 24 December 2001, p. 1.
50   *The Times*, 28 January 2002, p. 1.
51   House of Commons Debates, vol. 384, col. 321, 24 April 2002.

that equally suspect and threatening British citizens cannot be detained.[52] Next, the abiding nature of the declared emergency is disturbing – if the war against terrorism is to be won by eradicating all terrorism in the world, then there can be no expectation that the emergency will ever end or the security state will ever be dismantled. An alternative policing strategy by way of surveillance, calling in all the police powers in the Terrorism Act 2000, the Regulation of Investigatory Powers Act 2000 and elsewhere, would be more expensive. But it would be a feasible and more proportionate response. It might even be more productive to keep suspects under surveillance and, where possible, to charge them with offences.[53] Finally, whatever the position in late 2001, it must be doubted whether a sufficient level of threat can be said to persist after the elimination of the Taliban regime in Afghanistan, and after a thorough security trawl in the US and much of Europe. The undue persistence of repressive laws adversely affects most directly those against whom they are applied. But there is also a more subtle, collective detriment. The message given by western states of threat from other realms, especially the Islamic world, produces a response in progression by the politics of intolerance.

Outline of Legal Basis and Organization of Counter-terrorism[54]

Terrorism Act 2000

The Act is divided into eight parts, with six reflecting its substantive themes: proscribed organizations; terrorist property; terrorist investigations; counter-terrorism powers; miscellaneous offences (such as possession of items useful to terrorism); and extra measures relating to criminal process and policing powers confined to Northern Ireland. Among the innovations are a definition of 'terrorism', already described. There is also an attempt to subject a wider range of measures to judicial or quasi-judicial oversight – such as through a new independent commission to consider proscription orders and the judicial review of police detention 48 hours after arrest. There are some novel measures – such as the seizure of cash at borders – but these are relatively few and far between, and the Act is an occasion for clearer thinking rather than novel thinking. Consequently, some of the most eye-catching changes are structural rather than substantive. For the first time ever, anti-terrorism laws are stated comprehensively in one code, which draws together what was separate legislation for Great Britain, on the one hand, and Northern Ireland on the other. In this way, the laws in Britain and Northern Ireland are largely harmonized – save for the temporary extra inventory (Part VII) for Northern Ireland. One consequence is that some measures previously confined to Northern Ireland are now extended to Britain; on the other hand, the measures passed in 1998 to respond to Republican splinter groups have been limited to Northern Ireland. The legislation is intended to be not only comprehensive but also permanent, no longer requiring renewal or re-enactment save for

---

52　The discriminatory nature of the measure convinced Mr Justice Collins, in a Special Immigration Appeals Commission hearing, to declare the derogation to be in breach of Article 14; *The Guardian*, 31 July 2002, p. 1. Decision reversed in *A v Secretary of State for the Home Department* (2002) *The Times* 29 October).
53　Home Office and Northern Ireland Office, *Legislation against Terrorism*, Cm. 4178 (London: 1998), para. 5.6.
54　See Walker, *Blackstone's Guide to the Anti-Terrorism Legislation*.

the one part relating exclusively to Northern Ireland. To a significant extent, these betterments have now been compromised by the Anti-terrorism, Crime and Security Act 2001, which is neither wholly permanent nor comprehensive and, since it in part amends the Terrorism Act, degrades some of its predecessor's finer design features.

Conversely, it is as well to note what is absent from the Terrorism Act. One repeal concerns exclusion orders (allowing the removal of terrorist suspects from Britain to Ireland),[55] which had in fact already lapsed in 1998.

Another notable absentee is the power of internment without trial. This power had always been controversial, even though it had not been in use since 1975.[56] The power had actually been terminated by section 3 of the Northern Ireland (Emergency Provisions) Act 1998. Attempts to revive it were firmly resisted by the government, for while 'It does not rule out for all time the introduction of the power to intern...',[57] it would be 'a significant backward step at a time when we are normalizing the security situation in Northern Ireland'.[58] Although the stance of the Labour government against internment seemed very firm and principled, it has now been compromised by sections 21 to 23 of the Anti-terrorism, Crime and Security Act 2001, which allow for the detention without trial of certain asylum-seekers.

The third non-appearance concerns the offence of withholding information (formerly in section 18 in the Prevention of Terrorism (Temporary Provisions) Act 1989 (PTA)),[59] although a more focused offence dealing with financial institutions, formerly at section 18A of the PTA, is replicated as section 19 of the Terrorism Act. This particular omission has been wholly reversed by section 117 of the Anti-terrorism, Crime and Security Act 2001.

Anti-terrorism, Crime and Security Act 2001

This substantial legislative supplement is organized into fourteen parts. The first three deal with the forfeiture of terrorist property and seizure of terrorist cash. The overlap with the Terrorism Act is substantial, as Part I of the Anti-terrorism, Crime and Security Act 2001 actually replaces sections 24 to 31 of the Terrorism Act, while Part II makes amendments to other Terrorism Act measures on the same subject. Only Part III of the Anti-terrorism, Crime and Security Act 2001 treads into new territory, dealing with the freezing of foreign property held by United Kingdom institutions.

Next, Part IV addresses immigration and asylum matters pertaining to terrorism. There are three elements here. The most controversial is the detention without trial of foreign persons denied asylum on national security grounds or because of their inter-

---

55 Walker, *The Prevention of Terrorism in British Law*, chap. 5; Home Office and Northern Ireland Office, *Legislation against Terrorism*, Cm. 4178 (London: 1998), para. 5.7.

56 R.J. Spjut, 'Internment and Detention without Trial in Northern Ireland 1971-75', *Modern Law Review*, 49, 1986, p. 712.

57 Home Office and Northern Ireland Office, *Legislation against Terrorism*, Cm. 4178 (London: 1998), para. 14.2.

58 House of Lords Debates, vol. 613, col. 1054, 16 May 2000, Lord Falconer.

59 It was recommended for repeal by the *Inquiry into Legislation against Terrorism*, Cm. 3420 (London: 1996), para. 14.24; and the Home Office Consultation Paper (Home Office and Northern Ireland Office), *Legislation against Terrorism*, Cm. 4178 (London: 1998), para. 7.17.

national crimes. This measure has been the subject of a derogation under Article 15 of the European Convention. Just 11 detention orders have been issued, several of which are being contested. In addition, there is an attempt to short-circuit any claim to asylum by making the tribunal focus upon the Secretary of State's reasons for denying the claim. Part IV also deals with the retention of fingerprints in asylum and immigration cases.

Parts VI to X govern dangerous substances and acute vulnerabilities. The dangerous substances include weapons of mass destruction (Part VI) and pathogens and toxins (Part VII).[60] The acute vulnerabilities are nuclear and aviation facilities (Parts VIII and IX). The measures bolstering their security also encompass the specialist police forces assigned to their protection (Part X, sections 98 to 101). Other aspects of Part X (sections 89 to 97), as well as extracts from Parts XI (sections 102 to 107), mainly consist of amendments to Terrorism Act policing measures.

Next, there are various new criminal offences spread around the Anti-terrorism, Crime and Security Act 2001. Some are in Parts XI and XIII of the Act. More controversial is Part V, concerning offences motivated by religious hatred, which were officially depicted as necessary to send a signal that Muslim communities were not to be victimized. The first conviction concerned Ifitkar Ali, who issued anti-Semitic pamphlets.[61]

Finally, incorporated within Parts XIII and XIV of the Act are miscellaneous matters such as the implementation of European Union obligations and structural matters. In regard to the European Union aspect, it is intended that the Act should facilitate rapid implementation of, *inter alia*, the Council Framework Decision on Combating Terrorism (*Proposed Framework Decision on Terrorism from the Commission*, COM (2001), 521), which establishes minimum rules for the constituent elements of criminal acts and penalties in circumstances of between two and twenty years' imprisonment. The proposal for a Council Framework Decision on a European arrest warrant (*Decision on a European Arrest Warrant from the Commission*, COM (2001), 522), which introduces a pan-European arrest and extradition procedure,[62] is to be implemented by primary legislation and not under the 2001 Act.

The omissions from the 2001 legislation are again significant. Aside from changes during the passage of the Bill, one prominent non-appearance concerns the introduction of identity cards. Their utility had been considered by Lord Lloyd[63] but rejected because foreigners would not have them and they are too easily forged or stolen. The administrative difficulties of not just issuing cards but in keeping the details up to date are also enormous. There are also worries that checks could result in racial harassment.[64] Next, the criminalization of mercenary activities was put on the agenda because of reports that British Muslims had travelled to Afghanistan intending to fight for the

---

60   See further: Foreign and Commonwealth Office, *Strengthening the Biological and Toxin Weapons Convention*, Cm. 5484 (London: 2002).

61   *The Times*, 4 May 2002, p. 2.

62   See House of Lords Select Committee on the European Union, *Counter-Terrorism: The European Arrest Warrant Procedure* (2001-02 HL 34); House of Lords Debates, vol. 629, col. 1142, 10 December 2001, Baroness Symons.

63   *Inquiry into Legislation against Terrorism*, Cm. 3420 (London: 1996), para. 16.31.

64   A. Beck and K. Broadhurst, 'National Identity Cards', *Policing and Society*, 8, 1998, p. 40.

Taliban regime. The issue has been considered by the Legg Report,[65] although it mainly concerned their relationship with government (arising out of the role of Sandline[66] as a surrogate for British policy in Sierra Leone). Perhaps more relevant was the report on the Sierra Leone affair by the Foreign Affairs Committee,[67] which pointed to the Foreign Enlistment Act 1870 as an 'antiquated piece of legislation ... passed on the outbreak of the Franco-Prussian war'. The UK government has now responded to these concerns by the publication of a consultation paper, *Private Military Companies: Options for Regulation*,[68] the focus of which is commercial military services and their uses and relations with governments and multinational corporations, leaving unchanged the position of British Muslims who seek to graduate from *madrassas* to more violent action.

The Other Anti-terrorism Laws, including International Law

Terrorism Act is depicted as the primary code relating to domestic counter-terrorism powers but was never intended as the only source of legislation against terrorism, nor does it operate in this way even in conjunction with the Anti-terrorism, Crime and Security Act 2001.

Many of the offences directly relating to terrorist actions, whether in domestic law, such as the Explosive Substances Act 1883, or in international law, such as the Aviation and Maritime Security Act 1990[69] remain unincorporated. Issues of sentencing are also found outside the specialist terrorism legislation (especially in the Northern Ireland (Remission of Sentences) Act 1995 and the Northern Ireland (Sentences) Act 1998) and in the practice of the courts in cases such as *R.* v. *Hindawi* (concerning a Jordanian convicted of conspiring to commit terrorist acts).[70] Next, the laws relating to the use of force, especially lethal force, remain unchanged, despite concerns from the European Court of Human Rights[71] and scrutiny by the Bloody Sunday Inquiry.[72]

There is also a growing body of international process law. Over several decades, international treaties have been developed to respond to terrorism. They relate to hijacking and attacks upon aircraft, ships and related installations (the Aviation Security Act 1982, and the Aviation and Maritime Security Act 1990), diplomats (the Internationally Protected Persons Act 1978), hostages (the Taking of Hostages Act 1982),

---

65 *Report of the Sierra Leone Arms Investigation*, 1997-98 HC 1016.

66 See http://www.sandline.com/.

67 UK Foreign Affairs Committee, 1998-99 HC 116, para. 92; see also (Diplock) *Report of the Committee of Privy Counsellors* appointed to inquire into the recruitment of mercenaries, Cmnd 6569 (London: 1976).

68 UK Foreign Affairs Committee, 2001-02 HC 577. Also see Foreign Affairs Committee, *Private Military Companies*, 2001-02 HC 922.

69 See P. Wilkinson and B.M. Jenkins, *Aviation Terrorism and Security* (London: Frank Cass, 1999); G. Plant, 'Legal Aspects of Terrorism at Sea', in R. Higgins and M. Flory (eds), *Terrorism and International Law* (London: Routledge, 1997).

70 *R.* v. *Hindawi* 1988, 10 Cr App R (S), 104.

71 *McCann, Savage and Farrell* v. *UK*, App. no. 18984/91, Ser. A vol. 324, (1995); *The Times*, 9 October 1996, 21 EHRR 97; *Jordan, McKerr, Kelly and Shanaghan* v. *UK*, App. nos. 24746/95, 28883/95, 300054/96, 37715/97, judgment of 4 May 2001.

72 See http://www.bloody-Sunday-inquiry.org.uk/. See F. Ni Aolain, *The Politics of Force* (Belfast: Blackstaff, 2000); D. Walsh, *Bloody Sunday and the Rule of Law in Northern Ireland* (Dublin: Gill & MacMillan, 2000).

nuclear installations and materials (the Nuclear Material (Offences) Act 1983) as well as dealing with procedural issues such as extradition (the Suppression of Terrorism Act 1978). This list has now been supplemented by two further treaties, the United Nations Convention for the Suppression of Terrorist Bombings[73] and the United Nations Convention for the Suppression of the Financing of Terrorism.[74] In so far as their implementation is not already dealt with elsewhere in the Terrorism Act, it is the subject of sections 62 to 64.

The trial of the Lockerbie suspects in the Netherlands shows that the law against international terrorism cannot operate in isolation but may be moderated by the demands of politics and practicalities.[75] The International Criminal Court, founded by the Rome Convention, cannot deal directly with 'terrorism'.[76] The UK government views it as unsuitable because of difficulties of definition and the production of sensitive evidence.[77] Nevertheless, the deeds of terrorists may fall within admissible heads of jurisdiction, such as crimes against humanity.

Plans were afoot even at the time of the passage of the Terrorism Act to strengthen other aspects of counter-terrorism laws. For example, there were designs to improve extradition procedures, especially in the context of western Europe.[78] These ideas were raised again at the time of the Anti-terrorism, Crime and Security Act and may be implemented by order under section 111 once agreed at a European level. Another Home Office paper, *Animal Rights Extremism: A Strategy Document,*[79] promised further reforms to deal with tactics designed to intimidate the officers and employees of companies or units (such as at universities) involved in research that harms animals. These measures duly appeared in the Criminal Justice and Police Act 2001. By section 42, the police are given broad powers to direct protestors (or perhaps journalists)[80] away from the residence of another where it is reasonably believed that the presence of the protestors amounts to harassment or is likely to cause alarm or distress. section 45 then allows for 'confidentiality orders' to be issued by the Secretary of State (for Trade and Industry) under an amendment to the Companies Act 1985.

Organizational Overview

Terrorism has long shaped policing organizations in the United Kingdom. Within the Metropolitan Police in London, a Special Branch was formed in 1883 to respond to an

---

73   A/RES/52/164, Cm. 4662 (London: 1997).
74   A/RES/54/109, Cm. 4663 (London: 1999).
75   See A. Klip and M. Mackarel, 'The Lockerbie Trial', *Revue Internationale de Droit Penal*, 70, 1999, p. 777; *Lockerbie Trial Briefing*, http://www.ltb.org.uk/; *Lockerbie Trial*, http://www.thelockerbietrial.com/.
76   See D. McGoldrick, 'The Permanent International Criminal Court', *Criminal Law Review*, 1999, p. 627; International Criminal Court Act 2001.
77   *Government Response to the Foreign Affairs Committee, Foreign Policy and Human Rights*, Cm. 4299 (London: 1999), p. 3.
78   See UK Home Office, *The Law on Extradition: A Review* (London: 2001).
79   UK Home Office, *Animal Rights Extremism: A Strategy Document* (London: 2001).
80   See L. Hickman, 'Press Freedom and New Legislation', *New Law Journal*, 151, 2001, p. 716.

Irish bombing campaign at that time.[81] The Special Branch (SO12) remains the mainstay of police intelligence-gathering operations against political violence, and the London version has been replicated in other police forces throughout the country, most notably in Northern Ireland.[82] A separate Metropolitan Police squad with a more operational focus and responding to more defined threats and incidents emerged in 1970 in the shape of the Bomb Squad – renamed as the Anti-Terrorist Squad (SO13) in 1976 – with national coverage.[83]

In the background to the overt policing structures are the intelligence services: the Security Service (MI5) dealing with domestic threats; the Secret Intelligence Service (MI6) responding to international threats; as well as the surveillance agency; the Government Communications Headquarters (GCHQ); and Army Intelligence.[84] The central mechanisms for the coordination and resourcing of the intelligence agencies are based in the Cabinet Office. For GCHQ and the Secret Intelligence Service, the Joint Intelligence Committee (JIC), which includes the Director General of the Security Service, agrees the intelligence requirements and tasking, subject to Ministerial approval. The Security Service's plans and priorities are reviewed annually by a separate Cabinet Office interdepartmental committee: 'SO(SSPP)'.

The decisive step in explicitly allowing the secret agents into the world of policing was taken a decade ago when the increased threat from terrorism and organized crime prompted shifts in power. Consequently, the Security Service took over Special Branch's role as the main terrorism intelligence-gathering agency in 1992. Next, the Security Service Act 1996 provided the Security Service with a greater profile in combating serious organized crime. Overall, the trend is away from local policing towards national agencies and, increasingly, away from policing to intelligence agencies. The trend has implications not only for the strategies being employed but also for issues such as democratic accountability.[85] Although the Director General of the Security Service is now a public figure[86] and the Service has even produced a glossy pamphlet about itself,[87] in the words of Tony Blair 'a photo opportunity and brochure may be a historic moment by our standards of government secrecy, but giving us more facts about the security

---

81 See R. Allason, *The Branch: A History of the Metropolitan Police Special Branch 1883-1983* (London: Secker & Warburg, 1983).

82 See http://www.met.police.uk/so/special_branch.htm. See Home Affairs Committee, *Special Branch* (1984-85 H.C. 71); Home Office, *Guidelines on Special Branch Work in Great Britain* (London: 1994); C. Walker, 'The Patten Report and Post-sovereignty Policing in Northern Ireland', in R. Wilford (ed.), *Aspects of the Belfast Agreement* (Oxford: Oxford University Press, 2001).

83 See http://www.met.police.uk/terrorism/index.htm. National coverage was confirmed in 1990: House of Commons Debates, vol. 187, col. 27, 4 March 1991.

84 See http://www.mi5.gov.uk/; http://www.cabinet-office.gov.uk/cabsec/1998/cim/cimrep3.htm; http://www.gchq.gov.uk/; http://www.army.mod.uk/intelligencecorps/. See P. Gill, *Policing Politics: Security Intelligence and the Liberal Democratic State* (London: Frank Cass, 1994); L. Lustgarten and I. Leigh, *In From the Cold* (Oxford: Oxford University Press, 1994).

85 R. Norton-Taylor, *In Defence of the Realm?: The Case for Accountable Security Services* (London: Civil Liberties Trust, 1990); G. Zellick, 'Spies, Subversives, Terrorists and the British Government: Free Speech and Other Casualties', *William and Mary Law Review*, 31, 1990, p. 773; Home Affairs Committee, *Accountability of the Security Service*, 1992-3 HC 265, reply at Cm. 2197.

86 See especially S. Rimmington, *BBC Dimbleby Lecture*, reported in *The Guardian*, 13 June 1994.

87 See *The Security Service* (London: HMSO, 1993).

service is no substitute for being able to scrutinize it through genuine accountability'.[88] The Intelligence Services Act 1994, section 10, does set up a Parliamentary Intelligence and Security Committee, but its performance has been baleful. The other concern is the observance of individual rights; for example, will privacy be properly respected either during surveillance or in respect of the retention of records?[89] The tasking of externally-oriented secret service agencies in ways that can involve activity within the United Kingdom (as under the Anti-terrorism, Crime and Security Act 2001, section 116) is further evidence of these worrying trends. section 116(2) amends the Intelligence Services Act 1994 so as to ensure that the full powers of the secret state (including GCHQ and the Secret Intelligence Service) can effectively be brought to bear against foreign terrorist threats by allowing both agencies to be authorized under section 7 to act in this country, provided that the intention is for those actions to have an effect only on apparatus located outside the British Isles or on material originating from such apparatus. Before this change, any authorized acts had to take place abroad. In addition, subsection (3) provides for the meaning of the prevention and detection of crime as set out in section 81(5) of the Regulation of Investigatory Powers Act 2000 to be applied to the Secret Intelligence Service. The same definition applies to the Security Service in the Security Service Act 1989. The effect is to clarify that the Secret Intelligence Service can act in support of evidence-gathering activities.

Focusing on the Security Service as the best documented node in this intelligence web, under the Security Service Act 1989,[90] the Security Service is allowed a wide mandate for its activities. It expressly includes by section 1(1) 'the protection of national security and in particular, its protection against threats from ... terrorism...'. In practice, terrorism has formed the major part of its work during the past decade since the passing of the Cold War. This growing emphasis and expertise was given further impetus on 8 May 1992, when the UK's Secretary of State announced:[91]

> The Government have now decided that the lead responsibility for intelligence work against Irish republican terrorism in Great Britain should pass from the Metropolitan Police Special Branch to the Security Service.

The decision was prompted partly by concern about the failure to counter IRA activities in Britain, and it was also alleged that there was also pressure from the Security Service, searching for new work for agents at a loose end following the end of the Cold War. More rationally, the Security Service could argue that the police lacked the experience and skills necessary to penetrate the IRA, which were akin to counter-espionage rather than anti-crime techniques.[92]

---

88 *The Guardian*, 17 July 1993.
89 *Hilton* v. *UK*, Application no. 12015/86; *Hewitt and Harman* v. *UK,* App. no.12175/86; *Nimmo* v. *UK,* App. no.12327/86; *R* v. *Secretary of State for the Home Department, ex p Ruddock* [1987] 1 WLR 1482; *A.G.* v. *Guardian Newspapers* [1987] 1 W.L.R. 1248, (No. 2) [1988] 2 W.L.R. 805, [1988] 3 W.L.R. 776.
90 See I. Leigh and L. Lustgarten, 'The Security Service Act 1989', *Modern Law Review*, 52, 1989, p. 801; W. Finnie, 'The Smile on the Face of the Tiger', *Northern Ireland Legal Quarterly*, 41, 1990, p. 64. The Secret Intelligence Service and GCHQ are governed by the Intelligence Services Act 1994; see J. Wadham, 'The Intelligence Services Act 1994', *Modern Law Review*, 57, 1994, p. 916.
91 House of Commons Debates, vol. 207, col. 297, 8 May 1992.
92 See S. Farson, 'Security Intelligence v. Criminal Intelligence', *Policing & Society*, 2, 1991-1992, p. 65.

Having made the switch in 1992, it is far from clear how successful the Security Service has been in its lead role, as many of its activities remain in the shadows and are also aimed principally at prevention and disruption rather than overt prosecution. However, there is evidence of impact at two levels.

First, some cases have been reported in which it is clear that the secret services have taken the lead. For example, Fintan O'Farrell, Declan Rafferty and Michael McDonald were convicted in May 2002 of attempting to acquire weaponry for the Real IRA after being lured into a meeting in Slovakia with Security Service agents pretending to represent the Iraqi government.[93]

Second, terrorism has become the prime focus for the Security Service. By 1993,[94] it accounted for 70 per cent of the workload of the Security Service, with 26 per cent expended on international terrorism and 44 per cent on Irish and other domestic groups, although this figure had fallen back to 53 per cent by 1999 because of the reduction in Irish terrorism (down to 30.5 per cent, compared to 22.5 per cent for international terrorism).[95]

These intelligence strategies, characterized by central control and an absence of close legislative or parliamentary scrutiny, have emanated since 11 September 2001 in the form of organizational changes in relation to the policing of financial institutions. As part of an Action Plan on Terrorist Financing,[96] a Terrorist Finance Team has been established within the Economic Crime Unit at the National Criminal Intelligence Service.[97] This is intended to be a multi-disciplinary task force, which will improve financial intelligence skills and investigate the possible use of underground (Hawala) banking systems in the transfer of terrorist assets.

Even before 11 September 2001, greater police attention to intelligence-gathering was evidenced first through a reorganization of the policing of animal rights extremists by the setting up of a specialist unit in the National Crime Squad.[98] Another example is the establishment of the National Hi-Tech Crime Unit (NHTCU), launched within the National Criminal Intelligence Service (NCIS) in April 2001.[99] The NHTCU is tasked with the key role in the response to cyber-crime, especially as practised by serious and organized crime. The NHTCU's ability to gather evidence has been reinforced by Part XI of the Anti-terrorism, Crime and Security Act 2001, which establishes that, under section 102, the Secretary of State can issue a voluntary code of practice relating to the retention of 'communications data' by 'communications providers' which will give guidance to communications providers as to the basis for retaining – on national security and crime prevention grounds – communications data beyond the period that they require for their own business purposes.[100] The enhanced perception of the vulnerabilities of networks to

---

93 *The Times*, 3 May 2002, p. 3.
94 See *The Security Service* (London: HMSO, 1993). See also *Central Intelligence Machinery* (London: HMSO, 1996).
95 A detailed chart may be found on http://www.mi5.gov.uk/threats.htm.
96 House of Commons Debates, vol. 372, col. 940, 15 October 2001, Gordon Brown.
97 See http://www.ncis.co.uk/press/46_01.html; http://www.ncis.co.uk/ec.html.
98 See *The Times*, 27 April 2001, p. 2.
99 See http://www.nationalcrimesquad.police.uk/nhtuc/nhtcu.html.
100 See Walker, *Blackstone's Guide to the Anti-Terrorism Legislation*, chap. 5.

terrorist attack has also resulted in the appointment within the Cabinet Office of a Central Sponsor for Information Assurance and Resilience.[101]

International Cooperation

The implementation of international treaties relating to terrorism has been delineated above, and in most respects the UK government has been more enthusiastic than many counterparts about the development and implementation of these treaties. Aside from any moral justification, a pay-off in terms of combating the IRA has also been a motivating factor.

Much recent attention has focused upon European Union-based cooperation, where more progress may be possible than on a wider stage. The Third Pillar of the (Maastricht) Treaty of the European Union of 1992 deals with cooperation in the area of Justice and Home Affairs. Article K.1 of the Treaty on European Union (TEU) defined asylum policy, external border controls, immigration policy, combating drug addiction and international fraud, judicial cooperation in civil and criminal matters, customs cooperation and police cooperation in action against terrorism, drug-trafficking and other serious international crime as 'matters of common interest'. By Article K.2, member states were to consult and exchange information and then adopt joint positions, draw up joint action and draft conventions for national adoption. Now, under Articles 29 to 42 of the Amsterdam Treaty of 1998, the revised Title VI covers fewer areas (since some were translated into an enforceable part of the European Communities Treaty – the former Third Pillar policies on visas, asylum, immigration and other policies connected with the free movement of persons).

Much of the activity under the Third Pillar is in the nature of consultation, coordination and audit. However, various formal measures have arisen, some of which have required national implementation, including:

(a) the 1995 Convention drawn up on the basis of Article K.3 of the Treaty on European Union on simplified extradition procedure between the member states of the European Union;[102]

(b) the 1996 Convention drawn up on the basis of Article K.3 of the Treaty on European Union relating to extradition between the member states of the European Union;

(c) framework decisions adopted under Article 34 of the Treaty on European Union on the execution in the European Union of orders freezing property or evidence, on joint investigation teams, or on combating terrorism;

(d) the Convention on Mutual Assistance in Criminal Matters between the member states of the European Union, and the Protocol to that Convention, established in accordance with Article 34 of the Treaty on European Union; and

---

101 Defence Committee, *Defence and Security in the United Kingdom*, 2001-02 HC 518, para. 125.

102 See C. Gueydan, 'Cooperation between Member States of the European Community in the Fight against Terrorism', in R. Higgins and M. Flory (eds), *Terrorism and International Law* (London: Routledge, 1997).

(e) the establishment of Europol and also the Convention on Mutual Assistance and Cooperation between Customs Administrations.[103]

The pace of negotiations under these provisions quickened after 11 September 2001, and a pathway was provided to the rapid national implementation of any agreements by section 111 of the Anti-terrorism, Crime and Security Act 2001, which allows a government minister to issue regulations (a) for the purpose of implementing any obligation of the United Kingdom created or arising by or under any Third Pillar measure or enabling any such obligation to be implemented, (b) for the purpose of enabling any rights enjoyed or to be enjoyed by the United Kingdom under or by virtue of any Third Pillar measure to be exercised, or (c) for the purpose of dealing with matters arising out of or related to any such obligation or rights. Here, as elsewhere, the government advised that for practical reasons it is not possible to divide terrorism from other serious crime especially in relation to the funding of terrorism.[104] However, some reassurance was offered, including the insertion of a time limit in section 111 of 1 July 2002 so as to point power in the direction of the existing European Union anti-terrorism proposals rather than future, unimagined measures. It also included the precise specification in section 111(2) of the European sources of the pending legislation.[105]

The purpose of section 111 is to avoid legislative delay in the implementation of new, and possibly urgent, countermeasures. Rather than primary legislation, there can be secondary legislation, and the scope of the regulation-making power is very wide. By section 111(3) it includes 'any such provision (of any such extent) as might be made by Act of Parliament', but subject to a list of limitations in section 111(4) and (6), which in particular rule out retrospective rules, the creation of any power to legislate, or the creation of a criminal offence beyond a specified severity.

Following the attacks of 11 September 2001, a series of meetings were held under the umbrella of the Justice and Home Affairs Council of the European Union to bolster existing measures against terrorism.[106] It met on 20 September 2001 and agreed two proposals for Council Framework Decisions. One, the Council Framework Decision on Combating Terrorism (Proposed Framework Decision on Terrorism from the Commission, COM (2001) 521), establishes minimum rules for the constituent elements of criminal acts and penalties in circumstances of between two and twenty years' imprisonment. In this way, an EU definition of terrorism is constituted. Arguments abound as to whether this definition of 'terrorism' is sufficiently limited or whether it might capture forms of public disorder arising from political protest. A serious degree of impact is required by Article 3, but not necessarily any form of organization or sustainability. It may be an academic argument, for the UK government has opined that

---

103 See Cm. 5020 (London: 2000). The extension of the purview of the Europol Convention based on Article K.3 of the Treaty on the European Union, on the Establishment of a European Police Office (Europol Convention) with Declarations (Cm 3050, London: 1995, and Cm 4837, London: 2000) to terrorism was approved by the European Union's Justice and Home Affairs Council in 1998 and began to be implemented in 1999. See E. Marotta, 'Europol's Role in Anti-terrorism Policing', *Terrorism and Political Violence*, 11, 1999, p. 15.
104 House of Lords Debates, vol. 629, col. 599, 3 December 2001, Baroness Symons.
105 House of Lords Debates, vol. 629, cols.1142 and 1160, 10 December 2001.
106 See F. Reinares (ed.), *European Democracies Against Terrorism* (Aldershot: Ashgate, 2000); Walker, *Blackstone's Guide to the Anti-Terrorism Legislation*, chap. 10.

'the proposal does not go further than existing UK legislation, which is considered to be adequate and not to require change.'[107]

The second proposal, for a Council Framework Decision on a European arrest warrant (Decision on a European Arrest Warrant from the Commission, COM (2001) 522), introduces a pan-European arrest and extradition procedure.[108] In terms of substance, the 'European arrest warrant' will be used both for the purposes of arrest and surrender (unlike the normal two stages of extradition) and can in some circumstances also trigger search powers. The warrant travels between judicial authorities without any executive or diplomatic input. At most there is a judicial examination of the arrest warrant within ten days of the arrest (Article 15) unless the requested person consents to 'surrender' to the issuing state. The decision must be given within 90 days (Article 20). The offences, as defined by the law of the issuing member state, shall, under the terms of this Framework Decision and without any limitation as to double criminality of the action, give rise to a surrender pursuant to a European arrest warrant, including: membership of a criminal organization, laundering of the proceeds of crime, high-tech crime, murder, grievous bodily injury, kidnapping, illegal restraint and hostage-taking. It should be emphasized that there is no recognition whatever of any 'political offence' exception. The Framework Decision must be applied by the end of 2002, despite concerns about individual rights, whether the listed offences are specific enough, the position of the specialty rule, and the absence of a presumption in favour of bail and rights of appeal.[109]

In addition to these two Framework Decisions, the Justice and Home Affairs Council set a whole range of other work in motion in September 2001,[110] including:

- the implementation of Article 13 of the Mutual Legal Assistance Convention (Convention on Mutual Assistance on Criminal Matters between the Member States of the EU (OJ 2000 C 197/1)) concerning joint investigation teams;
- giving greater prominence to Eurojust, the EU's public prosecutions unit (see Decision 2000/799/JHA setting up a provisional Judicial Cooperation Unit (Eurojust) (OJ 2000 L 324/2), and Europol (there are only seven counter-terrorism specialists within its staff of 224) at the centre of the EU's counter-terrorism programme;
- requesting the Commission to submit proposals for law enforcement authorities to have access to communications data and calling for more urgent action on national contact points in the European Judicial Network. The European Judicial Network was created in July 1998 and links the mutual legal assistance units (Joint Action 98/428/JHA establishing a European Judicial Network (OJ L 191, 7.7.98));
- requesting the EU Police Chief's Operational Task Force (established in 1999) to organize an *ad hoc* meeting of heads of EU counter-terrorist agencies;
- requesting cooperation between military intelligence agencies;

---

107 House of Lords Committee on the European Union, *UK Participation in the Schengen Acquis,* 1999-00 HL 34, Appendix 3.
108 See House of Lords Select Committee on the European Union, *Counter-Terrorism: The European Arrest Warrant Procedure,* 2001-02 HL 34.
109 House of Lords Committee on the European Union, *UK Participation in the Schengen Acquis,* 1999-00 HL 34, Appendix 3.
110 See SN 4019/01, SN 4019/1/01, 12579/01, 12800/01, and 12800/1/01 REV 1.

- creating a new EU Intelligence Chief's Task Force to begin meeting regularly;
- instructing the Article 36 Committee to work out a simpler and quicker evaluation and assessment mechanism in order to find a procedure for assessing national anti-terrorist arrangements on the basis of legislative, administrative and technical procedures (following the Commission's Communication on Cyber-crime (COM (2000) 890). Examples given are legislation on 'administrative telephone-tapping' and a 'list of terrorist organizations';
- instructing the EU Working Party on Terrorism to draw up an inventory of national measures to combat terrorism;
- drawing up a common list of proscribed groups by Europol, anti-terrorist units and intelligence agencies (further to the Joint Action 98/733/JHA of 21 December 1998 adopted by the Council on the basis of Article K.3 of the Treaty on European Union, on making it a criminal offence to participate in a criminal organization in the member states of the European Union, *Official Journal* L 351, 29.12.1998);
- reviewing EC and EU financial legislation to ensure that banking systems comply with anti-terrorism investigations and automatic exchanges of information about terrorist funding; reviewing immigration and asylum legislation to be examined 'with reference to the terrorist threat'; seeking to devise a Framework Decision on the execution of orders freezing assets or evidence and to widen its scope to terrorist offences, building upon the Council Recommendation of 9 December 1999 on cooperation in combating the financing of terrorist groups (*Official Journal* C 373, 23.12.1999).

The foregoing list of ongoing work would appear to encompass a substantial catalogue, which may justify the UK government's argument that section 111 is necessary to avoid legislative overload. However, the government has indicated that it will not implement the European Arrest Framework Decision by way of section 111 but will resort to primary legislation.[111] This leaves its main programme, as now specified in section 111(2), the 1995 and 1996 Conventions under Article K.3 on Extradition, the Framework Decision on Combating Terrorism, the Mutual Legal Assistance Convention, plus a possible Framework Decision on asset freezing and a possible Framework Decision on setting up joint investigative teams.

Other measures relating to European Union cooperation in the fields of home affairs and policing include the Schengen *acquis*. The United Kingdom's relationship with the Schengen *acquis* has been complex.[112] As part of the integration of Schengen provisions into the Treaty on European Union (TEU) and the abolition of internal border controls by the Amsterdam Treaty, the Schengen protocol provides that the Schengen *acquis* applies only to the thirteen states that have signed the Schengen agreements. Under Article 4 of this protocol, the United Kingdom and Ireland 'may at any time request to take part in some or all of the provisions of this *acquis*', and if they do so request, the response will be determined by unanimous decision of the other thirteen. Protocol 3 recognizes the special travel arrangements with Ireland and stipulates that the United Kingdom will

---

111 House of Lords Debates, vol. 629, col. 1142, 10 December 2001, Baroness Symons.
112 See House of Lords Committee on the European Communities, *Schengen and the United Kingdom's Border Controls*, 1998-99 HL 37.

continue to exercise border controls regardless of Article 14 of the TEU. Protocol 4 accepts that the United Kingdom (and Ireland) remain outside the existing Schengen arrangements, although they can opt in to measures concerning the EU external frontier and asylum, while remaining outside any arrangements made in future for EU internal frontiers. In 1999, the UK government decided to opt in to various Schengen measures, although not to any that required abandoning border controls.[113] A further statement was made in 2001[114] to cooperate in a range of measures, including a Commission proposal for a Council regulation concerning the establishment of 'Eurodac' for comparison of the fingerprints of asylum applicants and certain other aliens (title subsequently amended to 'Council Regulation concerning the Establishment of "Eurodac" for the Comparison of Fingerprints for the Effective Application of the Dublin Convention'). UK participation has yet to come into effect, as it is subject to a further unanimous decision of the Council that all the conditions for participation have been met. [115]

There is growing European cooperation in crime control aside from the context of the European Union. For example, the Council of Europe's Cybercrimes Convention[116] requires member states to implement provisions related to interception of communi-cations, preservation and disclosure of traffic data, production orders, search and seizure of stored computer data, real-time collection of traffic data, interception of content data, and mutual assistance.

Further afield, one of the important, but very shadowy, forms of cooperation against terrorism concerns the United Kingdom's participation in the ESCHELON interception system.[117] The system is a global system for intercepting communications, operating under a long-standing UK-US agreement for sharing technological spying capacities and data, with the participation of Canada, Australia and New Zealand. Spy satellite networks are alleged to enable the system to intercept any telephone, fax, internet or email message. The system was condemned by a resolution of the European Parliament on 5 September 2001, in the light of a report on the existence of a global system for the interception of private and commercial communications (ECHELON interception system).[118]

Conclusions

It will be interesting to see how international political machinations shape the future working of legislation. Will an 'ethical' foreign policy[119] demand priority for the rantings of foreign dissidents, or will healthy trade relations and smooth diplomacy carry the day? Either way, it would be a fine development if, having been fortified with these sweeping

---

113 House of Commons Debates, vol. 327, cols. 380-2wa, 12 March 1999, Jack Straw.
114 House of Lords Debates, vol. 363, cols. 152-153wa, 1 March 2001.
115 See House of Lords Committee on the European Union, *UK Participation in the Schengen Acquis,* 1999-00 HL 34.
116 ETS 185, Strasbourg, 2001.
117 See http://www.cyber-rights.org/interception/echelon/; http://www.echelonwatch.org/; http://hermetic.nofadz.com/crypto/echelon/echelon.htm.
118 2001/2098(INI)) FINAL, A5-0264/2001 Parl.
119 House of Lords Debates, vol. 580, col. 129, 15 May 1997, Baroness Symons.

powers, the UK state could have the confidence and ability to rely primarily on 'normal' policing powers and upon its extensive contingency planning and networks.[120] However, as the UK government perceives itself as living in threatening and troubled times, the legislation can probably look forward to a long and active life.

Even if the legislation does persist for some time, it may be predicted that it will continue to be largely peripheral in effect. More important factors in dealing with terrorism will comprise firstly normal police powers and criminal offences and regular techniques of investigation and securitization. These must operate alongside cooperation and vigilance on the part of the public who provide, even in terrorist cases where there is an emphasis on proactive intelligence-gathering, much of the policing capability of society. International cooperation is also core to the response to more fluid and global vulnerabilities and Third Millennium terrorism.[121] Beyond the legal field, effective contingency planning and preventive measures are of enormous significance.[122] Above all, there must be a vibrant and inclusive democracy, which can discern the difference between vituperative and politically immature hot air and violence with the potential to spill blood and which holds its nerve and its cherished values in the face of the heat and light of the terrorist spectacular.

---

120 See Civil Contingencies Committee and Secretariat, http://www.co-ordination.gov.uk/terrorism.htm.
121 See Foreign Affairs Committee, *Foreign Policy Aspects of the War Against Terrorism*, 2001-02 HC 384.
122 See Cabinet Office, *The Future of Emergency Planning in England and Wales* (2001); Department of Health, *Health Protection* (2002); Defence Committee, *Defence and Security in the United Kingdom*, 2001-02 HC 518, paras. 158 and 256.

3 Irish Experiences and Perspectives

Dermot Walsh

Nature and Extent of Terrorist Activity

Introduction

Terrorist activity in Ireland is, and always has been, generated primarily by conflict over the role of Britain in the government of Ireland and, in particular, over the constitutional position of Northern Ireland.[1] Between 1800 and 1922 the whole of Ireland was ruled directly from London as part of the United Kingdom of Great Britain and Ireland. In the British general election of 1919 most of the Irish seats in the United Kingdom's Parliament were won by members of the Sinn Fein party who had stood on a policy of abstention. They promptly withdrew from Westminster and declared the establishment of their own independent parliament and government in Ireland. Almost immediately, the Irish Republican Army (IRA), a paramilitary body associated with Sinn Fein, embarked upon a guerilla warfare campaign aimed at forcing a British political and military withdrawal from Ireland. This campaign culminated in the signing of the Anglo-Irish Treaty between the self-proclaimed Irish government and the government of the United Kingdom in 1921. The Treaty made provision for the establishment of an Irish Free State with its own government that was almost completely independent of the United Kingdom.[2] These arrangements only applied to 26 of the 32 counties of Ireland. They did not extend to the six north-eastern counties (Northern Ireland), which were to remain part of the United Kingdom.

---

1 J. Lee, *Ireland 1912-1985: Politics and Society* (Cambridge: Cambridge University Press, 1989; F. Jones, *History of the Sinn Fein Movement and the Irish Rebellion*, 3rd ed (New York: Kennedy & Sons 1921).

2 See N. Mansergh, *The Irish Free State: Its Government and Politics* (London: George Allen & Unwin, 1934).

M. van Leeuwen (ed.): *Confronting Terrorism*, pp. 37-55
© 2003 Kluwer Law International. Printed in the Netherlands.

The Treaty was accepted by a narrow majority in a referendum in the 26 counties. The minority, however, refused to accept the exclusion of the six counties and a bitter civil war broke out between the newly established government in Ireland and the anti-Treaty forces. The latter conceded defeat by 1923 but did not disappear entirely. They assumed the military and political authority of the IRA and Sinn Fein and committed themselves to achieving the reunification of all Ireland's 32 counties by force.[3] To this end they used the state as a base to organize and direct attacks against targets in Northern Ireland, most particularly during the periods 1939-1948 and 1958-62. While these attacks never managed to pose any major security threat to either state, the very fact that the IRA continued to exist and engage in such activities was viewed in Ireland as a serious terrorist threat to the established constitutional order in the state.[4]

The IRA and Republican Terrorism

In 1969 when serious communal violence broke out within Northern Ireland, the IRA proved totally unprepared and incapable of protecting the minority Catholic population against attack from elements within the majority Protestant population.[5] This resulted in the formation of the Provisional IRA, which in turn assumed the political authority and objectives of the IRA. The new organization proved to be a much more potent and active force than its predecessor. Fed by the deep sense of alienation prevalent in large sections of the Catholic minority community in Northern Ireland which, in turn, was fuelled by repressive political and security policies,[6] the IRA managed to sustain an unprecedented campaign of violence from 1970 until the ceasefires in 1994 and 1997.[7]

The weaponry and resources that have been at its disposal over the past 30 years clearly mark the IRA as one of the major terrorist organizations of the twentieth century. Its armoury over the years has included: handguns, armalite and kalashnikov rifles, sub-machine-guns, heavy machine-guns, RPG rocket launchers, anti-aircraft missiles, hand-grenades, mortar bombs and semtex explosives. It has developed a high degree of sophistication in bomb-making, including bombs made from agricultural fertilizer. From the late 1970s supply never seemed to be a problem. Major shipments were received from Libya's Colonel Gaddafi in the 1980s, while others were purchased on the black market with seemingly inexhaustible financial resources acquired from robberies and 'legitimate' business fronts. Despite major seizures north and south of the border over many years, it was apparent that the IRA was still very well stocked with arms when it called its

---

3   See T.P. Coogan, *The IRA: A History* (Lanham MD: Roberts Rinehart, 1995); and J. Bowyer Bell, *The Secret Army: The IRA* (Dublin: Poolbeg Press, 1998).
4   The Irish Constitution makes provision for only one army, one national legislative authority and one national executive authority. It also enshrines government policy to pursue the unity of Ireland by peaceful means.
5   The minority Catholic population in Northern Ireland broadly consider themselves to be Irish and feel a close affinity with the rest of Ireland from which they were cut off in 1921. The majority Protestant population broadly consider themselves to be British and are firm supporters of the maintenance of the border between Northern Ireland and the rest of Ireland.
6   See D. Walsh, *Bloody Sunday and the Rule of Law in Northern Ireland* (London: Macmillan Press, 2000).
7   See T.P. Coogan, *The IRA* (Dublin, Fontana, 2000) and J. Bowyer Bell, *The IRA 1968-2000* (London: Frank Cass 2000); P. Taylor, *Provos: the IRA and Sinn Fein* (London: Bloomsbury, 1998).

ceasefires in the 1990s. Most of these arms were secreted in underground bunkers in Ireland.

It is not possible to be precise about the size of the IRA in terms of personnel. Active membership has fluctuated from time to time in response to recruitment patterns, changing internal organizational structures and operational strategies and wastage through capture (arrest, conviction and imprisonment), resignations/retirements and deaths. For much of the 1970s and 1980s it is estimated that active membership would have reached a peak of a few thousand. In the late 1980s and early 1990s, however, it is believed that this would have decreased to a few hundred.

An important feature of the IRA campaign has been the political support role played by Sinn Fein.[8] It has portrayed the IRA campaign as a continuation of the struggle to secure complete British military and political withdrawal from the whole island of Ireland and, thereby, to rescue the Catholic minority in Northern Ireland from the plight to which they were abandoned by acceptance of the 1921 Treaty. Tapping into this historical legacy and its enduring consequences has ensured at least a tacit toleration of the IRA and its campaign among significant sections of the community in Ireland. It has also provided a political context in which at least some of the IRA's actions could acquire a certain legitimacy. Sinn Fein has begun to develop this political base, particularly since the IRA ceasefires. Already it is one of the major political parties in Northern Ireland and is emerging as a significant political movement in Ireland. Currently, it has two seats in the Northern Irish government, 18 seats in the Northern Irish Assembly, 108 seats in local councils throughout Northern Ireland, four seats in the United Kingdom's Parliament, five seats in the Irish Parliament and 62 seats in local councils throughout Ireland.

The IRA's political manifesto includes the establishment of an Irish Republic of 32 counties, totally independent of Britain. It has always been vague, however, about the political complexion of this Irish Republic. The focus has been on the primary objective of British withdrawal and to that end it has managed to draw and retain support from across a broad church of socialists and conservatives. In the mid 1970s a more avowedly Marxist terrorist organization was formed, the Irish National Liberation Army (INLA) with its political wing the Irish Republican Socialist Party (IRSP). It has always been a much smaller organization based largely in urban Catholic communities in Northern Ireland. While it shares with the IRA the basic objective of forcing British withdrawal from Northern Ireland, this is combined with a very clear commitment to the estab-lishment of a workers' republic consisting of the 32 counties of Ireland. Although the INLA's organization and membership have always extended across the whole island of Ireland, its membership and terrorist attacks have been concentrated largely within Northern Ireland.

While the vast majority of shootings and bombings by republican terrorist organ-izations (IRA and INLA) have been carried out in Northern Ireland, there has also been considerable activity in Ireland. From the 1970s until the ceasefires in the mid-1990s these activities included: shootings, bombings, robberies, kidnappings and ransom demands, punishment beatings, smuggling, gunrunning, training in the use of arms and explosives as well as planning and preparation for terrorist operations outside the state.

---

8   See P. Taylor, *op. cit.*; B. O'Brien, *The Long War: the IRA and Sinn Fein* 3rd ed (Dublin: O'Brien, 1999).

The incidence of such terrorist activities has generally varied from year to year, with the 1970s and 1980s witnessing the most active periods.

For the most part, republican terrorist operations in Ireland have not been aimed directly at the institutions of this state. They might be portrayed generally as support operations necessary to maintain the organizations and/or to support the campaign in Northern Ireland. Nevertheless, several of these operations have resulted in the murder of 12 members of the Irish security forces. Most of these murders have been the result of operations that did not go according to plan. Some, however, such as the murder of Garda Jerry McCabe by the IRA in the course of a robbery carried out when the peace process was in motion, were so callous that it would be difficult to describe them as unintended consequences. It is also worth noting that some terrorist operations in Ireland were carried out directly in pursuit of the organization's political aims. A notable example was the murder of Lord Mountbatten and three other persons on holiday in Ireland in 1979. Lord Mountbatten was a senior member of the British royal family and former naval officer. As such, he would have been regarded as a prime target by the IRA.

The IRA called a ceasefire in 1994 to facilitate political negotiations aimed at a resolution of the constitutional conflict over the status of Northern Ireland. Frustration at the slow pace of the negotiations prompted a temporary breakdown in the IRA ceasefire in 1996, but it was restored in 1997 and has been maintained officially ever since. The negotiations ultimately resulted in the signing of the Good Friday Peace Agreement in 1998 and a major watershed in the IRA campaign.[9] Sinn Fein's acceptance of the Agreement, with its clear recognition that the status of Northern Ireland as part of the United Kingdom could be changed only by peaceful means, represented a seismic change in the republican position. Not only had Sinn Fein accepted the existence of Northern Ireland but they agreed to participate in its governance and to seek to achieve its unification with the rest of Ireland only through peaceful means. The military campaign to force a British military and political withdrawal from Northern Ireland was over. There still remained the problem of the IRA's huge arsenal of weapons and those of the other terrorist organizations. The Peace Agreement envisaged that these would be decommissioned and legislation has been enacted to facilitate this. In 2001 the first act of decommissioning of the IRA's arms was reportedly carried out. There has since been a second. Not only have these been hugely symbolic acts in themselves, but they also confirmed the IRA's support for Sinn Fein's political strategy.

While the Good Friday Peace Agreement and events consequent to it have largely removed the source of IRA violence, they have not totally eradicated the problem of terrorism associated with the constitutional status of Northern Ireland. The IRA still exists as an unconstitutional army. It still has access to a huge arsenal of arms and as such may still be considered to pose a potential threat to the state. A more realistic threat is presented by two splinter groups that broke away from the IRA, styling themselves the Continuity IRA (CIRA) and the Real IRA (RIRA). Although both are very small, they have been active in preparing and transporting arms and explosives within the state for use in Northern Ireland and Britain. While their level of activity generally pales in comparison with the levels associated with the IRA in the 1970s and 1980s, one was

---

9   See *Agreement Reached in the Multi-Party Negotiations* (otherwise known as the Good Friday Peace
     Agreement).

responsible for the bombing in Omagh (Northern Ireland) that claimed the lives of 29 people in 1998, the greatest single atrocity in the 30 years of violence.

Loyalist Terrorism

The conflict over the constitutional status of Northern Ireland has also generated a threat from Protestant terrorist organizations.[10] In 1912 political moves to grant a measure of self-governance to Ireland prompted the establishment of the Ulster Volunteer Force (UVF).[11] This was a paramilitary organization based in the British/Protestant community concentrated in the north-east of the island. Its primary objective was to resist by force, if necessary, self-governance or any such move towards weakening the status of Ireland as part of the United Kingdom. While the UVF was active in Northern Ireland until the 1920s, it remained largely dormant from then until the late 1960s when it resumed its terrorist campaign against Catholics.[12] The other major Protestant terrorist organization, the Ulster Defence Association, was formed in the early 1970s in Northern Ireland. Its primary objective was to resist any political reforms that would give greater recognition to the Irish tradition in Northern Ireland and weaken the British ethos. In practice, many of the violent activities of both terrorist organizations can be classified as sectarian attacks on Catholics in Northern Ireland.[13] Like the republican terrorist organizations, they have spawned a number of smaller splinter groups.

Although none of the Protestant (loyalist) terrorist organizations have a base or organization in Ireland, they have posed a constant threat to the Irish government. The sum total of their attacks across the border have been relatively small in number over the past thirty years and, for the most part, have consisted of planting incendiary devices in shops, public order incidents and bomb hoaxes. One devastating attack in 1974, however, took the form of exploding bombs without warning in crowded parts of Dublin and Monaghan.[14] Thirty-three people lost their lives. The Irish government therefore had to remain on the alert for such attacks, particularly at times of acute political and security tension in Northern Ireland.

International Terrorism

Terrorism associated with campaigns and conflicts in other parts of the world have not had any direct impact in Ireland. While it is believed that individuals associated with Islamic terrorism have lived in Ireland from time to time, there is no concrete evidence that they have ever used Ireland as a base for planning or launching terrorist attacks. Four individuals believed to have links to al-Qaeda were arrested by gardai in Dublin in December 2000 in the context of an FBI investigation into a plan to bomb Los Angeles

---

10   See, for example, J. Cusack and H. McDonald, *UVF* (Dublin: Poolbeg, 1997); and P. Taylor, *Loyalists: War and Peace in Northern Ireland* (New York: TV Books, 1999).
11   See A.T.Q. Stewart, *The Ulster Crisis* (London: Faber & Faber, 1967).
12   See Cusack and McDonald, *UVF*.
13   See Taylor, *Loyalists.*
14   See D. Mullan, *The Dublin and Monaghan Bombings* (Dublin: Wolfhound Press, 2001).

airport, but they were subsequently released without charge. There was also a suspicion that individuals with al-Qaeda connections based in Ireland may be engaged in preparing fake travel and identification documents.[15] However, no charges have ever been brought on foot of such suspicion. Ironically, the only concrete evidence of such an offence to emerge publicly concerns Robert McFarlane, a former USA Assistant Secretary of State, who allegedly travelled to Ireland on an Irish passport under the name of Sean Devlin in the course of what subsequently became known as the Iran-Contra affair. Although he was later pardoned in the USA for his involvement in this affair, his use of an Irish passport was never explained.

Irish involvement with international terrorism is much more likely to take the form of the IRA either receiving arms and training from, or contributing the same to, revolutionary terrorist organizations in other parts of the world. It is known, for example, to have strong links with the ETA organization in the Basque country and is currently under investigation for suspected links with the FARC organization in Columbia.

International organized crime seems to find Ireland a more attractive base than international terrorism. Ireland has served as a convenient gatepost to Europe for drug smugglers, particularly from South America. It would also appear that organized crime gangs, particularly from east European states, are taking advantage of the recent influx of refugees and asylum seekers to provide cover to set up a base for their operations in Ireland. All of this is in addition to the well-established links between the home-grown organized crime gangs and counterparts in the Netherlands and eastern Europe. While a clear distinction can be drawn between organized crime and terrorism, it is still worth taking note of these developments, as it is not always possible to maintain the distinction in Ireland. Indeed, the Irish government has a firmly established policy of deploying its anti-terrorist measures against organized crime. Moreover, there is evidence of cross-fertilization between organized crime and some of the Irish terrorist organizations, particularly INLA and the Protestant terrorist organizations in Northern Ireland.

Perceptions of the Terrorist Threat

The IRA and Republican Terrorism

Since the establishment of the state, government perceptions of the terrorist threat have always been dominated by the conflict over Northern Ireland. Republican organizations pursuing the reintegration of the national territory by force have always been considered a threat to this state, even though most of their violent attacks actually occurred within Northern Ireland and Britain. The fact that they are organized within the state, have regularly used the territory of the state to conduct support operations for attacks outside the state and pose a threat to the constitutional order within the state mark them out as the government's primary terrorist concern. For as long as the constitutional status of Northern Ireland was in dispute, the government considered that these organizations presented a real terrorist threat, even during times when they were relatively dormant. The activities of these organizations and their political support groups have always been

---

15   J. Cusack, 'FBI turns spotlight on al-Qaeda's Dublin operations', in: *Irish Times*, 31 July 2002.

monitored and members have been the subject of regular surveillance by the police. Legislative measures aimed at countering their activities have been retained throughout the history of the state.

Between 1972 and 1994 the threat posed by the IRA and INLA was considered to be so acute that it drained resources away from ordinary law enforcement activities throughout the state. All members of the police service were expected to contribute to intelligence gathering on the movements and activities of members of republican organizations, hundreds of police officers at any one time were transferred from their ordinary law enforcement activities to work primarily on anti-terrorist operations, regular cash movements to and from banks and post offices throughout the state were given police escorts, whole sections of some prisons were given over to the incarceration of terrorist prisoners and many judges were assigned to work in the Special Criminal Court dealing with terrorist suspects.

The IRA and INLA ceasefires and the associated peace process, which resulted in the Good Friday Peace Agreement in 1998, have had a marked impact on government perceptions of the terrorist threat posed by republican organizations. To some extent this was due to a very significant decrease in the number of armed attacks in Northern Ireland and Britain and related activities within Ireland. More fundamentally, it can be attributed to the historic acceptance by the broad republican movement of the Peace Agreement, with its acknowledgement that the status of Northern Ireland as part of the United Kingdom could be changed only by peaceful means. This, in turn, indicated an implicit acceptance by the republican movement that the institutions of the Irish state were legitimate, and that the IRA should begin a process of disarmament and ultimately stand down as the self-proclaimed army of the Irish Republic.

The government responded to these developments by embarking upon a programme of early release of republican prisoners, the transfer of a significant number of police officers from terrorist-related duties to ordinary crime and by the establishment of an expert committee with a remit to 'review the need for the Offences against the State legislation in the light of the contribution that the Good Friday Peace Agreement should make to the normalization of security arrangements while taking into account the continuing threat posed by international terrorism and organized crime'.

It does not follow that the government no longer perceives republican organizations as a significant terrorist threat. The ceasefires, the Peace Agreement, the decommissioning of some weapons and the improvement in the security situation do not conceal the fact that the IRA still retains its organization and a substantial armoury. Until it has fully disarmed and dissolved itself it is likely that it will remain a major concern for the government. This concern is fuelled by the fact that the IRA has engaged in occasional armed actions both within and outside the state. Most of these take the form of 'punishment beatings' and attacks on alleged drug-dealers within communities where the IRA is strong. There is also evidence that the IRA has attempted to import arms and continue to train and recruit members.

The perceived threat posed by republican organizations is also fuelled by the emergence of splinter groups since the Good Friday Peace Agreement. These groups present a serious terrorist threat. While many of their operations have been intercepted by security forces in both Northern Ireland and Ireland, they have managed to stage some high-profile attacks, such as the Omagh bombing.

Loyalist Terrorism

The threat perception of terrorism in Ireland from loyalist sources has tended to fluctuate from time to time over the past three decades. They have been considered most dangerous at times of political developments impinging upon the constitutional status of Northern Ireland, such as the Sunningdale Agreement of 1974, the Anglo-Irish Agreement of 1985 and the Good Friday Peace Agreement of 1998. Their modus operandi in recent years has largely consisted of the occasional bomb planted in retail outlets or at police or government targets. It would appear that efforts to combat the threat posed are largely confined to patrolling the border with Northern Ireland and contact with security forces in Northern Ireland. Since the loyalist terrorist organizations do not have networks or membership bases within the state, it is difficult for the Irish security forces to monitor their movements and activities directly.

International Terrorism

The threat perception of international terrorism in Ireland has been very low. Increasingly, however, the police have been paying more attention to Islamic terrorist networks as evidence has emerged that they are using Europe to establish bases and supply networks. Since 11 September 2001 the security services are paying more attention to the possibility of attacks on targets associated with western interests in Ireland, and the possibility that Ireland might be used as a base from which to launch attacks on western interests outside the state. It is also believed that the unprecedented number of refugees coming to Ireland in recent years has included individuals with links to Islamic terrorist organizations.

Media Perceptions

Media perceptions of the terrorist threat can differ depending on the source of the threat and the media outlet in question. Media coverage of domestic terrorism over most of the last thirty years has been dominated by factual reporting. There has been relatively little evidence of attempts to downplay or sensationalize the nature and extent of terrorist activity. The volume and incidence of terrorist activity spoke for itself. Accordingly, during the 1970s and 1980s when robberies, kidnappings, gun and bomb attacks were a regular occurrence, terrorism was a significant public concern. In the aftermath of the ceasefires and the Good Friday Peace Agreement, however, it would appear that public opinion is more inclined to the view that the domestic terrorist threat has largely dissipated. In public opinion surveys, terrorism does not feature as a significant concern compared to problems such as violent crime, organized crime, corruption, environmental pollution and public health.

Since the ceasefires and, in particular, the Good Friday Peace Agreement, the right-wing press have displayed a tendency to exaggerate the nature and extent of the terrorist threat posed by republican organizations. Their perception would appear to be that the threat from these sources is greater than the government seems prepared to concede. This is reflected in the style and tone in reporting actual terrorist incidents and in the content of regular feature articles. Other press and media outlets confine themselves to the factual reporting of terrorist incidents coupled with more balanced assessments of their implications.

In the aftermath of 11 September 2001 the media highlighted the threat posed by Islamic terrorism. Extensive coverage of the aftermath of the attacks on New York and Washington and the American-sponsored 'war on terrorism' has included regular assessments of the threat of terrorist attacks affecting Ireland. For the most part these have focused on the collateral damage that would be inflicted on Ireland as a result of an attack on the nuclear reprocessing facility at Sellafield in the United Kingdom. Shannon airport has also featured as a possible target in the media, as it is being used as a refuelling stop for American aircraft en route to Afghanistan. Media coverage of the possible effects of such attacks and the dangers of biological terrorism have captured the public imagination

Legal Basis for Anti-terrorist Measures

Article 28.3.3 of the Irish Constitution makes special provision for the declaration of an emergency by both houses of the legislature in time of war or armed rebellion. For this purpose 'time of war' is defined to include an armed conflict in which the state is not a participant, but in respect of which each house of the legislature has resolved that the conflict has given rise to a national emergency affecting the vital interests of the state. The first declaration of emergency under these provisions was issued in September 1939 on the commencement of the Second World War. Although the War ended in 1945, each house of the legislature failed to adopt the necessary resolutions terminating the emergency until 1976. Even then the rescission of the 1939 resolutions was followed immediately by the adoption of new resolutions declaring a fresh emergency arising out of the armed conflict in Northern Ireland. These were subsequently rescinded in 1995 in response to the IRA ceasefire.

The vital significance of a declaration of emergency under Article 28.3.3 is that it protects against constitutional challenge any law that is enacted and expressed to be for the purpose of securing the public safety and the preservation of the state in time of war or armed rebellion.[16] By using this magic formula the legislature could, for example, enact laws imposing whatever restrictions it deemed appropriate on an individual's liberty, freedom of expression, freedom of association and right to due process without the fear of such measures being challenged successfully under the fundamental rights provisions of the Constitution.[17]

While a number of measures were enacted under the cover of Article 28.3.3 during the Second World War, none of them survived beyond 1946. Only one measure was ever enacted under the cover of the 1976 declaration of emergency and that remained in force for only one year and was not renewed.[18] Nevertheless, it was a significant anti-terrorist

---

16   See G. Hogan and G. Whyte Kelly: *The Irish Constitution* 3rd ed (Dublin: Butterworths, 1994).

17   The only limitations are that it cannot be used to protect a law that purports to confer legislative authority on a body other than the legislature, or to protect a law that purports to reintroduce the death penalty.

18   See D. Morgan, 'The Emergency Powers Bill Reference I and II' (1978) 13 and (1979), *Irish Jurist* 67 and 252.

measure. Its primary feature was provision for the detention of terrorist suspects for seven days without charge.

The relative absence of emergency legislation in Ireland, despite the effects of the armed conflict in Northern Ireland, can be explained by the existence of the Offences against the State Act 1939 and its subsequent additions and amendments.[19] These have always provided the state with the essential executive and judicial powers considered necessary to combat terrorism. While the various measures have not been enacted under the cover of Article 28.3.3 and, as such, are subject to constitutional review, it will be seen that they bear some characteristics normally associated with emergency legislation. It should also be pointed out that the Offences against the State measures have been enacted specifically to combat terrorist activity. They are in addition to the standard measures available to combat ordinary crime and, generally, can be described as being more draconian than the 'ordinary' criminal justice measures.[20] Having said that, there is nothing in the powers and procedures introduced by the Offences against the State legislation that specifically confine their application to terrorist activity. They can, in appropriate circumstances, be used against 'ordinary criminal' activities. Increasingly, the state has been deploying them for this very purpose, particularly in the fight against organized crime.[21]

The Offences against the State legislation does not create an offence of terrorism per se. Indeed, Irish law does not recognize a distinct offence of terrorism, nor does it provide a definition of terrorism. However, the Offences against the State legislation does create a number of offences that might typically be committed by terrorist organizations, but that are not specifically confined to such organizations and their members. The scope and content of these offences clearly reflect the state's desire to suppress attempts by the IRA and other republican organizations to pursue the reintegration of the national territory by force. They include: usurpation of the functions of government; obstruction of the government; obstructing the President; unauthorized military exercises; interference with military or other employees of the state; membership of an unlawful organization; directing an unlawful organization; and training in the making or use of firearms. Other related offences include treason[22] and sedition.[23]

Many of these offences are framed in extremely broad terms in the sense that they criminalize actions or words that have no connection with terrorism or any activity that ought to be outlawed in a society based on respect for basic principles of democracy and

---

19   Subsequent amendments and additional measures are: Offences against the State (Amendment) Act 1940; Offences against the State (Amendment) Act 1972; Criminal Law Act 1976; Offences against the State Act 1985; and the Offences against the State (Amendment) Act 1998. There are other minor piecemeal amendments contained in general criminal justice enactments.

20   For a general discussion, see G. Hogan and C. Walker, *Political Violence and the Law in Ireland* (Manchester: Manchester University Press, 1989).

21   See: *Report of the Committee to Review the Offences against the State Act, 1939-1998 and Related Matters* (Dublin: Stationery Office, 2002); also D. Walsh, 'The Impact of Anti-subversive Laws on Police Powers and Practices in Ireland: The Silent Erosion of Individual Freedom', *Temple Law Review*, 62, 4 (1989), p. 1099.

22   See Article 39 of the Irish Constitution, and the Treason Act 1939.

23   Article 40.6.i of the Irish Constitution states: '[t]he publication or utterance of blasphemous, seditious or indecent matter is an offence which shall be punishable in accordance with law'. Sedition is recognized as an offence at common law.

the rule of law.[24] A seditious document, for example, is defined in such broad terms that the offence of possession of a seditious document will be satisfied by possession of an academic paper that argues that the government is not the lawful government of the state, or a document that tends to undermine the authority of the state.[25] Clearly, this constitutes a gross interference with freedom of expression and political debate.

The offence that has been used most frequently over the past 30 years is membership of an unlawful organization. Although it has been used exclusively against republican organizations seeking to achieve the reintegration of the national territory by force, the actual definition of the offence is so broad that it can be used against bodies that are pursuing political or economic objectives by purely peaceful means. For example, it includes any organization that 'promotes, encourages or advocates the non-payment of moneys payable to the Central Fund or any other public fund or the non-payment of local taxation'.[26] The government can issue a suppression order against any such organization if it is of the opinion that it is an unlawful organization. The legislation also includes provisions that make the task of the prosecution easier than it otherwise might have been in obtaining convictions for membership. Conviction is not dependant on proof that the individual went through a process of joining the organization or that the organization claims the individual as a member. It can be proved by matters such as: the opinion of a police officer that the individual is a member; any association on the part of the person that might lead to a reasonable inference that he is a member; possession of a document that indicates support for the organization; the failure to deny a published report that he is a member; and the failure to answer any police question relating to the individual's suspected membership.

The Offences against the State legislation provide the police with exceptional powers of arrest and detention; stop, question and search in public places; and entry, search and seizure. These are complemented by significant restrictions on the individual's right to silence. While these measures were designed for use in the investigation of terrorist offences, they can also be used against ordinary crime. Indeed, some of them can be used against persons who are not actually suspected of involvement in any criminal offence at all. Section 30 of the Offences against the State Act 1939, for example, permits the arrest and detention of an individual not just where he or she is suspected of committing a relevant offence, but also where he or she is suspected of having information about the commission of such an offence by others. It is not necessary that he or she should have any involvement in the offence. Individuals can also be arrested and detained under the power where they are suspected of being about to commit an offence; that is, before they have done anything that carries a criminal penalty. Persons arrested under this power can be detained without charge for a maximum of 72 hours. The normal maximum power of detention without charge is 12 hours.[27]

In addition to these special powers, the police can use all of their ordinary powers and procedures in the investigation and detection of terrorist activity. The most notable of

---

24 Some of these offences are recommended for repeal or substantial amendment by the Committee to Review the Offences against the State Acts 1939-1998 and Related Matters.
25 See Offences against the State Act 1939, s.10(2), for the definition.
26 Offences against the State Act 1939, s.18(f).
27 For a detailed account of police powers of arrest and detention, see: D. Walsh, *Criminal Procedure* (Dublin: Round Hall Sweet & Maxwell, 2002), at chapters 4-6.

these is the power to intercept postal and telecommunications messages in accordance with the provisions of the Interception of Postal and Telecommunications (Regulations) Act 1993.

Although the Offences against the State legislation technically constitutes ordinary legislation, two major parts bear many of the features of emergency legislation. These concern the provisions on internment and the establishment of special criminal courts. Internment can be introduced simply by a government proclamation declaring that internment is necessary to secure the preservation of public peace and order.[28] Once introduced, any minister of the government may order the arrest and detention without trial or time limit of any person who, in the opinion of the minister, is engaged in activities that are prejudicial to the preservation of public peace and order or to the security of the state. It has been introduced twice, from 1939-1946 and from 1957-1962, in response to renewed IRA activity. While it remains available as an option, the Irish government has refrained from resorting to it during the past thirty years.

Of much greater significance in practice over the past thirty years are the provisions governing special criminal courts. These come into effect when the government issues a proclamation declaring that it is satisfied that the ordinary courts are inadequate to secure the effective administration of justice and the preservation of public peace and order and that it is therefore necessary for the provisions governing special criminal courts to come into effect.[29] The government last issued such a proclamation in 1972 in response to the level of IRA activity in the state, and it has remained in force ever since.[30]

Pursuant to the proclamation and the relevant provisions in the Offences against the State legislation, the government has established a Special Criminal Court.[31] Trial in this Court is by three judges sitting without a jury, whereas trial for serious offences in the ordinary courts is by a single judge sitting with a jury of twelve citizens chosen at random from jury panels that have been drawn up from the electoral register. Guilt in the ordinary courts is determined exclusively by the jury deliberating in secret, whereas in the Special Criminal Court it is determined by the three judges who issue a single judgment.[32] All offences created by the Offences against the State legislation, as well as those scheduled pursuant to the 1939 Act, are normally tried in the Special Criminal Court.

Controversially, the Director of Public Prosecutions (DPP – the State Prosecutor) can also refer any case (irrespective of the offence involved) for trial in the Special Criminal Court where he certifies that in his opinion the ordinary courts are inadequate to secure the effective administration of justice in the case at hand.[33] There is no appeal against the DPP's decision to route a case through the Special Criminal Court.

---

28 Offences against the State (Amendment) Act 1940.
29 Offences against the State Act 1939, Part V.
30 Special Criminal Courts have previously been established from 1939-1946 and from 1961-1962.
31 For further detail, see Hogan and Morgan, *Political Violence and the Law in Ireland*.
32 For a detailed account of trial procedure in the special criminal court and in the ordinary courts, see: D. Walsh, *Criminal Procedure*, at chapters 19 and 20.
33 For criticism of this power, see the decision of the UN Human Rights Committee in *Kavanagh* v. *Ireland*. For proposals on reform, see the *Report of the Committee to Review Offences against the State Acts, 1939-1998 and Related Matters*.

Organization and Remit of Anti-terrorist Units

Counter-terrorist operations are primarily the responsibility of the Garda Siochana (police service), with contributions from the military and the Revenue Commissioners. Ireland does not have a separate secret service agency. This function is discharged from within the Garda Siochana.

The Garda Siochana is a national police service that is legally and constitutionally independent from the government in operational policing matters.[34] It is composed of 11,650 individual members, all of whom possess the full range of police powers and duties conferred by law. They are organized in a pyramidal structure of hierarchical ranks, with the rank of Garda at the bottom and the rank of Garda Commissioner at the top. While each individual member of the force can exercise his or her own discretion in the exercise of police powers and duties conferred upon them by law, they function as a cohesive unit under the administrative direction and control of the Garda Commissioner. The latter sets the operational policies and priorities for the force, exercises control over the allocation of resources within the force, and can establish distinct units within the force from time to time and is the disciplinary authority for the force. Although the Commissioner and the senior officers in the force are appointed (and can be removed from time to time) by the government, the Commissioner is generally independent of the government in the management of the force. The government has no formal authority over the contents of the Commissioner's operational policies, priorities and decisions in organizational or policing matters. However, since it ultimately determines the amount and allocation of budgetary resources available to the force, the government can exert influence in these matters. The Commissioner's receptivity to government wishes is enhanced by the fact that his appointment and removal lies very firmly in the hands of the government.

All members of the Garda Siochana have a responsibility to combat terrorism, just as they have a responsibility to combat crime. Some specialist units within the force, such as the National Drugs Unit and the Bureau of Fraud Investigation, deal with terrorist activities from time to time as these impact upon their particular remit. However, there are three units within the force that concentrate primarily, although not exclusively, on terrorism. The largest of these is the Special Detective Unit, commonly known as the Special Branch. Its membership is drawn from the ranks of the Garda Siochana and it operates under the administrative direction of a Chief Superintendent who, in turn, is answerable to the Assistant Commissioner, Crime and Security (C Branch). These members work in plain clothes and conduct policing operations throughout the state, including undercover surveillance and the arrest and interrogation of terrorist suspects. They are normally armed.

The work of the Special Branch is complemented by the National Surveillance Unit. As its name suggests, its function is to engage in the surveillance of individuals who are suspected of involvement in serious or subversive crime, including terrorism. Authorized postal and telecommunications intercepts, for example, would normally be carried out by

---

34   See D. Walsh, *The Irish Police: A Legal and Constitutional Perspective* (Dublin: Round Hall Sweet & Maxwell, 1998).

this unit.[35] Although it is a centralized unit headed by a Chief Superintendent specifically appointed for the task, its membership is drawn from the ranks of the Garda Siochana. Just like the Special Branch, it has been created purely as a matter of internal management organization and comes under the general responsibility of the Assistant Commissioner, Crime and Security (C Branch). Its members are normally armed in the course of operations.

Closely associated with the National Surveillance Unit is the Intelligence Section. In effect this is the state's secret service. Nevertheless, it is not established on the basis of distinct legislation or regulations. Like the National Surveillance Unit and the Special Branch it is merely a creation of internal management organization. It is headed by a Chief Superintendent who, in turn, is answerable to the Assistant Commissioner, Crime and Security (C Branch). The Section's members are drawn from the ranks of the Garda Siochana. They do not have any special powers or status over and above those of their colleagues in the force. It is just that they specialize in the assessment of intelligence information. The Section itself does not engage in surveillance or in the acquisition of intelligence in the field. For this it relies on the National Surveillance Unit, with which it works closely, and the Special Branch and general detective branch. As the state's secret service, its remit extends beyond domestic terrorism to include international terrorism and, indeed, any threat to the security of the state, irrespective of from where it comes.

It is also worth mentioning the Emergency Response Unit. This is an armed unit within the Garda Siochana specially trained to respond at short notice to incidents involving a threat of armed violence. While its remit is not confined to terrorism, inevitably it is most likely to be deployed in order to deal with terrorist threats.

The defence forces have played a significant role in combating terrorism in Ireland over the past thirty years. This has mostly taken the form of providing armed support to the police in specific operations, manning road checkpoints on the border, the transport of terrorist prisoners and escorting large consignments of cash by road. There is also a military intelligence branch within the defence forces, which is established as a matter of internal management organization within the defence forces with all of its members drawn from the defence forces. Very little is known about its internal organization and activities. It would appear, however, that a significant part of its work involves monitoring the threat of terrorism from internal and external sources. While members of the defence forces do enjoy certain powers of arrest over citizens, there is no evidence to suggest that these powers are used in the investigation and detection of terrorist activities. The Revenue Commissioners do not have a distinct anti-terrorist unit. Terrorism comes within their remit indirectly where terrorist activity takes the form of importing arms and ammunitions, profiteering from unlawful imports and exports, money-laundering through 'legitimate' businesses and tax evasion on the profits of 'front' businesses. This work is undertaken through the same units and procedures that apply to such activities from a non-terrorist source. It normally involves close cooperation with the Garda Siochana and, where appropriate, the defence forces and naval service.

The prosecution of all serious crimes in Ireland is the function of the Director of Public Prosecutions (DPP). There is no separate agency for prosecuting terrorist crimes.

---

35   See D. Walsh and P. McCutcheon, 'Ierland', in P. Tak (ed.), *Heimelijke Opsporing in de Europese Unie* (Antwerp: Intersentia Rechtswetenschappen, 2000).

They are prosecuted along with all other serious crimes by the DPP. Moreover, there is no separate unit within the DPP's office for dealing with terrorist crimes. They are dealt with by the same individuals and through the same processes and rules as ordinary crimes. The only difference is that where there is a suspected terrorist involvement in a case, the DPP will normally send it for trial in the Special Criminal Court.

Accountability for Anti-terrorist Operations

Accountability for anti-terrorist operations is primarily delivered through the account-ability of the members of the units engaged in such activities. The members of the anti-terrorist units within the Garda Siochana are accountable for their actions in the same manner and to the same extent as members of the Garda Siochana generally. For the most part, there are no special exemptions or special procedures applicable to actions or decisions taken for the purpose of combating terrorism. The primary external account-ability mechanisms for the Garda Siochana are: Parliament, the law, and the complaints procedure.[36] All of them, however, suffer from serious shortcomings from the perspective of transparency and effectiveness. These shortcomings are generally more acute in the context of terrorism.

Members of the Special Branch, National Surveillance Unit and the Intelligence Section are answerable to the Assistant Commissioner, Crime and Security in the same manner as any member of the criminal investigation units in the force. The Assistant Commissioner is answerable to the Commissioner who is answerable to the Minister for Justice, Equality and Law Reform who, in turn, is answerable to the Dail (the House of Parliament whose members are elected directly by the people). At least in theory, therefore, those engaged in anti-terrorist operations are subject to a direct chain of democratic accountability. The practice, unfortunately, is very different. While the Minister does convey information to the House from time to time about anti-terrorist operations that have given rise to serious public concern, more often than not he will plead national security interests to block potentially embarrassing scrutiny. In any event the Minister's capacity to deliver democratic accountability for the police is limited by the fact that he has no executive control over police operations. He is merely answering on behalf of the Garda Commissioner who does have the executive authority. Accor-dingly, he can do little more than convey whatever information the Commissioner makes available to him.

Up until recently Parliamentary Committees have held out better prospects for the delivery of effective democratic police accountability. They could call senior police officers before them to answer questions about their strategies and operations. While national security interests could always be used to limit the effectiveness of these committees, at least they had the advantage of being able to call to account directly those who did have executive authority in operational policing matters. At the time of writing, the capacity of these Committees to deliver police accountability is under threat as a result of a decision of the Supreme Court upholding a legal challenge by police officers

---

36   See Walsh, *The Irish Police.*

to the capacity of a parliamentary committee to question them about their involvement in a fatal shooting of an unarmed civilian.[37]

Members of the police force are answerable to the law to the same extent and through the same procedures as ordinary citizens.[38] They do not enjoy any general exemption or privilege for actions or decisions taken in the context of law enforcement or terrorist operations. They can be prosecuted for criminal infractions, sued for civil wrongs and be judicially reviewed for operational policies and decisions. In practice, however, it can prove difficult to maintain a successful action in the courts against the police for operational matters.

Criminal complaints against the police will be investigated by the police themselves and the decision whether to initiate a criminal prosecution will be taken on the basis of the police investigation report. Despite thousands of citizen complaints against the police in the past two decades, very few have resulted in criminal prosecutions and not even one has resulted in a conviction. Civil actions for damages are generally much more successful. Substantial sums have been paid out in recent years as compensation for police wrongdoing in the investigation and detection of crime and terrorist activity. It does not follow, however, that the civil action delivers effective accountability. There is reason to believe that many civil actions are not initiated or pursued as a result of the police applying pressure on the citizen to drop the action, or a reluctance on the part of the citizen concerned to risk the time, expense and emotional energy that a civil action necessarily entails.

Judicial review of operational policies, while a theoretical possibility, is a very poor accountability prospect. The courts afford a very broad area of discretion to the Garda Commissioner in the formulation of his operational policies, strategies and priorities. They are notoriously reluctant to second-guess him in such matters. Indeed, there has been no case in which the Commissioner's operational policies or strategy have been declared unlawful. It is also worth noting that the courts will not normally order the Garda Commissioner to disclose documents or information for any purpose where the Commissioner claims that such disclosure would be prejudicial to national security or would not be in the public interest because it would reveal the identity of a police informer or otherwise jeopardize an ongoing criminal investigation. These matters are particularly acute in the terrorist context.

A separate independent complaints procedure was introduced in 1987 to deal with citizen complaints against the police.[39] Although many thousands of complaints have been made through this procedure over the past fifteen years, very few have actually been successful. There are several reasons for this. While the procedure is described as independent, each complaint is in fact investigated by the police themselves, albeit under the supervision of an independent board. The decision of whether to refer an individual case to a disciplinary tribunal is taken by the independent board, but on the basis of the report of the police investigation. Another major problem with the procedure is the strict admissibility requirements that a complaint must satisfy before it can be dealt with through the procedure. There is also a strong suspicion that the police have brought

---

37   See *Maguire and others v Ardagh and Others* Supreme Court, 11 April 2002.
38   See Walsh, *The Irish Police.*
39   See Walsh, *The Irish Police.*

pressure to bear on complainants not to pursue their complaints. Whatever the reasons, about 60 per cent of complaints are not pursued after they have been lodged, and many complaints are not lodged at all because of general lack of confidence in the procedure.

There is a particular feature of the complaints procedure that can reduce its usefulness even further in the specific context of terrorism. If the report of a complaint investigation is likely to affect the security of the state, the Garda Commissioner must be notified. He can make further enquiries into the matter and report to the Minister for Justice, Equality and Law Reform and consult with the Complaints Board before the report can be finalized. In effect this enables the Commissioner to frustrate the full investigation of a complaint where he is concerned that the investigation will touch on matters of state security. In practice this is most likely to happen when a complaint is lodged concerning Garda action in the context of an anti-terrorist operation.

Accountability for the actions of the military intelligence branch and the Revenue Commissioners in anti-terrorist matters suffers from all of the weaknesses described above. Indeed, they are even less accountable by virtue of the fact that they are not subject to an 'independent' complaints procedure and their actions are generally less visible than those of the Garda Siochana.

International Terrorist Cooperation

Ireland is generally a keen participant in international cooperation against terrorism and organized crime. It has a long history of cooperation with the authorities in the United Kingdom in combating terrorism associated with the conflict in Northern Ireland. While this cooperation has suffered during times of political tension between the two governments, it has generally been strong since the signing of the Anglo-Irish Agreement in 1985. This Agreement made provision for regular meetings between senior police chiefs on either side of the border with Northern Ireland to discuss security matters of common interest. There is also a streamlined extradition procedure between the two jurisdictions and a facility whereby terrorist crimes committed in one jurisdiction can be prosecuted in the other.[40] While the Irish courts have on occasions refused the extradition of republican suspects on the ground that the offences for which they were wanted were political offences, or offences connected with political offences, the Irish authorities have not demonstrated any reluctance to pursue prosecutions against such suspects for offences committed in Northern Ireland.

Cooperation with authorities in Britain and Northern Ireland, both through the formal procedures and informally between police personnel on either side of the border, has produced some notable security successes. Several terrorist operations have been intercepted and significant arms finds made as a result of this cooperation. As yet, however, there is no facility for hot pursuit across the border, or joint investigations or operations between the police and security services on either side of the border.[41] Arguably, the

---

40   See Walsh, *Criminal Procedure*, chapter 3.
41   See S. Dunn, D. Murray and D. Walsh, *Cross-Border Police Cooperation in Ireland* (Limerick: University of Limerick, 2002)

investigations into the Omagh bombing have been hampered by the lack of a joint investigative team.

At the European level, Ireland is a keen supporter of cooperation against terrorism and organized crime. Generally, it uses the same mechanisms and procedures for both. It has signed up to and implemented the European Convention on Extradition and the European Convention on the Suppression of Terrorism. While it does not yet have a SIRENE bureau, it participates fully in Europol. It also has liaison officers in the Irish embassies of some European capital cities in order to facilitate cooperation on terrorism, organized crime and general criminal matters. In addition, there are substantial regular contacts between the personnel in specialized police and customs units and their counterparts in other European states. While these methods and procedures have proved very useful in combating IRA activity on the European mainland, they have had most relevance in practice for investigations into activities of organized crime gangs, drug traffickers and traffickers in human beings.

Ireland has a strong record of cooperation against crime and terrorism with several countries outside Europe, in particular the United States. For example, it has a formal extradition treaty with the United States and maintains regular channels of communication with the FBI. These channels have proved productive in combating IRA gunrunning operations. Although it is too early to point to concrete evidence, it is likely that these same channels will be used to convey information about the movements and activities of Islamic suspects to the US authorities in the wake of 11 September 2001.

General Conclusions

The discourse on terrorism in Ireland throughout the twentieth century was dominated by the IRA's campaign to secure British withdrawal from Northern Ireland by the use of force, and the methods employed by the state in response. The ferocity of that campaign, particularly during the 1970s and 1980s, coupled with the threat posed to the stability of the Irish state by the IRA, provoked a reaction from the state that would not be appropriate in dealing with ordinary crime and political opposition in a democracy based on respect for human rights. As often happens, however, the agencies of the state grew accustomed to their exceptional anti-terrorist methods and powers. Increasingly, they were employed to deal with organized crime, ordinary crime and lawful forms of political opposition and anti-establishment activities. As the level of terrorist activity has declined and the threat from the IRA has receded, so the use of these powers and methods against non-terrorist activity has become more pronounced. Exceptional police powers and special criminal courts that were introduced to deal with terrorism are now used extensively against persons suspected of non-terrorist crime. They have become integrated into the ordinary criminal justice system along with the general lack of adequate accountability that has been a feature of them.[42]

---

42 See Walsh, 'The Impact of Anti-subversive Laws on Police Powers and Practices in Ireland'; and 'Organized Crime and the Normalization of Anti-terrorist Laws in Ireland', paper presented to Conference on Legal Aspects of Emergency Regimes: International and Comparative Perspectives, Minerva Centre for Human Rights, Tel Aviv, 2000.

A disturbing aspect of these developments is that they are happening largely by stealth, without any open public debate or legislative authorization. Admittedly, pursuant to its obligations under the Good Friday Peace Agreement, the government established a committee to review the need for retaining the anti-terrorist measures in the peaceful environment that was expected to ensue from the Agreement. The committee, composed largely of police and government officials, has submitted its report which broadly endorses the use of the exceptional measures to combat non-terrorist crime. Inevitably, this will devalue the currency of exceptional anti-terrorist measures and will fuel the arguments of those who maintain that resort to such measures does more long-term damage to the body politic than could ever be done by the terrorist.

4 Democratization and State Responses to Protracted Terrorism in Spain

Fernando Reinares

Spaniards have consistently perceived terrorism as one of their two main public concerns – together with unemployment – since the late 1970s, as their polity was undergoing a process of democratization following nearly four decades of dictatorship. Nowadays it is no longer considered a major threat to democratic stability, as was the case some twenty years ago, but a protracted violent phenomenon that systematically violates human rights and disrupts basic political processes common to tolerant polities. This chapter summarizes and assesses state responses to this prolonged problem in a context of political change.[1] More concretely, the fundamental problem has been and still is that of ETA (an acronym for *Euskadi ta Askatasuna*, meaning Basque Homeland and Freedom), a terrorist organization formed during the 1960s amid the crisis of Francoism (1939-1975), as a radicalised expression of Basque ethnic nationalism. ETA has claimed responsibility for well over 80 per cent of the more than 1000 people killed in Spain as a result of terrorist actions between 1968 and 2001. It remains a major source of concern for the citizens of Spain as a whole and the Basque country in particular, even if its violence progressively declined in frequency throughout the 1980s and more so along the 1990s, a long way from the dramatic escalation that took place precisely during the period when the country underwent a process of regime change.

The average yearly number of fatalities attributed to ETA was 81 between 1978 and 1980, 34 between 1981 and 1990, and 16 between 1991 and 2000. It should be noted that ETA perpetrated just seven assassinations a year between 1968 and 1977, that is under the dictatorship and before Spain's first free elections. Paradoxically, however, this

---

1   Research underlying this contribution was made possible thanks to a grant from the Spanish Inter-ministerial Commission for Science and Technology (*Comisión Interministerial de Ciencia y Tecnologia*), SEC2000-1039.

M. van Leeuwen (ed.): *Confronting Terrorism*, pp. 57-70

operational decline caused by changing political conditions and state responses has modified both ETA's internal structures and victimization patterns. For instance, the range of targets has been successively amplified, from mainly military and police personnel at the beginning to civilians killed often highly indiscriminately outside the Basque country and, finally, to Basque elected politicians from local to national levels of government, university professors, journalists, business people or judges, among other categories of persons explicitly known for not endorsing Basque nationalist propositions. Basques themselves coincide with the rest of Spanish citizens in considering terrorism and unemployment to be their main issues of public concern.

ETA was practically the only terrorist organization active in Spain during the 1990s, killing 161 citizens, including children and elderly people, during the decade. One single assassination in 1993 was attributed to the GRAPO (*Grupos de Resistencia Antifascista Primero de Octubre*, or First of October Anti-fascist Resistance Groups). This left-wing terrorist organization had been particularly active during the period of transition from authoritarian rule and the beginning of the new constitutional regime, killing some 70 people in those days, but it had become a residual group since the mid-1980s. Right-wing terrorist organizations, not surprisingly also active during Spain's years of political change, caused nearly 40 fatalities as they tried to bring about an involution of the democratization process, but they vanished shortly after the failure of an attempted *coup d'état* in February 1981. The remaining terrorist events registered between the mid-1970s and the late 1980s were perpetrated by a few even smaller groups associated with the radical left and other peripheral nationalist movements, or were actions of strictly international terrorism.[2] In addition, the GAL (*Grupos Antiterroristas de Liberación*, or Anti-terrorist Liberation Groups), a vigilante terrorist organization linked to some state authorities and members of the security agencies, caused the deaths of 27 people between 1983 and 1987, mostly in south-western France, as part of a campaign intended to intimidate members and sympathizers of ETA living there. During the 1990s the GIA (*Groupes Islamiques Armés*, or Armed Islamic Groups) from Algiers was found to have some mobility structures along the Mediterranean coast in Spain. And already in the new millennium, supporting segments of al-Qaeda have been detected and 18 Islamic fundamentalists suspected of belonging to its global terrorist network have been detained. In none of these cases, however, is there evidence of (planning for) violent actions inside the country.

From Conflict Regulation to Anti-terrorist Agreements

Governmental anti-terrorist policy in the context of liberal democracies typically includes a varied, although not necessarily coherent or consistent combination of political, juridical and police measures, implemented in the context of increasing international cooperation.[3] Even if it is not to be exclusively understood as an anti-terrorist measure, the process of democratization was itself considered by Spanish citizens in general and

---

2   Fernando Reinares, 'Sociogénesis y Evolución del Terrorismo en España', in Salvador Giner (ed.), *España: Sociedad y Política* (Madrid: Espasa Calpe, 1990), pp. 353-396.
3   Fernando Reinares, *Terrorismo y Antiterrorismo* (Barcelona: Ediciones Paidós, 1998), pp. 131-173.

political elites in particular as the factor most likely to bring about the end of domestic civil violence. In other words, during the immediate post-Franco period, terrorism was not perceived as a major threat to political stability and the democratization process. Reactionary members within the armed forces were at that time considered the most serious menace. In fact, full amnesty was granted, between November 1975 and October 1977, to nearly 900 members and collaborators of ETA who had been exiled or imprisoned under the dictatorship, thus facilitating their integration into the new political situation and fostering the disappearance of that terrorist organization to which they belonged. In addition, political symbols forbidden by authoritarian rulers, such as the Basque flag designed within the nationalist movement, or *ikurriña*, as well as those of other opposition movements under the dictatorship, were legalized by January 1977. The Basque vernacular, also known as *euskera*, as well as other autochthonous tongues different from Castilian, ceased to be prohibited and were soon recognized as official languages. True, both full amnesty to those criminalized in the past for their involvement with ETA as well as the recognition of cultural and symbolic elements of a collective identity could have been adopted faster. The delays contributed to the radicalization of popular demands as evidenced in frequent street demonstrations that in these immediate post-Franco years were all too often met with severe police repression. This, in turn, contributed to the persistence of sympathetic attitudes towards the terrorist organization for rather a long period of time, before the public at large came to generally reject the terrorists.

The first free elections after the end of Francoist dictatorship took place in June 1977. The emerging state legislative power – where the moderate UCD (*Unión de Centro Democrático*, or Democratic Centre Union) gained a relative majority of parliamentary seats and the PSOE (*Partido Socialista Obrero Español*, or Spanish Socialist Workers Party) became the main force in the opposition – consensually drafted a democratic Constitution that was approved in a referendum and enacted by December 1978. New general elections were then called in March 1979, producing results similar to the previous ones. But it was the formal establishment of a Basque Autonomous Community that political elites and public opinion widely perceived as a conflict-regulation development that was expected to exert, in the short term, a critical impact on the evolution of ETA. The new political and territorial entity was a responsive outcome designed to satisfy widespread collective demands within three provinces (Alava, Guipúzcoa and Vizcaya). Navarre remained outside the process because the large majority of its people rejected formal incorporation into an encompassing Basque political entity. However, in another referendum held in October 1979 the citizens of the other three territories ratified a statute of autonomy agreed by their political representatives, both nationalists and non-nationalists, and the central government. Basques elected their own parliament in May 1980 for the first time. The resulting party system, which has changed relatively little over the past two decades, is characterized by high levels of fragmentation and polarization.[4] Although the PNV (*Partido Nacionalista Vasco*, or Basque Nationalist Party) has received the largest share of valid votes ever

---

4   Francisco J. Llera, Los Vascos y la Política. El proceso político vasco: Elecciones, partidos, opinión pública y legitimación en el País Vasco, 1977-1992 (Bilbao: Universidad del País Vasco, 1994), pp. 13-33; and Juan J. Linz, Conflicto en Euskadi (Madrid: Espasa Calpe, 1986), pp. 295-366.

since, it is crucial to note that the Basque electorate remains deeply divided over its support for nationalist and non-nationalist parties. However, the political branch of the ethno-nationalist terrorists, initially known as Herri Batasuna (HB, United People) and nowadays simply Batasuna (Unity), has rarely received the votes of more than 10 per cent of the electorate in the Basque Autonomous Community.

Indeed, the success of democratization and self-government as processes of conflict regulation was only partial in the short term, as far as terrorism was concerned. Such differential impact was highly dependent on the distinctive logics adopted by the two then existing factions into which ETA has been divided since the mid-1970s, namely *ETA politico-militar* or ETA (pm) and *ETA militar* or ETA (m).[5] The former terrorist group acknowledged the importance of the ongoing political transformations and decided in 1982 not only to abandon violence altogether but to dissolve the entire underground structure as well. In order to lower the cost of exit from terrorism, initially allowing for the effective self-dissolution of ETA (pm) and subsequently trying to affect the internal cohesion of any remaining terrorist organization, the central government simultaneously introduced social reinsertion measures based on individual pardons. As a result of the institutional move, nearly 250 former militants and collaborators in the various ETA factions had requested and benefited from these social reinsertion measures by 1990. However, as the leaders of ETA (m), the only faction that has persisted until the present day (this is why it is commonly referred to simply as ETA), perceived how these measures were negatively affecting the maintenance of their clandestine organization, they attempted to raise the cost of exit by threatening all those militants and collaborators who opted for reinsertion or were likely to do so. To make the threat credible, two ETA gunmen in September 1986 killed a female former member of the terrorist directorate who had decided to accept the social reinsertion measures in 1985, while she was walking with her four-year-old son through the main square of a small village in Guipúzcoa where she had been born. Women leaders, by the way, were rare in an underground group overwhelmingly dominated by male activists.

As the effectiveness of social reinsertion measures declined, the authorities in May 1989 introduced penitentiary provisions aimed at dispersing imprisoned members of terrorist organizations in general and the then nearly 500 members or collaborators of ETA (m) across the country, instead of concentrating them in just a few prisons. The aim was to make it more difficult for the underground leaders to exert strict control over the inmates and their relatives, a task usually performed through designated lawyers and subordinate associations related to the support network arranged around and for the terrorist organization. This governmental initiative aimed at undermining the internal cohesion of jailed militants and, by extension, of the terrorist organization at large. As a result of the penitentiary initiatives being introduced, well over 100 inmates sentenced because of offences related to ETA (m) had opted for reinsertion measures by 1995. Both the reinsertion measures of 1982 and the penitentiary dispersal initiative of 1989 have been maintained by successive central governments. Moreover, as of 1996 when the liberal conservative *Partido Popular* (PP, Popular Party) gained access to the central executive, competences on the penitentiary institutions, which had traditionally been

---

5   Fernando Reinares, 'The Political Conditioning of Collective Violence: Regime Change and Insurgent Terrorism in Spain', *Research on Democracy and Society*, vol. 3, 1996, pp. 297-326.

ascribed to the Spanish Ministry of Justice, for the first time became part of the Ministry of the Interior, needless to say the crucial government department as far as anti-terrorist policy is concerned. While these measures were implemented in the context of a broad political consensus comprising anti-terrorist matters, they proved to be quite effective in stimulating individual dissociation from the terrorist organization, renunciation of violent methods and acceptance of measures aiming at reinsertion in society.

Formal political agreements among the main parties and other relevant collective actors, both at the autonomous and state level, seem to be associated not only with the formulation but also with the effectiveness of anti-terrorist policy. In general terms, the broader the political consensus behind governmental measures to counter terrorism, the better the results eventually obtained throughout its implementation would tend to be. In this respect, the so-called Pact of Madrid, subscribed to in November 1987 by a large majority of the political parties presented in the national parliament, and even more importantly the subsequent Pact of Ajuria Enea for the pacification and normalization of the Basque country, signed in January 1988 in Vitoria by the main nationalist and non-nationalist parties of the Basque Autonomous Community, were both highly influential on the adoption and implementation of governmental anti-terrorist measures, at least until the mid-1990s. A similar agreement was reached in October 1988 in Pamplona by the most prominent political and social forces of Navarre. These pacts aimed at providing favourable conditions for citizens to mobilize against ETA and its supporters, although their main political effect was probably that of aligning the Basque Nationalist Party with the other democratic parties, thus trying to isolate the undemocratic radical formations within the nationalist sector. However, PNV leaders decided in the early 1990s to look for alliances with other nationalist formations, such as Herri Batasuna, despite the latter being a non-democratic party clearly subordinated to ETA. By the mid-1990s, the *Partido Popular*, then a rising force among the Basque electorate and already the main opposition party in the central parliament, also became critical of reinsertion measures, thus openly contradicting the existing agreements. These developments brought the Pact of Ajuria Enea and similar accords to a virtual end.

Furthermore, the Basque Nationalist Party went as far as secretly signing alternative agreements with another smaller nationalist party (*Eusko Alkartasuna*) and ETA itself in August 1998 and September 1999, and a third agreement shortly later, although this time publicly and encompassing a number of legal nationalist parties, trade unions and other associations, the *Pacto de Lizarra* or *Pacto de Estella* (Agreement of Lizarra or Estella, depending on the denomination of the site where it was subscribed). The basic purpose of all these agreements was to constitute a nationalist front, thus trying to advance nationalist proposals and imposing them on the Basque people as a whole, presumably in exchange for ending terrorist violence. All these anti-system developments prompted the two main parties at the national level, PP and PSOE, which also account for about one-half of the electorate within the Basque Autonomous Community and even more than two thirds of the votes within Navarre, to sign an agreement in defence of civil liberties and against terrorism (*Acuerdo por las libertades y contra el terrorismo*) in December 2000. Actually this is the first properly anti-terrorist pact since the consolidation of democracy in Spain. As the pact clearly states, their proponents would only incorporate the PNV provided that this party decides to side with other democratic parties, even if they are not nationalist, instead of establishing alliances with other nationalist groups regardless of their democratic credentials. Besides agreement on adopting mechanisms for joint decision-making on anti-terrorist initiatives and stimulating citizens' reactions to terrorism, the national anti-terrorist pact, which was endorsed by a large number of other parties and entities from civil society in the following months, wanted to make it clear that in a democracy the use of terrorist violence can never extract political advantages or rewards of any kind, and solemnly committed the signatories to provide continuous assistance to victims of terrorism.

As to the issue of negotiating with the terrorists, the consensus reached at the end of 2000 by the PP and the PSOE emphasizes, in the case of ETA, that Basque citizens have their own autonomous institutions and elected political representatives, while the terrorist organization solely aims at violently imposing minority, exclusive and explicitly xenophobic goals upon the whole population. Therefore, political negotiations between a democratic responsive government and a terrorist organization are ruled out, as has been the case in the past with respect to ETA as well as other terrorist organizations active in Spain.[6] Legitimate authorities have twice engaged in significant conversations with leaders of ETA: first with those of ETA (pm) in 1981; and later with leaders of ETA (m), in 1989. A third rather unsuccessful and even irrelevant meeting took place late in 1998, but the leaders of the declining terrorist organization were already engaged in a joint strategy with the Basque Nationalist Party aimed at creating a nationalist front. However, the central issue of all these contacts was always that of possible legal initiatives to facilitate the renunciation of terrorism. Offering political concessions of any kind in return for an end to violence has never been considered.

The victims of terrorism are no doubt among the people most firmly opposed to any kind of talks with the terrorists. Among the institutions and actors involved in the internal security sector, the *Asociación de Víctimas del Terrorismo* (AVT, Association of Victims of Terrorism), together with similar civic entities formed within the Basque country, constitutes the most influential interest group since at least the late 1980s. Founded early in 1981, the AVT has concentrated efforts on lobbying both managers of the state bureaucracy and responsible politicians for introducing legislative proposals, as well as on offering legal and psychological assistance to all those affiliated – around 1,800 individuals by the year 2002 – most of them relatives of persons who have been killed or wounded in an act of terrorism. As a result of this dedication a unified legislation protecting the victims of terrorism became a reality, although only as late as 2001. The *Asociación pro Derechos Humanos* (APH, Association for Human Rights) also played a somewhat minor role in the same policy network during the late 1970s and throughout the 1980s. But the victims of terrorism who gathered in associations have contributed as well to the prevention of revenge actions against the terrorists and thus to the spread of sectarian violence among the Basques. The implicit acknowledgment of this important fact, as well as the need to satisfy their moral demands and material rights, led the signatories of the national anti-terrorist pact to establish a unitary foundation to support the victims of terrorism (*Fundación Víctimas del Terrorismo*).

---

6   Florencio Domínguez Iribarren, *De la Negociación a la Tregua: El Final del ETA?* (Madrid: Taurus, 1998), pp. 17-104; Robert P. Clark, *Negotiating with ETA: Obstacles to Peace in the Basque Country, 1975-1988* (Reno: University of Nevada Press, 1990), pp. 73-221.

In the framework of this new anti-terrorist pact, new measures have also been promoted to deal with the array of groups and entities that provide resources to terrorist organizations, groups and entities acting under the command of leaders from the terrorist organization. Basque radical nationalism is a sector arranged from within and around ETA; it is the environment of subordinate specialized groups and entities that mobilize the human, material and symbolic resources that a terrorist organization needs to persist over time.[7] More precisely, a major political decision on anti-terrorist policy was adopted in the middle of 2002, when the Spanish Parliament approved new legislation on parties that allows the executive, upon request from the Parliament, to demand judicial procedures intended to outlaw political groups unwilling to condemn terrorism or maintaining links with a terrorist organization. In this context, there is overwhelming accumulated evidence on the relationship between Herri Batasuna or Batasuna, on the one hand, and the terrorist organization ETA on the other. For instance, a few hundred Batasuna members have been sentenced in court for their implication as militants or collaborators of the terrorist organization. Therefore, even if this initiative has prompted some debate among politicians and public opinion in general, a controversy linked in the Basque country to the cleavage between nationalists and non nationalists, a large majority of those who are representatives, as well as the people they represent, are in favour of the new law on parties. Actually, it is expected that in the near future judges might outlaw Batasuna, the still legal or tolerated branch of what remains of the terrorist organization known as ETA.

Anti-terrorist Legislation and Law Enforcement

Francoism confronted insurgent terrorism through indiscriminate repression and the use of militarised institutions. Official violence was, under these circumstances and particularly when deployed against ETA, conducive to the loss of state legitimacy in the Basque country and the growth of a public opinion that was sympathetic to the terrorist organization. During the democratic transition and the years of democratic consolidation, the emerging political elites had to remove these practices and reform the agencies, introducing new ones in accordance with the rule of law and the principles of an open society. But due to the intrinsic characteristics of the political change experienced, gradual and reformist rather than rapid and revolutionary, many of these reforms took place rather slowly, to the extent that indiscriminate repression by police forces when presumably performing operations against terrorism happened while the existing legal framework was being replaced. All this resulted in the counter-productive application of some legislative and proactive measures against terrorism, which during some critical years unintentionally contributed to sustaining significant and lasting popular support for the terrorists. It is estimated that nearly half of the Basque adults perceived ETA members as either patriots or idealists in 1978, whereas only 7 per cent of those inter-

---

7   José M. Mata, *El Nacionalismo Vasco Radical* (Bilbao: Universidad del País Vasco, 1993); and Peter Waldmann, 'From the Vindication of Honour to Blackmail: the Impact of the Changing Role of ETA on Society and Politics in the Basque Region of Spain', in Noemi Gal-Or (ed.), *Tolerating Terrorism in the West* (London: Routledge, 1991), pp. 1-32.

viewed in public opinion surveys would call them plain criminals. In 1989, less than one-quarter of the same citizens referred to the terrorists as patriots or idealists, and the number of those who portrayed them simply as criminals was more than doubled as compared to the previous decade.[8]

In January 1977, the National Court was created in Madrid to deal with serious organized crime and terrorist offences. This implied a fundamental jurisdictional change, since terrorist crimes would be dealt with, from that moment on, by ordinary judges instead of military courts, as had been the case previously. Likewise, following the broad *Pactos de la Moncloa* (Moncloa Agreements) which were signed in October 1977 by most of the parliamentary parties in order to secure the democratization process despite a severe economic crisis, new provisions adapted to both the international environment and the emerging political context progressively replaced the fragmented and confusing legislation on terrorism inherited from the dictatorship. But it would not be until December 1978, when terrorist activity had already started its dramatic escalation, that the first constitutional law to combat terrorism was proclaimed. It included special provisions on increasing condemnatory sentences, extending otherwise normal detention periods and establishing limitations to the judicial control over searches of domicile and the interception of private communications. As it will be argued, some of these provisions were intended to facilitate police investigation. Far from being effective for these purposes, however, such legislation resulted instead in a worrying number of proven cases when detainees were subject to mistreatment and even torture enforced by state security agencies that were still unreformed and largely devoid of a professional culture adapted to the emerging democratic regime.[9]

Interestingly enough, a significant change in the ideological orientation of the governing party, from the centrist position of UCD to the leftist but moderate orientation of the PSOE, did not initially result in a different legal approach to terrorism. On the contrary, the Socialist Party, thanks to its absolute majority in both houses of the Spanish Parliament as a result of the general elections held in October 1982, promoted a new law as from December 1984 but along the same lines of previous existing norms. Such legislation, probably the most important of its kind and controversial as well, applied during 1985 and 1986. However, at the end of 1987 the Constitutional Court overturned some of the new provisions, such as the extension of the detention period up to ten days. This special anti-terrorist legislation was finally derogated in May 1988, not only because of the unconstitutional provisions already mentioned but also because of the political consensus on anti-terrorist measures reached early in 1988, when the main political parties of Spain as a whole and in particular those of the Basque country signed the Ajuria Enea Agreements. Some of the non-controversial provisions contained in the derogated special legislation were subsequently incorporated in ordinary legislation. For instance, articles 571 to 580 within Chapter V of the new Penal Code approved in November 1995, when the PSOE was still in control of the central government, are devoted to terrorist crimes.

---

8   Llera, *Los Vascos y la Política*, pp. 97-119; and Linz, *Conflicto en Euskadi*, pp. 617-665.
9   Oscar Jaime, *Policía, Terrorismo y Cambio Político en España, 1976-1996* (Valencia: Tirant lo Blanch, 2002), pp. 219-262; and Antonio Vercher, Antiterrorismo en el Ulster y en el País Vasco: Legislación y medidas (Barcelona: Promociones y Publicaciones Universitarias, 1991), pp. 279-347.

Early in 2001, the Penal Code was modified so as to include new provisions that were adapted to changes observed in terrorist practices since the mid-1990s. Reacting to widespread popular mobilizations against ETA inside the Basque country, ETA leaders designed a plan to complement terrorist actions such as car bombs or assassinations perpetrated by formal militants with other kinds of violent activities, typically committed during the weekends by some 150 teenagers socialized within a subculture of hatred and exclusion, with the purpose of systematically harassing Basque citizens who declare themselves not to be nationalists. Therefore, in addition to violent activities aimed at subverting the constitutional order and seriously threatening public peace, terrorist offences now also include (1) criminal actions intended to intimidate part of a given population as well as social or political collectives, (2) terrorist actions perpetrated by individuals aged between 18 and 21 who will otherwise face special courts, (3) the praise or justification of terrorism, and (4) the humiliation of the victims of terrorism and their relatives. Likewise, those condemned for terrorist offences will no longer be eligible for public office for at least twenty years, and terrorist actions against elected representatives in local institutions have been put on a par with those suffered by members of other state bodies. Meanwhile, judges of the National Court initiated legal action on the financing of terrorism and on entities providing support to terrorist organizations, simply by applying the Penal Code. As a result, some youth gangs, groups seeking to maintain control over ETA members in prison and even a newspaper sympathetic to the ethno-nationalist gunmen, all of them belonging to the complex network created over the years and directed by leaders of the terrorist organization, were finally decreed illegal.

Concerning the police response to terrorism, it is important to remember once again that during the immediate post-Franco and the democratic transition periods, security agencies and security agents were those of the previous authoritarian regime. Surely affected by conditions of uncertainty, the two existing and still militarised security agencies – namely *Policía Nacional* (National Police) and *Guardia Civil* (Civil Guard) – were then unreceptive and even opposed to the conflict regulation initiatives adopted by the government to deal with terrorism in general and the threat posed by ETA in particular. In addition, information services within these state security agencies were truly precarious and lacked any coordination. Security agents, trained and indoctrinated under the preceding authoritarian regime, were prone to disloyalty, and their officials were often directly or indirectly involved with both domestic and foreign right-wing extremists. Certainly, police branches associated to the surveillance and persecution of political dissent during the dictatorship were dismantled at the end of 1976. However, some of the state functionaries who belonged to these units were later assigned to new anti-terrorist operations as from 1977, when the incidence of terrorism was relatively low and violent actions perpetrated by the GRAPO appeared even more worrying than similar incidents attributed to ETA's factions. Nevertheless, terrorism was not a priority on the governmental agenda during these days. As a result, police responses had a rather low profile during this period in comparison with those common in the early 1970s, that is, still under the dictatorship. Arguably, too, the new authorities shared a certain distrust of the existing security forces.[10] Political elites still believed that democratization was likely to cause the demise of terrorist organizations, a belief that lasted at least until the middle

---

10   Jaime, *Policía, Terrorismo y Cambio Político en España, 1976-1996*, pp. 167-217.

of 1978, when terrorist violence escalated dramatically for nearly two years. These two years were precisely the critical period of time when the Spanish Constitution was drafted and promulgated, and when the Basque statute of autonomy was negotiated and approved as well.

As terrorism perpetrated by ETA escalated at the end of the 1970s, the government of Spain finally decided to establish special police units in the Basque country, rather unsuccessfully trying to coordinate resources between agencies. UCD politicians preferred the National Police as the agency with responsibility for internal security issues in those days. At the same time, the Minister of the Interior went abroad looking for advice on how to counter terrorism properly. In July and November of 1978, for instance, he travelled to the Federal Republic of Germany and the United Kingdom, respectively, to find out about specialized anti-terrorist units and appropriate information-gathering systems. The executive wanted to increase the number of agents, create intelligence services and modernize technical resources within the police, in order to fight better the now unequivocally perceived threat of terrorism. However, as terrorism continued to escalate, the civilian Minister of the Interior was replaced in April 1979 by an army general. This could be seen as an anomaly in the context of functioning democracies, which can only be understood taking into consideration the menace of a military uprising as a result of deliberate terrorist provocation, and the fact that such an appointment actually lasted less than one year. During this period, a central government delegation for security matters was opened in the Basque Autonomous Community and also in the Autonomous Community of Navarre, headed by another general linked to the National Police. In February 1980, special operational groups and anti-terrorist units, from both the National Police (*Grupos Especiales de Operaciones*) and the *Guardia Civil* (*Unidades Antiterroristas Rurales*) were deployed in the Basque country.

It was not until mid-1980 that a new Minister of the Interior, again a civilian, decided for the first time to create a unified command for fighting terrorism, headed by a police commissioner. The same minister successfully ordered the suppression of violent extreme right-wing groups, which were still committing acts of terrorism against left-wing parties and sympathizers. Following the unsuccessful *coup d'état* in February 1981, four army companies were assigned anti-terrorist operations in the Basque country, although strictly limited to border surveillance and only until the end of summer 1981 when these army companies were replaced by units belonging to the *Guardia Civil*. Again in 1982, military personnel were assigned to the protection of public buildings and installations. Beyond surveillance and protection, the democratic government of Spain was always cautious during these years not to involve the armed forces in internal security issues, contrary to the experience of Northern Ireland. Besides, surveillance operations by army companies turned out to be inefficient for the containment of terrorism. When the Socialist Party formed the executive as a result of the October 1982 general elections, the new governing politicians initially opted for continuity in issues concerning police response to terrorism. Soon, however, the new Minister of the Interior decided to favour the *Guardia Civil* as the preferred agency in the fight against terrorist organizations for a number of reasons, in particular the remarkable discipline already existing within that agency. The *Guardia*'s prominence had become obvious by the end of the 1980s and has persisted until the present day. It has been unaffected by governmental changes, most recently the fact that the PP has been the party in government since its victory in the 1996 general elections.

What about police efficacy and efficiency in the fight against terrorism, as these parameters evolved from the transition from authoritarian rule to a consolidated new democracy? It is estimated that only one-third of the nearly 5,700 people arrested between 1977 and 1987 by the state security agencies for alleged terrorist offences in relation to ETA were finally prosecuted by judges.[11] Clearly, between the late 1970s and well advanced 1980s, the main purpose of detentions seemed to be that of obtaining information about the terrorist organization and its collaborators, so as subsequently to use this information in specific police operations. The need for information useful in counter-terrorism operations prompted a large number of detentions by the police for the primary purpose of collecting information on the terrorists and those who were offering them direct support. All this no doubt facilitated further police responses and therefore had negative effects on the terrorist organization, contributing to a decrease in its violent activities. Nonetheless, it also seems true that such behaviour produced widespread anger and resentment among affected sectors of the Basque population because of police abuses and not uncommon cases of torture. It thus facilitated the reproduction of affective adhesion and even a significant amount of popular support to ETA, and therefore ETA's persistence over time as a protracted terrorist organization.

Similar consequences in terms of popular discontent and lasting sympathy towards ETA can be attributed to the terrorist violence practised during the transition from authoritarian rule by right-wing extremists, including those of Basque origin, and a number of Italian neo-fascists associated with reactionary members of the state security agencies. They killed 10 people in France and 23 others inside Spain between 1975 and 1981, choosing their victims presumably because of their direct or indirect relationship with ETA. Between 1983 and 1987, a similar campaign of terrorist activity was carried out, for which the already mentioned GAL claimed responsibility. This terrorist organization was secretly arranged by police officials, who recruited mercenary assassins among organized criminals of Marseilles and Lisbon, some of them already implicated in earlier terrorist activities against ETA and its supporters, and who benefited from the passivity and allegiance of some prominent politicians. They targeted members and sympathizers of ETA who where living across the border in southwestern France, although surprisingly around half of the 28 people killed had no links whatsoever with the ethno-nationalist terrorist organization. Spain, fortunately, was by then a functioning democratic regime where the rule of law was finally applied to these policemen, gangsters and some politicians belonging to the Socialist Party who were involved with the GAL. They received severe court sentences for their illegal activities. The families of their victims have received monetary compensation through funds extracted from the state budget, as in the cases of relatives whose loved ones were killed by other terrorist organizations, including, of course, ETA.

Police counter-terrorist operations became much more discriminate and selective after 1988. No single episode of illegal violence in the state's response to ETA has been reported since then. For instance, the number of people suspected of crimes associated to ETA who were detained by security agencies between 1988 and the end of 1997 amounts

---

11   Domínguez Iribarren, *De la Negociación a la Tregua*, pp. 201-221.

to nearly 970, about one-fifth of all those arrested during the previous decade. More importantly, the judiciary formally prosecuted well over 60 per cent of those arrested. Interestingly enough, together with the decrease in the number of suspects arrested and the selective character of police detentions since the late 1980s, ETA's terrorist activity continued to decline as well. This process was assisted by the increasingly more selective policing of terrorism, reforms operated within the state security agencies and, of course, political decisions adopted with that purpose as part of the already mentioned Pact of Ajuria Enea.[12] Moreover, the Basque Autonomous Community's police force, fully and exclusively dependent of the Basque Autonomous Community's government, engaged in counter-terrorism as from 1986, although it would not be until the end of 1989 that the *Ertzaintza*, as this law enforcement agency is also known, proactively acted against the gunmen of ETA (m). As expected, the terrorist organization reacted by killing two autonomous police officials in the early 1990s.

All these changes in the police response to terrorism have been crucial in emotionally dissociating important segments of the Basque population from ETA and have contributed to the progressive reduction of support for the terrorist organization. Basque public opinion throughout the 1980s increasingly exhibited negative attitudes towards ETA's militants. Since the late 1980s and throughout the 1990s, citizens' mobilizations against violence became commonplace and were articulated in a number of associations such as for instance the *Coordinadora Gesto por la Paz* (Gesture for Peace), which became a prominent social feature in villages and cities across the Basque country.[13] Since the mid-1990s, ETA and its followers have reacted to this social trend by physically and aggressively confronting demonstrations against terrorism and, as indicated in paragraphs above, by targeting in particular Basque citizens who are not nationalists. Actually, all the elected political representatives at various levels of government who belong to either the Basque section of the PP or that of the PSOE suffer direct and daily persecution from ETA sympathizers and collaborators, to the extent that they have to be permanently protected by the Basque autonomous policemen, National Police agents or even private bodyguards. An amazing and dramatic fact that is probably unique in the context of European liberal democracies. Between 1996 and 2000, almost 5,000 episodes of street harassment and intimidating actions against these people and their families – a variety of more limited terrorism usually practised by gangs of youngsters outside formal membership of ETA but in open support of the terrorist organization – have been reported in the Basque Autonomous Community and Navarre, in addition to the more common terrorist attacks perpetrated by ETA gunmen which during that same period caused 47 fatalities.

---

12 Fernando Reinares and Oscar Jaime, 'Countering Terrorism in a New Democracy: The Case of Spain', in Fernando Reinares (ed.), *European Democracies Against Terrorism: Governmental Policies and Intergovernmental Cooperation* (Aldershot, Hampshire: Ashgate, 2000), pp. 119-145.
13 María J. Funes, 'Social Responses to Political Violence in the Basque Country: Peace Movements and their Audience', *Journal of Conflict Resolution*, vol. 42, 1998, pp. 493-510.

International Cooperation and 11 September 2001

ETA became a terrorist organization and transnationalised its activities at about the same time. Its alleged main goal, shared by the large majority of its members, is the creation of a Basque independent state where there would be only one official language, namely *euskera*, and a single exclusive national collective identity, despite the Basque country being a plural society in political, cultural and linguistic terms.[14] Moreover, an independent state comprising four Spanish provinces and three other territories in France. For the purpose of mobilizing resources and developing strategies, the terrorist organization has crossed the border between these two countries since its inception, although violence has been directed only to targets inside Spain, while refuge and sanctuary have been sought in France. Therefore, anti-terrorist measures implemented by Spanish governments have been objectively limited by ETA's transnationalization and the approach to the phenomenon adopted by the French authorities. Actually, ETA found a comfortable sanctuary in south-west France from the late 1960s until well into the 1980s. The terrorist organization was widely perceived among French politicians, intellectuals, public opinion and mass media circles as an anti-Franco armed group whose members qualified for political asylum, even after Spain successfully underwent a democratic transition and consolidation, processes that were severely disrupted and seriously threatened by terrorism. French apparent ignorance of these facts, particularly of the Basque autonomous institutions already functioning, and inhibition with respect to the terrorist sanctuary – behaviour most probably calculated in order to remain free from peripheral nationalist violence – caused the indignation of Spanish political elites and citizens, both to the left and the right of the political spectrum.

Cooperation against terrorism between the two neighbouring states started in the mid-1980s, following the celebration of bilateral inter-ministerial seminars every semester since 1983, which facilitated a better knowledge of the political situation in Spain among French politicians, as Spain was about to become a new member state of the European Community in 1986.[15] One and a half years prior to that, in July 1984, the French and Spanish Ministers of the Interior, both belonging to socialist parties, signed a document detailing the modalities of anti-terrorist police cooperation. These *Acuerdos de la Castellana* (Agreements of the Castellana, named after the avenue in Madrid where they were signed), became the most important accords ever reached between the two countries in combating ETA, inaugurating a period of cooperation that was subsequently developed to mutually satisfactory degrees by the late 1990s. However, the dynamics of bilateral police and judicial cooperation tended to oscillate, accelerating as parties of the centre-right formed the French executive and becoming less intense when the left was governing. Ideological positions in this case made a significant difference. Nevertheless, the outcomes of this cooperation have been increasingly effective in apprehending terrorists, dismantling the terrorist infrastructure and disrupting their finances. Before police and judicial collaboration became substantial, hundreds of ETA members were living undisturbed in French localities not far from the border with Spain, whereas ETA

---

14   Fernando Reinares, *Patriotas de la muerte. Quiénes han militado en ETA y por qué* (Madrid: Taurus, 2001), in particular pp. 85-119 and 151-176.
15   Sagrario Morán, *ETA entre Francia y España* (Madrid: Editorial Complutense, 1997).

has now been reduced to a few dozen activists staying clandestinely and more often than not away from the Pyrenees.

In accordance with its demand for bilateral cooperation with France and other states – particularly West European and Latin American – against ETA, the government of Spain, irrespective of the party in charge of the executive, has consistently supported multilateral arrangements in the fight against transnational or international terrorism, both among liberal democratic regimes in the context of western Europe as well as in the framework of the United Nations. For example, the explicit inclusion of terrorism as an objective of police cooperation between member states of the European Union, as it appears in the text of the Europol Convention signed in July 1995, was added in April 1995 to the draft at the insistence of the Spanish executive, which argued that if Europol was to justify its existence, then surely it had to deal with terrorist activities that systematically violated human rights and disrupted the democratic political process in a number of member states.[16] Interestingly, however, previous drafts of the Convention discussed since 1993 did not include preventing and combating terrorism among Europol's objectives. Even more interesting is the fact that European governments reluctant in the recent past to include terrorism as an objective of European police cooperation were more than ready to advance multilateral initiatives against such violent phenomenon following the attacks of 11 September 2001 in New York and Washington. This collective shift in attitudes may surely help to explain why the government of Spain succeeded shortly after these catastrophic events in achieving certain goals that it had been pursuing for a long time, concerning police and judicial cooperation within the European Union. In particular, the Framework Decision on the European arrest warrant, included within the Action Plan against Terrorism formally adopted by a special European Council on 21 September 2001, to supplant the system of extraditions between member states.[17]

---

16 Jaime, *Policía, Terrorismo y Cambio Político en España, 1976-1996*, p. 305.
17 More details on EU policies in the chapter by Monica den Boer.

5   The French Approach: Vigour and Vigilance

Nathalie Cettina

France is a rich subject for the study of terrorism: for 30 years, the country has been swept by waves of internal and international terrorism, involving a variety of movements and targets. These wide-ranging terrorist campaigns have compelled the French authorities to introduce an anti-terrorist policy based on a high-performance system that is unique in Europe.

Terrorist Activity

Internal Terrorism

Between 1972 and 1987, at a time when the *Organisations Communistes Combattantes* (OCC) were using Europe as their chosen battlefield, France experienced a wave of revolutionary and anti-imperialist terrorism, led from 1979 onwards by the group *Action Directe*.[1] Their violent attacks began with explosives and machine-gunfire targeting tangible symbols of capitalism and the government. In 1984, they turned their attention to representatives of industry and of the military. After the group's former leaders were stripped of their powers at Vitry-aux-Loges in 1987, the organization collapsed and died out.

---

1   Between 1972 and 1978, the organizations preceding *Action Directe* were the *Nouvelle Résistance Populaire, the Groupe d'Action Révolutionnaire Internationaliste* (GARI), the *Brigades Internationales*, and the *Noyaux Armés Pour l'Autonomie Populaire* (NAPAP). See Michael York Dartnell, *Action Directe: Ultra-left Terrorism in France, 1979-1987* (London: Cass, 1993).

M. van Leeuwen (ed.): *Confronting Terrorism*, pp. 71-94
© 2003 Kluwer Law International. Printed in the Netherlands.

Today, the Basque[2] and Breton[3] movements have lost most of their violence. Over the past 25 years, internal terrorism in France has been sustained only by Corsican nationalist and separatist demands.[4] Gradually, through a series of internal restructurings, mergers and government interventions, this Corsican terrorist movement has become more extreme. Originally represented by the politico-military *Front de Libération Nationale Corse* (FLNC), the movement split into two sections at the beginning of the 1990s: the *FLNC Canal Historique* and the *FLNC Canal Habituel*. A number of smaller groups emerged over the decade (such as Resistanza, Corsica viva), each with an official political party as a front. The nature of the attacks changed throughout the 1990s: the FLNC's infamous *nuits bleues*, consisting of extensive assaults on administrative buildings in Corsica, were followed by a settling of scores between rival nationalist factions which has intensified since 2000. Towards the end of the 1990s, a number of the informal groups resulting from schisms between movements solidified, resulting in the assassination of the Prefect of Corsica, Claude Erignac, in Ajaccio on 6 February 1998. Since then, the French government has introduced a negotiation process, the *Accords de Matignon*, intended to provide a legislative and governmental response to demands from the various official Corsican nationalist movements. However, the cessation of violence has not been a precondition for negotiations.

International Terrorism

Early in the 1980s, France suffered the consequences of its active policies in the Middle East: the support given to Iraq in the war against Iran, that given to Israel against radical Palestinians,[5] and France's traditional positions in Lebanon, which was contested by Syrian expansionists. The Israeli invasion of Lebanon in 1982 had a destabilizing effect, which was partly accountable for the escalation of violence against westerners.

---

2   From 1976 onwards, *Iparretarrak*, the '*organisation socialiste révolutionnaire de libération nationale*', engaged in violent acts targeting tangible symbols of the government (e.g., *commissariats, gendarmeries*) with the aim of obtaining their autonomy then the independence of the Basque region. Although it lost its leader at the end of the 1980s, the movement did not die out. In a primitive form, it continued to launch a few minor attacks in Basque territory. In 1994, a new youth movement called *Gazteriak* emerged, along the same lines as the Spanish *Jarrai* movement, which became notorious for violent demonstrations during which its members hurled Molotov cocktails. In recent months, ETA members have shot down police in the Basque area of France. See Xavier Crettiez and Jérôme Ferret, *Séparatismes violents: le silence des armes* (Paris: La documentation Française/IHESI, 1999).

3   In Brittany during the 1970s a movement for regional autonomy developed, driven by the *Front de Libération de la Bretagne* (FLB) and the *Armée Révolutionnaire Bretonne* (ARB). Although this movement remained rather small, it engaged in terrorist acts against tangible symbols of the government. From 1996 onwards, after years of silence, they resumed their bomb attacks on public buildings and facilities (attack on the law courts of Rennes in July 1996, a bomb planted in front of the tax office in Morlaix on 5 March 1999, explosive device placed in the reception of the tax collector's office in Paimpol on the night of 8 March 1999). The Bretons are fundamentally nationalists, as testified by the assistance and sanctuary given by some Bretons to Spanish Basque nationalists during the 1990s. See Crettiez and Ferret, *Séparatismes violents: le silence des armes*.

4   Robert Colonna d'Istria, La Corse au XXe siècle: histoire des heurts et des malheurs d'une province française (Paris: France-Empire, 1997).

5   Early in the 1980s, French President François Mitterrand was not opposed to the founding of a Palestinian state, but he wanted the PLO to recognize Israel's right to exist.

Since 1980, France has intermittently been a battlefield for reprisals and terrorist acts between immigrant communities – first between the Palestinian and Israeli communities,[6] then between the Armenian and Turkish communities.[7]

Progressively, as the Palestinians in Lebanon were attacked by the Israeli armed forces, supported by France and the United States, every person, group or country opposed to the recognition of the Palestinian cause became a target for terrorist acts instigated by Palestinian dissidents.[8] The explosion on a Paris-Toulouse train on 22 March 1982 was the first in a series of murderous terrorist attacks on France, targeting first its economic and political interests,[9] then its people.[10] In the same period, in exchange for practical and financial support from the Syrian secret services, the ASALA movement launched a series of attacks on the French capital.[11]

Islamist terrorism in France in 1985 and 1986 was both politically and religiously motivated, a sort of jihad. On behalf of the Iranian Ayatollahs, backed by the Syrian regime, the *Comité de Solidarité avec les Prisonniers Politiques Arabes et du Proche-Orient* (CSPPA) bathed Paris in blood,[12] and the Hezbollah and Islamic jihad groups abducted French nationals in Beirut. Suppression of the terrorist network responsible for the attacks and the diplomatic initiatives intended to settle certain contentious issues allowed the diplomatic arm-wrestling between Paris and Tehran to be resolved by the end of the 1980s. As a result, the terrorist threats from the Middle East to France and French interests came to a halt.

From 1993 onwards, France's support of the Algerian government's policy towards Islamists made French nationals in Algeria – and France itself – into jihad targets. In December 1994, an Air France Airbus was hijacked, and a violent terrorist campaign swept through Paris and the provinces in 1995 and 1996.[13] An indiscriminate terrorism was rekindled, similar in its form and targets to that of the 1980s, although less intense.

---

6 On 3 October 1980, a bomb attributed to the Abu Nidal group exploded in the synagogue of the rue Copernic in Paris. This was the first attack of this kind in France, killing four people and injuring around twenty.

7 On 4 March 1981, two members of the Turkish embassy in Paris were killed by ASALA. In September 1981, ASALA members took staff of the Turkish consulate in Paris hostage.

8 On France's foreign policy during this period, see Gilles Ménage, *L'œil du pouvoir*, II and III (Paris: Fayard, 2000 and 2001).

9 On 3 April 1982, FARL assassinated Yacov Barsimentov, Second Secretary of the Israeli embassy in Paris; on 22 April 1982, the rue Marbeuf attack, attributed to Carlos, took place; and on 20 July 1982, there were explosions both at the Leumi bank in Paris and at the Ganco company (which did business with Israel). Both were attributed to *Action Directe*.

10 On 9 August 1982, anti-semitic machine-gunfire on the terrace of the Goldenberg restaurant, rue des Rosiers, in Paris, killed six and injured 22; on 19 November 1983, a bomb in the Paris restaurant *l'Orée du Bois* injured 30; on 22 December 1983, the Paris restaurant *le Grand Véfour* was bombed; on 31 December 1983 a bomb in the Saint-Charles station in Marseille killed five and injured 40; on 31 December 1983, a bomb in the Paris-Marseille TGV train at Tain-l'Hermitage killed two and injured eleven.

11 On 21 July 1982, a bomb exploded in a dustbin on the Place Saint-Michel, injuring fifteen; on 23 July 1982, a bomb in the Drugstore Saint-German injured two; and on 15 July 1983 a bomb in the Paris-Orly airport killed eight and injured 60.

12 Attacks at the Galeries Lafayette, Galerie du Claridge, Point-Show, Gibert, Hôtel de Ville, and the rue de Rennes.

13 List of attacks:

  • 24 December 1994: hostage taken on an Air France Airbus at Algiers airport. [Cont.]

The French case is indicative of the Islamist networks' ability to establish themselves in the west.[14] Throughout the 1980s, Muslims described as 'fundamentalists' emerged from a politicized fringe of the supposed Muslim 'community', linked either to the Sunni Muslim Brotherhood, ready to resort to violence for their cause, or to the Shiite sect, made up of Iranian, Iraqi and Lebanese members. Since the beginning of the 1990s, in the troubled suburbs of large towns, the second generation of Muslims in France (young people often of French nationality) has been progressively 're-Islamized'. Rebelling against a society that welcomed their parents but from which they feel excluded, and whose values they reject and may even hate, these youths respond through local associations to the mobilization of the Islamist networks. The Algerian FIS has encouraged the expression of this social rejection in order to exploit it for its cause. Islam has been used to create a community that incites these youths to clash with the society in which they live, driving away any chance of social integration.[15] The consequences for communities badly in need of a frame of reference have been dire, ranging from suburban violence and the provision of practical support to the Algerian Islamists, to terrorism. In the most violent areas (Créteil, Argenteuil, La Courneuve, Bobigny and Montreuil), the Islamists have been able to recruit a large number of militants to fight for the triumph of Islam, a war of which the newly militant were previously unaware. Although the Algerian problem was perceived as a mutual confrontation between France and Algeria, it was motivated by a Salafist desire to destabilize the world.

After 1995, the source of the threat became harder to identify. It was no longer a question of a 'mutual confrontation', but of a fragmented movement. The terrorist networks severed their ties with professional organizations, the threat became global and

---

- 11 July 1995: assassination of Sheikh Abdelbaki Sahraoui, the imam of the rue Myrrha mosque in Paris and co-founder of the Algerian FIS.
- 25 July 1995: bombing of a B line RER train at Saint-Michel station, killing eight and injuring 84.
- 17 August 1995: attack near the place Charles de Gaulle in Paris, wounding seventeen, of whom three were seriously injured.
- 26 August 1995: a gas canister was found on the TGV railtracks between Lyon and Paris, level with Cailloux-sur-Fontaine, Rhône.
- 3 September 1995: attack on the market of the boulevard Richard-Lenoir in Paris, injuring four.
- 4 September 1995: an explosive device was defused in the public toilets on the place Charles-Vallin in Paris.
- 7 September 1995: a car bomb detonated in front of a Jewish school in Villeurbanne, Rhône, injuring fourteen.
- 6 October 1995: attack near the Maison-Blanche underground station, lightly injuring thirteen.
- 17 October 1995: attack on the C line of the RER between the Musée d'Orsay and Saint-Michel stations, injuring 29, of whom five were seriously injured.
- 3 December 1996: attack on the B line of the RER, at the Port-Royal station, killing seven.

14 These Islamist terrorist networks are much more pernicious than state terrorism or nationalist movements fronted by legal organizations, since they have no clearly identifiable leader. The French authorities are therefore unable to open a dialogue or negotiate with them, as they were able to negotiate with Iran to liberate hostages held in Lebanon in 1988.

15 This refusal to integrate continues to spread in many large urban areas in France, fuelling the rebellion against institutions. Juvenile delinquency, or the delinquency of young adults, is a real social problem at the heart of the political debate. It is the consequence of a loss of authority of the police and the courts, but also of parents and the school system. The French authorities are faced with young people who refuse to become part of a society they revile. These rootless youths are all too easily absorbed into the ranks of Islamists propagandists driven by hatred of the west.

anti-terrorist services throughout the world had trouble seeing what was happening. Between 1996 and 1999, the networks multiplied in Europe, promoting jihads throughout the world by fund-raising and issuing false papers. This kind of network action has shown itself to be the operating mode of the al-Qaeda 'organization',[16] which brings together a collection of individuals and groups, uniting fanatical Sunni Muslims in jihad. It is not just the young and troubled who are mobilized: individuals within western society are also recruited. Swayed by activist Islamist teachings, some of these individuals even lay down their lives in their efforts to wage jihad in the west.[17]

Before the 2000 European Football Cup, France launched a vast operation in collaboration with Germany, Belgium, the Netherlands and Italy to dismantle those Islamist networks most likely to strike. However, the anti-terrorist services lacked the information necessary to evaluate the networks' capabilities properly. The arrest of Ahmed Ressam in the state of Washington on 14 December 1999 changed this: it became obvious that the terrorist network was global, with agents in Africa, Asia and the United States. Terrorism had spread irreversibly, and although the specialized anti-terrorist services suspected something was being planned, they were unable to predict how terrible it would be.

Between December 2000 and April 2001, the Italian, German and French services uprooted an Islamist cell that had planned to attack Strasbourg cathedral in December 2000.[18] On 12 September 2001, the public prosecutor's office in Paris launched a preliminary investigation into the possible existence in France of accomplices to the attacks in the United States. Since then, several branches of networks have been dismantled in France. Some of the individuals concerned were already known by the police to have taken part in the logistics of the Algerian *Groupe Islamique Armé* (GIA). France serves as a safe haven for activists, where they can recruit members and raise funds for jihad. To let these networks grow would be to risk seeing them take violent action in France one day, perhaps even in the form of suicide attacks.

Threat Awareness

After the rue Marbeuf attack on 22 April 1982, terrorism ceased to be seen as just one of many types of criminal act, and became a priority for national security. The French have learned to adapt to anti-terrorist measures; the current terrorist crisis is not something new to France. For the past ten years, there has been a political consensus between left and right, condemning terrorist acts and agreeing on the policy towards international attacks. Anti-terrorism is no longer a dividing issue.

---

16 Al-Qaeda is not a structured and hierarchic entity, as it is perceived in the West. It is made up of individuals, groups and followers with no land of their own, who have pledged their allegiance to jihad throughout the world.

17 This trend suggests, worryingly, that western societies may be being infiltrated from inside by propagandists sufficiently powerful to convert integrated individuals or even nationals, and to teach them to participate in the destabilization and destruction of those same societies.

18 After 11 September 2001, and in the early months of 2002, the French anti-terrorist services continued to dismantle the network, part of the al-Qaeda movement, which was preparing to attack Strasbourg again.

The intransience of the threat during the Gulf War called for the reinforcement of the anti-terrorism system. Priority was given to operations. The mobilization of armed soldiers, *gendarmes* and police in civilian areas within France, in a spirit of surveillance, prevention and protection, was held to be an innovative method in crisis management, known as the Vigipirate Plan. The Plan was widely acclaimed. By establishing practical coordination in the field, the Vigipirate plan became the ace in the deck of the vigilance measures available to the government under the say of the French Prime Minister. A clear system of surveillance was put in place. However, the services mobilized were required neither to gather intelligence, nor to carry out the functions of the *Police Judiciaire* (the criminal investigation department). Their job was to dissuade and to reassure – in short, to protect. The Plan features two types of mobilization. 'Basic' mobilization calls for the raising of public awareness and the intensification of vigilance, and 'reinforced' mobilization requires the police, the *Gendarmerie Nationale*, customs and the *Sécurité Civile* to come together to safeguard those 'vulnerable points and networks' within the province of each of these services. Under the warning system of the Vigipirate Plan, police and *gendarmes* work together to define the reinforced local surveillance measures around high-priority establishments and vulnerable points, such as the *métro* or stations. The overall plan is documented in a step-by-step guide for the police and *gendarmes*, helping them to establish quickly where they should intervene, and to define their respective roles clearly.

In each of France's *départements*, the Prefect is responsible for implementing the Vigipirate Plan locally. This involves coordinating the relevant services and adapting the preventative system to the region, taking into account factors such as the susceptibility of certain locations, the proximity of an international border or the concentration of immigrants in their region.

The use of the Vigipirate Plan – a socialist initiative – by a right-wing government during the 1995 Algerian terrorist crisis demonstrated the unanimous recognition of its effectiveness and the protection and reassurance it offers. In a few years, Vigipirate had become the most prized active prevention measure in France. Since then, the anti-terrorist system has been maintained in a constant state of alert, and the Vigipirate Plan has been in continuous effect: for the past six years, its *'Attentifs ensemble'* posters have been displayed on public transport and in stations and airports. Despite its rigorism (proof of a strict anti-terrorist policy involving the armed forces), the Vigipirate system has not been contested or rejected by the people, who see in it a real assumption of responsibility for their protection. The residents of town centres, mainly in Paris, have been able to meet the public authorities' request for vigilance. They are asked to be watchful and alert, and to help the police. Active prevention becomes the business of all. Simple passers-by or travellers become part of the system, contributing both to their own safety and to that of their fellow citizens.

In speaking about the plan, politicians were careful not to incite panic, emphasizing alertness, vigilance and caution instead. From the beginning, the President of the Republic indicated that the danger perceived should not lead one to confuse action with agitation, but should instead arouse 'calm, concern and determination.'

As a result, in the hours following the 11 September 2001 attacks, the first thing that the French authorities did was to bolster the anti-terrorist system already in constant alert. France is experienced in this, and the country and people were automatically and visibly protected: 4,500 additional men (police, *gendarmes* and military) were mobilized in vulnerable public and private areas (the *métro*, RER, stations, airports, shopping centres and department stores); almost 6,000 were mobilized in Paris; and all regions were put on alert. Dustbins and automatic luggage lockers were put out of service. The French people were not alarmed, as they had lived through this kind of situation before and so accepted all the more willingly the checks put in place. Nor did they avoid public places. The French have a great deal of experience of terrorist crises and, more specifically, of Islamist offensives, although that did not lessen their shock at the horrific images of the 11 September attacks.

The existence of restless activist networks came as no surprise to the French anti-terrorist services, which had been working on Islamist networks since 1994. Well before 11 September 2001, the intelligence services had received information about Islamist networks ready to strike inside France. At the start of September 2001, armed with information about plans to attack American interests in Paris, anti-terrorist judges were able to launch an investigation into the activities of individuals who proved to be linked to Osama bin Laden's movement.[19] France's vigilance ensured that after 11 September, the services knew where to dig to try to uncover active or dormant networks within the country. Thanks to their experience, the French services were better able to anticipate the methods of the international branches of the terrorist network, even if these were not sufficiently exposed. It is fair to add that for years, France's European partners had all too often responded indifferently to French requests for international cooperation in this matter.

Today, the danger is still great. Terrorist acts in Europe are all too likely, and the threat will not go away even if the al-Qaeda network was entirely eradicated. The French most fear those radical Islamist networks that are already inside the country, likely to target American interests in France (such as the US embassy or Disneyland Paris) as well as French citizens (by bombing public places).

The aerial threat is taken very seriously. France has fortified its aerial defences so that any suspicious aircraft can be diverted or shot down. A battery of surface-to-air missiles has been installed at the site of the La Hague reprocessing installation, and at the submarine base on Ile Longue in Finistère. Civil aviation is also carefully monitored. But here, as elsewhere, the weakness of the security services is that they can enforce preventative measures against known types of attack, but are unable to predict new terrorist methods. This is why, in December 2001, an individual at Roissy airport was able to board a plane with an explosive charge hidden in his shoe. Thanks to the alertness and courage of the staff and passengers on board, he was prevented from detonating the charge mid-air. However, constant vigilance is clearly not enough, and there is still much work to be done to ensure that each aircraft is safe, from the boarding phase onwards.

Terrorism is both dramatic and out of the ordinary: as such, it finds in the media a permanent and powerful intermediary. This is not to say that the French media is a mouthpiece for terrorists.[20] On the contrary, the media conveys the anxieties and fears of

---

19 Of the 60 Islamists arrested in this case, 30 members of the Begal network were charged.
20 However, intentionally or unintentionally, the media has sometimes served as a mouthpiece for terrorists. On occasion, the media have presented the nationalist terrorists and those driven by leftist ideas as 'soldiers' or 'social heros', underlining the dramatic appeal of their cause and way of life when, [Cont.]

the people, and becomes a communication channel between citizens and the authorities. Any overstatement by the press reminds those in power of their duty to protect the nation by appropriate means. The events of 11 September 2001 and the subsequent anthrax attacks in the United States gave rise to media debates on the level of protection in France against such terrorist acts. The possibility of biochemical attacks has further fuelled an emerging paranoia, manifested in debates about infection and the increasing number of fake 'contaminated letters' within the country.

France is aware that the battle against Islamist terrorism does not depend only on America's military intervention in Afghanistan. In order to defeat the terrorists, each European state must focus on internal security, block criminal finances and dismantle networks in their country before they grow any further. This strategy requires international cooperation, and a broad and long-lasting collaboration between the police and the judiciary. The French government has been campaigning assiduously for stronger teamwork between states, from formulating anti-terrorist plans in the forum of the United Nations, to bringing its drive and support to the efforts of the European Union.

The Anti-terrorist System

In France, the security services involved in anti-terrorism[21] are grouped according to four principles: specialization, centralization, systematic coordination and relationship networks.

Specialization

The first principle is specialization by function and by focus with regard to judicial inquiry, information-gathering, prosecution and investigation. The increase in terrorist acts in France throughout the 1970s compelled the police and intelligence services to ensure that some of their agents specialized in specific anti-terrorist techniques. This specialization, as well as an increase in qualified staff numbers, was taken further in reaction to the development of an international and indiscriminate terrorism in the mid-1980s.

POLICE JUDICIAIRE
Founded at the end of the 1960s, the *6ᵉ Division Centrale de la Police Judiciaire* (*6ᵉ* DCPJ, also known as the *Office de répression des atteintes à la sûreté de l'Etat et des*

---

in reality, the acts of these groups were marked by a murderous violence. The position taken by certain French newspapers in favour of the Baader group at the beginning of the 1970s is one example.

21   Three ministries are involved in the fight against terrorism. The powers of the Ministry of the Interior are shared out between the *Police Judiciaire*, the intelligence services, and an intervention service. Within the Ministry of Defence, anti-terrorism makes up a small part of the duties of the *Gendarmerie Nationale*, the *Direction de la Protection et de la Sécurité de la Défense* (DPSD) and the *Direction du Renseignement Militaire* (DRM). The *Direction Générale de la Sécurité Extérieure* (DGSE) intervenes against terrorist intrigues abroad. Lastly, the public prosecutor's office (*'le Parquet'*) handles prosecutions; magistrates conduct the investigations and pass sentence on terrorists.

menées subversives) made its mark in the 1990s as a centralizing anti-terrorist service throughout the country.[22] The division's 50 superintendents and inspectors are divided into two sections: (1) the 'separatist' section, which focuses on Basques, Corsicans, Bretons and French West-Indians; and (2) the 'international' section, specializing in Middle-Eastern and Islamist terrorism, the Kurdish problem, European terrorism and leftism. The 6ᵉ DCPJ's national jurisdiction allows it to gather intelligence via the regional services of the *Police Judiciaire* (the SRPJ), the *Brigade Criminelle* of the Parisian police, the *Gendarmerie Nationale*, the *Sécurité Publique* and the *Police de l'Air et des Frontières*. It also receives intelligence gathered by the *Renseignements Généraux* (RG) and the *Direction de la Surveillance du Territoire* (DST). The Division has proved an undeniable success. A real expert in anti-terrorism, it was promoted in 1998 to the rank of *Division nationale anti-terroriste* (DNAT), thereby expanding both its duties and its means.

The intensity of the terrorist problem in certain vulnerable areas has forced local *Police Judiciaire* services to adapt their approach. The Paris police headquarters houses a division of the *Police Judiciaire* called the *Brigade Criminelle*. Since 1978, the division has mobilized its anti-terrorist section, the SAT, whenever a terrorist act takes place in the capital. The *Brigade Criminelle* was highly active during the attacks from the Middle East in 1986 and those of 1995 and 1996. The SAT has established itself as an unavoidable anti-terrorist service in Paris, an area that it shares, sometimes reluctantly, with the DNAT.

The Bordeaux SRPJ has special anti-terrorist units in Pau and in Bayonne; and the SRPJ in Ajaccio considers itself primarily as an anti-terrorist service.

The DST's staff are also empowered to act in the capacity of the *Police Judiciaire*. The service's judicial involvement in matters relating to terrorism became apparent in the course of 1986. In investigations of large, international terrorist cases, the DST is allowed to issue its own rogatory commissions. In practice, however, these cases often involve a joint seizure with the *Brigade Criminelle* or the DNAT. In recent years, the DST and the *Brigade Criminelle* have been granted jurisdiction with regard to the Islamist networks linked to al-Qaeda, to the detriment of the DNAT.

INTELLIGENCE

Before 1990, the intelligence services in France had been used to thinking of the enemy in terms of governments or structured organizations. In the course of the 1990s, they had to learn how to deal with a pyramid network consisting of many dispersed groups, making it virtually impossible to identify and capture the leaders. The services had to broaden their field of investigation to include entities that were not obviously terrorist in nature, but on their way to becoming it.

In 1975, the DST, responsible for managing the foreign threat within France, established its own anti-terrorist division. From 1982 onwards, this division prepared itself to fight 'those activities [inside France] inspired, supported or initiated ... by

---

22 The law of 9 September 1986, pertaining to anti-terrorism and against attacks on state security, restored to the *Police Judiciaire* those duties of repressing terrorism that it had somewhat lost since 1981.

foreign powers [constituting] a threat to security'.[23] Anti-terrorism remains a priority for the DST today. With around 100 men in its anti-terrorist division, the service studies the structures of violent movements in order to be able to predict what they are likely to do next; this is an extensive task demanding an ongoing investment of staff and resources. To achieve this task, the DST has both operational units (shadowing groups) and an analytical service.[24] Over time, the service has been able to adapt its methods, posting liaison officers abroad and becoming an expert on the Islamist issue. Its dedication to the fight against international terrorism has led to some spectacular arrests, including those of Anise Naccache and Carlos in 1994. In addition, the intelligence provided by the DST to the *Police Judiciaire* has ensured the success of a number of anti-terrorist operations.

In 1976, a memorandum from the *Direction Générale de la Police Nationale* made the *Direction Centrale des Renseignements Généraux* (DCRG) responsible for 'the research and centralization of information regarding internal terrorism'.[25] The DCRG's role is to identify problems and to inform the decisions of the regional and governmental authorities by making the government aware of the political and socio-economical climate in France. In short, the DCRG identifies the threat and evaluates its components, such as its finances, techniques and logistical support systems. Today, of the DCRG's 3,000 agents, over 100 work full-time on terrorist activities. Their national jurisdiction has allowed them to intervene in cases of Arab terrorism within France (the DCRG has equipped itself with a working group on Islamist terrorism from within French society), Corsican terrorism and the Basque terrorism of the Iparetarak and ETA, when members of these groups seek refuge in France. This service has constantly adapted its means and its approach in response to the changing nature of the terrorist threat.

In 1988, the existing *Sous-direction de la recherche* was created within the DCRG, specializing in the surveillance of factions with terrorist tendencies. Some of its assignments are operational in nature, and so are entrusted to the *Section Opérationnelle de Recherche et de Surveillance* (SORS), responsible for following up the objectives. These assignments consist either of initiating surveillances, or coordinating the *Police Judiciaire*'s existing surveillances. The rest of the DCRG's work is entrusted to the *Sous-direction de l'analyse*, of which two subdivisions fulfil a special anti-terrorist role: (1) the 'dissension and violence' section; and (2) the 'foreigners and minorities' section, which monitors foreign communities within France. The DCRG does not require a rogatory commission, and therefore has more freedom to act. It prefers to work through human informants or sources.

The police headquarters in Paris houses its own section of the DCRG, the RGPP.[26] In the early 1990s, anti-terrorist activities within the Paris police were managed by a section of the RGPP known as the *9e section*, comprising all the operational units. In 1995, the

---

23 Decree of 22 December 1982. The DST consists of 1,300 officials, divided between a central service and eight regional units, made up of brigades or special units in large cities, and posts in the *départments d'outre mer*.

24 The DST's '*secret défense*' classification severely limits any description of its units or of its activities, including the infiltration by DST agents of organizations abroad. The DST prefers to recruit individuals at the very heart of the target organisation. 'Identifying someone as a member of a given organization, manipulating him, meeting him clandestinely, that's the basis of our work,' says a former DST director.

25 Note no. 643 of 19 March 1976. The RG had actively participated in the urban fight against the FLN.

26 The RGPP has jurisdiction in the following *départements*: Hauts-de-Seine, Seine-Saint-Denis, Val-de-Marne, Val-d'Oise, Yvelines, Essonne and Seine-et-Marne.

RGPP was very active in Islamist circles, as attested by the centralization of intelligence work and the creation of a *13ᵉ section* named *Islam-radical,* consisting of around 30 staff. This section contains a 'mosque' group, whose duties include deciphering the sermons of the imams. During the 1995 terrorist crisis, hundreds of RGPP officials were assigned to anti-terrorist activities, with a core team of 200 people.

Created by decree on 5 April 1982, the *Direction Générale de la Sécurité Extérieure* (DGSE) is an undercover espionage service responsible for gathering intelligence from abroad in order to inform the French government of the political, economic, scientific and even military activities of certain countries. The service is also responsible for detecting any anti-French movement abroad. During the 1970s, when anti-terrorism became a serious concern, an anti-terrorism and anti-subversion operational section was created, the service's networks in the Middle East were reinforced and the service began tracking the terrorist Carlos. The DGSE's *Direction renseignement* consists of a unit specialized in anti-terrorism, with around 100 agents and with 'plants' in the Middle East and Latin America. This unit fulfils those duties fundamental to any intelligence service: research, analysis and dissemination of information. The DGSE is also responsible for ensuring that sources are both reliable and secure, as well as resisting any attempts by enemy agencies to infiltrate the service. However, the staff and resources placed at its disposal have proved to be insufficient to achieve these objectives.

The globalization of the criminal world over the past decade has shattered the internal/external demarcation that previously existed between the RG, DST and DGSE with regard to terrorist activities. Each must learn to work with the others as much as possible, bringing their special competences to a shared field of intervention.

The *Gendarmerie Nationale*'s function is to provide logistical support. Its role within the counter-attack system enables it to safeguard intelligence missions, to protect vulnerable civilian sites of national interest, and to intervene in threatened areas. The *Gendarmerie*'s chief advantage is that it consists of networks covering the whole country, and so is always close at hand.

In light of a jihad raising its ugly head in very diverse places in the world, the need to establish analysis and prevention units became clear. Since the early 1990s, France has introduced units responsible for preparing inventories of terrorist risks. This has primarily taken place within the framework of the military. The *Direction de la Protection et de la Sécurité de la Défense* (DPSD) is responsible – purely on a preventative basis and exclusively in the military field – for managing the terrorist threat likely to target the staff, equipment and buildings of the Ministry of Defence.

One of the units created was a small division of the *Direction du Renseignement Militaire* (DRM) known as the *Mouvements Terroristes et Subversifs,* which focuses on learning to predict the potential threats to French armed forces throughout the world, and to pinpointing the emergence of large movements and those in a state of transition.

The role of the *Secrétariat Général de la Défense Nationale* (SGDN), one of the French Prime Minister's services, is to attempt to detect potential risks and to serve as the custodian of anti-terrorist plans.

Finally, in response to an increase in hostage-taking (by terrorists as well as other criminals), the French Ministries of Defence and the Interior have recruited staff specially trained in direct intervention in crisis situations. In 1976, the *Gendarmerie Nationale* set up the first service designed to respond directly to the shock caused by violent actions:

the *Groupement d'Intervention de la Gendarmerie Nationale* (GIGN). The *Police Nationale* equipped itself in 1972 with a *Brigade de Recherche et d'Intervention* (BRI). This was replaced in 1985 by the RAID.

Centralization

The second of the four principles is centralization. In passing the law of 9 September 1986 pertaining to the fight against terrorism and to the attacks on state security, the French Parliament effectively centralized the anti-terrorist effort in Paris. The four judges of the *14ᵉ section* of the public prosecutor's office in Paris, a section created by the 1986 law, are authorized to claim any case relating to terrorism that they consider sufficiently sensitive to merit dealing with at a national level.[27]

With regard to the investigative courts *(l'instruction)*, most of the terrorist cases were put under the jurisdiction of four judges within the Galerie Saint-Eloi in Paris's *Palais de Justice*. Initially, each magistrate was responsible for one of four types of case: Corsican, Islamist, Palestinian or Basque. The cases have subsequently been shared out according to requirements, and each judge has some Islamist cases. The choice of the police service receiving rogatory commission (the DNAT, *Brigade Criminelle*, SRPJ Ajaccio or SRPJ Bayonne) remains entirely at the discretion of the magistrate. For the sake of effectiveness, the same case is frequently referred simultaneously to two services.

The public prosecutor's office in the court of appeal in Paris has also developed an anti-terrorist specialization. In both the *cour correctionnelle*, which has jurisdiction for misdemeanours, and the *cour d'assises*, the prosecuting magistrates have become specialists who maintain permanent links with the *14ᵉ section* and the examining magistrates. This system ensures that each party has the same understanding of the procedures and the cases are processed faster. In effect, the magistrate has been reinstated at the side of the police officer and the intelligence services so that he can be kept informed of the investigations.

The last aspect affected by this centralization is the sentencing of terrorist crimes. A *cour d'assises* without jury was established in Paris in 1986, but the magistrates called to sit there were not specialized in anti-terrorism.

The 1995 crisis called for the reinforcement of the specialist judicial structures, and regular meetings between magistrates and police officers were organized. As of March 1994, the responsibility for following up the Islamist networks within the Ministry of Justice was given to a new *Bureau de Lutte contre le Terrorisme*,[28] which mandated that any undertaking with Islamist activist associations must be broken up, and that at the slightest suspicion of the presence of an Islamist network, the specialized police services

---

27   The magistrates of the *14ᵉ section* divide cases between themselves in the following manner: the head of the section has the ETA cases; a second magistrate has the Islamist and Kurdish terrorist cases; and the third is dedicated solely to the Chalabi Islamist case file, due to its size and scale (164 accused and 69 detained). A fourth magistrate is responsible for the cases of Iranian and Palestinian terrorism and espionage. The cases concerning the 1995 attacks and the Corsican case files are shared out between the four.

28   This name was given to it on 15 January 1996. The Bureau's objective is to drive, control and coordinate the initiation and exercise of public action.

and judicial powers in Paris must immediately be involved. The public prosecutor's office has opened Islamist case files according to the strategic direction provided by the Bureau.

The preventative role that has been given to the judicial system has resulted directly in the reinforcement of identity checks, the uncompromising prosecution of instigators of false bomb scares and a greater legal vigilance towards the circulation in France of leaflets with Islamist connotations inciting anti-semitism and racial hatred.

Systematic Coordination

The third principle is systematic coordination at operational and institutional levels. Faced with the emergence of an international terrorism mobilizing all of the security forces, the French authorities sought to enhance the coordination between services in order to make them more effective. [29]

On 8 October 1984, the *Unité de Coordination de la Lutte Anti-terroriste* (UCLAT) was established within the Ministry of the Interior, under the leadership of an official of the *Police Nationale.* UCLAT connects all the services involved in dealing with terrorist problems, bringing their representatives together once a week. The unit intervenes in specific terrorist cases, by ensuring the relevant information changes hands, and by using the *Police Judiciaire* as a natural link with the magistrates' bench. UCLAT is also responsible for the global follow-up of the terrorist threat. It has access to the intelligence gathered abroad by the network of liaison officers posted in Italy, Spain, Germany and Belgium.

Since 1995, UCLAT has played a substantial part in preventative operations targeting Islamist circles, designed to dismantle fundamentalist networks in France and challenge Islamist militants. It distributes intelligence to the services, and encourages them to rise above any rivalry and share information. UCLAT makes the system more transparent by ensuring that the role and responsibilities of service are clear.

In order to enable effective coordination between French government ministries in times of crisis, the *Comité Interministériel de Lutte Anti-terroriste* (CILAT), composed of political and administrative officials, and the *Conseil de Sécurité Intérieure* (CSI) were merged, bringing together the ministers concerned.

---

29   Authorities taking charge of coordination at an institutional level is attested by the creation of the *Bureau permanent de Liaison Anti-terroriste* (BLAT) in 1982; the *Cellule Anti-terroriste de l'Elysée* on 24 August 1982; the *Unité de Coordination de la Lutte Anti-terroriste* (UCLAT) on 8 October 1984; the *Comité Interministériel de Lutte contre le Terrorisme* (CILAT) in 1982; the *Conseil de Sécurité Intérieure* (CSI) in 1986; and the *Service Central de Lutte Anti-terroriste du parquet de Paris* (SCLAT), under the law of 9 September 1986.

Relationship Networks

The fourth and last principle regards the relationship networks among players, which are crucial for the anti-terrorist system to operate properly.[30] Communication and the exchange of information depend largely on the will of the police and magistrates, and on the character and levels of trust and sensitivity of the players. The measures taken to coordinate the services should not impose constraints on these services, but should instead be seen as a contract for exchanges between them.

Despite the progress achieved through the implementation of these four principles, there is still much room for improvement. To date, the progress has been circumstantial, dependent on both the players and on the stakes.

Persistent Problems

The measures taken to strengthen France's anti-terrorist system have failed to resolve three endemic problems.

The first problem concerns the rifts between services, which specialization and centralization have not succeeded in mending. There is a permanent coordination problem in France in respect to security issues, which is strongly restated with each terrorist campaign. Ill-prepared for an internal threat, these services were taken by surprise by the leftist movement that developed in France during the 1970s. The police and intelligence services did not work together in the best of circumstances, and the inevitable conflicts of jurisdiction were coupled with jealousy and rivalries.

As of the 1980s, the emergence of an external threat from the Middle East led the political authorities to take the fight against terrorism in hand, resulting in the increase in the number of specialized services and commanding authorities, such as the *Cellule Anti-terroriste de l'Elysée,* created in 1982. The result of this increase has been an overlapping of jurisdictions and fields of intervention, as well as a series of factors undermining coordination: partitioning, conflicts between individuals, the politicization of the units, a failure to exploit intelligence to the full and an inability to predict what might be at stake.

This squabbling between factions has shown itself to be deeply rooted. The terrorist acts of 1995 and the resulting destabilization led to new tensions between the various intelligence services, among the various *Police Judiciaire* services, between the *Police Judiciaire* and intelligence services, between the police and *gendarmes*, and between the police and the justice system; each falling back into their own 'corporate' mindset. If, over time, this hostility has given way to a forced coexistence, traditional rivalries rapidly resurface as staff numbers increase.

These rivalries and conflicts have made their way into the management of internal as well as international terrorism, as demonstrated by the many problems and irregularities that held up the investigation into the assassination of Prefect Erignac in 1998. These were the result of discrepancies in the approaches of the police, the judiciary and certain

---

30   In the context of anti-terrorism, the term 'network' refers to an anarchic, uncertain development, of variable duration, of personal relationships among players.

individuals involved, each wanting to impose themselves and to move forward independently, using their own methods.

The situation today is paradoxical. On the one hand, the way in which the anti-terrorist system works has vastly improved, as shown by its many victories. On the other hand, there is a crisis at the very heart of the system, as the various players put their personal interests first, opening the way to a series of blunders. As one police officer puts it, 'there is a very good anti-terrorist system in France – but it relies on people'.

The second problem is that the political authorities often seem unable to recognize the constraints faced by the police. Generally, politicians do not learn from past experience, and are too concerned with obtaining rapid results, thereby underestimating the need for coordinated security services. In fact, the timetables of the police officer and the politician are two separate things, although the political authorities are unwilling to accept this. In addition, political leaders have always distrusted the intelligence services, fearing their power and often unsure how to use them. However, to be really effective, an operation must be backed and supported by a clearly defined political action.

The third problem is that networks, although effective when they work well, are shifting and impermanent structures. If the staff changes, the networks burst and die. If the system is to be improved, it needs to move beyond circumstantial cohesion to the spontaneous integration of all those involved.

Legislation

The specialized and centralized services required the support of a body of legislation. From 1986 onwards, the legislature adopted an anti-terrorist legislation that has been supplemented in response to each new terrorist crisis.

The law of 9 September 1986, pertaining to the fight against terrorism and the attacks on state security, provided a definition of the terrorist act for the first time: 'any offence connected with a one-man or collective undertaking, aiming to seriously disturb the peace through intimidation or terror'. The legislature introduced a specific legal regime for this type of crime, although it did not create a specific terrorist charge. The procedures were adapted to make it easier for the police to act. In dealing with terrorist organizations made up of scattered branches and many members, it had become impossible for the *Police Judiciaire* to carry out the necessary checks or to consult seized documents within the custody period of 48 hours. The legislature therefore increased the maximum custody period to four days (Article 706-23 of the *Code de Procedure Pénale*). Equally importantly, police searches, house searches and the seizure of evidence no longer required the approval of the person concerned. Those measures apply to everybody (i.e. French citizens and to non-citizen residents of France). The magistrate's means against terrorism were also augmented. The legislature increased sanctions, automatically linking the *interdiction de séjour* (banishment from France or from certain regions in France) to the main penalty. This severity was counterbalanced by a system reducing or exempting from the penalty those terrorists who cooperated with justice. However, terrorism was not set as a separate charge: in 1986, the legislature confined itself to instituting a specific legal regime for certain crimes and offences in relation to activities or undertakings falling within the definition of terrorism.

Following the Algerian Islamist attacks in 1995, Law 96-647 of 22 July 1996 completed the anti-terrorist legislation. A specific and separate terrorist charge was created.[31] For the charge to apply, three factors must be established: an intentional relationship between the act and the one-man or collective undertaking; the presence of a terrorist undertaking; and a psychological (intimidation) and physiological (terror) aspect whereby an atmosphere of panic has been created within the population.

The purpose of the charge is for anti-terrorist police officers and magistrates to be able to act on findings that 'for lack of a criminal charge, did not previously constitute grounds for proceedings'.[32] It provides the means to act against recruitment and support networks within the destabilized Muslim community, which is vulnerable to extremist ideas, or against those who harbour terrorists, without whom they could not operate.

Groupings of foreign people or people under foreign control, whose activities may run counter to the interests of the French state, were also felt to be a source of concern. The law of 22 July 1996 introduced 'the criminal liability of legal entities' (*la responsabilité pénale des personnes morales*, Article 422-5 of the *Nouveau Code Pénal*). Within the context of Islamist activism, this made it possible to charge foreigners who use a social or religious pretext, such as facilitating integration or safeguarding the national culture, to provide assistance and support to terrorists.

The law of 22 July 1996 also introduced another crucially important charge: 'conspiracy in connection with a terrorist undertaking' (Article 421-2-1 of the *Nouveau*

---

31 Article 421-1 of the *Nouveau Code Pénal* sets out that:

> 'The following acts constitute acts of terrorism, when they are "intentionally" in connection with a one-man or collective undertaking, aiming to seriously disturb the peace through intimidation or terror (Law 96-647 of 22 July 1996):
> 1 Any deliberate attacks on the life or integrity of a person, kidnapping and illegal confinement, the hijacking of aircraft, ships or any other method of transport, defined in book II of the current code;
> 2 Theft, extortion, destruction, damage and deterioration, as well as offences regarding information technology, defined in book II of the current code;
> 3 Offences regarding combat groups and disbanded movements as defined in Articles 431-13 to 431-17, as well as offences defined in Articles 434-6 and 441-2 to 441-5 (Law 96-647 of 22 July 1996);
> 4 The manufacture or possession of machines or devices designed to kill or to explode, defined in Article 3 of the law of 19 June 1871, repealing the decree of 4 September 1870 concerning the manufacture of weapons of war;
>   the production, sale, import or export of explosive substances, defined in Article 6 of Law 70-575 of 3 July 1970, reforming laws regarding gunpowders and explosive substances;
>   the purchase, possession, transportation or illegitimate carrying of explosive substances or devices made with the help of those substances, defined in Article 38 of the decree-law of 18 April 1939 determining the regime with regard to materials of war, weapons and munitions;
>   the possession, carriage or transportation of weapons and munitions of the first and fourth categories, defined in Articles 24, 28, 31 and 32 of the decree-law of 18 April 1939 (Law 96-647 of 22 July 1996); the offences defined in Articles 1 and 4 of Law 72-467 of 9 June 1972 prohibiting the perfecting, manufacturing, possession, storage, purchase and transfer of biological weapons or weapons based on toxins; and
>   the offences foreseen by Articles 58 to 63 of Law 98-467 of 17 June 1998 relating to the application of the Convention of 13 January 1993 on the prohibition of the perfecting, manufacture, storing and use of chemical weapons and on their destruction (Law 98-467 of 17 June 1998);
> 5 The receipt of the product of any of the offences listed in points 1 to 4 (Law 96-647 of 22 July 1996).'

32 Alain Marsaud, *Rapport fait au nom de la commission des lois*, French National Assembly, no. 2406, 29 November 1995, p. 6.

Code Pénal). Previously, participation in a terrorist activity could only be prosecuted under the same charge as offences related to a terrorist act. From this point onwards, it became a specific charge, incurring harsher penalties. The police and magistrates needed to be able to proceed to the dismantlement of a terrorist network on the basis of such violations as, for instance, the use of false number plates or the bearing of weapons on the public highway. The 'legal proceedings begun against X for conspiracy' charge incurs a custody period, during which time the necessary checks can be made and the necessary confrontations and hearings can be held. With this evidence in hand, the officials are then entitled to pursue the case centrally. The charge can extend to all the individuals who took part in the logistics behind the terrorist activity, be it by disseminating an Islamist magazine, or obtaining forged identity papers. This has proven to be an invaluable tool for the services of the *Police Judiciaire*, and has become the fundamental legal justification for their activity. Without it, the management of Islamist terrorism since 1994 would not have been as effective.

The law of 30 December 1996 allows seizures of evidence, searches and house searches to be conducted at night (between 10pm and 6am) as well as during the day, both within the framework of an investigation and in the case of an emergency.

Determined to be rigorous, the legislature also increased the penalties for terrorist acts relative to other crimes (Articles 421-3 to 421-5 of the *Nouveau Code Pénal*). The upper time limit for *peines correctionnelles* (so-called 'minor penalties') was raised from five to ten years, allowing the *cour correctionelle* to intervene in cases previously dealt with by the *cour d' assises*. The judgment of terrorist offences in the *cour correctionelle* allows the evaluation of the support given by individuals for a terrorist mission, even if they did not directly take part in its execution. The durations of the additional sentences were also increased.[33] The statute of limitations for the sentences and for the state's case – twenty and thirty years, respectively – is longer today in terrorist law than it is under the *droit commun* (ordinary law).

Most recently, in response to the attacks in New York on 11 September 2001, the legislature has added anti-terrorist provisions designed to strengthen the means of the police services, in the *Sécurité Quotidienne* (day-to-day security) law passed on 15 November 2001. These provisions will continue to apply until 31 December 2003. Under this law, police checks in public places have become more stringent. In those areas not directly accessible to the public at airports, airport outbuildings and harbours, the police are allowed to search people and their hand luggage. The check can take the form of a visual inspection, or if the owner consents, a hand search. With the permission of the person concerned, police are also allowed to 'pat down' individuals in a brief body search. Any freight, postal parcels, merchandise, aircraft, ships or other vehicles in these areas may also be checked.

Private security forces in public places are allowed to inspect visually and, with the owner's consent, hand search his or her hand luggage. They can also 'pat down' people with their permission. Police agents are entitled to search moving, stationary or parked vehicles on the public highway or in places accessible to the public. This had never

---

33 Suspension of civil, civic and family rights; prohibition from engaging in a public function or professional or social activity that had served as the framework for the offence; banishment from certain areas or from France.

previously been granted, as it was considered an attack on people's right to freedom of movement.

In a preliminary investigation, seizures of evidence, searches and house searches are authorized at the request of the public prosecutor, provided that the authorization is granted by the *juge des libertés et de la detention*.

The law also mandates regular watchdog inspections to monitor the conduct of those staff carrying out security or defence missions, those with access to protected areas, those using equipment or products of a dangerous nature, and those involved in missions with a potential risk to the people or to the peace. It also states that, wherever necessary, the hearing and interrogation of an individual, and the confrontation of several, may be held 'remotely', as long as the methods of communication involved do not compromise the confidentiality of the information exchanged.

The terrorist charge is extended to include the financing of a terrorist undertaking by providing, gathering or managing funds, values or goods in the knowledge that they will be used to commit terrorist acts.

The obligation of telecommunications companies to erase or render anonymous any data relating to a communication as soon as that communication is completed is mitigated by the need to be able to stop criminals from using new communication technologies for unlawful ends. At the request of the public prosecutor of the Republic, the *juridiction d'instruction* (the investigative courts) or the *juridiction de jugement* (the courts in which criminal cases are heard and judged), encrypted information may be deciphered.

Today, the magistrates consider that anti-terrorist legislation should be further reinforced to create an augmented charge of conspiracy, which would grant them more power in dealing with those networks on the verge of attacking.

Civil Liberties

The laws passed and the centralization and specialization of the services have not met with unanimous approval. The wording of each piece of legislation intended to strengthen anti-terrorist law has been greeted by reservations and criticisms.

The issues are complex. How can one fight legally against a network? How can one justify the extension of the procedures and powers of the police to individuals who are not strictly speaking terrorists, but move in activist circles? How should one treat offences committed by members of movements known to be terrorist, but which fall entirely within the letter of the law? Are the legal measures taken proportional to the threat to society? Could the same results not be achieved under the *droit commun*? These are the questions that were asked of the judiciary with respect to its responses to the terrorist campaign of 1995.

Between 1995 and 1999, wide-ranging police operations and the investigation and prosecution of the Chalabi case caused a general outcry from associations of lawyers,[34] which was then spread by the International Federation for Human Rights (IFHR) and by the media. Each of these bodies strongly criticized the workings of anti-terrorist justice,

---

34   The Chalabi case concerns the use of France as a safe haven for the establishment of networks aiming to convey equipment from Germany and Turkey to Algeria, through Marseille, Spain or Morocco.

accusing the French legal system of a *'justice spectacle'*,[35] whereby human rights were being violated and the legislation was being applied in a way that had somehow gone astray.

According to these critics, anti-terrorist justice is too quick to classify people as proven or potential terrorists on the basis of their convictions or the company they keep. The press spoke of 'suspicion towards all immigrants', of 'more and more suspects', of 'an approach tantamount to an all-round raid'. Immigration, religious fundamentalism, the ideological and cultural links of immigrants with their country of origin and the threat of terrorism were all too quickly linked together. The IFHR saw this as a usurpation of power, leading to 'abuse', 'excesses' and 'worrying drifts'.

The targets for this criticism included the establishment in 1994 of a detention centre in Folebray by the French Minister of the Interior for foreign Islamists in France likely to support or take part in terrorist activities (before their exile), and the mass arrests in Islamist circles throughout France between 1995 and 1998. In spring 1996, the arrests of Bretons for the support that they had given to Spanish Basques were met with incomprehension, as the French people questioned whether the Vigipirate Plan justified the mobilization of the infantry in public places, or the surveillance and searches of the public and their personal effects. The judicial phase of the proceedings against the Chalabi network was the subject of much controversy with regard to the duration of the preliminary investigations, allegedly illegal enforcement of provisional detention, irregularities in the course of the interrogations, excessive use of the 'conspiracy in connection with a terrorist undertaking' charge, the inadequacy of the evidence, the 'cynical exploitation of the fear of immigrants' in 'preventive raids' in Islamist circles, and the lack of sufficient distance between the magistrates and the public prosecutor's office, the bench magistrates and the police officers. These 'drifts' were said to result from the identical treatment of all suspects, and a failure to sort out the key players from the rest. People were allegedly being detained without sufficient charges, and as a result, a debate on how terrorist networks operate was opened.

These criticisms need to be put in perspective. The legislature's sole intention has been to give police officers and magistrates an adapted legal arsenal, which nevertheless respects personal freedom. It is not appropriate to question the workings of the judicial system when it has proved itself effective. The system is motivated by a concern for professionalism and success, as well as the desire to prevent potential terrorists from escaping the anti-terrorist net. It is thanks to provisions such as 'criminal conspiracy in connection with a terrorist undertaking' that anti-terrorism is able to advance and defeat the enemy.

The *Sécurité Quotidienne* law, which reinforced anti-terrorist legislation after the attacks of 11 September 2001, was met by a chorus of disapproval. It was perceived as a restriction of personal freedom that would have no effect on terrorists, but would strike at the very heart of democracy. The extended checks carried out on people and their personal effects, including their cars, have been denounced, in particular by the IFHR and the *Syndicat de la Magistrature* (the French magistrates' union), as attacks on people's privacy and their freedom of movement. It has been said that the sole effect of the law

---

35 International Federation for Human Rights, *Rapport d'enquête sur l'application de la législation anti-terroriste*, 21 January 1999.

would be an exponential increase in the number of checks directed at those who look foreign, and in the number of people without papers sent to detention centres.

The means placed at the disposal of police officers and magistrates must be appropriate to a dispersed enemy, without striking at the foundations of democracy. This requires the careful consideration of each of the parties involved, so that the government cannot be accused of making anti-terrorism a graveyard for personal freedom.

Success

Despite criticisms, the French anti-terrorist system has shown great determination in the fight against enemies with a plethora of personalities, motivations, and organizational structures.[36]

Since 1994, the operation to dismantle Islamist networks inside France, and their branches abroad, has shown impressive results. A number of covert channels of support for the Algerian guerrilla have been ruptured. On each occasion, stocks of weapons, ammunition, transmission equipment, forged identity papers and essential equipment were seized. Several hundreds of militant Islamists have been placed behind bars. The terrorist groups active in France in 1995 (the Kelkal group in Vaux-en-Velin[37] and the groups in Chasse-sur-Rhône and Lille) were dismantled within three months, and many of their instigators and supporters have been imprisoned. The information obtained from questioning both the leaders and followers of these groups has enabled the services to strike decisive blows to the infrastructure of Algerian Islamists within France. The firm policy of repression in Corsica since the end of 1996 has led to both arrests and indictments, although many cases remain unresolved.[38]

The mills of justice have ground remarkably quickly. Since December 1996, 34 people suspected of having belonged to an Islamist terrorist network established in France at the end of the 1980s, and of wanting to destabilize Morocco, have been tried before the *12e chambre correctionnelle* of the Paris courts.[39] In November 1997, an Islamist network that had participated in the 1995 attacks appeared before the *cour correctionnelle* of Paris. The trial of the Chalabi network began in September 1998: the enormity of the case file slowed proceedings down considerably, although the investigation has moved forward at a constant rate. To finish, in the case relating to the 1995 attacks, 24 defendants were sentenced in June 1999 in the *cour correctionelle* for 'conspiracy in connection with a terrorist undertaking', and some of them were brought before the *cour d'assises* for the assassination of Imam Saharaoui on 11 July 1995, among other charges. Within four years, the members of the logistical support networks

---

36 This determination led to the achievements against the Islamist terrorists in 1995, admired by many European countries.

37 Named after the young second-generation Arab immigrant enlisted by GIA agents in the defence of the Algerian Islamist cause and used to set the bombs in place during the attacks in 1995. He was on the run in the region of Lyons when he was shot down by the police on 29 September 1995.

38 For the past three years, the alleged assassin of Prefect Erignac, Yvan Colonna, has escaped police detection, although his accomplices have been arrested. The resurgence of assassinations between nationalists over the past two years has failed to lead to a single arrest, due to the lack of a serious 'trail'.

39 On 9 January 1997, the two leaders of terrorist networks were sentenced to eight years imprisonment; the other 32 received sentences of one to five years.

for the terrorists in Paris, Lyons and Lille, as well as the instigators of the attacks, were arrested and handed over to justice.

After almost ten years of persistent investigation and despite the difficulties facing the police, the trial relating to the UTA attack on a DC10 plane on 19 September 1989, in which 170 people were killed above Ténéré, finally took place. The sentencing *in absentia* of six members of the Libyan secret services to life imprisonment testifies to the capacity of the anti-terrorist system to take a firm stand when faced with what was believed from the start to be an act of state terrorism.

France in an Anti-terrorist Partnership

The fact that terrorism may be an international enterprise was driven home by the tragic events of 11 September 2001. The political authorities' statements of principle in favour of solidarity between states are not enough; it is vital to establish a practical collaboration between the police officers and magistrates of different countries. Both the will and the ability to act must be shared.

Well before September 11, the anti-terrorist services in France had requested the cooperation of their European partners in the fight against Islamists, separatists and extreme leftists. The specific nature of terrorism calls for police services to work together. These are currently a collection of specialized anti-terrorist services, between which the processing of information is divided rather than centralized. Any collaboration and exchange of information takes place through networks of personal relationships.

However, upon closer inspection, the level of cooperation varies according to the nature of the parties involved. The RG and DST intelligence services have set up sections responsible for liaising with their foreign counterparts. The RG's *liaison extérieure* section is responsible for the follow-up of exchanges (notes, faxes or direct contacts) with the information services of the European Union's member states. The DST has long invested in international cooperation, and its international relations division has joined forces with a number of European services with which it has preferential relationships.[40] Faced with a terrorist threat that comes from further and further away, the DST has extended this web of relationships to the whole world. The exchanges between intelligence services depend on trust and discretion: intelligence is a people business, made up of contacts and networks.

To some extent, the intelligence services in Europe do work together.[41] In spring 2000, Belgium and the Netherlands, responsible for organizing the European Cup football matches that year, asked the European – and particularly the French – services for information on the terrorist risks. The countries began to collaborate, and have continued to do so. However, the information exchanged is often not of the highest quality, due to common rivalries between intelligence services even within countries, especially when different ministries are involved.

---

40   The DST is in communication with the following agencies: MI5 and MI6 (United Kingdom); BND, BVF and BKA (Germany); CESID and CGI (Spain); SISMI, SISDE and the *Carabinieri* (Italy).

41   Informal encounters initiated in the 1970s, including the so-called *Club de Berne*, have continued since.

Following the emergence of an anti-terrorist specialization in the countries that have experienced terrorism, the various criminal investigation services have also formed basic relationships. The 'it's their problem, nothing to do with me' attitude has gone. However, it is not yet a real collaboration: the investigative techniques and procedures remain specific to each state, acting as barriers between the services.

The collaboration between magistrates is still fragile, due to legal and procedural differences, but also because of the lack of specialization and centralization in the judicial anti-terrorist systems of a number of countries. Between some countries, on a given case, a certain appreciation of the need for collaboration has been developed, as between France and Spain. But there is no real partnership between states. As soon as the evidence and suspects are abroad, it becomes immensely difficult to investigate or brief a case. All too often, the requests for mutual assistance are met slowly and reluctantly. This was true in the cases of Rachid Ramda, Abou Farès and Abdelkrim Dénèche at the time of the investigations into the 1995 Islamist attacks in France. Working with foreign partners requires an international mind-set. To date, this mind-set is barely there. France's requests for assistance have either been ignored, or dealt with inadequately. The countries that collaborate most with France in the judicial context are those that have already had to deal with terrorist crises and have a similar legal system. France works very well with Spain, and obtains good results with Belgium and Italy. In contrast, the common law countries have found it difficult to collaborate, as have those countries that were unaware of increasing terrorist tendencies among radical Islamists, hiding behind the protection of personal freedom in order to refuse France's requests for assistance. The same goes for the Nordic countries, and in particular for the United Kingdom, which realized all too late that they were an ideal safe haven for Islamist activists.

Finally, the instruments of the European Union (the European Councils, programmes, action plans, joint actions, and resolutions) have proposed a number of measures to improve cooperation, but these have long been perceived by the French police and magistrates as theoretical and impractical solutions.

Since 11 September 2001, there has been an awakening with regard to the international nature of the terrorist threat and the need for all countries in Europe to pool their efforts. This tragedy will hopefully convince countries relatively unscathed by terrorism to date, such as the Nordic countries, to stand by their neighbours and respond to their requests for help. For the services to be able to work as a team, each country needs to have understood the real nature of terrorism. Magistrates are travelling to meet their counterparts more frequently, and informal meetings are increasingly taking place.

For the collaboration to become stronger, the legislation and procedures of each country will need to be harmonized. Each member state will need to recognize the validity of the procedures followed in another country. The recent commitment to set up a European warrant for arrest between now and 2004 will help this process, but it is still taking far too long.

The increase in the number of networks and types of activity to be monitored will require agents to be more versatile and mobile, and the techniques available for acquiring and processing information will need to be reinforced. This implies the use of liaison officers to ensure effective collaboration between the member states of the European Union, as the essential go-betweens for the criminal investigation departments and intelligence services. France has already been using liaison officers in this manner for some time.[42] Liaison magistrates should also be posted in the courts of each country. [43]

The police and national magistrates, who are used to working in closed circles within bilateral relationships, will need to be convinced of the credibility of international organizations such as Interpol, Europol and Eurojust. They must be educated as to how these bodies can help them most.

Political solidarity between the European member states in the fight against terrorism should no longer be thwarted by economic, commercial, military and strategic interests. Since 11 September 2001, the states have made a commitment not to refuse requests for help from other countries. It is the least that one can expect of them.

Conclusions

The events of 11 September 2001 have proven that anti-terrorism is essentially a task of anticipation and prediction, and one in which the intelligence services have failed. Their methods need rethinking. Both in France and abroad, they must improve and diversify their techniques for obtaining information, by combining technical and human sources. The practice of infiltration must be developed, and they must learn to make better use of the wealth of information that is openly available. Intelligence staff must learn to tune their ears to society automatically, to use its channels of communication and to exploit the information gained.

Terrorism can be compared to a complex jigsaw puzzle: its pieces are many and diverse, consisting of individuals, channels, financing networks, external influences and structures. To understand the overall picture and defuse the threat, each of these pieces needs to be monitored and understood. This can only be achieved if all the services work together. It is not enough to collect information; intelligence staff need to know how to use and analyse it to draw conclusions, predict risks, learn about plans being hatched, understand the way in which members of a network function and what they are looking for – in short, they need to be able to determine what terrorists are capable of doing, when, where and how. Achieving this will take time. The intelligence services will need to adapt their approach, relying more on intuition and on insights into cultures and traditions. They will need to operate as if in a permanent state of emergency in order to ensure that their specialist and analytical capabilities are at their strongest at all times.

Perhaps the intelligence services should be equipped with a small consultancy unit of sociologists, historians, political experts and philosophers, as well as weaponry experts, nuclear scientists and chemists. This would allow agents to understand the terrorist methods and thought processes better. In addition, intelligence staff must be brought up to standard. The services in France do not currently recruit people who are highly educated in extremely specialized fields. France is lagging in this respect.

What is needed is an intelligence world that is lawful, undivided, and has its own culture. The challenge in the fight against terrorism is to put intelligence work back at the

---

42　The liaison officers in France were reconnected to UCLAT during the centralization of the police.
43　The liaison magistrates posted in France come from the Netherlands, Germany, Italy and Spain.

heart of society, to treat it as a political undertaking, and to ensure that it is no longer a separate world that is viewed with suspicion, distrust and fear.

6 Terrorism in Italy: Receding and Emerging Issues

Giuseppe de Lutiis

The Historical Background

It seems inappropriate to begin a report on terrorism in Italy in recent years without mentioning, however briefly, the lengthy period from 1969 to 1984 when Italy experienced its harshest and most extensive terrorist attacks, of diverse origins and with apparently conflicting aims.

According to the records of Italy's Ministry of Internal Affairs, between 1 January 1969 and 31 December 1987 there were 14,591 politically motivated violent attacks on people or objects in Italy.[1] The attacks varied greatly, from assault and murder to the use of Molotov cocktails and explosives. Between 1976 and 1980, when terrorism in Italy was at its most virulent, a total of 9,673 violent acts occurred; on average, five incidents a day. In 1979, the worst year of all, there were 2,513 violent acts, with an average of seven politically motivated violent incidents every 24 hours.

Between December 1969 and August 1980, in addition to terrorist acts committed by members of opposing ideological camps (the neo-Fascists and the extreme left), there were several of what appeared to be indiscriminate terrorist incidents. In particular, six atypical and unclaimed attacks took place, and were deemed part of what was dubbed a 'strategy of tension'.[2] It is difficult to give a concise definition of this strategy, but the most appropriate explanation seems to be the following, from a judicial sentence:

---

1 Source: Ministry of Internal Affairs; see also *Corriere della Sera*, 25 January 1988. The total also includes attacks from abroad, and specifically the two attacks by Arab terrorists at Fiumicino airport on 15 December 1973 and 27 December 1985.
2 List of attacks:
- 12 December 1969: attack in a Milan bank, killing 16 and injuring 88. [Cont.]

M. van Leeuwen (ed.): *Confronting Terrorism*, pp. 95-109
© 2003 Kluwer Law International. Printed in the Netherlands.

'The term "strategy of tension" usually refers to the concept of a strategy of which the objectives are generally kept secret, and which aims to physically and psychologically condition the dynamic movements within society and the political system, as well as the interaction between them; this may include "political" murders and massacres.'[3]

Those responsible for these attacks (some of whom were later identified among young people leaning to the extreme right) went unpunished for a long time. This was because the investigations, although conducted with great commitment by the Italian magistrates, were sabotaged by the factions of Italy's military secret service, which protected the guilty parties. This was due less to any ideological affinity between the military secret service and the terrorists (although in some cases, this affinity probably did exist), but more because the killings fitted within a general destabilization strategy aimed at shifting the country's political centre of gravity to the right, creating the conditions for the establishment of an authoritarian government 'in the public interest'. Many years later, the magistrates confirmed, albeit in an interlocutory sentence, that the neo-Fascist perpetrators of the first of these terrorist attacks (Milan, 12 December 1969) had been in contact with US intelligence service agents, and that these agents had been aware of the attacks that were being planned.[4]

In the mid-1980s, terrorist attacks from the extreme right all but ceased. The left continued to engage in terrorist activity until 1988, although the attacks became less frequent over time. The only type of violent crime that really persisted and even worsened was that committed by the Mafia. In the Cold War years, many governmental investigative agencies fighting this ancient criminal organization, which dates back to the nineteenth century, did no more than arrest the individual assassins, without touching the leaders. A number of researchers believe that this approach may have been politically motivated, in the aim of tolerating the existence of Mafia groups to guarantee effective opposition to the left and to trade unions supported by the left in those areas where the groups had managed to establish themselves strongly.[5] During this period, the investigative agencies were prepared only to arrest individual, low-ranking members of the Mafia, and only if there was strong proof for a specific and serious offence.

In the 1980s, Mafia organizations became more aggressive, killing dozens of government representatives. Among these were eight magistrates, two politicians, three members of the police force and of the *Carabinieri*, and the Prefect of Palermo. Three of

---

- 31 May 1972: a car loaded with dynamite exploded in a town near Gorizia, in Venezia Giulia, killing three *carabinieri* and injuring two.
- 17 May 1973: bombing of a crowd in front of the police headquarters in Milan, killing four and injuring twelve.
- 28 May 1974: explosion in a square in Brescia during a trade union demonstration, killing eight and injuring 94.
- August 1974: explosion in a train from Florence to Bologna, killing twelve and injuring 44.
- August 1980: attack at the Bologna railway station, killing 85 and injuring 200.

3   Court of Justice of Venice, Investigations Office, *Sentenza: ordinanza di rinvio a giudizio contro Cicuttini Carlo più 33*, p. 411.
4   Court of Justice of Milan, sentence of 30 June 2001.
5   G. Di Lello, 'La vicenda di Salvatore Giuliano', *Storia d'Italia: Annali 12, La criminalità* (Torino: Einaudi, 1997); A. Silj, *Malpaese; Criminalità, corruzione e politica nell'Italia della prima Repubblica, 1943-1994* (Roma: Donzelli, 1994); N. Tranfaglia, *Mafia, politica e affari, 1943-91* (Bari: Laterza, 1992).

these attacks, killing Judge Rocco Chinnici (29 July 1983), Giovanni Falcone (23 May 1992) and Paolo Borsellino (19 July 1992), caused veritable blood baths through the large amount of explosive used. In addition to the targeted victims, thirteen others – mostly bodyguards to the magistrates – were killed.

Summer 1993 was marked by five serious attacks in Rome, Florence and Milan. Some of these targeted basilicas and other monuments of high artistic value. Although some citizens were killed, the attacks appeared to be timed to harm as few people as possible: they took place in the middle of the night, in places usually deserted at that time. This leads one to deduce (as confirmed later by those Mafia members who collaborated with investigators) that the purpose of these crimes was to imply that similar and equally destructive attacks could also be carried out during the day, killing many and destroying Italy's artistic heritage. One should note that in the years leading up to these attacks, the magistrates had increased their efforts to strike at Mafia leaders for the first time.

Terrorism in Recent Years

Apart from the Mafia attacks listed above, between 1989 and 1995 no significant terrorist activity was recorded in Italy. Both right-wing and left-wing extremists confined themselves to the propaganda of their respective doctrines.[6]

Prime Minister Prodi's report on the intelligence and security policy of the first six months of 1996 refers to types of cooperation between extra-parliamentary right-wing extremists and Islamist fundamentalists. In addition, in the first few months of 1996, the level of aggression from anarchic revolutionary groups increased. Two attacks, one of which failed, were attributed to these groups, although no clear evidence was found. The report for the second half of 1996 refers to the threats posed by former anti-communist fighters from Afghanistan:

> 'Since the early 1990s, Islamist terrorist groups have been able to count on the presence, in crisis areas, of veterans of the war in Afghanistan, who returned to their home countries after the retreat of the Soviet army and have filled the ranks of militant fundamentalist Islamist groups and organized crime. Due to the highly professional skills these Islamist veterans have acquired, their strong ideological motivation and substantial and diversified financial support, they are a valuable reinforcement to the terrorist groups.'[7]

The next report to the Italian Prime Minister, concerning the first half of 1997, expresses concern about a possible coming together of the Italian extreme right and Islamist fundamentalists. It states:

---

6   During this period, there were only two attacks by left-wing terrorists. On 2 September 1993, gunshots were fired at the outside wall of the US Air Force base in Aviano (Pordenone), and a bomb was thrown into a building housing military staff. On 10 January 1994, there was an attack on the NATO Defence College in Rome. In both cases, no one was harmed.

7   Senate of the Italian Republic, *Relazione sulla politica informativa e della sicurezza*, communicated to the Italian Prime Minister's Office on 18 January 1997, doc. XXXIII, no. 2, pp. 31-32.

'Some of the extreme-right groups, who share with radical Islamist regimes a common hatred of the western system, continue to show a specific interest in these regimes, in which they have long had close partners who also provide financial support.'[8]

This report also contains an explicit reference to possible terrorist attacks from Islamist groups:

'In recent months, there has been a noticeable increase in the acquisitions of information by Islamist factions, particularly from the Middle East, for the purpose of planned attacks in Europe. The services have therefore focused their intelligence activities on detecting potential threats of attack to the national territory, and particularly those threats of a foreign or religious nature.'[9]

As early as 1997, the Italian intelligence and investigative agencies were aware of the threat from Islamist fundamentalist groups. The Prime Minister shared this concern, but the broader political class remained unaware. The resurgence of terrorism from the extreme left was also underestimated, despite the fact that a high-ranking crime-prevention police officer had warned the Parliamentary Commission on the Investigation of Terrorism of the risk of the return of various types of terrorism.[10] Another reason why the warning within the report was not heeded sufficiently was because there was no specific terrorist activity in Italy in 1997 and 1998, with the exception of an armed assault by Venetian secessionists on the bell tower in St Mark's Square in Venice.[11] Due to its media coverage, the incident provoked an uproar, but Venetian secessionism exhausted itself within a few years, and became subsumed within legal political action for strong regional autonomy.

On 20 May 1999, Italy was rudely awakened from the illusion that the country no longer had to deal with terrorism when Professor Massimo D'Antona, a consultant to the Minister of Labour Antonio Bassolino, was shot six times near his home in Rome. The *Brigate Rosse* (Red Brigades) claimed responsibility for the murder. In the preceding months, there had been noticeable agitation in left-wing opposition circles, partly due to Italy's military intervention in Kosovo. However, there had been no reason for anyone to expect a homicidal attack on a high-ranking official. The crime itself was obviously committed by professionals, and the perpetrators left no clues whatsoever as to their identity. The fact that even after three years not one of the perpetrators had been arrested illustrates the professionalism of the attack. Professor D'Antona was assassinated at a time when the *Nuclei Territoriali Antimperialisti* (Territorial Anti-Imperialist Nuclei), made up of revolutionary left-wing groups that until then had expressed themselves

---

8   Senate of the Italian Republic, *Relazione sulla politica informativa e della sicurezza*, communicated to the Italian Prime Minister's Office on 1 August 1997, doc. XXXIII, no. 3, p. 15.
9   Senate of the Italian Republic, *Relazione sulla politica informativa e della sicurezza*, communicated to the Italian Prime Minister's Office on 1 August 1997, doc. XXXIII, no. 3, p. 23.
10 Parliamentary Commission of Inquiry into Terrorism in Italy and the Failure to Identify those Responsible for the Massacres, session of 18 December 1996, *Audizione del prefetto Carlo Ferrigno*.
11 On 9 May 1997, a group of eight members of the secessionist group *Padano*, armed with sub-machine-guns, held the St Mark's Square bell tower for a few hours, and broadcast a brief communication, also transmitted on the long-wave national public network. They received quite a harsh court sentence, but this was subsequently reduced by the Court of Appeals, and the eight were freed.

almost exclusively through writings against NATO, had begun to step up their actions because of the growing tension in the Balkans. They escalated their activities to burning cars with AFI (American Forces in Italy) number plates, owned by soldiers based in Aviano, and to attacking offices of the *Democratici di Sinistra*, a party that, according to the terrorists, had betrayed the internationalist and pacifist ideals of the left. On 19 March 2002, there was a terrorist attack on a politically sensitive target, Professor Marco Biagi, consultant to the Minister of Labour Roberto Maroni. This attack took place during a difficult confrontation between the government majority and the opposition on the subject of making employees redundant 'without just cause', just four days before a trade union demonstration that was to be attended by three million people. This assassination was committed in cold blood and extremely professionally, proving that the perpetrators were not youngsters committing their first terrorist act. The killers' intentions appear to be exclusively political, aiming to inject a terrorist variable into political conflicts. Furthermore, the lengthy document emailed to many in the days following the attack, and claiming responsibility for it, suggests that the terrorists have access to sources close to the Ministry of Labour. This appears to link this attack to the murder of Professor D'Antona.

As for right-wing terrorism, in the second half of 1999 a movement known only as the *Movimento Antisionista* (Anti-Zionist Movement) made itself known through two attacks in Rome. The first targeted the *Museo Storico della Lotta di Liberazione* and the second a cinema showing a film about the Holocaust.[12] In fact, with the exception of these two attacks and a third in Rome on 22 December 2000, when an explosive device was planted at the entrance to the offices of an extreme-left-wing newspaper, right-wing extremist groups have tended to engage in various expressions of racism on banners or in chants at football matches and in anti-immigration demonstrations, rather than in terrorist acts. The person who attempted to detonate the device was a former militant member of a 1980s' right-wing terrorist group, and was seriously injured when the bomb exploded.

Right-wing subversion expresses itself through radical, if not typically Nazi, groups. These groups take advantage of the complex problems resulting from immigration from Third World countries, and try to engage less educated young people in intolerance and

---

12   On the subject of right-wing extremist groups, Prefect Ansoino Andreassi, Central Director of the *Polizia di Prevenzione,* stated to the Parliamentary Commission of Inquiry into Terrorism:

> 'It has been proved that the *Movimento Politico Occidentale,* as well as other neo-Fascist and neo-Nazi groups, received money transfers from two well-known persons, Roberto Fiore and Massimo Morsello, who had been *Terza Posizione* supporters and who had hidden for a long time in London where, over the years, they started large businesses.
>
> As they are no longer wanted by Italian Justice ... they have recently reappeared in Italy to manage *Forza Nuova,* a movement they created which is now active in several provinces with the aim of participating in the election campaigns.
>
> In addition to *Forza Nuova* there is another radical right-wing organization, *Fronte Nazionale Italiano,* which shares the same ideological foundation and consequently the same hostility to the social policy of integration, especially with regard to immigration. [This hostile position consists of] anti-Americanism and the defence of Catholic fundamentalism, similar to the thesis made public by the English *Third Position*, the French *Front National* and the Spanish *Falange*.'

Parliamentary Commission of Inquiry into Terrorism in Italy and the Failure to Identify those Responsible for the Massacres, session of Wednesday 1 December 1999.

racial discrimination. In this context, one phenomenon that has caused serious problems for the public order is the coming together of extreme-right militants and the most extremist fringe of football fans.[13] The resulting young group is the real novelty in right-wing circles. While in the past, football 'hooligans' constituted a source of recruitment for organized right-wing groups, today they have achieved autonomy from the traditional organizations and manage their own field of action. These 'ultra' supporters have brought to the world of football a new kind of conflict, which has nothing to do with sporting competition and stems directly from the clashes of street politics. However, this phenomenon seems unlikely to increase in the coming years, because the right-wing *Alleanza Nazionale* party, part of the government coalition, is seeking to limit its expansion.

In brief, there is a risk that this type of terrorism will return to Italy, but hopefully this does not present any imminent danger. The right-wing and left-wing extremist groups do have international connections, but these seem limited. That said, the members of one of the subversive left-wing groups, the *Nuclei Territoriali Antimperialisti-Partito Comunista Combattente*, have agreed a pact for action with the Greek terrorist groups *Mavros Asteria* and *17 Novembre,* according to documents circulated by these members in June 2001.[14]

In contrast, extremist Islamist groups appear to have penetrated Italy in some depth, with many dangers. Prime Minister Giuliano Amato's report on Italy's security and intelligence policy of the first half of 2000 explicitly mentions the conversion to Islam of extremists, who then remain in contact with other fundamentalist groups in Italy and abroad in the name of joint opposition to the US and Israel.[15] One should note how the *Nuclei Territoriali Antimperialisti*, in a 1999 document, sang the praises of Osama bin Laden as a 'champion' of anti-imperialism, whose actions had proven his determination to fight the United States, global superpower, to the very end.[16]

There is no evidence of terrorist risks directly linked to immigrant populations in Italy. Of course, it is possible that international terrorist organizations are taking advantage of the flow of hundreds of thousands of immigrants into Italy to conceal their members among them in order to get them into the country. This risk is higher among people coming from Arabic or Islamic countries. Links between these populations with organizations abroad may be the result of previous participation in international networks, such as al-Qaeda or similar organizations, although one cannot exclude the recruitment of new members in Italy, mainly in the Islamic cultural centres. However, it

---

13   Ministry of Internal Affairs, *Rapporto sullo stato della sicurezza in Italia*, 9 February 2001, p. 331.
14   Gianni Cipriani, 'Sul G8 grava il pericolo greco', *Il Nuovo*, 25 June 2001
       (http://www.ilnuovo.it/nuovo/foglia/0,1007, 58126,00.html).
15   Senate of the Republic, *Relazione sulla politica informativa e della sicurezza*, communicated to the Prime Minister's Office on 11 September 2000, doc. XXXIII, no. 9, p. 11. This aspect had already been noted during the Parliamentary Commission's session of 18 December 1996, during which Prefect Ferrigno, then Central Director of the *Polizia di Prevenzione*, had declared: 'It seems important to draw attention to a socio-cultural phenomenon which has developed since the 1980s – and I must emphasize this, given its peculiarity at this time – the conversion of some Italian citizens to the Islamic Shi'ite religion. It has been noticed that a number of young followers of subversive right- or left-wing groups have taken to the Muslim faith and identified with the fundamentalist ideology and anti-imperialist themes, which breathes new life into their political stance.'
16   Gianni Cipriani, 'Sul G8 grava il pericolo greco'.

is widely acknowledged that Arabic terrorist groups, like most other terrorist groups (with the exception of some anarchists) are rigidly compartmentalized. It is therefore extremely difficult to evaluate whether there is a firm connection between these organizations and the Muslim communities in Italy. One can only state that there is no obvious connection.

The problems resulting from the high level of unemployment among immigrants seem to fall into the category of common crime and do not appear to be connected with terrorism, even though unemployment, and the despair that comes with it, may lead certain individuals to embrace terrorist causes. Many immigrants involved in illegal activities, such as drug trafficking or prostitution, were already engaged in this kind of activity before entering Italy. These immigrants mainly come from the Balkans, Albania, Montenegro and Serbia, and in most cases they belong to criminal organizations in their own country. Integration has mostly proved a problem in northern Italy, where the *Lega Nord* (Northern League) political party focuses much of its propaganda on emphasizing the dangers of extensive immigration. Problems have occurred predominantly in those areas where immigration has been turbulent, which has made smooth integration with the local communities difficult.

Threat Awareness

Over the past ten years, Italy's security and intelligence organizations have effectively monitored subversive movements from both the extreme right and the extreme left. As potential terrorist threats appeared to be solidifying (i.e., over the last four to five years), these organizations have been able to indicate, without fail, where the threat would re-emerge.

These warnings were not adequately reflected in the media's account of the various attacks during this period. What has been lacking in politics, research and in the press is an overall analysis connecting episodes separated by time and space. This kind of analysis would have allowed the public to gain a clearer and broader understanding of these terrorist movements, which are less intense and have fewer supporters than those afflicting Italy in the 1970s and 1980s. However, the murders of Professor D'Antona and Professor Biagi stand out, even among the diversity of terrorist attacks that Italy has experienced in the past, as they appear to be clearly distinct from other acts committed by the 'resurrected' *Brigate Rosse*, which showed some restraint (by setting fire to the cars of US citizens without ever targeting people, for instance).

With regard to the awareness of danger, before the events of 11 September 2001 Italians had only a vague and generic perception of Islamist fundamentalism. After the New York attacks, their attitude changed, partly because of the presentation and interpretation of events by the media. Italians began to overestimate the danger of attack in major Italian cities, and in the first weeks even changed some of their habits. For example, the number of passengers using Rome's underground system decreased considerably, with a corresponding increase in road traffic. However, this change in behaviour lasted for only about ten days.

In November and December 2001, a fairly calm debate developed in the press about the appropriateness of continuing to focus attention on terrorist attacks, by dedicating a large number of pages to these topics more than two months after 11 September 2002. The government did attempt to persuade the media to reduce the column inches given to these issues, and media interest seemed to decrease spontaneously in the second half of December 2001. The public's fear of attacks in Italy seemed to fade at the same time, although some intelligence circles feared a possible terrorist attack on St Peter's Basilica in the days around Christmas 2001.

Italy did not experience problems involving letters containing anthrax spores. There were a few isolated incidents of letters containing white powder, but it was immediately clear that these were jokes in bad taste. This was ascertained so quickly that there was no time for the population to panic.

The Anti-terrorist Organizations

The anti-terrorist organizations in Italy report to the Ministry of Internal Affairs and the Ministry of Defence. The *Polizia di Prevenzione* (Prevention Police) report to the first, while the *Reparto Operativo Speciale dell'Arma dei Carabinieri* (Special Operational Corps of the *Carabinieri*) reports to the second. The two secret services SISDe (*Servizio per le informazioni e la sicurezza democratica*, or Service for Information and Security of Democracy) and SISMi (*Servizio per le Informazioni Militare*, or Service for Military Information and Security) operate under the authority of the Ministries of Internal Affairs and Defence respectively. Finally, an Italian branch of Europol has been working in close cooperation with the police forces of other European countries for a few years now.

The *Direzione Centrale per la Polizia di Prevenzione* (Central Directorate of the Prevention Police) was created by decree of the Minister of Internal Affairs on 31 January 1978, and was originally called UCIGOS (*Ufficio Centrale per le Investigazioni Generali e le Operazioni Special*). UCIGOS received its current name by decree on 8 April 1991, and consists of a general investigation service and an anti-terrorist service. This anti-terrorist service is made up of three main divisions: the first specializes in fighting right-wing subversion and terrorism; the second in fighting left-wing subversion and terrorism; and the third in combating international terrorism. The third division is also in charge of the relationship with the police forces of other countries. There is a separate, fourth division for special operations, known as the *Nucleo Operativo Centrale di Sicurezza* (Central Operational Group for Security), a group of approximately 300 men specifically trained for high-risk interventions.

UCIGOS was created during the reform of the secret services and the dissolution of a previous security service that had reported to the Ministry of Internal Affairs.[17] It filled the void created when it was decided that the officers of the new secret services would not have the same status as officers of the *Polizia Giudiziaria* (Judicial Police). UCIGOS was in direct contact with the political offices of each *Questura* or precinct, which are now called DIGOS (*Divisione per le Investigazioni Generali e le Operazioni Speciali* – Division for General Investigation and Special Operations). These functions are now exercised by the *Direzione Centrale per la Polizia di Prevenzione*.

---

17   Law 801, 24 October 1977.

In December 1990,[18] the *Carabinieri* created the special operational group *Raggruppamento Operativo Speciale* (ROS), to conduct anti-terrorist investigations, among other duties. ROS was originally conceived as a central structure composed of departments, and a peripheral structure functionally dependent on the central structure and divided into crime-fighting sections to counter the most important forms of political and common crime and to ensure maximum coverage of Italy. Until 1998, ROS did have a central investigative role, but the decree issued by the Ministry of Internal Affairs on 25 March 1998 withdrew those central investigative functions and replaced them with a coordinating role. Nowadays, ROS is divided into four sections: the first operates in the field of organized crime, such as the Mafia; the second in the fields of drug-trafficking and kidnapping; the third conducts operational analyses of organized crime; and the fourth is responsible for analysing and fighting criminal subversion and domestic and international terrorism.

Law 801 of 24 October 1977 reformed the Italian secret services and created SISMi and SISDe. SISMi is responsible for Italy's military security at home and abroad, and SISDe is charged with protecting the state's institutional and political interests from anyone acting against these interests, including political subversion. SISDe is therefore the service in charge of fighting terrorism, but in the current phase, whereby the greatest danger is from organizations based abroad, SISMi actively supports SISDe. In April 1995, SISMi had 2,223 members of staff and SISDe had 1,339.[19] In both cases, these numbers lagged considerably behind the original plans for staff numbers (and no official data is available for subsequent years). In January 2002, some newspapers reported that the government intends to increase staff numbers in the two services, but for the time being this is no more than a journalistic indiscretion.

The intelligence services perform their duties independently from the police forces and the *Carabinieri*, although they can, of course, ask for specific information. Furthermore, once they become aware of criminal activity, they are obliged (at least in theory) to communicate this information to the magistrates via the police, although they have the right to delay the communication if there is cause to believe that such a delay is indispensable to gather additional information. The secret services do not have, nor have they ever had, the right or powers to hold, interrogate or arrest people. If this were to occur, it would be a grave violation of citizens' rights, given that no lawyer would be present and no legal safeguards would be provided.

The Italian Penal Code has long included articles prescribing specific penalties for terrorist acts. In the late 1970s, some very restrictive norms were introduced, imposing heavy sentences for individuals who, while not participating in the actual execution of violent actions, belonged to the terrorist group responsible. After the events of 11 September 2001, it became clear that new legislation regarding penalties and prosecution was required. The first piece of new legislation was the decree of 18 October 2001, which

---

18   Decree-Law 324 of 13 November 1990 made provisions for the establishment of central and interprovincial police services (the *Guardia di Finanza, Polizia di Stato* and *Carabinieri*) to ensure a connection between investigations concerning organized crime. The *Carabinieri* created the *Raggruppamento Operativo Speciale* on 3 December 1990.

19   Report of the Parliamentary Committee for the Intelligence and Security Services and State Secrets, *Primo rapporto sul sistema di informazione e sicurezza*, communicated to the Italian Prime Minister's Office on 6 April 1995, pp. 28-29.

was altered to become Law 438 on 15 December 2001 and introduces the charge of 'international terrorism' and the newly defined category of 'association for the purpose of international terrorism'.[20] Until then, the contents of Article 210-bis of the Penal Code did not adequately cover terrorist actions initiated in Italy in preparation for operations abroad. It was all the more important to fill this gap in the law, as it appears that Islamist terrorists tend to consider Italy a safe haven in which to set up bases from which they can carry out attacks in neighbouring countries. Through the introduction of this newly defined criminal charge, this gap has been closed, and the magistrates are now in a position to act on the basis of a system of specific and pertinent norms.

Furthermore, the new law determines that officials of the judicial police cannot be punished if, in the course of specific police operations and 'with the sole aim of acquiring evidence regarding crimes committed with the objective of creating terror', they 'receive, replace or hide money, weapons, documents, narcotics, goods or items which are used to perpetrate such crimes, or otherwise hinder the determining of their origin, or make their use possible', either 'directly or through another person'.[21] During such investigations, police officers may utilize documents, assume identities or go undercover to stimulate or enter into communication with individuals or contacts in communication networks. This new Article legalizes a practice that is sometimes used by police officers in anti-drug-trafficking operations.

Despite this reform, there is a lack of coordination between the various public prosecutors, who may accidentally investigate the same groups and persons at the same time. During the fight against the Mafia at the beginning of the 1990s, the *Direzione Nazionale Antimafia* (National Anti-Mafia Directorate) was created as a central organization for information on the anti-Mafia activities of the various precincts. There is no similar central body for the anti-terrorist fight, and it is possible for magistrates investigating the same terrorist group in different cities to be unaware of each other's activities and search for evidence that has already been gathered elsewhere. The lack of centralization of the Judicial Police and the magistrates means that some activities are duplicated in part, or even in full at times. In order to resolve this, some advocate the creation of a *Procura Nazionale Antiterrorismo,* similar to the *Direzione Nazionale Antimafia*. Others believe that it would be easier to give the *Direzione Nazionale Antimafia* responsibility for coordinating the fight against terrorism. There are those, however, who fear that this solution would place too much power and information in the hands of such a small group of magistrates. This objection may be well founded, but there is no doubt that if domestic or international terrorism became a major problem again, the creation of a centralized body would immediately become indispensable.

---

20 Article 1 of Law 438 of 15 December 2001, which amplifies Article 270-bis of the Penal Code, reads as follows: 'within criminal law, terrorism also takes place when acts of violence are directed against a foreign state and international institutions and organizations' (as published in the *Gazzetta Ufficiale*, no. 293, 18 December 2001).

21 Article 4 of Law 438 of 15 December 2001.

International Anti-terrorist Cooperation

Any cooperation between the secret services of countries allied in the fight against terrorism takes place in confidence, and in the absence of official or at least reliable information it is therefore difficult to evaluate from the outside. For the same reasons, it is almost impossible to evaluate the overall activities of the secret services, even though what emerges in the Italian Prime Ministers' reports between 1996 and 2000 does suggest, as we have already seen, that these secret services have understood the dangers from Islamist fundamentalism.

With regard to anti-terrorist collaboration between the police forces of different countries, it is probably necessary to ensure that it becomes permanent, and not the kind of collaboration that it is currently, which only delivers results in crisis situations and even then after a delay. There seems to be a total absence, or at least a deficiency, of permanent planning.

The existing cooperation also suffers from differences in legislation between states. In some countries there are no specific anti-terrorist laws, and terrorist acts are punished as common crimes. Other countries have laws or other legal instruments that explicitly use the terms 'terrorism' and 'terrorist'. As mentioned earlier, the Italian Penal Code has for some time contained specific articles dealing with terrorist crimes or attempts to subvert the democratic order. With regard to jurisprudence, in recent years there have been differences in interpretation concerning the objective of terrorism and the objective of subversion of the democratic or constitutional order. Some hold them to be equivalent and others believe that they are distinct. The Court of Cassation, which holds the prevailing opinion, has declared that the two categories are separate:

> 'The aim of terrorism is to create terror among the people through indiscriminate criminal actions, i.e., actions that are directed not against individuals, but against what they represent ... if individuals are targeted, this is independent of their function in society; the actions are meant to create terror in order to weaken trust in the existing order and weaken its structure. Subversion, by contrast, is directly aimed at subverting the constitutional order and undermining the pluralistic and democratic composition of the state by taking apart its structures, by preventing the state from functioning properly or by diverting it from the fundamental principles that are the essence of the constitutional order.'[22]

It follows from this that the law only punishes organizations that have a terrorist programme against a foreign state, and not those with a non-terrorist subversive plan, because Article 270-bis of the Penal Code determines that planning to attack a foreign state through violent acts constitutes terrorism and not subversion. In fact, Law 438 only introduced the concept of 'international terrorism', and not a broader definition.

The profound changes in the nature of the crimes and in the operating modes of members of terrorist organizations show just how inadequate the traditional forms of judicial and police cooperation are in the fight against this type of crime. Some countries have legislation that is strongly protective of suspects' rights, and that does not permit the extradition of foreigners for crimes such as *associazione sovversiva* (subversive asso-

---

22   See Giuseppe Narducci, 'Nella differenza tra atti terroristici ed eversivi i confini del 'nuovo' reato', *Diritto e Giustizia*, vol. III, no. 3 (Milan: Giuffré, January 2002).

ciation). Many of those who joined terrorist groups in the 1970s and 1980s were accused of these crimes in Italy if there was insufficient evidence of their direct participation in crime, assaults or other specific offences. Many Italian left-wing terrorists found refuge in France, and still live free there as they are only accused of *associazione sovversiva*, for which France has not granted extradition, even for those given heavy sentences by the Italian courts.

In recent years, terrorism has operated increasingly through international networks that often take advantage of the legislative gaps caused by geographical limitations to the scope of investigations. They also take advantage of the differences in approach between different EU member states. EU member states must therefore make every necessary effort to harmonize their policies in this area, and consequently their legislation, by developing joint legal propositions and reinforcing the collaboration between the judiciary and the police forces. The agreement on the European arrest warrant is a first important step. One must mention, with deep regret, that Italy has taken an incomprehensible and highly limiting position by adopting a law regulating the verification of documentation requested from the judicial authorities of other countries, thereby creating serious obstacles to international judicial cooperation. Furthermore, the Italian government continues to have reservations about the European arrest warrant. It is disconcerting, to say the least, that political self-interest has so far prevailed over the pressing need to create new and efficient instruments in the fight against terrorism.

Cooperation between magistrates, police and security officers of the different European countries must be increased by adopting common legislation, for instance, in the critical area of asset-freezing, thereby implementing Resolution 1373 of the United Nations Security Council.[23] Above all, the proposal for a framework prepared by the European Commission with regard to the fight against terrorism must be implemented rapidly by all member states, in view of the fact that only six member states have specific anti-terrorist legislation.

Possible Civil or Human Rights Violations by Anti-terrorist Services

At present, the Italian media and public do not appear to be particularly concerned about potential violations of the civil rights of Italian citizens or foreign citizens residing in Italy who might be investigated in connection with subversive Islamist networks in Italy. There have been no changes in the legislation concerning the legal safeguards for citizens under investigation or accused of criminal acts.

However, some legal experts have pointed out that under Article 270-bis, according to which the protected interest is the 'democratic order' in Italy, activities directed against another state could not be considered as punishable offences. More generally, some have raised the problem of whether all violent acts should be considered as terrorist acts, even when directed against dictatorships that deny fundamental human rights, or promote ethnic violence or civil war.

The Italian Minister of Public Function with authority over the secret services, Franco Frattini, caused some concern at the end of November 2001 when he announced

---

23   Resolution 1373 was adopted by the UN Security Council at meeting no. 4385 on 28 September 2001.

in a newspaper column an imminent reform of the secret services that amounted to an increase in the investigative powers of these services without the obligation to inform the magistrates or to obtain judicial permission for wire-tapping and electronic eaves-dropping.[24] This announcement was criticized for the way in which it was made – it had not been agreed beforehand with the members of the Parliamentary Committee on Intelligence and Security Services, and the statement became public in an interview with the press – and it clearly implied restrictions of civil rights. The Italian government chose not to persist in this reform project, and two weeks later another newspaper ran a story on the guidelines of another reform project that was being prepared by the Parliamentary Committee.[25] According to this report, the legal limits within which secret service officers could operate would be extended in comparison to the existing law, but less drastically than would have been the case for the original proposal. In any case, this increase would take place under the control of the Parliamentary Committee. In both projects, irregular operations had to be authorized beforehand by the Italian Prime Minister. The full drafts of the proposals were not made public, and therefore they cannot be evaluated in any depth. In December 2001, however, the Parliamentary Committee on Intelligence and Security Services did present a public report on the subject of the possible reform. This report introduced a new legal definition of intelligence, as the 'gathering and analysis of information which could not be obtained otherwise, and which is useful for the protection of national security'.[26] This document indicates that within the Committee, there are two schools of thought on how the new law may define the demarcation between what officers can and cannot be authorized to do. The majority of the Committee members believe that it is enough to indicate those legal interests that require absolute protection and cannot in any way be exposed to risks, even by those acting undercover and in the name of a superior public interest. By way of example, the Committee cites acts 'aimed at endangering or harming life, physical integrity, personal freedom, health or public safety'.[27] A few members of the Committee believe that it is preferable to indicate all cases of conduct that require authorization. In their opinion, this would ensure that the political body responsible for granting authorization acts within a well-defined framework and not at its own discretion.

The issue of reforming the secret services has been under discussion for a while in Italy, but it is likely that reform will be implemented within a relatively short period. The need for reorganization emerged after the discovery in the mid-1980s that after the reform of 1977 the secret services had behaved in a manner that court sentences found to be criminal.[28] The need became more urgent after the fall of the Berlin Wall, which was hoped would lead to more relaxed international relations. Moreover, whereas before 11 September 2001 the reform that was both expected and desired was one that would

---

24   See *Il Corriere della sera* of 25 November 2001 and the daily newspapers on the following days.
25   See *La Repubblica* of 14 December 2001.
26   *Report of the Parliamentary Committee for Intelligence and Security Services and State Secrets on the Different Options for Reforming the Functions and Structures of the Intelligence and Security Services*, communicated to the Prime Minister's Office on 13 December 2001, doc. XXXIV, no. 1, p. 10.
27   *Report of the Parliamentary Committee for Intelligence and Security Services and State Secrets on the Different Options for Reforming the Functions and Structures of the Intelligence and Security Services*, communicated to the Prime Minister's Office on 13 December 2001, doc. XXXIV, no. 1, p. 10.
28   Fifth Court of Justice of Rome, sentence of 29 July 1985.

extend the protection of citizens' rights and the powers of the Parliamentary Committee, after the attacks on the United States it seems probable that the secret services' powers of autonomous investigation may be extended, even when they violate the Penal Code. For instance, wire-tapping and electronic eavesdropping could take place without prior authorization. It can only be hoped that these measures, which without any doubt affect citizens' rights, will be counterbalanced through the Parliamentary Committee's increased powers of control.[29]

With regard to recent events, there have been no reports of potential violations by the secret services, the police or the *Carabinieri* of the civil rights of suspected citizens or their followers. Nor have their been any reports – even in the press – of allegedly illegal acts committed by investigators dealing with Islamist terrorist groups. One should note that even during the times when the fight against terrorism was at its most bitter, there were only a few incidents of violence against terrorists by law and order officials. These abuses cannot be compared to those that have occurred in other European countries. Furthermore, in 1981 police reform introduced many constitutional rights that the police had not enjoyed before, including the right to form trade unions. This reform drew the forces of law and order closer to the principles laid down in the Italian Constitution. As has been well documented, serious violations took place in Genoa the night after the G8 meeting on 21 July 2001. Although a Parliamentary Committee was rapidly formed to investigate the violence of the demonstrators and the police, the true reasons for these abuses have not been clearly established. In general, the conduct of the police in keeping the public order has been proper, unlike their behaviour in the 1950s and 1960s. There have been very few episodes like those at Genoa, and they were all far less serious.

In summary, it can be said that the events of 11 September 2001 have not led to significant violations of the rights of Italians or those of foreigners residing in Italy.

Final Evaluation

If terrorism is understood to be 'the systematic use of extreme violence and violent threats in the aim of achieving public or political objectives',[30] then it can be said that in recent years there have been isolated terrorist events of diverse origins. It is more difficult to determine with any certainty whether one or more terrorist organizations have been operating in a methodical way. From an operational point of view, the terrorist cell that in all likelihood carried out the attacks against Professors D'Antona and Biagi appears to be

---

29 The Parliamentary Committee for Intelligence and Security Services and State Secrets was founded in 1977, at the same time as the reform of the secret services, which sanctioned their duplication. It had only extremely weak powers of control, as it was not authorized to enter into the detail of the services' operations, but was entitled solely to require information about the general lines of their activities. In subsequent years, the Committee achieved a partial enlargement of its powers, not so much through changes in the legislation, but because of the personal goodwill of the Italian Prime Ministers and the services' directors, who provided more detailed information. One should note that the Committee's activities are always confidential, with the exception of some reports that it decides to send to the Italian Parliament, which then become public. For many years now, many political leaders have been fighting for the amplification of the Committee's powers of control through legislation.

30 W.T. Mallison Jr. and S.V. Mallison, 'The Concept of Public Purpose Terror in International Law', *Journal of Palestine Studies*, vol. IV, no. 2, 1974-75, p. 36.

highly professional, unlike the groups of similar origin that are active in the north of Italy. However, investigators are picking up signals that the different organizations are coming together in a union that is probably imminent, if not already complete. This would obviously present a grave danger, because it would create a direct bridge between the professionalism of the *Brigate Rosse-Partito Comunista Combattent* (BR-PCC, or Red Brigades-Combating Communist Party) and the presumably higher number of members belonging to the other groups.

With regard to the problems posed by the fundamentalist Islamist networks' plans to launch new attacks on the United States and US allies, investigations in Italy have proven the presence of various al-Qaeda cells and other Islamist groups that, as stated above, tend to consider Italy as a base from which to prepare attacks abroad.

In conclusion, it appears essential to improve the skills and overall professionalism of the secret service agents in Italy, by means of a major staff recruiting programme and by hiring young people with an in-depth knowledge of the world of international finance and the relevant areas of the various terrorist groups. On this note, it seems that a number of agents from the *Guardia di Finanza* are now joining the military secret service, which is extremely positive.

The police and *Carabinieri* have brought in a new generation of recruits over the last ten years and appear to be well prepared to face new crises. As for the magistrates, they acquired a high level of professionalism during the period of terrorism in the 1970s and 1980s. They (or some of them) must acquire new knowledge about the problems and operating modes of international terrorism, but this is likely to be resolved within a short time-frame. Should Italy experience significant terrorist acts again, the idea of creating a *Direzione Nazionale Antiterrorismo* (National Anti-terrorism Directorate) should be reconsidered.

7 Terrorism in Germany: Old and New Problems

Stefan Malthaner and Peter Waldmann

Terrorism and Counter-terrorism in Germany: An Overview

When commandos of an elite counter-terrorism unit stormed a hijacked Lufthansa airliner in Mogadishu, Somalia, on 18 October 1977, killing all but one of the terrorists and freeing all the hostages unharmed, the incident marked the end of a more than six-week stand-off between the German state and the left-wing terrorist organization Red Army Faction (RAF). Palestinian terrorists had conducted the hijacking operation in support of a terrorist campaign to coerce the German government into releasing the RAF's founders Gudrun Ensslin and Andreas Baader from prison. Earlier in 1977, members of the RAF had murdered the Federal Attorney General and a leading bank manager; finally on 5 September 1977 they had kidnapped the prominent industrialist Hans Martin Schleyer. The night after the plane was rescued, Andreas Baader and two of his comrades committed suicide and Mr Schleyer was killed by his kidnappers.

The picture of terrorism in Germany is dominated by assassinations and bombings committed by left-wing terrorist groups, particularly the RAF, with the events of late 1977 marking a peak in the public's memory the of the terrorist threat to Germany, and a major incision in the country's post-war history. After the RAF's campaign came to an end in the early 1990s, terrorism in a narrow sense – that is, requiring more or less permanent organizational structures and a degree of strategic planning of terrorist attacks – did not occur in Germany. However, in addition to violent activities of a militant left-wing scene, the 1990s saw an outbreak of right-wing and racist violence of an unprecedented scope.

This chapter seeks to provide an overview of terrorism and political violence in Germany, the way it was perceived, and corresponding reactions. The first part briefly

M. van Leeuwen (ed.): *Confronting Terrorism*, pp. 111-128
© 2003 Kluwer Law International. Printed in the Netherlands.

sketches the different manifestations of terrorist violence as well as the organization and legal basis of counter-terrorism in Germany; and the second part describes government and public perceptions of the various forms of terrorism and political violence. A final paragraph offers a tentative interpretation of the relationship between different forms of political violence and the perceptions and reactions that they induce, the main interest lying on a comparison of reactions to left-wing terrorism on the one hand and reactions to right-wing violence on the other hand.

Left-wing Terrorism in Germany: The Red Army Faction

In the early 1970s, various rather small left-wing terrorist groups emerged as a violent fall-out of the 1968 student revolt, among which the Red Army Faction, also known as the Baader-Mainhof Gang, became the most notorious.[1] Only two years after its emergence, following a series of bombing incidents in which five people were killed and more than 50 injured, most of the first-generation members of the RAF were captured. During the following years a second and a third generation of RAF terrorists set out to free imprisoned members and to continue their struggle.

The events of 1977 were followed by a number of arrests and drop-outs, but in the mid 1980s the RAF started another offensive of assassinations and bombings. One of these incidents, the murder of a US soldier – the only reason being to get hold of his ID card to enter US military facilities in Frankfurt – produced criticism among RAF supporters and groups of prisoners, raising in some of them doubts about the justification of violence of this kind. The incident marked the beginning of a process of internal discussions and factionalism among members, prisoners and supporters, which ultimately brought an end to the RAF's terrorist campaign. However, until 1991 the group continued to assassinate economic and political leaders, among them Alfred Herrhausen, who was killed in November 1989 by a bomb of exceptional technical sophistication. During the almost 30 years of the organization's existence, terrorism committed by the RAF killed more than 40 people and injured about 100 more.

In 1992, then German Minister of Justice Klaus Kinkel started an initiative to end terrorist violence by offering to reconsider the sentences of some long-term RAF prisoners, which coincided with the increasing insecurity among activists about the violent strategy. In April 1992 the RAF published a statement declaring a provisional ceasefire. The group has not assassinated officials since then, even after a RAF member and a policeman were killed in a botched arrest operation in 1993. In April 1998, after another four years of inactivity, the RAF finally declared its disbandment, stating an obvious fact rather than publishing any veritable decision on their part.

In the 1990s, left-wing violence predominantly took the form of violent hooliganism and street riots perpetrated by so-called Autonome who act within a loosely structured, militant extremist left-wing scene, united by a diffuse form of anarchism and the use of violence. While Autonome during the mid-1990s were involved in severe street battles

---

1   Other left-wing terrorist groups were, for example, the 'Movement 2 June' (*Bewegung 2. Juni*) and the 'Revolutionary Cells' (*Revolutionäre Zellen*).

with police and in violent anti-nuclear-power protests, they recently took part in riots surrounding anti-globalization protests in Gothenburg, Genova and other places.

Right-wing and Racist Violence

Terrorist violence in the 1970s and 1980s was not only perpetrated by extremist left-wing groups. From 1979 to 1983, groups and individuals motivated by racist and right-wing ideologies, and in most cases linked to extremist right-wing and Nazi organizations, committed a number of terrorist bombings and murders, killing a total of twenty people and injuring many more.[2] By the mid-1980s, however, almost all perpetrators of right-wing terrorist crimes had been arrested and tried.

The organized right-wing extremist and Nazi scene, from which many of the terrorists had emerged, was factionalized and weakened by internal disputes and rivalry by the end of the 1980s.

With the beginning of the 1990s, right-wing violence re-emerged in a different shape. Shortly after Germany was reunited in 1989/90, the country was shaken by an outbreak of right-wing and racist street assaults, riots, violent hooliganism and fire-bombing attacks, directed mainly against foreigners and accommodation for asylum-seekers. The year 1992 marked a sad peak in this development with more than 1,500 violent incidents and a total of 17 people killed by arson attacks and assaults by right-wing gangs. A number of pogrom-like incidents, for example in September 1991 in Hoyerswerda and in August 1992 in Rostock, gained particular public attention, when crowds of up to several hundred youths attacked buildings serving as accommodation for asylum-seekers with the onslaught lasting for several days and the police unable to get the situation under control. Atrocities reached another shocking high when in November 1992 and May 1993 the homes of Turkish immigrants were set on fire and three women and five children were killed in the flames.[3]

Violent crimes motivated by right-wing and racist ideologies in the early 1990s were committed in most cases rather spontaneously by gangs of local youths, only one-fifth of the perpetrators having contacts with right-wing or Nazi organizations. Many of the perpetrators, however, identified themselves with the skinhead scene and culture, shown in their appearance and lifestyle. The skinhead movement is a form of violent and in Germany predominantly racist hooliganism, which has existed to a limited extent since the late 1980s in the western as well as in the eastern part of Germany. It proliferated during the course of the 1990s, and in some circles it increasingly took the form of a juvenile subculture.[4]

---

2   Out of these twenty people, twelve alone were killed in a bombing incident at the *Oktoberfest* in Munich in 1980.

3   Bundesministerium des Innern, *Verfassungsschutzbericht 1992* (Bonn: Bundesministerium des Innern, 1993), pp. 70-78.

4   Helmut Willems, Stefanie Würtz and Roland Eckert, *Analyse Fremdenfeindlicher Straftäter* (Bonn: Bundesministerium des Innern, 1994); Helmut Willems, 'Development, Patterns and Causes of Violence against Foreigners in Germany: Social and Biographical Characteristics of Perpetrators and the Process of Escalation', in Tore Biorgo (ed.), *Terror from the Extreme Right* (London: Frank Cass, 1995), [Cont.]

While violent incidents took place in all parts of Germany, the eastern states represented a particular focus of right-wing extremist violence. Between 30 and more than 40 per cent of all violent crimes occurred there, although these states account for only one-fifth of Germany's overall population. In addition, attacks differed in their basic characteristics. Incidents in the eastern states tended to be more violent and to be perpetrated more openly, while in the western states right-wing organizations tended to play a greater role and attacks were perpetrated more secretly.[5]

Although statistics compiled by the German Federal Criminal Police Office (BKA) show a substantial decline in the number of right-wing violent crimes after 1993/94, fire-bombing incidents in particular stabilized on a level significantly higher than before 1991. In the year 2000, the number of violent incidents again rose considerably, by approximately 30 per cent, particularly in the western states. These statistics, however, include only crimes reported to the police and classified as right-wing extremist incidents. While the basic trend shown by these statistics seems to be fairly correct, they have nevertheless been criticized for neglecting a large part of actually occurring incidents, because of the victims' reluctance to contact the police and the requirement of an alleged motivation directed against state order for the crime to be registered as a right-wing extremist crime. While official statistics list a total of 36 people killed as a result of right-wing violence during the 1990s, NGO and media sources, not unreasonably, estimated the death toll from 1990 to 2000 at 93, others even at more than 130.[6] In part in reaction to this criticism, in 2001 the BKA adopted a new definition system, introducing the categories of 'politically motivated crime' (which is not necessarily directed against the state order itself) and of 'hate crime'. The result of these new categories on reporting and statistics are not so far known.[7]

The increase of right-wing violence in 2000 in particular reflected a proliferation of violent street attacks against people (which rose by about 40 per cent), with the murders of a Mozambique citizen and a homeless person in July 2000 being the most appalling incidents. In addition, attempted arson attacks, particularly on a Jewish synagogue, and a bomb explosion in September 2000, which severely injured members of a passing group of Jewish immigrants from Russia, gained particular public attention. After two probably right-wing bombing incidents in 1998 and 1999, the recent events raised fears of the emergence of a new right-wing terrorism. So far, however, there are no further indications supporting this assumption.

---

pp. 167-168; Armin Pfahl-Traughber, 'Die Entwicklung des Rechtsextremismus in Ost- und Westdeutschland', *Aus Politik und Zeitgeschichte*, 39/2000, 22 September 2000, pp. 8-10.

5   Heinz Lynen von Berg, 'Rechtsextremismus in Ostdeutschland seit der Wende', in Wolfgang Kowalsky and Wolfgang Schroeder (eds), *Rechtsextremismus: Einführung und Forschungsbilanz* (Opladen: Westdeutscher Verlag, 1994), pp. 101.

6   Bernd Wagner, 'Zur Auseinandersetzung mit Rechtsextremismus und Rassismus in den neuen Bundesländern', *Aus Politik und Zeitgeschichte*, 39/2000, 22 September 2000, p. 32.

7   Bundesministerium der Innern, *Erster Periodischer Sicherheitsbericht* (Berlin: Bundesministerium des Innern, 2001) pp. 267 and 275.

International Terrorism in Germany

While during the 1970s and 1980s several serious international terrorist incidents took place in Germany (including the hostage taking of Israeli athletes by Palestinian terrorists at the Olympic Games in Munich in 1972), international terrorism during the 1990s affected the country only marginally. German citizens were attacked abroad, but terrorist incidents in Germany itself were comparatively limited in scope, attacks being primarily aimed at targets related to a conflict in the terrorist organization's country of origin or against traitors or rival terrorist groups. German facilities were targeted mainly as a by-product of a campaign against a foreign country or simply to attract public attention.

The main source of terrorist violence perpetrated by foreigners in Germany during the 1990s was the Kurdish separatist organization PKK (Kurdish Workers' Party). From 1992 onwards the organization pursued a campaign of arson attacks against Turkish shops, community centres, embassies, etc., peaking in 1995 when more than 180 such incidents took place. This campaign finally came to a halt, but in 1999, after the arrest of PKK leader Abdullah Ocalan by Turkish security forces, Germany was rocked by a series of riots, fire-bombing incidents and hostage-takings, which, however short-lived, caused extensive damage and injured a number of people.

Besides these groups, a number of foreign terrorist organizations – such as the Lebanese Hizb'allah, the Palestinian Hamas, and the Algerian GIA – did have branches in Germany.[8] The activities of these organizations in Germany were, however, pre-dominantly non-violent, ranging from fund-raising and recruitment to political propaganda. While members of these organizations were in some cases charged with building up a criminal organization, they generally tried not to stir up things in a country that was valuable to them as a place to rest and to raise economic and political support.

The emergence of a different terrorist threat to Germany was indicated in December 2000 by the arrest of an Islamist terrorist cell in Frankfurt, allegedly affiliated with Osama bin Laden's al-Qaeda network, which apparently had planned an attack on the Strasbourg Christmas market and other targets, thereby posing a direct threat to German interests.

The 11 September 2001 attack on the United States of course also proved to be a fundamental incision for Germany. While the event was of great significance for the whole world, indicating the emergence of a terrorist threat of new dimensions, it was of particular relevance for Germany as some of the hijackers had been living for several years in the country and some preparations for the attack had possibly been done in Germany. Before leaving for the United States to be trained as pilots, three of the main hijackers had been studying in Hamburg; the suspected leader of the group, Mohammed Atta, since 1992; Marwan al-Shehhi and Ziad Jarrah since 1996. Three other persons who had been living in Hamburg are suspected of having planned to take part in the attack (but failed to obtain visas) and of having transferred money to the hijackers while they

---

8   While about 800 Hizb'allah members are estimated to be active in Germany, about 250 persons are believed to support Hamas in various ways, and about 350 to belong to the Algerian GIA. See Bundesministerium des Innern, *Verfassungsschutzbericht* 2000 (Berlin: Bundesministerium des Innern, 2001), pp. 173-178.

were being trained in the US.[9] In Germany itself, no terrorist attacks perpetrated by individuals affiliated or sympathizing with al-Qaeda did take place since September 11th. However, the detonation of a truck bomb in front of a Synagoge in Tunesia on April 11th, 2002, killing 19 people, among them 14 German tourists, and several arrests revealing plots to carry out attacks in the country, demonstrated that a direct threat existed for Germany, too.

Counter-terrorism in Germany

The Organization of German Security Forces

The organization of counter-terrorism in Germany is structured by the country's Federal Constitution, ensuring a far-reaching autonomy for the sixteen states or *Länder*. While law-making is to a high degree centralized at the Federal Parliament and the Federal Government, law enforcement and internal security in general are primarily the responsibility of the states. Each state has its own police force, including a State Criminal Police Office and specially trained anti-terrorism units, which account for more than 85 per cent of total law enforcement personnel in Germany. The Federal Criminal Police Office (*Bundeskriminalamt*, BKA) and the Federal Border Police (*Bundesgrenzschutz*, BGS), both federal police forces and the latter including the elite counter-terrorism unit GSG 9, account for the remaining 15 per cent. In addition, each state does have an internal intelligence agency, the so-called Office for the Protection of the Constitution (*Verfassungsschutzamt*).

Concerning counter-terrorism, however, there does exist a considerable degree of centralization. The BKA, in addition to its responsibility for various central databases and specialized forensic technology, and the Federal Attorney General are in charge of criminal investigations in a variety of terrorist crimes, including terrorist activities directed against the Federal Government and international terrorism. The BKA, with its vast technological capabilities and considerable manpower, eventually has a principal role in the response to terrorist activities, however not in an exclusive sense, but as a leading coordinator and mediator between state authorities. Terrorism investigation takes place in cooperation between federal and state forces: there are several committees, regular meeting groups, and councils as well as joint investigation groups, which have been installed to minimize friction in this process.

The Federal Office for the Protection of the *Constitution (Bundesamt für den Verfassungsschutz*, BfV) has a similar leading role among the internal intelligence agencies. State agencies are obliged to report gathered intelligence to the federal *Verfassungsschutz* which maintains central database systems, while the BfV in addition can gather intelligence in the states on its own. Foreign intelligence-gathering is exclusively the responsibility of the federal intelligence agency or *Bundesnach-richtendienst* (BND).

German intelligence agencies are governed by restrictions and are controlled in various ways. As a result of the strict separation of law enforcement and intelligence-

---

9   *Der Spiegel* 48/2001, *Die Zeit* 66/2001.

gathering functions in the outline of the German security structure, intelligence agencies do not have any police powers, which means that they are not authorized, for example, to arrest and question people or search homes, and the passing of information from intelligence agencies to law enforcement is restricted by a number of conditions. Yet, the cooperation between BKA and BfV is described as close, and the information flow between the two bureaus is considerable.

Democratic control over the intelligence agencies is exercised by the Parliamentary Control Commission, a parliamentary subcommittee that intelligence agencies and the government are obliged to report to and that has, under certain conditions, the right to visit the agencies, view documents, and interview officers. The Federal Data Protection Commissioner (*Bundesbeauftragter für den Datenschutz*) is in charge of controlling the government's and authorities' compliance with data protection laws. While the efficacy of this control is hard to assess, defences of privacy in Germany are estimated to be comparatively strong.[10]

Counter-terrorism Legislation

Legislation concerning terrorist crimes is not concentrated in a specific Terrorism Act, but laws dealing with terrorist offenses, the regulation of terrorist investigations, etc., are spread over the penal code as well as the penal procedures code. These laws nevertheless represent a specific set of terrorism legislation and are interconnected in various ways, with Article 129a (§129a StGB) being the central regulation. Article 129a prohibits setting up, being a member, and supporting a terrorist organization. Various laws, particularly procedures regulations restricting some defendants' and defence attorneys' rights, and some extended police search and arrest competences, are restricted to cases of Article 129a.[11]

Another set of regulations relevant for counter-terrorism is the so-called political penal law, which prohibits various forms of (non-violent) political extremist activity, such as continuing banned extremist organizations, brandishing banned extremist symbols (including Nazi symbols), and incitement of racial hatred. While political extremist associations fighting against the constitutional order can be banned by the German Minister of the Interior, extremist political parties can only be prohibited by the Federal Constitutional Court.

International Cooperation

Germany has traditionally been a very committed advocate of international counter-terrorism cooperation, concerning the development of international norms and agreements on terrorism as well as the international cooperation of security forces.

---

10   Katzenstein, *West Germany's Internal Security Policy*, (Ithaca: Cornell University Press, 1990) p. 61.
11   Katzenstein, *West Germany's Internal Security Policy*, pp. 32-33; Uwe Berlit and Horst Dreier, 'Die Legislative Auseinandersetzung mit dem Terrorismus', in Fritz Sack and Heinz Steinert (eds), *Protest und Reaktion* (Opladen: Westdeutscher Verlag, 1984), p. 167.

Particularly in the 1970s and 1980s, the Federal Government championed a number of resolutions and conventions on a European level and within the United Nations, among them the European Convention on the Suppression of Terrorism (1977), and it took a particular interest in developing and expanding international institutions such as Interpol, Trevi, and Europol.

In addition, German security policy included an emphasis on police cooperation through, for example, the exchange of police officers and international police meetings and conferences. Besides, cooperation with states in eastern Europe includes technical assistance, training programmes, and financial support to obtain modern equipment. As a result, and particularly through the permanent exchange of contact officers, German police authorities developed a very close cooperation with many European law enforcement authorities and US agencies. Police authorities actually prefer this direct and often rather informal form of cooperation over institutionalized forms such as Europol, as they are able to contact foreign officers much faster and can build on trust developed in years of personal work relations.

International cooperation is, however, restricted by the German Constitution and legislation, forbidding, for example, the extradition of suspects subject to capital punishment in the requesting country. The passing of data on individuals is in addition restricted by data protection regulations. This leads Katzenstein to the conclusion: 'Thus even though the Federal Republic is the most persistent advocate of international and police cooperation in western Europe, its own policies illustrate the restraints that inhibit full cooperation'.[12]

Threat Perceptions and Reactions to Terrorism in a Dynamic Perspective

The threat from the various and successive forms of terrorism and political violence throughout Germany's history was perceived in fundamentally different ways. This section sets out to describe perceptions as well as reactions to terrorism and right-wing violence by linking them to the specific characteristics and patterns of the different forms of political violence.

RAF Terrorism: Perceptions and Reactions

During the 1970s, left-wing terrorism became, in the government's as well as in the general public's perception, the main threat to internal security and triggered extensive reactions and measures, which in some cases were criticized as excessive. A considerable part of German legislation on terrorism and significant changes in the layout of various security services developed in response to the perceived challenge of terrorism during that decade.

Soon after its emergence, the Baader-Mainhof Gang was taken very seriously by political as well as by police authorities. Search operations and road blocks, etc., of an unusual scale had been conducted even before any actual bombing incidents took place.

---

12   Katzenstein, *West Germany's Internal Security Policy*, p. 63.

Arrested terrorists were submitted to a rather special treatment, initially solitary confinement, later in a specially constructed maximum security prison including an attached court building where terrorist trials were held. At the same time, a number of legislative changes were introduced to secure the feasibility of the trials (see below).

In early 1977, then West German Minister of Justice Hans Jochen Vogel explained the special measures with the particular threat posed by the group: 'Not that people are killed – however terrible that is – is the main characteristic of this terrorism. Its main characteristic is the frontal attack against our state, our society and against the fundamental consent of the intellectual and political forces on which the order of our state and society rests'.[13]

During late 1977 the terrorist campaign, as well as the state response, culminated. Germany was gripped by a series of dramatic events: the terrorist assassinations, the kidnapping and dramatic negotiations, and finally the hijacking. All this grew in the public consciousness to a major crisis by the ruthlessness and scope of the deeds as well as by the government's massive reaction, involving crisis committees and one of the most extensive police operations seen in German history.[14] In a speech held before the German Parliament, Chancellor Schmidt made clear his view of the situation: '[This deed] is an attack against our community, based on the principle of liberty, itself, against every human community, and in that, against each and every of us personally'.[15]

This threat perception was largely shared by the general public. A survey conducted in 1977 found that almost two-thirds of the respondents held the opinion that terrorism had created a serious crisis for the German state. A similar share of respondents favoured a harsh response from state authorities.[16]

The situation also had an effect on the parliamentary and political culture. From the mid-1970s a debate emerged, predominantly initiated by conservative politicians and the media, blaming leftist politicians, intellectuals and artists for sympathizing with the terrorists' aims or motivations. It had a stifling effect on political communications and culture, contributing to the late 1970s being characterized as a 'time of lead'.

Government reactions to left-wing terrorism in the 1970s particularly took the form of legislative measures and a reorganization of the security services responsible for counter-terrorism. One main result was a significant acceleration of the security services' expansion and modernization, a process that had already begun in the 1960s. Another consequence was the increasing centralization of counter-terrorism responsibilities and competences in the country's federal system.

In 1972 and 1973 the federal government and state governments launched a security programme involving legislative and organizational changes, putting the Federal Criminal Police Office (BKA), until then a central agency for relevant data, in charge of *inter alia* certain forms of terrorism and political violence, giving it genuine investigative authority. The BKA under its ambitious director Horst Herold became the main instrument of Germany's response to terrorism, coordinating the efforts of the State

---

13 Cited in Hans-Gerd Jaschke, *Streitbare Demokratie und Innere Sicherheit* (Opladen: Westdeutscher Verlag, 1991), p. 170.
14 At the height of RAF terrorism, in 1976 and 1977, about 100,000 police officers were involved in the search for the terrorists; see Katzenstein, *West Germany's Internal Security Policy*, p. 48.
15 Cited in Jaschke, *Streitbare Demokratie und Innere Sicherheit*, p. 253.
16 Katzenstein, *West Germany's Internal Security Policy*, p. 35.

Criminal Police Offices and pioneering new ways of information technology and computerized search methods. The office grew from about 1,200 officers and employees in 1960 to a staff of more than 3,300 in 1980.

In the hunt for suspected terrorists, the BKA developed a highly sophisticated, computerized, mass data comparison search method called *Rasterfahndung*, which cross-checked a profile generated from characteristics of known cases with mass data obtained from various sources. While the office put immense technology and manpower into the search for terrorists, only few terrorists were actually arrested as a result of this effort.[17]

Also in response to terrorism, particularly the 1972 hostage tragedy at the Olympic Games in Munich, the specialized anti-terrorism commando unit GSG 9 was set up as a part of the Federal Border Police, which established a formidable reputation after the successful recapture of the hijacked Lufthansa airliner in Mogadishu in 1977. Specially trained commando units were also set up by the majority of state police forces until the mid-1970s.

Between 1970 and 1980 the West German Bundestag introduced a number of changes to the criminal code as well as to the criminal procedures code, in many cases chronologically and factually closely related to terrorist incidents or terrorism trials. The amendments introduced, revised or extended regulations prohibiting various forms of support for terrorist organizations, including the mere expression of support or approval. The failure to cooperate with law enforcement authorities was also made a punishable offence. In addition, the new regulations provided, for example, extended search and arrest powers to police in cases of suspected terrorists and restricted the rights of defence attorneys and defendants in court. The higher control to which attorneys and defendants were exposed was a reaction to a number of incidents, in which lawyers or their employees had allegedly or evidently supported the terrorists by passing messages to outside members and in one case allegedly smuggling weapons to the prisoners. Collaboration took a special turn in the case of one attorney's office, out of which fifteen staff members went underground to join the RAF. However, various of the amendments introduced in the 1970s were criticized for violating standards of fair trial and for providing unrestricted powers to the police by specifying only vague conditions and restrictions, while at the same time scepticism was voiced about the usefulness of several of the regulations in the fight against terrorism.[18]

---

17 Out of 60 arrested RAF terrorists, some 20 were caught by foreign police forces and 30 as a result of citizen cooperation; see Katzenstein, *West Germany's Internal Security Policy*, p. 48. One expert commented: 'By the end of 1978, only eight terrorists had been apprehended as a direct result of all the highly complex, expensive, and sophisticated [...] search procedures [...]. It was not clever detective work nor the activities of the BKA's famed "finger squads" that tracked down Germany's top terrorists; it was the alertness of old ladies, landlords, a garbage collector, and other assorted amateurs'; see Schiller cited in Katzenstein, *West Germany's Internal Security Policy*, p. 66.

18 Sebastian Scheerer, 'Gesetzgebung im Belagerungszustand', in Erhard Blankenburg (ed.), *Politik der Inneren Sicherheit* (Frankfurt am Main: Suhrkamp, 1980), p. 128; and Berlit and Dreier, 'Die Legislative Auseinandersetzung mit dem Terrorismus', pp. 286-290.

Perceptions of Right-wing Violence in the 1990s

Right-wing and racist violence from the early 1990s onwards was soon perceived, particularly by federal and various state authorities and security forces, to be a serious threat to internal security and public order, and was reacted to with considerable firmness. After some years of rather limited priority, the events of summer 2000 produced intense political pressure, propelling right-wing violence to the top of the federal government's political agenda for some time and opening doors for a more thorough understanding of the threat posed by right-wing violence. Still, in some states and particularly in some affected areas on the local level, authorities tend to neglect the problem or its scope.

The 1991 and 1992 outbreaks of extremist right-wing and racist violence also produced an extensive media echo and shock and outrage among the German population. The public outrage mobilized a broad variety of social actors and from October 1992 numerous mass gatherings, commemoration services and marches were organized in many major cities, attended by hundreds of thousands of people.

Among politicians and officials, right-wing violence came to be recognized after Hoyerswerda and Rostock as a serious threat to public order and security as well as a danger to Germany's international reputation, which had been severely damaged by the incidents, which had been observed in alarm and with consternation in many countries.

In response, a number of states, such as Saxony for example, set up special investigation groups, and at the end of 1992 a committee to coordinate the fight against extremist right-wing violence was set up by the Federal Ministry of the Interior.

Yet the administration of justice by the courts in various cases of right-wing violent crimes in the early 1990s came to be criticized for handing out rather modest sentences and for only slowly progressing legal proceedings in some cases.[19]

A tool of particular importance in the government's response to right-wing violence proved to be the prohibition of extremist organizations. In 1992 and 1993 alone, the Federal Minister of the Interior banned five associations of right-wing extremists. At the same time a number of leading activists were tried and sentenced, leaving the organized right-wing scene considerable weakened and uncertain.

Another aspect of government perception, because a majority of the perpetrators were teenagers or young adults, was to consider right-wing violence to be a problem of juvenile violence and criminality, which lead in the early 1990s to a number of pedagogical measures and programmes, such as street workers and youth centres. After 1994, when the number of right-wing extremist and racist violent incidents – particularly arson attacks and riots – decreased, public and media attention diminished significantly. Until 2000, right-wing and racist violence gained only occasional and rather limited public and media attention, although the overall number of incidents remained, compared to pre-1991 levels, considerably high.

---

19 Until a decision by the Federal Court in 1994, courts classified fire-bombing attacks on refugees' or foreigners' homes as 'arson', which is a far less serious crime than 'attempted murder'. Monika Frommel, 'Fremdenfeindliche Gewalt, Polizei und Strafjustiz', in Konrad Schacht, Thomas Leif and Hanelore Janssen (eds), *Hilflos gegen Rechtsextremismus: Ursachen, Handlungsfelder, Projekterfahrungen* (Cologne: Bund-Verlag, 1995), pp. 148-153.

Among federal officials and politicians responsible for internal affairs and security, however, a perception of right-wing violence as a problem that had to be dealt with did exist, and police measures continued on a routine level. In addition to ongoing investigations, the police conducted various search operations and seizures against right-wing activists and dealers in Nazi music and books, and the German Ministry of the Interior issued further prohibitions of extremist organizations.

Among local authorities and in some state governments, however, right-wing extremist violence was often not recognized to be a major problem or was seen primarily as a form of juvenile violence. Many mayors or local politicians tended (and still tend) to play down violent incidents and the overall scope of the local extremist scene. The activities of non-governmental organizations and initiatives that have emerged since the mid-1990s – drawing attention to the threat from right-wing extremism, organizing cultural events, compiling independent studies and assisting victims of violence – were often not welcomed by local authorities, which feared damage to their town's reputation and considered the view to be exaggerated.

In some cases, parts of the local population allegedly approved of right wing violent deeds, in other cases at least agreed to the perpetrators' cause if not their deeds. In general, right-wing and xenophobic attitudes are shared by a not insignificant minority of the German population. Surveys found between 10 and 25 per cent of all Germans agree to various xenophobic and right-wing opinions. These attitudes are distributed unevenly. Approval is strongest in the eastern states.[20]

The outbreak of right-wing extremist violence in summer 2000 once more produced intense media attention and alarmed politicians, particularly in the federal government, which since September 1998 had consisted of a coalition of Social Democrats and the Greens. Government officials had already stressed the importance of combating right-wing extremist violence in 1999 and early 2000, declaring it a main focus of government policy. Yet until summer 2000 no major measures had been initiated. In August 2000 Chancellor Gerhard Schröder gave voice to government perceptions when he explained that he considered right-wing violence to be a danger to internal peace and to Germany's international reputation, which had to be checked, among other things, to prevent foreign investors from leaving Germany. He acknowledged that mistakes had been made in the fight against right-wing and racist violence: 'Too often, we all have just not realized the problems that do exist in this field'.[21]

The immense political pressure produced by the extensive media attention and public debate led to the initiation, in some cases rushed, of various measures in 2000 and 2001. One line of reaction, promoted particularly by the German Minister of the Interior Otto Schily, was stepping up repressive actions. In September 2000 two right-wing skinhead

---

20 Corinna Kleinert and Johann de Rijke, 'Rechtsextreme Orientierungen bei Jugendlichen und jungen Erwachsenen', in Schubarth and Stöss (eds), *Rechtsextremismus in der Bundesrepublik Deutschland*, pp. 172-181; Manfred Küchler, 'Xenophobie im internationalen Vergleich', in Jürgen Falter, Hans-Gerd Jaschke and Jürgen Falter (eds), *Rechtsextremismus: Ergebnisse und Perspektiven der Forschung* (Opladen: Westdeutscher Verlag, 1996), pp. 257.

21 *Der Spiegel* (http://www.spiegel.de), 12 August 2000 and 29 August 2000. Wolfgang Thierse, President of the German Parliament and an MP with a most persistent and sincere concern about right-wing violence, similarly stated that right-wing extremism in the eastern states 'had too much been glossed over' (*Der Spiegel*, 23 August 2000).

organizations were banned, showing, according to Otto Schily, that: 'the government is moving against extremist activities with all due firmness'.[22] At the same time, the government gave instructions to examine the possibilities of having the right-wing extremist party NPD prohibited by the Federal Constitutional Court. In addition, security services on the federal as well as on the state level initiated a number of preventive measures, among them various initiatives by the police to visit and talk to potential perpetrators and their parents at home, and a coordinated programme to assist right-wing activists willing to leave the scene.

On the other hand, the Federal Government launched a number of programmes promoting civil society and democratic culture initiatives, showing a growing awareness of this aspect of the threat from right-wing extremism and violence. An umbrella organization was set up to mobilize and bring together local non-governmental initiatives, and a programme to support their activities financially was started. Publicity campaigns were launched.

Perceptions and Reactions Concerning International Terrorism

During the 1990s, international terrorism in Germany posed a rather limited threat to internal security and was basically perceived as such and fought on a routine level. While the PKK campaign of arson attacks and violent protests gained considerable attention, it was not seen as a direct threat to German interests. Yet due to the significant number of violent incidents, in some cases aimed at facilities or personnel of the German security services, and due to the large number of PKK activists in Germany, the PKK was seen as a potential threat that had to be controlled and checked. In 1993 the PKK and a number of aligned organizations were prohibited, and during the following years several activists were convicted and further associations banned.

In a general perspective, international terrorism, after a series of large-scale terrorist incidents throughout the world in the 1990s, was perceived as a serious and growing threat to national security, and Germany, as a close ally of directly threatened countries like the US, UK and France, was also perceived to be affected by this development.[23] However, for Germany itself, this threat remained rather abstract, although closely observed by intelligence and law enforcement agencies.

As an indication of a possible direct threat to German interests, the arrest of a group of Islamist terrorists in Frankfurt in December 2000, obviously planning violent attacks in western Europe, was observed with alarm by German security services. The incident, however, gained rather modest attention in the media and the general public.

The attack on the United States on 11 September 2001 was a watershed for security politics world-wide and, of course, proved to be a cardinal incision for Germany too, fundamentally altering threat perceptions and security priorities. As was true for most governments in the western hemisphere and around the world, the events of 11 September were seen as an attack on the entire free world and on its fundamental values.

---

22 Bundesregierung, *Bulletin der Bundesregierung*, Berlin, 14 September 2000.
23 Kurt Schelter, 'Internationaler Terrorismus und Organisierte Kriminalität', in Bundesministerium des Innern (ed.), *Aspekte der Inneren Sicherheit* (Bonn: Bundesministerium des Innern, 1996), p. 19.

As it became clear that some of the hijackers had been living in Germany, a large-scale investigation was initiated involving various security services, including a 600-strong special commission of BKA and Hamburg police officers. Although there were no indications of terrorist attacks being planned against Germany itself, international terrorism came to be considered the paramount threat to national security after the attack on the United States. Chancellor Schröder explained: 'We are in the midst of a decisive and probably long-term fight against international terrorism'.[24] And Germany was ready, as Schröder made clear, to engage in this fight on a military level; the times when Germany was not expected to play more than an assisting role in the struggle for international peace and security were now definitely over.[25]

This perception was shared by the general public to a certain extent only. The vast majority of respondents questioned in late September believed, the world was not going to be the same after the attack.[26] Another survey found 57 per cent holding the opinion that the US was right to retaliate with military force, although only 37 per cent thought that Germany should participate in this military action.[27]

Soon after the 11 September 2001 attacks, the German Federal Government initiated a variety of actions to counter the threat of international terrorism. Crisis management teams were set up in the Federal Chancellor's Office and other ministries, and the protection of sensitive German, U.S., U.K., and Israeli facilities as well as aviation security was increased considerably. In late September 2001, the government decided upon a first package of measures. It included an additional fund of some 1.5 billion euros to improve internal and external security, covering the costs for a total of 2300 extra personnel for various agencies, mainly BKA and BfV, and a special fund for the German armed forces. In addition, the package included several amendments, particularly article 129b StGB, making support for and membership in a foreign terrorist organization a punishable offence. Also, a change to the Organizational Law now allows extremist religious organizations to be banned by the German Ministry of the Interior. While the abolition of the so-called Religion Privilege for organizations was passed by the Bundestag quite soon, allowing an Islamist organization in Cologne to be banned in mid December, the parliament hesitated to agree to 129b StGB, anxious not to include freedom struggles considered legitimate. The bomb explosion in Tunisia on April 11th, however, significantly accelerated the decision making process, and two weeks later the bill was passed.

As part of the ongoing investigation, the bank accounts of suspected affiliates of Osama bin Laden were frozen. In addition, from 1 October 2001 onwards, a *Raster-fahndung* (the same computer-based mass-data comparison search method used against the RAF) was started to find possible terrorists. While the measure was criticized by some for discriminating against people of Arab origin, even security officials were rather sceptical about the success of the method against terrorists like the 11 September hijackers, as only a very sketchy profile of possible suspects could be compiled.[28]

---

24   Bundesregierung, *Bulletin der Bundesregierung,* 19 September 2001.
25   Bundesregierung, *Bulletin der Bundesregierung,* 11 October 2001.
26   Allensbach Institut für Demoskopie, *Terror in Amerika: Die Einschätzungen in Deutschland* (Allensbach: Allensbach Institut für Demoskopie, 2001).
27   Zweites Deutsches Fernsehen (http://www.zdf.de), 9/2001.
28   *Die Zeit* (http://www.zeit.de), 41/2001.

A second package of measures was decided upon by the government in December 2001. It came into force in January 2002, introducing, *inter alia* various amendments extending the competences of the BKA and the Federal Office for the Protection of the Constitution, facilitating intelligence transfers between security services, increasing the screening of visa and asylum applicants, and opening the possibility for adding biometric characteristics such as fingerprints to ID cards and passports to ensure correct identification.

The extension of intelligence agencies' competencies – concerning, for example, the right to obtain information from banks, telecommunication companies and other service providers – attracted strong criticism for violating personal privacy and civil liberties, as did the plan to add fingerprints to ID cards, particularly because of the questionable benefit of the measure in the fight against terrorism (as it would take several years until all German citizens were provided with new documents).[29]

The German public nevertheless seemed willing to endure restrictions of civil liberties in order to ensure public security. A survey conducted in late September 2001 found that 74 per cent of the respondents were generally willing to accept limitations of civil liberties for the sake of security. However, only 44 per cent were ready to accept extended legal possibilities for telephone-tapping and electronic surveillance of private homes.[30]

In Conclusion: Proposal of a Tentative Interpretation

Threat Perceptions and Characteristics of Terrorist Violence

The cases laid out above show significant differences in the way that German authorities perceived and reacted to various forms of political violence.

Terrorism by the RAF, even during the kidnapping of Mr. Schleyer in 1977, objectively never posed a threat to the German state itself or the country's political order. In comparison to other European terrorist organizations, the RAF was a rather small group, not exceeding 20-30 members, and casualties from its terrorist campaign were comparatively limited (however serious and tragic the individual incidents were). Authorities, however, reacted exactly as if terrorism did present such a threat. It was considered, as Jaschke put it: 'a direct attack on the state itself'.[31] This interpretation by state authorities and politicians, with its corresponding reactive measures and political criticism falling silent and leftist politicians being discredited, produced a political situation that was called by Scheerer a 'symbolical state of siege'.[32]

Right-wing violence on the other hand never produced a similar reaction and never mobilized state authorities in a comparable way, although in 1992 the death toll from extremist right-wing and racist attacks exceeded that of left-wing terrorism during its most violent year. While right-wing violence was perceived to be a serious problem of

---

29 *Die Zeit* (http://www.zeit.de), 41/2001; *Frankfurter Allgemeine Zeitung*, 29 October 2001.
30 *Der Spiegel* (http://www.spiegel.de), 38/2001.
31 Jaschke, *Streitbare Demokratie und Innere Sicherheit*, p. 168.
32 Scheerer, 'Gesetzgebung im Belagerungszustand', p. 120.

public order and an embarrassing social problem, it was neither considered a major crisis nor a threat to the state or the political order, and state reactions, however extensive, never took the character of an all-out mobilization.

These discrepancies in perception can be explained in various ways, one being the Cold War as the international context during the 1970s and 1980s leading to a greater sensitivity to a 'communist threat'. In contrast, the thesis presented here is that state perceptions and reactions were induced by certain features of the violent deeds, their targets and perpetrators as well as by the basic nature of the different forms of political violence.

The mere structure and modus operandi of a terrorist organization like the Red Army Faction suggest a far more serious and persistent threat. While the RAF was a tightly knit, cell-shaped terrorist organization conducting kidnapping, bombing, and assassination operations against high-profile targets in a considerably sophisticated manner, right-wing and racist attacks were perpetrated spontaneously by groups of local youths and were directed against members of minorities such as immigrants or homeless people. In addition, many perpetrators could soon be arrested and the right-wing scene in general was easily infiltrated, leading to the impression of a rather easily controllable and short-lived threat.

In a more fundamental sense, perceptions are essentially shaped by the underlying character of the different forms of terrorist violence. Left-wing terrorism is at its core a strategy of provocation directed against the state, calling into question the legitimacy of government itself. In this, a terrorist deed per se is a challenge to state authority, meant to demonstrate the government's injustice and illegitimacy on a strategic level by provoking a state overreaction and forcing the government to show its 'real face'. Governments generally appear to find it very hard to evade this pattern of provocation and reaction, as terrorist incidents generate immense political pressure to show strength and react firmly.[33]

Right-wing and racist violence on the other hand does not follow this pattern of terrorism. While the perpetrators might well reject the current form of government, right-wing violence is not a provocation of government power and does not challenge the very legitimacy of the state. It targets marginalized sectors of society and right-wing militants often see themselves as carrying out actions in support of the larger society's 'real interests' or as 'restoring order'.[34] Right-wing violence can be interpreted as a form of vigilantism as described by Rosenbaum and Sonderberg.[35] In contrast to left-wing terrorism, which refers to and is perpetrated in the name of an alternative state and a future social order, however vague, the point of reference of vigilante violence is a factual or perceived status quo, which from the perpetrators' point of view has to be 'defended' (or restored), even if by violating the very laws on which this order rests.[36]

---

33 Peter Waldmann, *Terrorismus: Provokation der Macht* (München: Gerling Akademie Verlag, 1998), pp. 27-39.

34 One of the perpetrators of an arson attack in a small town in eastern Germany in 1991, for example, explained in 2000 that he felt that people were agreeing with their deeds and that he merely did the dirty work for local residents; see WDR, 20 March 2000.

35 H. Jon Rosenbaum and Peter C. Sonderberg, 'Vigilantism', *Comparative Politics,* July 1974, vol. 6, pp. 541-570.

36 Rosenbaum and Sonderberg, 'Vigilantism', p. 542.

While left-wing terrorism generally induces extensive reactions, right-wing violence therefore produces a tendency to see it not as a threat to the state and the political order but as an embarrassing and possibly serious but rather manageable social problem, resulting in the danger of underestimating its scope and persistence despite loose organizational structures and underestimating the threat that it poses to society and democracy.

Seen from this perspective, international terrorism can be judged ambivalently. International terrorism can take the form of an immediate provocation when it targets a state considered to be the direct enemy, questioning the government's or government policy's legitimacy. On the other hand, when international terrorist attacks in a certain country target facilities or personnel of a foreign state, or if they are primarily meant to produce public and media attention, they do not have the character of a direct provocation of a state government. In these cases, however, violent attacks in particular can pose an indirect provocation by their sheer scale, challenging the state's ability to maintain internal security. International terrorism for Germany during the 1990s was a rather abstract and potential threat or a problem of public order that was dealt with on a routine level. Yet after the 11 September 2001 attack on the United States, international terrorism was perceived by the German government, as is true for many countries, to be the major, if not an existential, threat to national security. Although there were no indications of any threat of terrorist attacks against Germany itself, the event triggered reactions and measures of an extraordinary scale.

This reaction can be explained in various ways. The sheer scale of the attack, of course, induced perceptions of an existential threat. In addition, the enmity towards the western hemisphere in general that was present in the perpetrators' and the alleged mastermind's motivation, and the fact that the attack was directed against the heart of the west's leading superpower, suggested a threat to US allies too. Solidarity with the US also required doing everything possible to prevent attacks against the US being prepared in Germany.

Germany itself was not attacked on September 11th, and government and popular perceptions and conciousness are not affected and shaped to the extent the U.S. was. Still, the attack, in its scale as well as in the perpetrators' characteristics, indicated a global terrorist threat, leading to widely shared perceptions of an immediate danger, and eventually to a globalization of threat perceptions.

Counter-terrorism Measures as Political Symbolism

The understanding of the challenge that terrorism poses to governments helps to identify mechanisms of authorities' reactions. Terrorist events, as unexpected, spectacular attacks that gain extraordinary public and media attention, as well as by the implicit provocation of state power, produce severe political pressure on governments from various sides to react firmly, showing strength, capability and readiness to act, and to satisfy the public demand to guarantee public security. As mentioned above, it seems quite difficult to evade this mechanism of provocation and (over-)reaction.

In this situation, governments show a tendency to produce actions that in part seem inadequately or not at all suited to counter the specific threat against which they were introduced. Counter-terrorism initiatives and 'action packets' passed in the wake of terrorist attacks tend to include measures directed against security problems or persons only loosely connected with the current threat, measures with a doubtful or rather improbable effect on the terrorist campaign, or measures with an effect only after such a long period of time that they are factually irrelevant for the solution of the current problem.

While these reactions can be interpreted as overreactions or misjudgements, they can also be understood as symbolic political measures.[37] From this perspective, some actions taken in the wake of terrorist attacks have a predominantly symbolical function, that is, they are taken to demonstrate the governments' strength and capabilities, to restore a feeling of security in the general public and to counter the symbolical challenge to state authority and legitimacy, rather than for their actual outcome in reducing terrorist activity.

The primarily symbolic function of various amendments passed in the wake of RAF terrorism in the 1970s has been described by Scheerer, who explained this as part of a 'healing process' of the symbolically injured state authority.[38]

Some measures introduced after 11 September 2001 can also be seen as mainly symbolic actions, such as the inclusion of fingerprints in ID cards, for example, which was the subject of an extensive debate, but did not actually bear any relevance to countering the immediate threat of international terrorism.[39]

Political symbolism is, of course, inherent in politics. Measures with primarily symbolical functions, however, can have a sizeable effect in restricting civil rights and liberties and thus must be weighed accordingly.

---

37 The concept of symbolic politics, emphasizing symbolic functions of political measures as opposed to their instrumental functions, was championed by *inter alia* Murray Edelmann (1976/1988). Treiber discusses reactions to RAF terrorism from this perspective (1984).

38 Scheerer, 'Gesetzgebung im Belagerungszustand', pp. 128-130 and 132-133.

39 Other examples might be seen in measures to facilitate intelligence transfer between security services and step up pressure on Islamist organizations, which is not entirely unreasonable, but the problem with the Hamburg group was that agencies did not have any hints at all that they could have passed and none of the hijackers was a known Islamist activist or belonged to any formal Islamist organization.

8 The Mysteries of Terrorism and Political Violence in Greece

Mary Bossis

Political Violence in Greece: Experiences and Threat Perceptions

In comparison to many other European countries, Greek terrorism has been remarkable for its longevity and consistency.[1] For the past quarter of a century, Greek terrorist groups have been using the same tactics. Yet they have avoided detection or capture, and hence they have come to be surrounded by a certain mythical aura.

Greek terrorism first appeared after the fall of the dictatorship (junta) in 1974, at a time when many indigenous terrorist groups in the rest of Europe had already been active for some years. Most attacks in Greece have been perpetrated by two groups: the Revolutionary Organization 17 November (hereafter 17N) and the Revolutionary People's Struggle (hereafter ELA). Later, a number of short-lived organizations claimed a few casualties, only to disappear again. Finally, during the 1990s, a new organization (according to some, an offspring of ELA), calling itself Revolutionary Nuclei, appeared.[2] The activities of these three groups deserve some special attention in an analysis of Greek experiences with indigenous terrorism.[3]

---

1   For an analysis of the concepts of terrorism and political violence, see Mary Bossis, *On Defining Terrorism* (Athens: Travlos, 2000).

2   Overall, terrorist organizations in Greece, including the numerous short-lived or short-term organizations, number approximately 250 (source: Greek Ministry of Public Order, as was published in the Newspaper *Ta Nea*, 10 November 1999).

3   Mary Bossis, *Ellada kai Tromokratia: Ethnikes kai Diethneis Diastasseis* [Greece and Terrorism, National and International Dimensions] (Athens: Sakoullas, 1996).

M. van Leeuwen (ed.): *Confronting Terrorism*, pp. 129-145
© 2003 Kluwer Law International. Printed in the Netherlands.

17N: Actions and Motivations

17N struck for the first time on 23 December 1975, the first year after the fall of the dictatorship, by assassinating CIA station manager Richard Welch.[4] It stunned the public and the authorities, which at first refused to acknowledge 17N's existence. During these early years, 17N 'purged' (a tactic called catharsis) a number of individuals who had been connected with the military junta that had ruled Greece with an iron hand. 17N 'executed' members of the junta's torture system, or American CIA agents whose support of the dictatorship had left the Greek people with strong anti-American feelings.

This was a turbulent time for Greece. Demonstrations were the order of the day and anti-American feelings were intense in the aftermath of the hated colonels' regime.[5] 17N aimed to win the sympathy of the Greek people, who at the time believed that the Greek state was failing to meet their desire for justice by punishing those individuals who had been active in the junta's repressive policies.

The authorities (the government and the police) and the people were surprised in 1976 when E. Mallios, police captain during the junta and accused of torture, was shot down by 17N. Shortly after the attack, the French newspaper *Libération* published the first 17N proclamation, in which the organization claimed responsibility for both attacks.[6] 17N explained the reasoning behind its targeting and gave an account of its methodology. When in January 1980 17N targeted P. Petrou, the former deputy commander of the riot police (MAT), which had been active under the junta, and his driver Stamoulis, the proclamation sent to the press was immediately acknowledged as authentic.[7]

17N proclamations have always been extensive and well written, and were widely read. The early ones suggested an ideology consisting of a particular form of Marxism-Leninism, 'seasoned' with liberal doses of patriotism, according to the circumstances and the choice of target. 17N targeting, in particular, has attracted much debate and attention in the media. The organization selected its victims within a specific group of enemies or opponents, in order to send a message to that group as a whole.

During the 1980s, 17N assassinated a number of non-Greek targets of little or no renown among the general public.[8] This has raised the question of why and how the organization was capable of accessing data concerning the past careers of these virtually anonymous victims, and to track them down and assassinate them.

---

4   It is widely believed that the name 17N is related to the university students' uprising, on 17 November 1973 against the military dictatorship. Since the fall of the junta, the date has been honoured with demonstrations that usually end at the American embassy in Athens. However, 17N has never explained its choice of name. For a detailed historical analysis of 17N, see George Kassimeris, *Europe's Last Red Terrorists: The Revolutionary Organization 17 November* (New York: New York University Press, 2001).

5   The *New York Times*, 17 December 1979, mentioned nearly 200 bombings of cars belonging to US military personnel and associates in 1975; 120 in 1976; and 84 in 1977.

6   Kassimeris, *Europe's Last Red Terrorists*, p. 74, mentions the *Libération* edition of 24 December 1976.

7   Between the Mallios and Petrou cases many attacks occurred. Some were claimed by ELA. The others were not claimed at all, except for the assassination of another junta collaborator called Babalis, whose death was claimed by the Group June '78. See Mary Bossis, *Ellada kai Tromokratia*, p. 121.

8   Attempt to assassinate Judd in 1984; Chandess in 1984; Nordin in 1988; Carros in 1988. Each was held responsible for the US military presence in Greece. Due to lack of official explanations as to where the 17N 'discovered' the specific targets, a number of scenarios and hypotheses have appeared, but were never verified. See Mary Bossis, *Ellada kai Tromokratia*, p. 131.

In the first years of its activities, 17N ended its proclamations with a salute to the 'ongoing struggle towards socialism'. It ceased doing so as the bipolar system gradually came to an end. 17N's proclamations have ideologically evolved over time, while maintaining their distinctive brand of socialism. In the case of attacks against a foreigner, 17N has habitually provided a brief biography of the target as well. Later, 17N explained its continued targeting of American representatives by pointing at the American involvement in 'imperialist wars', as was the war against Iraq of 1991. 17N referred to the US army as a 'criminal genocide machine'.[9] Other 'imperialists' were also punished: thus British Brigadier Saunders was shot on 6 June 2000 because 17N disagreed with NATO's bombardment of formerYugoslavia.

The 17N proclamations have been widely discussed in the media, investigated by the police, and have usually been authenticated. 17N's 'patriotic' claims have never referred to any particular political party. Greek political parties have all consistently condemned terrorism and have denied any ideological or organizational links to indigenous terrorist groups.

17N: An Elusive Organization

During the 26 years of its existence, 17N has managed to remain an extremely elusive organization until summer 2002, when it finally lost cover. According to open sources, the police, in spite of considerable effort, were unable to uncover the identities of the perpetrators. 17N were masters of hiding. There was no evidence available in open sources concerning their membership, recruitments, financial transactions, sponsors, training grounds, hiding places, possible movements outside the country, and so on, all of which proved to be an excellent breeding ground for speculation.

The longevity of Greece's terrorist organizations, in particular 17N, has greatly concerned both analysts and public opinion. Why have the authorities been unable for so long to round them up or at least produce significant leads? One would think that Greece is too small for a 'phantom organization' to operate for such a long time. The terrorists have moreover emphatically placed themselves within a radically left-wing tradition – a political landscape that the Greek police authorities used to know inside out.[10]

This latter point needs some elaboration. From the end of the Second World War until the fall of the military dictatorship in 1974, when the Greek Communist Party was finally recognized as a lawful political party, Greek authorities had celebrated a string of 'successes' in their efforts to stifle left-wing activity. During this period, the 'Palace' – the highly conservative monarchy – and its puppet governments had mobilized all sorts of mechanisms,[11] both state and para-state, in order to dispose of what they considered to be the country's 'internal enemies'. They embarked on a merciless 'crusade' against 'left-

---

9 In the newspaper *Eleftherotypia*, 14 March 1991.
10 Mary Bossis, 'Political Violence: The Unique Greek Case', *Eleftherotypia*, *Afieroma*, 15 April 2000, pp. 20-21; also Mary Bossis, *Ellada kai Tromokratia*, p. 229.
11 The links between official state forces – such as the secret services, the gendarmerie and the army – para-state organizations of the far-right and underworld gangs were highlighted after the assassination of Grigorios Lambrakis (MP for the Unified Democratic Left (EDA), founder and Vice-President of the Committee for International Peace and Disarmament in Salonika in 1963.

wing elements'.[12] As a result, outlawed left-wing organizations were broken up and dispersed, their members tracked down, expelled, or imprisoned. Some political opposition was allowed, but its members always depended on 'official' channels of expression, while elections were never free. Until the collapse of the military dictatorship, the police had thus enjoyed an 'excellent' track record in controlling the political left. It therefore seemed natural to assume that under the new political constellation they would still have no problems in tracking down left-wing terrorists, once these started their actions in the mid-1970s. It should be noted that after the fall of the junta the police were not purged of junta elements due to the *stigmiaio* legislation, which judged their active participation in the military regime as a 'momentary' crime rather than a 'constant' one.[13]

But in fact, the police have been singularly unsuccessful, an amazing development that has been viewed with incredulity and suspicion, and has given rise to a huge amount of speculation. The threat emanating from 17N has, after all, been very serious for conservative elements in Greece's political elite. From its first appearance in 1975 until 2000, the organization carried out 101 attacks and has claimed responsibility for 23 assassinations.[14] 17N has also succeeded in robbing a military base in order to enrich its arsenal with rockets and other kinds of weapons, and the operation until summer 2002 remained an absolute mystery.[15] Investigations into the affair have been seriously flawed, with neither military nor civilian police able to come up with results. Indeed, the number of rockets or other weaponry stolen from the base still remains unclear.[16]

17N, in short, has been and still may be quite threatening to people in power.[17] Why then did the police fail to eradicate this dangerous organization during all these years? Is it because the perpetrators can count on the goodwill of many Greeks, who have not felt any sympathy towards the police for many years, mostly because of their oppressive

---

12   Their fighting methods included the use of numerous paid informers; see George Kassimeris, *Europe's Last Red Terrorists*, p. 165. This practice was bitterly but inconclusively debated in the Greek Parliament after the fall of the junta; see Greek Parliament, *Parliamentary Papers*, 12 April 1978, p. 2490; also 18 April 1987, p. 2725.

13   For this unique legislative approach, see D. Spinellis, *H eshati prodosia: Anamesa sto Parelthon kai to Mellon* [The Final Treason: Between the Past and the Future], Poinika-3 (Athens: A. Sakkoulas, 1979), p. 78.

14   Statement by the Greek Ministry of Public Order, Athens, as referred to in *Eleftherotypia*, 12 February 2002.

15   Raid on Sykurio military base on 24 December 1989. Another well-known case is known as the 'Vironas Police Station', where on 14 August 1988 six members of 17N dressed up as policemen, entered a police station, tied up the officers on duty, locked them in the station detention cell and walked out with their weapons, radios, station seals and police caps. The entire case was ridiculed by the Greek Press. Investigations have so far been fruitless. See *Ta Nea*, 15/16/17 August 1988.

16   The weapons have been recovered only very recently, in summer 2002. A number of the stolen rockets have been used by 17N, or at least the police claim that they belong to the stolen military arsenal. According to another version, the military had no knowledge of the actual amount of weapons stolen, due to lack of proper inventory in the base. In any case, the amount as well as the kind of weapons stolen remains a mystery. See *Ta Nea*, 14 August 1989.

17   Extensive discussions were published in the daily press concerning the safety of prominent Greek industrialists, news editors, newspaper owners or mass media owners in general, politicians, and police, etc. The same type of agony is shared by the foreign embassies, the American Embassy in Athens first and foremost. Quite often it is written in the daily press that almost 3,000 people are protected around the clock by the police. It is also widely known that a number of 'targets' use private security agencies to feel safe. See *Ta Nea*, 28 December 2001.

activities during the military junta? Still, the police managed well enough during the junta to suppress any form of opposition. Had the police suddenly become incompetent? Did they have strategic or tactical reasons for not bringing the terrorists to justice? Were these terrorist groups really 'invisible' or did they not exist at all and were there other forces at play? Again, the absence of tangible evidence, in a country where almost everything is known or easily approached and apprehended, has created a mythical aura around 17N. Even after the recent arrests, it may take time before these pressing questions can be fully answered publicly. The absence of evidence has also caused the persistent spread of unsubstantiated hypotheses that certain left-wing political forces associated to certain political parties have had a hand in terrorist attacks in the country – hypotheses that have damaged Greece's international standing. For an independent analyst, it is possible to highlight the pernicious mystery and analyse plausible and less plausible explanations, but impossible to get to the bottom of it. Most of the approaches are subjective and have the stigma of the political beliefs of the analyst.

End to a Mystery? The Arrests of Summer 2002

In summer 2002, following a failed attempt by a 40-year old man to place a bomb in Piraeus, the police could finally strike. They arrested dozens of 17N members, and judging from early information, the terrorists have been confessing freely. Experts are surprised by their lack of ideology and, for that matter, lack of intelligence. As far as they can see, it seems that 17N resembles none of the characteristics of other extreme left-wing terrorist groups in Europe.

Information available in early August 2002 indicated that not all 17N members had been arrested. It will no doubt take a long time before the investigations are completed, but on the basis of what was known at the time of writing, some familiar issues have now become even more intriguing. It is now almost certain that 17N was not, after all, a left-wing, theoretically informed revolutionary group. Rather, left-wing ideology has served as a cover and pretext for spreading terror. If this hypothesis is true, it raises the question of what forces have been behind the organization all this time? Why and how could the organization stay active for so long, given that Greek special security forces used to have the professional capacity to eradicate left-wing groups? Most states try to react quickly and effectively when faced with terrorism. Why has the Greek state machine functioned so sluggishly in dealing with 17N? The question is even more puzzling in light of the fact that the 17N attacks have so badly undermined Greece's international standing and domestic security.

ELA and Others

Next to 17N, ELA has been the most important Greek terrorist organization. Active since 1975 and finding its roots in the students' movements against the junta, it perpetrated well over 300 attacks, either on its own or in collaboration with other terrorist groups,[18] before mysteriously ceasing activities in 1995. For almost twenty years, ELA, unlike the 17N group, tried to avoid human casualties, limiting itself to attempts against property with symbolic value. ELA bombed American targets, European Union offices, ministries, embassies and industries, etc. After every attack, the organization (like 17N) sent a proclamation to the press, explaining the targeting and giving an in-depth account of the organization's opinion of the political, social and economic life of the country.[19] Then between 1992 and 1995, ELA diverted from its previous tactics of avoiding any casualties. This striking change has been explained by its cooperation with the '1 May' group (see below). ELA, although small in active members, was reportedly somewhat closer to a 'typical' terrorist organization than 17N. To judge by its statements and target selection, the organization was inspired by radical socialist convictions.

A comparison of statements sent to the media by 17N and ELA organizations reveals the differences between the two major terrorist organizations. They differed in style of writing, in the perceptions of wrongdoings of the authorities, and most importantly, in their ideology. ELA pursued an ideology within a 'socialist' model (as understood by the organization), while 17N remained in a Marxist-Leninist model with 'patriotic' elements. Comparison of their respective declarations thus argues strongly against any connection between the two terrorist organizations.

In addition to 17N and ELA, a number of other organizations have appeared, small but active enough to suggest a pattern. None of these small organizations have so far been rounded up, and no individuals have been arrested. Their activities have been concentrated on bombings, explosions and burning cars. In addition, there are many cases of attacks on vehicles and buildings, which should not be categorized or labelled as terrorist activities, as they fall into the category of social violence.

Although 17N was the most prominent lethal organization, a few other short-lived organizations have killed people. Thus, Group June 78 claimed responsibility for the assassination of P. Babalis, a junta collaborator and torturer. The organization disappeared after this one action,[20] and Group June 78 may have been an alias for an ELA fraction.[21]

Another terrorist organization, 1 May, claimed responsibility for several assassination attempts during the late 1980s,[22] and since this organization was active for a few years, it cannot be categorized as a 'single act organization'. Reportedly, 1 May struck up a partnership with ELA in 1992, which resulted in an attack on a bus transporting riot police that caused eighteen casualties.[23]

---

18   George Kassimeris, 'Greece: Twenty Years of Political Violence', *Terrorism and Political Violence*, vol. 7, no. 2, summer 1995, pp. 79-83.

19   During the 1980s it appeared with double names: ELA-Revolutionary Group of International Solidarity Christos Kasimis in 1986 (for attacks under the name of an ELA member who was killed in a police ambush during an attempt to arson the German company AEG in 1977); and ELA-1 May (under which it claimed a number of bombings and lethal attacks in 1990).

20   Babalis was assassinated on 31 January 1979.

21   Mary Bossis, *Ellada kai Tromokratia*, p. 237.

22   An attempt on the life of the Secretary-General of the Greek Labour Union, G. Raftopoulos, in 1987; and attacks on public prosecutors Samuel and Bernardos in 1989.

23   Kassimeris, 'Greece', pp. 79-83.

Other shadowy but murderous organizations with allegedly ideological agendas were more short-lived still.[24] The police call these organizations 'anarchic', but it is noteworthy that 'anarchism' is not considered a strong ideology in the 'off-stream' youth movements. A number of small youth organizations use the terminology, but they do not produce substantial evidence of any real knowledge of anarchic theory. However, it is common police practice to call these alienated and violent youths 'anarchic' when there is no substantial evidence or proof of any ideological background. Between 1995 and 2000 they claimed no less than 387 attacks,[25] and the authorities' utter inability to catch the perpetrators caused heavy criticism, especially during the 1990s.[26]

During the 1990s, and especially towards the end of the decade, organized crime attacks resembled terrorist activity, and the authorities were quick to define them as such.[27] The Greek Minister of Public Order even publicly attributed such cases to 17N, but 17N emphatically denied any involvement.

Finally, the 1990s witnessed the birth of the organization Revolutionary Nuclei. This group seems to lack a clear-cut ideology and is strikingly clumsy in its targeting. Indeed, it has already admitted killing someone unintentionally.[28] The amateurishness of this organization is a new phenomenon for Greek terrorist activity, as all of the organizations active over the last 30 years have been particularly careful not to make 'innocent' victims, so as not to produce public antipathy.

International Ramifications

No public evidence has been produced so far as to the existence of working connections or affiliations of Greek terrorist groups or grouplets with counterparts elsewhere in Europe. There have, however, been many speculations on such associations.

A number of incidents involving international terrorist activity in Athens have been linked to the Carlos network, and a few Greek citizens have been named as collaborators. The affair has become known as the STASI case, referring to the secret agency of former East Germany. After the reunification of East and West Germany, the German police handed their Greek colleagues a file referring to these cases. The media have speculated about the affair since then, but no Greek citizen has been arrested in connection with it, in spite of judicial and police cooperation on the issue between Greece and Germany. The STASI case remains one of constant interest, as Greek newspapers quite often mention

---

24 Mary Bossis, 'Political Violence', pp. 20-21. Thus the group Revolutionary Solidarity claimed responsibility for the assassination of psychiatrist M. Maratos in 1990, while the organization Social Resistance claimed the bomb attack against former minister Manos in 1988.
25 Greek Ministry of Public Order, Athens, in *Ta Nea*, 10 November 2000.
26 For example, an organization calling itself *Machimos Antarticos Sximatismos* (loosely translated, it means Fighting Guerrilla Formation), with short-lived activity, in 1997placed 1.5 kilos of dynamite in the house of the author, who is an International Relations Lecturer and expert on political violence. The perpetrators resented her knowledge of terrorism. The authorities did not make any public announcement concerning their investigations, and so far there are no publicly known arrests connected with the case.
27 The attempted assassination of Greek MP B. Michaloliakos from the opposition party New Democracy may have been a case in point.
28 Intercontinental Hotel bombing, spring 1999.

the slowness of the procedure and speculate on the names of the individuals allegedly involved. [29]

Incidents of international terrorism occurred in Greece in the 1970s and early 1980s, but the perpetrators usually concentrated on targeting their own nationals and not their host country's citizens. Their hit-and-run operations were annoying, mostly due to the international pressure exerted on the Greek government,[30] and in the majority of cases, some of which were quite serious, the attackers were arrested.

The Greek government had openly voiced its solidarity to the Palestinian people's struggle, while it condemned international terrorism.[31] At the same time, the Greek government demanded that Arab League member states prevent their citizens from using Greek soil in order to solve their differences.[32] In those days the American ambassador in Athens sent a memo to the Greek Minister of Foreign Affairs, accusing the Greek government of 'relations with Arab terrorist organizations [Abu Nidal], aiming to avoid terrorist activity in Greece'.[33] The Greek side angrily condemned the accusations, calling them 'unsustainable, suspicious, and ridiculous'. This heavy atmosphere in Greek-American relations continued during summer 1987, and although the Greek state reacted the same as other European states, it remained the target of American criticism.[34]

Most cases of international terrorism took place during the 1970s and early 1980s. Only four incidents occurred during the early 1990s, and since then there have been no reports of international terrorism in Greece.

Present-day Threat Perceptions in Government, the Media and the General Public

Greek authorities have recently focused on the challenge of preventing terrorist attacks during the Olympic Games, which will be held in Greece in 2004. The events of 11 September 2001 in the United States have, if anything, sharpened their concerns and stimulated their ambition of preventing such attacks in Greece. Police forces have stepped up security planning in order to guarantee the safety of the international sports event.

As for the Greek public, the events of 11 September 2001and the subsequent anthrax letter attacks in the US have caused a major change in threat perceptions concerning terrorism. Terrorism actually did not previously figure very high on the list of ordinary people's security concerns, but this has changed dramatically. It is, moreover, interesting to see how the Greek media have intensified their coverage, not just about the aftermath of the 11 September 2001 attacks but also about indigenous terrorism, particularly about 17N. The quality of their coverage has varied from informative to alarmist, as has been true of the media in other western countries reporting on the dramatic attacks in the US.

---

29   As in the newspaper *To Vima*, 6 January 2002.
30   *Daily Telegraph*, 9 June 1984; also *New York Times*, 9 June 1984.
31   *Eleftherotypia*, 5 September 1987.
32   *Vradini*, 29 December 1985; also *Neue Osnabrucker Zeitung*, 12 July 1984.
33   *Eleftherotypia*, 28 June 1987.
34   Mary Bossis, *Ellada kai Tromokratia*, pp. 165-171.

An ill-founded fear of receiving anthrax mail has gripped some Greek citizens – as happened in other countries during autumn 2001.[35]

Public meetings, seminars and conferences on international terrorism have vastly increased in numbers, if not always in quality. Many discussions are devoted to safety during the 2004 Olympics in particular and to the ability of the authorities to guarantee such safety. The US attacks on Afghanistan have also stimulated public debate, and this public debate betrays much scepticism about the 'war on terrorism'.

The drive in Brussels to produce new European legislation in order to fight terrorism has not been understood by all Greece's political parties as the best way of facing the new threats. Representatives of political parties have conducted long discussions on television. As in the past, they have disagreed on the use of new legislation, as new laws are viewed by some as rules that may breach civil and human rights.[36]

Greece's geographic position poses a number of problems that need to be examined carefully. The situation in the Balkans has been a reason for security concerns during the last decade, and even more so when in neighbouring Albania (1998) and Bosnia (October 2001 and March 2002) there have been deportations of members of the al-Qaeda network.[37] That affair raised a number of questions on future safety in the wider area and the possibility of 'sleeper cells' to be woken during the Olympic Games. The Greek and foreign press mentioned the possibility of extremists in Kosovo, southern FYROM (Former Yugoslav Republic of Macedonia), northern Albania or even Bosnia, where a number of mujahidin fighters remained behind after the war was over. The possibility that they will renew their affiliations and cause problems during the Olympic Games remains one of the headaches of the authorities in Athens.[38]

Finally, discussions on the new EU measures against terrorism have stirred up concerns in Greece regarding the defence of human rights, and reminiscences of the country's recent past have reinforced these concerns. The Greek Ministers of Justice and Public Order have given long interviews supporting the EU's legal approaches in order to soothe public temperament, stressing that they will not undermine human rights.[39]

Counter-terrorism Policies in Greece

Intelligence and the Police

The police, as stated before, have been singularly unsuccessful in their attempts to catch terrorists. Their failures have been explained – by way of justification – by a lack of legislation, incompetence of the police forces, lack of political will (especially that of the

---

35   *Ta Nea*, 2 December 2001; also radio station Sky, 12 December 2001.
36   *Ta Nea*, 14-15 December 2001.
37   The deported extremists were arrested in Cairo and put on trial. Two were later executed; the others serve prison sentences. See Steve Macko, 'Counter-terrorism Analysts Take Note of New Threats from Egyptian Terrorist Group', *ERRI Risk Assessment Services*, vol. 5-110, 20 April 1999; also Jailan Halawi, 'Albanian Returnees Executed', *Al Ahram*, issue no. 471, 2-8 March 2000, on the case of Bosnia's deportations. See *Eleftherotypia*, 31 March 2002.
38   *Eleftherotypia*, 12 April 2000.
39   *Express*, 21 September 2001.

socialist PASOK government), the role of the press, and by the indifference of the people who never viewed terrorism as a threat against the masses.[40]

The anti-terrorist squad – whose duty it is to unmask terrorists and deliver them to justice – is made up of approximately 350 police officers. The police and the intelligence agency (*Ethniki Ipiresia Pliroforion*, or National Intelligence Agency) are two different and quite separate organizations. The intelligence agency does not have the authority to arrest people, while many times in the past there have been cases of 'mixed authorities' with 'awkward' results. The intelligence agency does not publicize the work of its employees, but from notable failures in the past we can perhaps assume that it has not employed many academics.[41] The agency has dealt exclusively with the terrorist organizations, their ideology, modus operandi, frequency of appearances, and press releases concerning future hits, but with stunningly little success. It has been heavily criticized for its lack of insight into Greek terrorism. In spite of this, it has built a close relationship with journalists, to whom it gives 'exclusive' clues on investigations; the same kind of symbiotic relationship has, interestingly enough, also come about between the media and terrorist organizations.[42]

As already mentioned, the police were in the past the 'arm' of the military junta's suppressive strategy and were closely connected to the American agencies that supported the dictatorial colonels' regime. As a result, the police still do not enjoy the full confidence of the Greek people, and arguably, because of this historical distrust, Greek citizens will not denounce an acquaintance to the police. The persistent theory of widespread citizen support or sympathy towards terrorist organizations, on the other hand, has never cut any ice. There are no serious (statistical) data to prove the amount of 'sympathy' from the Greek people towards the terrorist organizations. During the 1990s, the government tried hard to break down the barriers between the police and the public in order to create better relations. Relations now are not hostile, yet at the same time they are not immensely friendly. Most people maintain their reserve, even if out of caution rather than dislike. For example, witnesses of terrorist acts have not testified in court, as they feared possible reprisals by the terrorists and felt that they could not trust the police to protect them.

Witness protection programmes were introduced in Greece at a late stage, because they were opposed by the political authorities in charge of the Greek Ministry of Public Order.[43] They argued that Greece was too small a country to 'hide' people and that implementing such programmes would mean a major work load for both the Ministries of Justice and Public Order. In addition, the principle of witness protection was at first introduced and discussed by a team of think-tank academics who were considered 'outsiders' by the police. By the end of 2000, the witness protection programmes finally became enacted, but they still await testing in practice.

---

40   *Ta Nea*, 11 May 1992; also the newspaper *Avriani*, 13 November 1986.

41   *Eleftherotypia*, 12 July 1984.

42   Russell F. Farnen, 'Terrorism and the Mass Media: A Systematic Analysis of a Symbiotic Process', *Terrorism: An International Journal*, vol. 13, no. 2, March-April 1990. See also *Eleftherotypia*, 7 and 15 March 1988.

43   The Greek Ministry of Public Order, in cooperation with the Ministry of Justice, is in charge of the legislation proposals concerning the issues of public safety and public order.

Confessions have also been extremely rare. Many of the 'usual suspects', mainly young people who were arrested and brought to court every time that there was a terrorist action, have pleaded not guilty and have been acquitted by the jury. Even those who did spend time in prison rarely admitted to having perpetrated terrorist acts. The conservative New Democracy Party has put the accusation that prominent socialist Greek politicians (the socialist PASOK party has been in government since 1981, with a three-year interlude) were supporting these 'usual suspects', or even maintained connections with 17N. These unsubstantiated claims have long figured in US intelligence agencies' and media reports, and still do.[44] The same accusations – which admittedly result from the lack of police arrests – were uttered against the Greek government by a former American ambassador.[45] One must keep in mind that the American intelligence agencies have been cooperating with their Greek counterparts since the beginning of terrorism in Greece, and the accusation certainly sheds a strange light on the quality of that cooperation.

Legislation

Even though the Greek penal code has provided full coverage for different crimes or criminal activities, the Greek Parliament over the past three decades has had bitter debates on the need to adopt specific anti-terrorist legislation.[46] Generally speaking, those who favoured explicit legislation mainly came from the conservative New Democracy Party, which argued that specific legislation was necessary in order to provide for the security of Greek citizens and to fight or preferably deter terrorism. The socialists (PASOK) and communists, by contrast, as well as the centre-left (EDIK) have opposed such legislation as superfluous and as a potential threat to democratic rights.

Law 774/1978 was the first attempt to introduce specific anti-terrorism legislation. It was largely based on the Italian and German models of the time.[47] The Greek government was confronted with indigenous terrorism and at the same time deeply concerned about terrorism in other European states, which climaxed during the 1970s. Discussions in the Greek Parliament pitted the governing New Democracy Party, which was proposing the legislation, against the left-wing opposition parties, which rejected it. The question of the definition of terrorism became an issue of heated discussions among politicians and in the media. The opposition parties claimed that Parliament should not pass a law on a phenomenon that had not been precisely defined.[48] The law as it came to be enacted defined a number of specific terrorist felonies and also made it a crime to give refuge to terrorists, but it did not present an overarching concept of terrorism. The sentences introduced for the various crimes were very heavy, including the death sentence, and the law authorized substantial financial rewards for informers whose reports resulted in the

---

44   Paul Pilar, 'Terrorism and US Foreign Policy', as reported in the Greek newspaper *Ependitis*, 29-30 December 2001.
45   Press interview with former US Ambassador Thomas Nails to the Greek television station Mega Channel in December 2001.
46   For the following paragraph, the author has made grateful use of Kassimeris's study *Europe's Last Red Terrorists*, especially pages 155-191; also Bossis, *Ellada kai Tromokratia*, pp. 149-163.
47   See the newspaper *Kathimerini*, 16 December 1990.
48   Greek Parliament, *Parliamentary Discussion Papers*, April 1978, p. 2405.

arrest of culprits. Unlike West German and Italian anti-terrorist legislation, however, the law did not increase police powers with regard to the collection of evidence (e.g. opening mail, examining bank records or detaining individuals for interrogation without specific charges.)[49] Opposition parties claimed that existing legislation was effective enough, and claimed that extra-legislative measures would merely be used against the people. PASOK representatives actually denied that the violence with which Greece had to deal was terrorist in character. They ascribed the attacks to 'fascist or anarchical elements' operating in the very margins of society.[50] The idea of introducing legislation on terrorism was viewed as a pretext to suppressing newly gained democratic freedoms.[51] These same concerns and criticisms were voiced during large public demonstrations in various major Greek cities. The protesters' anxieties about the new legislation were evidently inspired by bitter memories of Greece's recent past.

In 1983, one and a half years after elections had handed governmental power to the socialist party, Law 774/1978 was abolished, although in 1988 the PASOK government did ratify the European Convention on Combating Terrorism.[52]

The next legislation concerning terrorism was passed in 1990, a year after the assassination by 17N of P. Bakoyiannis, an MP with the New Democracy Party. Bakoyiannis was the first Greek MP to be murdered by terrorists, and his death greatly shocked the Greek people. 17N sent a long proclamation justifying their choice of target. Bakoyiannis's widow, who succeeded him in Parliament, was instrumental in promoting new anti-terrorist legislation, which was enacted after the New Democracy Party won the elections. Even though the 1916/1990 Law for the Protection of the Society against Organized Crime was not explicitly aimed against terrorism, it copied many of the articles of the abolished Law 774/1978. While it left out the death sentence, it vastly extended police powers to collect incriminating material and evidence.

The most controversial article in Law 1916/1990 enabled the district attorney to prohibit the publication of terrorist proclamations after a lethal attack. Article 6 was condemned as unconstitutional by the opposition parties, which claimed that it impinged upon the freedom of the press.[53] The media were indeed the first to be 'punished' by the new legislation. Almost six months after its enactment, 17N attacked a Turkish diplomat and sent its usual proclamation to the media. The newspaper *Eleftherotypia*, defying the ban, published 17N's proclamation entirely, while condemning the attack in no uncertain words, and soon six more newspapers followed.[54] The next day, seven editors were arrested on charges related to the anti-terrorist law. The public outcry was enormous, as the editors were charged with prison sentences. They remained in jail for a short period of time until a fine was paid on their behalf by the Athens Union of Newspaper Publishers, but this case opened an extensive rift between the media and the New Democracy Party. After winning the 1993 elections, PASOK abolished Law 1916/1990 after having formed a new government.[55]

---

49   Kassimeris, *Europe's Last Red Terrorists*, p. 156.
50   Kassimeris, *Europe's Last Red Terrorists*, p. 161.
51   Greek Parliament, *Parliamentary Discussion Papers*, April 1978, p. 2776.
52   Greek Parliament, *Parliamentary Discussion Papers*, April 1988, p. 5526.
53   Greek Parliament, *Parliamentary Discussion Papers*,, January 1990, p. 973.
54   *Eleftherotypia*, 6 June 1991.
55   Bossis, *Ellada kai Tromokratia*, p. 296.

Finally, in June 2001 under a PASOK government, both PASOK and New Democracy, cooperating on this controversial issue for the first time, voted in favour of Law 2928, 'Amendment of Provisions of the Penal Code and the Code of Penal Procedure and other Provisions on the Protection of Citizens from Punishable Actions of Criminal Organizations'.[56] This unique approach of both political parties, opponents for many years on almost all issues in Parliament, to vote for an anti-terrorism legislation, can be explained by a number of reasons. Firstly, the time was ripe; secondly, the 2004 Olympic Games were approaching; and thirdly the government wanted to escape from the international pressure it felt because of the continuing problems in putting 17N out of action. The Law is mainly directed against organized crime and criminal activity, but at the same time it is the toughest anti-terrorist legislation that has ever been passed with almost an absolute majority in the Greek Parliament. Article 9, for instance, is dedicated to witness protection. Article 2, which concerns the deportation of foreign citizens who are illegally in the country, is also considered a new approach. It is hoped that the new legislation will force a breakthrough in anti-terrorist investigations, which have been so unsuccessful during the past quarter of a century.

The Olympic Games of 2004

The Greek authorities' preparations for the 2004 Olympics are assuming momentum. Meanwhile, the negative publicity by foreign media has alerted mass public opinion to the issue of the police's ability to guarantee the safety of athletes and international visitors and to protect the international standing of Greece. The Olympics' security plan has been published in the media, and it consists of four interrelated plans.

(1) *Strategic Plan*: This covers providing safety in the widest sense during the Olympic Games for the athletic grounds and VIPs. It deals with anti-terrorist measures as well as measures against criminal activity, transportation in general as well as the transportation of athletes and VIPs outside the athletic grounds, such as in operas, cinemas and museums. It deals, in short, with recognizing all possible dangers and preparing written scenarios on how to avoid them.

(2) *Directional Plan*: This contains instructions for security personnel – either police officers, members of the armed forces or trained volunteers. It details, for instance, how to react on discovering a bomb under a vehicle, with the use of special equipment. Basic importance is given to the points of entrance to the Olympic Games, including special magnetic doors able to detect weapons and explosives. There will be special protected entrances for the public, officials and the media in order to avoid problems such as arose in Australia when a few people tried to grasp the Olympic flame. In order to achieve maximum protection, the immediate notification of all foreign representations, all their members and all their movements to the Greek authorities is considered absolutely necessary. The chain of command of security personnel is explained. There will be two persons in charge on every Olympic ground: one will be in charge of the organizational committee and the other will be in charge of security. They will be in constant com-

---

56   Greek Ministry of Justice, Law 2928, Art. 14, Athens, 2001, pp. 1-6.

munication, and the individual in charge of security will be in constant touch with headquarters.

(3) *Tactical Plan*: This approach includes the coordination of all involved mechanisms, such as athletes' transportation, fires where the games are in process, the replacement of vehicles, safe movement of the injured or wounded to hospitals, etc. In order to avoid problems, the scenarios include the smallest possible detail, and all hospitals will be on duty throughout the Olympic Games.

(4) *Operational Plan*: This is considered the most crucial, and deals with the security measures depending on the 'target'. The measures cover all the water games, press villages, and all the grounds in which the athletes will be circulating. This plan includes all the last-minute movements for those involved in the security apparatus, that is the police, the army and volunteers. It requires non-stop training and constant formulating of possible scenarios, either on paper or mock cases.

To date, almost 50,000 persons are being trained for providing security at the 2004 Olympics: 17-20,000 from the police; 7,000 from the army; 7,000 firemen and port police; 7,000 volunteers; and 5,000 private security experts. This number includes the 3-4,000 secret service agents, as well as the security guards of foreign athletes, who will be allowed to carry their own weapons (the latter are not trained in Greece). The Australian authorities, by the way, did not accept the same demand (that foreign bodyguards may carry arms) by the Israeli and the American secret services for the Olympic Games in Sydney in 2000. General command will rest with the Chief of Police and the General Director of Security for the Olympic Games. All security bodies will be under their command, and the army will function administratively and in civilian clothing. The entire operation is estimated to cost approximately 84 million euros, including technical preparations.[57]

The planning of the 2004 Olympic Games is a major headache for the Greek security services, but even more so for the Greek government, which wants the safest Olympics ever. Many foreign experts and security services have visited Greece and have participated in the Greek authorities' training procedures. The Greek Ministry of Public Order and the 'Athens 2004' operation have been collaborating closely with the security services of seven countries with expertise and knowledge on Olympic Games security: the US, UK, France, Germany, Spain, Israel and Australia. International cooperation is considered to be very important in ensuring the safety of the Games.

The 11 September 2001 events have altered the principal plans concerning security, and new issues of importance have been placed on the agenda. The issue of 'asymmetric threats' has become part of the security dialogue, and the possibility of suicide attacks using aeroplanes, electronic terrorism and biochemical warfare are all part of the new preparations. The Greek approach for the Games's safety is based on the Atlanta and Sydney models, accounting for the particularities of the situation in Greece.

Transportation of athletes is considered to be a primary issue in security preparations. Since not all athletes come from 'high risk' countries, there will be different security measures for their movements in and out of the grounds, based on the high-risk factor.

---

57   The four approaches were made public in the press by the Greek Ministry of Public Order, and they were published in *Eleftherotypia*, 30 December 2001.

Other participants, such as volunteers, drivers and required personnel will be checked or go through a screening process.

Preparing for the Olympic Games is one of the most difficult tasks imaginable for any government hosting them. Since the Munich Olympics in 1972, all states have altered their security mechanisms in order to prevent possible terrorist attacks. The 11 September 2001 suggests that no preparation is ever perfect or absolute, but the Greek approach has combined international cooperation and expertise in order to prevent problems as much as possible. Greece is well aware that it will be under heavy international scrutiny and dearly wants to prevent any calamity from happening.

A Few Words on Negative Press Reports regarding Security Measures for the 2004 Games

Negative publicity, mostly from foreign (especially US and British) newspapers, on the persistence of terrorist problems in Greece has angered Greek citizens. Such publications have become more offensive in tone since the announcement that Greece will host the Olympic Games in 2004. For example, on 14 May 2000 the American magazine *Time* claimed that the visitors to Athens in 2004 might mistake Greece for Afghanistan; on 24 June 2000 the British *Sunday Times* accused the PASOK government of collaborating with 17N; on 23 June 2000 the *Wall Street Journal* warned businessmen to stay away from Athens; on 9 December 2000, the *New York Times* hosted the opinion of an ex-CIA chief, who wondered if members of 17N would be on the welcoming committee for the foreign athletes; and on 8 January 2002 on the 'Sixty Minutes' show, one day before the Greek Prime Minister departed for an official trip to the US, the US television channel CBS held discussions and interviews with several people who claimed that the Greek government and PASOK were the only ones responsible for the continued existence of 17N. The show went as far as accusing President of the Greek Parliament A. Kaklamanis of being a supporter of the terrorist organization. The show deeply insulted the Greek government, and the Greek Prime Minister stated before his departure: 'The times when the Americans could pressure the Greek government are over. The times when the Greek Prime Minister would travel to the US in order to be told how to govern the country are over'.

Although it is impossible to predict the future, 17N attacks during the Games have now become extremely unlikely. They would have been anyway, if 17N had acted within its own tradition of courting the sympathy of the Greek public. The Greeks, it should be noted, are extremely proud of having the Games back in its country of origin, and cherish a very old and strong tradition of sportsmanship. It would be far more realistic for the foreign and the Greek press to focus on threats by international terrorist movements during the 2004 Games.

Concluding Remarks

Greece has had a long history of foreign intervention in its internal affairs. This 'cooperation' has hardly been a matter of free choice. Greece's dependency on foreign powers for its reconstruction after the Second World War meant that refusing cooperation in general, or specifically on matters of internal security, was never an option. Worse, throughout the period between the end of the Second World War and the collapse of military dictatorship, which roughly coincided with the height of the Cold War, Greek authorities felt obliged to exhibit their loyalty proactively and be cooperative towards the West and the United States in particular. They were supposed to 'purge' Greece of all communist 'elements', since at the time the main threat to public order and security allegedly came from the communists. In the context of this specific history, the pressure presently exercised on the Greek government by the US for intensification of cooperation touches a raw nerve, especially as this pressure is exercised through the use of negative travel advisories, in which Greece features as an 'unsafe' country.

In the recent past, two major separate trends developed in indigenous terrorism in Greece. Firstly, there have been the smaller organizations, such as the Anti-State Struggle and the Revolutionary Nuclei. Their activities have in some cases been lethal, but for the most part damage was done to inanimate targets such as buildings, offices and foreign-owned companies and vehicles. Their presence has been erratic: they appeared, they were active for some time, and then fell into inaction in order to reappear later. There is no saying whether they will emerge again in the future. Ideologically, they have lacked the potential of organizations such as ELA, but they have sadly contributed to Greece's reputation of having a major problem with terrorism. At the same time, occasional arrests and 'inadvertent' discoveries by the authorities have brought to light a curious link between the activities of these small organizations with common criminal activity, combined with a pitiable ideological vacuum, highlighted when such groups have claimed responsibility for attacks. According to some analysts, these elements seem to suggest that ideology in the case of these organizations is only a smokescreen. If this assumption is correct, the question obviously rises: a smokescreen for what and whom? So far, there have been no convictions in these cases, as charges could not be substantiated. This has stimulated speculations about the relation of these organizations with state (secret) services and para-state groups pursuing their own agendas. As the ideological preferences do not coincide with the past, the most probable expectation is that these new organizations, or the ones to appear in the future, will be more lethal and much more dangerous than their predecessors.

Secondly, there were the two major terrorist organizations. The political discourse employed by 17N and ELA was intelligent and ideologically sophisticated, which is why these two organizations have been compared to organizations that appeared in the rest of Europe after the revolutionary days of May 1968. Their evolution is well known. In Germany and Italy terrorist organizations were set up to mobilize public support 'in favour of the overthrow of capitalism'. They used violence in their ambition to impose the revolution. Leading members of these extremist groups have been arrested; the basis has fallen from under their ideological constructs with the collapse of communist regimes and they have by and large disbanded. Yet unlike the counterparts in France, Italy and Germany, members of ELA have not been apprehended, and 17N members only very recently. Yet assuming that ELA and perhaps even 17N members have been inspired by similar ideological motives, they have had to face the same historical evolution away from their ideological ideals. Capitalism seems globally triumphant, and communism has lost its appeal. In most places in the world, communist and socialist movements are in the process of reformulating their discourse and recasting their strategies, and political participation has radically changed. In these conditions, 'voluntary redundancy' would be a solution for Greek left-wing terrorists, possibly even an honourable one in their eyes – if only to preserve the aura around their previous existence. As ELA has ceased its activity since 1995, it is assumed (as a hypothesis) that it went through major internal or ideological differences, which in a way prevented the continuation of its previous existence. If the organization Revolutionary Nuclei is indeed a remnant of ELA, then the new formation is more dangerous than the older version, because it now lacks its former ideology and strategy. Finally, 17N did continue to act, but added a patriotic element in its proclamations. It remains to be seen whether it will still be capable of terrorist action after the recent string of arrests. The remarkable and worrisome 'rebirth' in Italy of the Red Brigades, with the assassination of an adviser to the Italian Minister of Labour on 19 March 2002,[58] was a cause of concern for the Greek authorities, as the Greek government is facing the same problems on social security issues as Italy. The possibility of a terrorist attack that imitates the Italian example has been a case of worry for the Greek police.[59]

As terrorism is drastically changing world-wide, it is considered natural that the changes will eventually enter the Greek political scene. With respect to countering terrorism, the authorities need to change policy drastically. Police authorities should limit themselves to maintaining the safety of society without allowing political considerations to determine their work. It is of urgent importance that the authorities win the public's trust, and they can only do so if they depoliticize anti-terrorist policies. In this connection it might help if in future the authorities, as has been the policy in a number of other European countries, allow a major role to non-political, academically trained experts in the analysis of terrorism in Greece.[60] It should be kept in mind that terrorism has specific causes. In order to counter the lethality of terrorism, the Greek authorities need to understand the origins, as well as the social, political and economic causes that would create terrorism in Greece. At the same time, they must understand and closely follow international trends in terrorism, as Greece is geopolitically located in a 'transit' area, and the constant evolution of the causes of terrorism in the Middle East may well eventually expand from the source and enter other countries, as has happened in the past. Terrorism will continue to be a major issue in the future, for Greece as well as for other countries in the world.

---

58 *Ta Nea*, 21 March 2002.

59 *Ta Nea*, 27 March 2002.

60 The establishment in 1994 of the Scientific Committee for the Analysis, Investigation and Planning against Organized Crime was at the time considered a major step forward in the scientific research, political approach and in-depth understanding of the historical-political-economic and social birth of terrorism in Greece. The think-tank was short lived due to the Greek authorities' animosity, which considered the analysts a 'foreign body'. As a consequence, it was dissolved in 1996.

9 The Netherlands: Structuring the Management of Terrorist Incidents

Erwin Muller

Introduction

Compared with the intensity and structure of terrorist problems in neighbouring countries, the Netherlands has known little terrorism over the past twenty-five years. As a consequence, academic research on terrorism and counter-terrorism in the Netherlands has been rare, and only a few Dutch scholars have written on this topic, although the Dutch National Security Service (*Binnenlandse Veiligheidsdienst* or BVD; recently renamed *Algemene Inlichtingen en Veiligheidsdienst*, AIVD) has written about terrorism and counter-terrorism in its published annual reports.

The Dutch lack of experience with massive terrorist attacks has brought with it one disadvantage: terrorism and counter-terrorism have been low on the political and judicial agenda. However, the terrorist attacks on the United States of 11 September 2001 have caused a temporary change in the first months after the attacks.

Terrorism in the Netherlands

In the Netherlands, several indigenous groups have committed acts of terrorism: the *Rode Jeugd*, South Moluccan youngsters and *RARA*.[1] The intensity of such attacks has been mild compared with other European countries, although the attacks by South Moluccan activists were serious enough.

---

1   J.A. Emerson Vermaat, 'Terrorist Sympathizers in the Netherlands', *Terrorism*, 1987, pp. 329-335.

M. van Leeuwen (ed.): *Confronting Terrorism*, pp. 147-163
© 2003 Kluwer Law International. Printed in the Netherlands.

A number of terrorist incidents have occurred in the last 25 years and some of these have had a major impact on the decision-making process. The unprecedented hijacking of trains in the 1970s by South Moluccan activists was crucial in this respect and a few remarks about the position of people of South Moluccan descent in the Netherlands are in order here. In colonial times, many male South Moluccans, the vast majority of them Christians, served in the Dutch Indian army. During the Japanese occupation of the Dutch East Indies at the time of the Second World War, they remained loyal to the defeated colonial power. After the Japanese were defeated and the Dutch East Indies gained independence to become Indonesia, many South Moluccans longed for an independent state of their own. The Dutch government sympathized but was unable to lend a helping hand. Over 10,000 South Moluccans immigrated to the Netherlands in the early 1950s, without giving up their hopes of a return. Partially as a consequence of this hope, they did not as a community integrate easily into Dutch society. At various intervals, South Moluccan activists have reminded a number of governments of their nationalist ambitions. More recently, they have also demanded (diplomatic) interventions to quell violence between Christians and radical Muslims in their homeland. Sometimes their actions took a violent character, as was notably the case with the hijacking of trains in the 1970s.

The Dutch government was utterly taken by surprise by the hijackings. It needed several years to develop a consistent policy on counter-terrorism. In addition to repressive methods to counter terrorism by South Moluccan activists, the Dutch government also developed a preventive and social strategy to integrate the South Moluccans in Dutch society. The mix of repressive methods and preventive and social measures succeeded in ending serious terrorist attacks, but in the meantime the South Moluccan actions came closest to any form of structural terrorism that the Netherlands has known.

Incidental terrorist actions have occurred in the Netherlands relatively frequently,[2] which means that anti-terrorist forces have been faced with ever-changing opponents. Preventing and controlling incidents calls for a different approach than countering a more structural threat. Dutch policies have so far largely been adapted to incident control. The following overview[3] reflects Dutch experiences with terrorism.

Dutch Political Terrorism

*   *Occupation of the Indonesian residence in Wassenaar by 33 South Moluccans, 1970.* The perpetrators, second-generation South Moluccans, wanted an independent state and blamed the Dutch government for not living up to earlier promises of help in that endeavour. Impatient with the 'polite' way of their elders, they turned to terrorism.[4]

---

2   A.J. Jongman, 'Trends in International and Domestic Terrorism in Western Europe, *Terrorism and Political Violence*, 1992, pp. 26-76.
3   In this overview the criminal kidnappings in the Netherlands are not mentioned.
4   See V. Herman and R. Van der Laan Bouma, 'Nationalists without a Nation', *Terrorism*, 1980, pp. 223-257; and C.H. Yeager, 'Mena Murai: The South Moluccans Fight in Holland', *Terrorism*, 1990, pp. 215-226.

A police officer died during the hostage-taking in Wassenaar. The crisis was ended when the occupiers surrendered.

- *Hijacking of a train at Wijster and hostage-taking in the Indonesian embassy in Amsterdam by South Moluccans 1975.*[5] South Moluccans captured and held a train and the Indonesian embassy. The Dutch government was again fully taken by surprise. The terrorists killed three hostages. The government started intensive negotiations and used South Moluccan mediators. After two weeks the hostage-takers surrendered. This form of negotiation became known as the 'Dutch approach'. The goal of this long negotiation was to exhaust the hostage-takers.[6]

- *Hijacking of a train at De Punt and hostage-taking in a school in Bovensmilde by South Moluccans, 1977.* South Moluccan terrorists again hijacked a train. At the same time they occupied a primary school. The hostage-taking of such young children particularly upset the Dutch government and public. The government tried again, but in vain, to end these crises through negotiations. After three weeks, it ordered a massive attack on the train and the school. Six terrorists and two hostages died in the process. The children had been freed some weeks earlier because of the outbreak of a contagious disease among them.

- *Hostage-taking in the Provincial Government in Assen by South Moluccans, 1978.* The last major terrorist attack by South Moluccans was directed against the Provincial Government Building in Assen, in the province of Drente. One hostage died. The newly installed government refused to negotiate, and after only 36 hours, it sent in the Marines. Another hostage died a month later because of wounds inflicted by the terrorists. No more major terrorist attacks were subsequently mounted by South Moluccans, although every few years there are riots concerning young South Moluccans. At Christmas 2000 South Moluccans were responsible for some smaller bomb attacks in the Netherlands. Dutch intelligence is still watching potential activists within the Moluccan community.

- *Bomb attack by RARA, 1987 and 1991.* RARA (*Radikale Antiracistische Aktie*; RARA is also Dutch for 'guess who?') was a small group that attacked multinationals with bombs. They wanted to protest against apartheid in South Africa. The attacks in 1985-1987 were concentrated on the Dutch multinational Makro, which owns a number of supermarkets in the Netherlands and in South Africa. Although there was substantial material damage, no casualties were involved in the bomb attacks. In 1991, RARA attacked the house of the State Secretary of Justice and the Ministry of Interior to influence Dutch policy on refugees and asylum-seekers. Although some persons were arrested, no one was convicted, and after 1991 there were no more attacks.

- *Assassination of Pim Fortuyn.* On 6 May 2002, the populist politician Pim Fortuyn was killed at the Media Park in Hilversum. Fortuyn was a successful leader of a new

---

5   R. Barker, *Not Here, But In Another Place: A True Story of Captors and Hostages* (New York: St Martin's Press, 1980); U. Rosenthal and P. 't Hart, 'Managing Terrorism', in U. Rosenthal *et al.* (eds), *Coping with Crises: The Management of Disasters, Riots and Terrorism* (Springfield IL: Charles C. Thomas, 1989), pp. 367-397.

6   D. Mulder, 'The South Moluccan Story', in P. Janke (ed.), *Terrorism and Democracy* (London: Macmillan, 1992), pp. 73-114.

political party that was expected to gain a major victory at the Dutch national elections on 13 May 2002 (and in effect did gain such a victory). In some polls, Fortuyn was mentioned as the next Prime Minister of the Netherlands. While it became known that the detained suspect had been professionally active in an environmental organization, he kept silent about his motivations throughout the following months, nor did he reveal whether he had prepared his act alone or in association with others.

Criminal Terrorism

- *Criminal hostage-taking in a farm in Deil by two bank robbers, 1973.* This kind of crime was new for the Netherlands, and the strategies and policies developed during this hostage-taking were used in the further development of counter-terrorist measures and policies in the Netherlands.
- *Hostage-taking of a church choir in a prison at Scheveningen, 1974.* The main actors in this event were imprisoned criminals, but they were aided by imprisoned PLO members. The situation was extraordinary also because of the premises where it took place. The hostage-takers demanded their freedom. The crisis was ended by force; no one died or was wounded; and the hostage-takers surrendered without resistance.
- *Hostage-taking of the passengers of a German bus, 1988.* A bus that had been hijacked in Germany was driven with hostages to the Netherlands. The Dutch authorities negotiated with the hostage-takers and gave them a controlled BMW instead of the bus. Most of the hostages were freed, but the hostage-takers took two of their victims back to Germany. The German police ended the crisis with force and one hostage died. This incident was the first example of a cross-border criminal terrorist incident involving the Netherlands.
- *Kidnapping of Colonel Van de Kieft, 1989.* Colonel Van de Kieft was kidnapped by a disturbed man, and the Dutch Intervention Team, attempting to free him, accidentally killed the Colonel instead of the kidnapper. The necessary procedures were not followed. This episode led to the further development of procedures for the use of violence during terrorist incidents.
- *Hostage-taking in Helden, Limburg, 2000.* Two criminals captured a peasant family and raped the daughters. The police knew that there was the possibility of continued rape but they did not intervene. The hostage-takers surrendered after they had given a press conference. They were arrested and sentenced to long terms in prison.

International Terrorism in the Netherlands

- *Hostage-taking in the French embassy in The Hague by the Japanese Red Army, 1974.* This was the first time that the Netherlands faced major international terrorism. Almost all the demands of the terrorists were met, including the freeing of a member of the Japanese Red Army detained in France. The terrorists fled with their friend and a substantial sum of money, but they did free their hostages unharmed. Still, this is a case of flawed counter-terrorism because no one was arrested and the government, which was taken utterly by surprise, complied with all the demands.

- *Killing of the British ambassador by the IRA, 1979.* The IRA killed the British ambassador, Sir Richard Sykes, in The Hague. This killing led to more sophisticated security concerning diplomats, and was the first time after the Second World War that a politically motivated killing of a specific prominent foreign individual had occurred in the Netherlands.
- *Bomb attacks on British soldiers carried out by the IRA, 1988.* The IRA attacked six British soldiers in two separate attacks. Three soldiers were killed; the others seriously wounded. The IRA claimed the attacks one day later. They demanded that the British leave Northern Ireland. There was no explanation of why they attacked in the Netherlands. There were no arrests.
- *Killing of two Australian tourists by the IRA, 1990.* In 1990 the IRA shot two Australian tourists in the marketplace in Roermond, mistaking them for British soldiers. The IRA later acknowledged responsibility and apologized. No arrests were made.
- *Bomb attacks on Spanish buildings by the ETA, 1989-1990.* The ETA bombed Spanish buildings and authorities in the Netherlands. There were no casualties but material damage was considerable. The bombing of the residence of the Spanish ambassador in The Hague forced the Dutch government to intensify security measures. There were no arrests.
- *Hostage-taking in the Greek residence by Kurdish separatists, The Hague, 1999.* In reaction to the capture of the Kurdish leader Öcalan, Kurdish activists occupied the Greek residence and some people in it were taken hostage. Occupations and demonstrations simultaneously occurred all over Europe. The action in The Hague was spontaneous. The authorities were once more taken by surprise. Most of the hostage-takers were arrested and convicted.
- *Bomb threat on tunnels in Amsterdam and Rotterdam, 2001.* Two weeks after the 11 September 2001attacks in the United States, authorities received a sophisticated looking threatening note indicating that some tunnels in Amsterdam and Rotterdam would be bombed. Although none of the authorities thought that the threat would be implemented, all possible security measures were taken. Dutch citizens were confronted with massive military force. No attack occurred. Nobody was arrested.

Some patterns can be discerned in this overview. Until the late 1960s, the Netherlands was spared any terrorist acts, but in the 1970s, various hostage situations and occupations occurred. In many cases, terrorists tried to pressurize the authorities by threatening human lives. In the 1980s, criminal kidnappings replaced politically motivated hostage-taking, and during that period no prominent terrorist movements were active in the Netherlands. The end of the 1980s and the early 1990s saw mostly bomb scares and bombings, raids on army barracks, arson and other types of violence, focused on objects rather than on persons. Those hit-and-run actions called for different measures from the authorities than hostage situations, in which the location of the terrorist was known and remained fixed: only when the terrorist could be arrested at the crime site were some convictions proved possible; in all other cases, the Dutch police and Public Prosecutors were not successful.

General Aspects of Counter-terrorism in the Netherlands

According to the Dutch scholar Fynaut, the Dutch response to terrorist and activist violence can best be described as 'composed'. Political violence, he argues, should not be stemmed by violence alone. Moreover, counter-violence should be 'organized and exercised as much as possible within the framework of the existing organization and operation of the police system'. [7]

This description captures the essence of counter-terrorist policies in the Netherlands. The authorities try to balance repressive power with preventive and social measures.

Legal Order versus Public Order

The central question in the discussion of powers before, during and after terrorist incidents is the relationship between the administrative and the judicial authorities (the Minister of Justice, the Procurator General and the Public Prosecutor versus the Minister of Home Affairs, the Queen's Commissioner and the Mayor). In the Proceedings of Parliament this choice is defended with the following argumentation:

> 'Since these are completed (and still continuing) criminal offences, the Minister of Justice is the first responsible authority in such cases. He must decide in close consultation with the Prime Minister, also Minister of General Affairs, and the Ministers of Foreign Affairs and Defence, and possibly with other officials involved. If a terrorist act occurs, however, interests related to public order are also at stake, and other measures of an administrative nature will also be required. It is important that judicial measures and measures related to public order are carefully harmonized.' [8]

In the early 1970s, the government primarily defined terrorism as a violation of legal order. That placed the responsibility for response to a terrorist act with the judicial authorities. The then Minister of Foreign Affairs wholeheartedly agreed with that construction, which made it possible to apply the hierarchical power structure of the Public Prosecution Department. Combating terrorism primarily became a matter for the national government, in particular the judicial bodies, and in 2002 this was still the basic structure for counter-terrorism in the Netherlands. To date, the responsibility for combating terrorism in the Netherlands has primarily been vested in the Minister of Justice. Over the years, however, it has become customary for judicial and administrative authorities to consult on the measures to be taken. The interaction between maintaining public and legal order during terrorist incidents was acknowledged.

---

7 C. Fynaut, 'Politiek geweld en de politiële bestrijding hiervan in Nederland', *Tijdschrift voor de Politie*, 1989, pp. 501-505.
8 *Bijlagen Handelingen Tweede Kamer 1972-1973*, 12000, VI, no. 11 [author's translation].

In the case of a terrorist attack, the Chief Prosecutor of the region has the lead. All his/her decisions have to be coordinated with the Mayor and Chief of Police involved. The coordination of security measures rests with the Department of the Interior. The *National Handbook Crisis Decision Making* is the main procedure for decisions.[9]

Legislation and Regulations

There is no specific Act in the Netherlands that governs procedures during terrorist incidents. There are merely (confidential) ministerial circulars and policy rules. Policy in the Netherlands is essentially still based on a 1972 letter from then Prime Minister Biesheuvel to the Dutch Second Chamber.[10]

Separate circulars and scenarios have been developed for various types of terrorist incidents. In 1976, a more general scheme for combating terrorism was drawn up: the Order on the Investigation of Organized Crime of a Terrorist Nature. In 1981 the Cooperation Scheme for the Control of Terrorist Crimes replaced that Order, and introduced the National Public Prosecutor for the Combat of Terrorism, who is in charge of coordinating investigations in the event of an imminent terrorist incident. The scheme is an attempt at regulating the exchange of information between the police, the Public Prosecution Department and the administrative bodies. The Special Investigation Department of the Central Criminal Investigation Department plays a pivotal part in this. In the 1990s a national structure for crisis management was formed, but it is not certain whether all forms of terrorism have been included in this structure.

The Netherlands has no special emergency legislation for terrorist incidents. The Civil Authorities Extraordinary Powers Act or the War Act, both of which grant far-reaching powers to political/administrative persons in authority, do not apply to terrorist acts.[11] The action taken during terrorist incidents is usually based on powers that exist in regular criminal law. Special (criminal) legislation for terrorist incidents has long been set aside as a form of 'overacting'.[12] In the early summer of 2002, the Dutch government, reacting to EU decisions, has produced a bill to make participation in a terrorist organization liable to punishment.[13]

The use of force in terrorist situations must meet the same conditions as the use of force in more regular situations. The police and the military must be extremely reticent, and instructions to use force must be described as accurately as possible. Even during terrorist incidents, operational units must observe the applicable instructions on the use of force. Subsidiarity and proportionality requirements are essential here.

---

9   *Handelingen Tweede Kamer: Lijst van vragen en antwoorden*, 31 January 2001, no. 27925.
10   Bijlagen Handelingen *Tweede Kamer 1972-1973*, 12000, VI, no. 11.
11   A.P. Schmid, 'Combating Terrorism in the Netherlands', *Terrorism and Political Violence*, 1992, pp. 79-110.
12   P. Klerks, *Terreurbestrijding in Nederland* (Amsterdam: Ravijn, 1989), p. 185.
13   *Wijziging en aanvulling van het wetboek van Strafrecht en enige andere wetten in verband met terroristische misdrijven (Wet terroristische misdrijven)*, Tweede Kamer der Staten-Generaal, 2002.

Anti-terrorist Units

In the Netherlands, combating terrorism is primarily a police task. The Dutch government has acknowledged the risk of an entirely separate anti-terrorist organization becoming isolated from the rest of society, and it has set up various Special Support Teams, in which the police and the military are handed specialist anti-terrorist tasks in addition to their regular work. These units can assist in the handling of terrorist incidents and they operate under the responsibility of the judicial authorities during a terrorist incident.

Figure 1   *Anti-terrorist Support Teams*

BBE-K	Armed Forces Special Support Team: marksmen
BBE-RP	National Police Force Special Support Team: marksmen
BBE-M	Marine Special Support Team: close combat fighting
BSB	Military Police Special Security Assignments Brigade: personal security
AEKL	Royal Army Cordoning Unit: cordoning the place of the incident

There is a thin line between the use of regular police services and these special units. The special (BBE) units can be engaged only with the approval of the Minister of Justice. Arrest Squads of the municipal and national police forces can be engaged with the approval of the Chief Public Prosecutor. In urgent cases, the authorities in charge can be informed of the use of Arrest Squads afterwards.

At the time of the 1990-1991 Gulf War, Dutch management of terrorist threats was decided upon for the decade to come.[14] In the event of an actual act of terrorism, the ministers of the Gulf Crisis Cabinet (the Prime Minister, the Deputy Prime Minister, and the Ministers of Foreign Affairs, Home Affairs, Justice, Defence and Economic Affairs) would have been in overall charge of countermeasures. The actual threat of terrorist acts was assessed by the 'Assessment Triangle', consisting of the Director-General for Safety and Public Order of the Ministry of Home Affairs, the Director-General for Police and Aliens' Affairs of the Ministry of Justice, and the head of the National Security Service. This 'Assessment Triangle' met on almost a daily basis during the first three months of 1991. If the BVD or the Central Criminal Investigation Department (CRI) had any information on a specific threat, that information was passed on to the relevant provincial and municipal authorities through the National Coordination Centre. After the Gulf War, the BVD and the Central Criminal Investigation Department regularly provided confidential threat analyses. After the attacks in the United States in September 2001, the Triangle was still operational. The national crisis response was coordinated on the basis of the *National Handbook Crisis Decision Making*.

---

14   A.J. Jongman and P. Klerks, 'Terreur', in U. Rosenthal and J. de Vries (eds), *Nederland en de Golfcrisis: Politiek, Media, Terreur* (Arnhem: Gouda Quint, 1993), pp. 109-139.

The Collecting, Exchange and Processing of Information

Various organizations collect, process and exchange information on criminal offences of a terrorist nature, and harmonization and coordination between these organizations is often problematic.

Firstly, the National Security Service (AIVD), under the political responsibility of the Minister of the Interior, is in charge of identifying activities and persons posing a potential threat to the democratic legal order or the safety of the state. One of the tasks of this Service is therefore to investigate and identify the threat of terrorist incidents. Its officers have no operational powers. The National Security Service uses Local Intelligence Services (*Plaatselijke Inlichtingen Diensten*, PIDs) of the local and regional police forces. Those Local Intelligence Services gather information related to acute or imminent breaches of the peace. The information is gathered at the request of the Mayor, who is politically responsible for public-order policy in his or her municipality, or at the request of the National Security Service. In 2002 a new law on the National Security Service was set in motion. This law gives the Service more authority to use intelligence methods. At the same time, the administrative and political control of the Service is improved. Under the law that went into force in May 2002, the National Security Service may also collect intelligence concerning other countries.[15]

Secondly, the Korps Landelijke Politiediensten (KLPD, National Police Forces) gathers information on persons and groups suspected of terrorist activities and attempts to draw up risk analyses of terrorism at a specific moment in time. Within this Force a central unit gathers and analyses all relevant police information on terrorists and potential attacks. The KLPD is not a formal intelligence agency, but it can gather information and act on it. The division of tasks and distribution of information between the National Security Service and the police requires a substantial amount of harmonization and coordination. With the consent of the National Prosecutor for the Combat of Terrorism, information of the National Security Service may be used in a criminal investigation. Since 11 September 2001, the National Security Service and the police are cooperating more closely in fighting terrorism, but there is still no full integration of the information concerning terrorism.

Criminal Intelligence Services (CIE) also operate within the police forces. The Central Criminal Investigation Department operates a national criminal investigation service. The Criminal Investigation Services focus on proactive investigation activities.

After the attacks in the United States, all these services have been working more closely together. Knowledge centres for terrorism have been formed. Obstacles against information collection were removed in the first months after the attack. The sense of urgency for better coordination and organization, however, diminished after a while.

The Taking of Hostages

In the 1970s, the Netherlands was suddenly faced with large-scale hostage situations, and its first activities in the field of anti-terrorism date back to that period.

---

15   See *Wet Inlichtingen en veiligheidsdiensten*, 2002.

Regulations

The first politically motivated hostage situation to occur in the Netherlands, at the Indonesian residence in 1970, was passed off as an incident. It did not give rise to the formulation of any rules on combating terrorism. Not until Israeli sportsmen were taken hostage during the Olympic Games in Munich in 1972 did the Dutch government begin to draw up policy rules.

After official preliminary talks and a meeting between the ministers of Justice and Home Affairs, the judicial *Hostage Circular* was drawn up in 1972 (13 October). A few months later, the Prime Minister sent the *Anti-terrorism Memorandum* to the Second Chamber of Parliament (1973). On 23 February 1973, the Minister of Foreign Affairs sent out a circular to the Queen's Commissioners on how to proceed in hostage and kidnapping situations, and that circular was based on the judicial *Hostage Circular*. In a committee of the Second Chamber, set up especially for that purpose, the *Anti-terrorism Memorandum* was discussed at a public meeting on 23 March 1973 and the policy outlined by the Ministers was adopted. In May 1974, the *General Guidelines on Police Action in Hostage or Kidnapping Situations* were sent to the Police Commissioners on a confidential basis.

Subsequently, the Netherlands was faced with a number of terrorist acts that had a serious psychological impact on society. The operational guidelines were adjusted after each terrorist incident. Finally, in 1978, the national policy on the handling of acts of terrorism were set down in the *Handbook on Hostage Situations* issued by the Minister of Justice. The operational guidelines in hostage situations were most recently revised in 1982. Since then, no changes (or in any event no public changes) have been made to the scenarios and guidelines.

Article on the Taking of Hostages

By way of implementation of the UN Convention on the Taking of Hostages of 1979, an Article was inserted in the Dutch Criminal Code making the taking of hostages a punishable offence. Partly in response to various kidnappings, the Minister of Justice proposed to Parliament to increase the punishment that could be imposed in relevant cases. Article 282A of the Dutch Criminal Code makes the taking of hostages and kidnapping punishable by law. Under that Article, a higher punishment can be imposed than used to be possible under Article 282 of the Criminal Code.[16]

1   A person who intentionally deprives a person of his or her liberty or keeps him or her
     so deprived with a view to forcing another party to do or refrain from doing
     something will be punished for the taking of a hostage with imprisonment of not
     more than fifteen years or a fine of the fifth category.

---

16   Author's translation. For the parliamentary discussion of the insertion of this Article, see TK 1987-1988,
      Bijlagen Handelingen, 20373.

2   If the offence leads to a person's death, the perpetrator will be punished with life imprisonment, or temporary imprisonment of not more than twenty years, or a fine of the fifth category.

Decision-making during Hostage Situations

The above-mentioned circulars and guidelines primarily set out the division of powers and what organizations and persons need to be warned. They also deal with the principles of the action taken by various government services. A detailed checklist sets out what must be done and when, emphasizing that no decision should be made on granting demands until the Minister of Justice or the State Secretary for Justice has been contacted. Two elements are emphasized in all the guidelines: the Minister of Justice is primarily responsible, since continuing crimes are involved; and the importance is stressed of realizing consultation and cooperation with judicial, administrative and police authorities.

The decision-making structure used in the 1970s during hostage situations still applies.

> 'As a rule, hostage situations constitute such a serious violation of legal order as to exceed the local and regional levels. The policy to be followed with regard to the demands made by the offenders and the steps to be taken in order to put an end to the hostage situation are therefore generally the responsibility of the national government, in particular the joint responsibility of the Ministers of Justice and Home Affairs. The final responsibility vests in the Minister of Justice. Naturally, this does not affect the statutory powers of the local authorities, *i.e.* the Procurator General/Chief Public Prosecutor and the Queen's Commissioner/Mayor, who, each in his or her own field and in so far as relevant, jointly take action in accordance with the instructions given by the national government.'[17]

Various scenarios and reports suggest that three decision-making centres must be set up in the event of a hostage situation: a crisis centre at the national level; a policy centre at the local level; and a command post at the hostage site. The decision-makers try to act in accordance with the following principles during hostage situations:

> 'The object of the government action is primarily to end the hostage situation while observing the following principles:
> a.   preventing injuries to the hostages;
> b.   preventing the perpetrators from realizing their intended object;
> c.   apprehending the perpetrators as soon as possible.'[18]

---

17   *Final Report of the Integrated Departments Working Party on Police Action in a Larger Context* (Dutch title: *Eindrapport Werkgroep Geïntegreerde Staven bij Politie-optreden in Groot Verband*, The Hague: 1982); Appendix C, p. 9.
18   *Final Report of the Integrated Departments Working Party on Police Action in a Larger Context* (The Hague: 1982); Appendix C, p. 9.

Assaults

Assaults are specified as bomb explosions and arson. They may be directed against either persons or buildings. Written and telephone warnings usually precede this type of assault.

Rules and Decision-making in the Event of Bomb Scares

Terrorists may give a warning before the assault. The 'Decree on the Action to be taken in the Event of Bomb Scares' of 1979 (OBM – bomb scare response – regulation) sets out the procedure on how to respond if the police, judicial authorities, government or other parties are confronted with a bomb scare. Although an interdepartmental working party on improvised explosives had already been set up in 1972, and the training of explosives' disposal officers was commenced in 1973, it was not until 1979 that the official procedure was put down in writing. Before 1979, improvised checklists were used.

The OBM regulation provides that the Mayor is responsible for the action taken in response to a bomb scare. Decisions on bomb scares are regarded as related to maintaining public order. The police must always be informed of bomb scares; only the police are authorized to carry out an explosives investigation after a bomb scare. The police can demand the evacuation of a threatened building through the Mayor. The Explosives Disposal Unit of the army is in charge of disposal of the (suspected) explosives and it operates under the Mayor's responsibility.

In 1992, a survey was conducted among the police on the action taken in the event of bomb scares. Each year, some 1,400 bomb scares occur in the Netherlands. The survey showed that the applicable rules and decision-making procedures are not yet generally accepted:

- At one-third of police forces, decisions are not always made by or in consultation with a trained leader of the explosives investigation team.
- Usually (in two-thirds of the cases) no agreements have been made with companies and Mayors.
- The OBM regulation is generally known, but in one-third of cases it is not or not fully applied.
- There is great variety in internal instructions. Many do not contain the minimum required or desirable information. Some even contain incorrect information.

During the last ten years there have been no new regulations or research on assault in the Netherlands.

Rules and Decision-making after Assaults

The police, judicial authorities and government have to respond in a very short time-frame during an assault, and the period after the event is dedicated to finding the perpetrators and reconstructing what has been destroyed. The investigation commences during these phases. Regional investigation teams are mostly used, which are set up on an *ad hoc* basis in response to specific assaults. In some cases, such an Investigation Support Team is lifted to a national level. The response during and after an assault is almost entirely in the hands of the judiciary. The judicial authorities and the police are supported by the technical expertise of the Explosives Disposal Unit and the Forensic Scientific Laboratory. The customary investigation rules apply, as set out in the Dutch Code of Criminal Procedure.

If any casualties or damage to property have occurred, the element of enforcement of public order will also play a part. It may be necessary to evacuate buildings, close off roads and make other decisions related to public order. In those cases, the Mayor, as the party primarily responsible for public order, will play a part in the decision-making process. In that case it will be necessary to harmonize the demands of the investigation with the maintenance of public order.

Counter-terrorism after 11 September 2001

Many measures were taken in the Netherlands after 11 September 2001 to intensify the combat of terrorism. It must be noted again that combating terrorism had little priority in the Netherlands before that date. Due to the infrequent occurrence of terrorist acts in the Netherlands, it had become the work of a few specialists. Executives and officers paid more attention to contingencies and breaches of the peace than to the threat of terrorism. This changed immediately after 11 September 2001, both with the authorities and with the general public. In late 2001, the Dutch considered international terrorism to be the most important threat.[19]

In the aftermath of the attacks, public debate focused on a number of issues related to terrorism, such as the status of the Kurdish Liberation Movement PKK. In the Netherlands, the PKK had not been seen as a terrorist organization for a long time. PKK sympathizers could freely move and act in the Netherlands as long as they respected Dutch law. The Dutch government had even provided support for some legitimate activities by the PKK in the Netherlands. At the same time, the PKK was prohibited as a criminal and terrorist organization in Belgium and Germany. In the discussions in Brussels about the European list of terrorist groups, the Netherlands took a controversial position on the PKK. By spring 2002, the topic of PKK status within the EU still had to be resolved, although a number of Dutch parliamentarians were arguing that the PKK should indeed be considered a terrorist organization. After the attacks in the United States, this policy of the Dutch government was heavily debated in the political arena, and it should be noted that, eventually, the Dutch government has not opposed the decision of the European Council to put the PKK on the list of terrorist organizations.

No terrorist incidents occurred in the Netherlands in the first six months after 11 September 2001, although there were several scares. As already noted, at the end of September 2001 four tunnels in Rotterdam and Amsterdam were closed after a bomb scare. There was also great unrest in the Netherlands for some time involving phoney

---

19   L. Wecke, *Terrorismebeeld in Nederland* (Nijmegen: Centrum voor Internationaal Conflict-Analyse en Management (CICAM), 24 October 2001).

'anthrax' powder letters. At the time of writing, it cannot be said that there is any demonstrable increase in the threat of terrorist incidents.

In response to the assaults of 11 September 2001, the Dutch government formulated a detailed Anti-terrorist and Safety Plan of Action.[20] The Plan of Action comprises a wide range of measures to be taken by almost all of the relevant organizations in the Netherlands. The Dutch parliament is kept informed of the progress of these activities by means of regular progress reports.[21]

The government has concentrated on the combination of measures after the attacks in the United States. Most interesting is the focus on the integrity of the financial sector. The government believes that if the authorities can get a hold on the financial structures and flows of the terrorists, a major contribution towards counter-terrorism would be made. Just before the attacks in the United States, the *Nationale Gezondheidsraad* or Board of Health published a report on bioterrorism and concluded that the Netherlands was not at all prepared for a biological terrorist attack.[22] After the attack on the US, the Dutch Minister of Health ordered smallpox vaccines to be produced for the entire Dutch population. Other measures are also useful for the improvement of counter-terrorism in the Netherlands, and it would be beneficial if an Anti-Terrorism Act were made in the Netherlands in which the responsibility and regulations for counter-terrorism were formulated.

Time will show to what extent these often-expensive measures will continue to receive the public and political support that they received in the first six months after the assaults of 11 September 2001 if no new terrorist incidents occur in the Netherlands.

Current Threat Perspectives

Expectations of the Dutch Security Service

In early 2001, the BVD published a report containing a risk assessment of terrorist threats to the Netherlands for the early twenty-first century. It is the first substantiated terrorist threat assessment to be published by the BVD, for whom assessing these risks is a professional priority.[23]

'The threat of terrorism to the Netherlands is largely a derivative of the international threat', the Service stated, naming American, British and Turkish interests or properties as examples for potential terrorism targets. 'The internationalization of terrorism has meant that violent political attacks may in principle take place anywhere in the world, including the Netherlands.' Still, the Service pointed at various relevant factors that may

---

20 *Bijlagen Handelingen Tweede Kamer 2001-2002*, no. 27925.
21 *The Derde voortgangsrapportage met betrekking tot het actieplan Terrorismebestrijding en Veiligheid, 2002* demonstrates the diversity of measures. It covers: prevention; issue of visa and possibilities of biometrical means of identification; security, safety and public order; investigation and prosecution; technological measures; integrity of the financial sector; and action against terrorism.
22 Nationale Gezondheidsraad, *Verdediging tegen bioterrorisme* (The Hague: 14 June 2001).
23 National Security Service, *Terrorism at the Start of the Twenty-first Century: Current Threat and Positioning of the Netherlands National Security Service (BVD)* (Dutch title: *Terrorisme aan het begin van de 21e eeuw; dreigingsbeeld en positionering van de BVD*, The Hague: Binnenlandse Veiligheidsdienst, 2001), pp. 15 and 16.

arguably draw special attention to the Netherlands from terrorists looking for targets: the Netherlands' strategic geographical position, with major nodes of international traffic (Rotterdam harbour; Schiphol airport); its position as host to a number of international courts (e.g. the Lockerbie trials; the Yugoslav tribunal) and offices charged with the verification of international agreements (such as the Organization for the Prohibition of Chemical Weapons, OPCW); and its role as host country to large groups of immigrants from various parts of the world. These immigrants may import violent conflicts from their homelands into their new country of residence (such as conflicts between Turks and Kurds, or among Afghans of opposite persuasions, etc). Finally, the Service mentioned the reputation of the Netherlands as a tolerant society, where many religious and political opinions, even outlandish ones, are generally respected and the judicial system is known for its mild punishments. In some cases it is likely that terrorists have deliberately opted to come to the Netherlands – either illegally or through the asylum policy – to hide here and to support their home organizations.

The BVD continued by noting that, unlike the situation in most neighbouring countries, homegrown terrorism did not presently play a significant role in the Netherlands. It did not exclude the risk of 'a certain continuum between failed integration, increased segregation, growing polarization and violent confrontation', but concluded that there were no indications that such a process would result in terrorism. In conclusion, the BVD report stated: 'there is no great risk that society will be confronted with terrorist attacks on Dutch territory in the near future. Nevertheless, there are many risk factors that require that the country be on its guard'. It also noted that the Netherlands arguably is attractive to terrorists as a place to stay unnoticed and prepare attacks elsewhere.

In its *Annual Report* for 2001, published in May 2002, the BVD obviously returned to the issue of terrorist threats. While maintaining most of its conclusions from *Terrorism at the Start of the Twenty-first Century*, it did note that in 2001 a (very) small number of cases had occurred of young Dutch Muslims being won over by foreign radical Islamic recruiters to join the 'Holy War' abroad. While the BVD had previously traced the activities of such recruiters to groups of fresh immigrants still staying in asylum centres, it now had to conclude that, even though on a very small scale, the tendency to radical Islamic violence was taking root among some Islamic Dutch citizens.[24]

The Security Service is now researching possible links between radical Dutch Muslims and individuals associated with al-Qaeda. It has intensified information-gathering on terrorism and cooperation with other security services in the Netherlands and abroad.

Shortly after the attacks on 11 September 2001 a terrorist cell made up of Algerian citizens was arrested in Rotterdam. It had been planning a bomb attack on the American embassy in Paris. The Dutch Security Service, which had spotted the cell before 11 September, is convinced that with this action they prevented a major terrorist attack.

The would-be terrorist Richard Reid stayed in Amsterdam before he tried to bomb a plane with a bomb in his shoe. Personnel and passengers arrested him in flight before he could implement his plan. Two Islamic Dutch boys of Moroccan descent from Eindhoven

---

24 National Security Service, *Jaarverslag* (Annual Report) 2001 (The Hague: Binnenlandse Veiligheidsdienst, 2002), p. 130.

were killed in Kashmir in a struggle with the police. According to the BVD, they had been recruited as *jihad* fighters. Finally, an ETA terrorist was arrested in a squatters' building in Amsterdam in late January 2002, just before the marriage of the Dutch crown prince.

New Risks

Are there new risks for terrorism in the Netherlands? The following considerations make it plausible that the number of terrorist incidents in the Netherlands may rise.[25] These considerations, it should be noted, also apply to other European countries.[26]

Firstly, it seems that the underlying motives of many terrorists are much more diffuse than in the past. Their aim is not to free specific prisoners or to liberate a specific country, but rather to overturn American imperialism and to protest against western capitalism. This makes it difficult to counter them by means of specific politics. It is not even certain that they do in fact pursue a specific object. In any case, no specific object is involved that can be geographically demarcated, nor are their acts motivated by economic or social deprivation. They are basically driven by a fundamentalist attitude to life, aiming to live and have others live in accordance with their strict regimes of laws and regulations, usually of a religious nature. These terrorists believe that such fundamentalism should not only dominate people's private lives, but should also dictate the organization of governments and states. Such fundamentalism aims at abolishing the separation of Church and State. It is not easy to predict what targets they find interesting. It seems that any object or person that can be seen as an example of American (or Israeli) or capitalist expansion or secularism could fall victim. Such 'symbolic' persons and objectives are frequently present in the Netherlands (as well as in other western countries).

Secondly, the primary object of these terrorists appears to be to instil fear for fear's sake. Fear is traditionally created by assaults at unexpected moments, in unexpected places against innocent people, but the aim now also seems to be to cause many casualties. It would appear that these terrorists wish to increase the number of fundamentalist governments. Their reasoning may be that if it is established that the leaders of western democracies are unable to guarantee the safety of their own citizens, those citizens will be more susceptible to alternative types of government. If the terrorist organization is able to commit brutal assaults several times in succession, people will become aware that the government can no longer guarantee their safety. The repetition of terrorist acts leads to a further escalation of fear. Dutch society, as any modern society, is vulnerable. There are many possibilities for terrorist attacks. It would not be difficult for terrorists to stop or hinder the functioning of Dutch society.

Thirdly, international terrorism today appears to be rooted primarily in religious fundamentalism. Although many people focus on Muslim fundamentalism, it is con-

---

25   E.R. Muller, 'Nieuw terrorisme', *Tijdschrift voor Veiligheid en Veiligheidszorg*, summer 2002.
26   See also W. Laqueur, *The New Terrorism* (Oxford: Oxford University Press, 1999); I.O. Lesser *et al.*, *Countering the New Terrorism* (Santa Monica CA: RAND, 1999); B. Hoffman, *Inside Terrorism* (New York: Columbia University Press, 1998); G.E. Schweitzer, *Super Terrorism* (New York: Plenum Press, 1998); and J. Stern, *The Ultimate Terrorists* (Cambridge MA: Harvard University Press, 1999).

ceivable that other forms of religious fundamentalism, such as sects, will also engage in terrorism. It appears to be difficult for the rationally oriented combat of terrorism to switch to value-related terrorism, as religious fundamentalism may also be named. The logic of the preparations and actions of religious fanatics is not always recognized in the western world. Dutch society is multicultural. Almost every religion and every nationality are represented in the Netherlands. This gives potential terrorists the opportunity to prepare for terrorism with little risk of being found out in time.

Fourthly, international terrorism is now the dominant form of terrorism. Terrorists make use of the freedom that is nowadays customary in international traffic. There are close ties between cells in different countries. Terrorists take up residence as respectable citizens in various countries. They live and work in accordance with the traditions and culture of the country in question. The terrorist cell in Rotterdam is one of the examples.

All these reasons point towards a possible increase in international terrorism in the Netherlands, although in the short term a rise in home-grown terrorism is not expected. There are no great political issues in the Netherlands nowadays. Most political demands are met in one way or another. But in connection with international terrorism, it is possible that some ethnic groups in the Netherlands will turn towards terrorism as soldiers of an international terrorist organization.

Conclusion

Terrorism is not a major problem in the Netherlands. But there are new risks because of its changing nature. The Dutch authorities have to prepare for more intensive terrorism in the future. They can use the experience with other kinds of crises such as natural disasters and rioting to this end.

The combat of terrorism in the Netherlands is set out in regulations only to a limited extent. Organization during terrorist incidents is usually improvised on the basis of previous incidents and the specific terrorist incident. Such a flexible response arguably has its advantages. Nevertheless, organizational forms have meanwhile been established in outline; the implementation of the policy they determine depends on the specific terrorist incident.

It is advisable to create a Terrorism Act in the Netherlands in order to streamline response to terrorist threats organizationally. The responsibilities of all involved authorities have to be described. This chapter argues that at present it is not clear who is responsible in what stage of a terrorism incident. Besides a Terrorism Act, it is crucial that Dutch citizens and authorities are more conscious about the possibility and risk of terrorist attacks in the Netherlands. The Netherlands' vulnerability is great because of its tolerant society. These are great values to the Dutch, but it is necessary to be realistic about the threats to these values. There is no objective reason why the Netherlands will be spared from terrorist attacks in the near future.

10 Swedish Experiences: Countering Violent Networks

Malena Rembe[1]

Introduction

Terrorism has not been a major problem of national security in Sweden. While very small numbers of representatives of various international terrorist groups have stayed in Sweden, they have not caused serious problems there. In addition, Sweden has its domestic groups of the radical 'left' and 'right'. These have mainly operated within the law, although there have been cases of destruction of property and even violence against persons. Meanwhile, the outbursts from certain activists in the margins of the large anti-globalist demonstrations during the Gothenburg EU Summit of 2001, and the strong reactions by Swedish law enforcement, have drawn wide international attention. These incidents cannot be labelled as terrorist, but a concise analysis is nevertheless deemed relevant here, as they have influenced government thinking on security issues in general, and particularly may illustrate the rise of radical networks and the difficulties that law enforcement forces have in fighting them.

The attacks on the United States of 11 September 2001 have made an enormous impact on threat perceptions and policy-making in Sweden. The Swedish government has supported or at least accepted the change from a 'criminal justice' to a 'war-making' model in the international fight against terrorism, following the American example. Proposals for new, expanded legislation and enhanced international investigative and legal cooperation in the 'fight against terrorism' have also been endorsed. Demand for new, more intensive cooperation between law enforcement and the military in the fighting of domestic political violence has been raised. There has also been a sharp rise in

---

1   The author has written this chapter in a strictly private capacity.

M. van Leeuwen (ed.): *Confronting Terrorism*, pp. 165-183
© 2003 Kluwer Law International. Printed in the Netherlands.

sentences of imprisonment pronounced in cases of violent resistance at anti-EU demonstrations. This chapter will analyse these changes and comment upon their potential consequences.

Swedish Experiences with Terrorism

International Groups and Networks with Presence in Sweden

No act of international terrorism has occurred in Sweden over the last decade. Going back a bit further, however, a few examples can be found. Croat activists murdered the Yugoslav ambassador in 1971 and hijacked a domestic flight in 1972. The hijacking resulted in the release of the perpetrators of the embassy murder.[2]

In 1975, two Japanese activists with ties to the Japanese Red Army (JRA) were expelled after preparing an attack on the Libyan embassy. Two other members of the same organization were expelled after planning an attack against Japanese targets in West Germany.[3]

In April 1975 a group of six former mental patients tied to the *Rote Armee Faktion* (RAF) occupied the German Embassy in Stockholm. They demanded the release of RAF leaders imprisoned in West Germany. The occupation ended with two hostages being killed and a number of others, including the terrorists, injured. The terrorists were immediately expelled to West Germany, a decision that the Minister of Justice Anna Greta Leijon might have regretted when 'Operation Leo' was revealed in 1977. According to the plan Minister Leijon was to be kidnapped and exchanged for those who had participated in the embassy occupation.[4]

Two Swedish citizens were arrested in 1980 for attempting to smuggle weapons into Sweden to be used against Israeli targets in Denmark. They also planned to murder the Saudi king. The Swedes received prison sentences while four foreigners connected to the group were expelled to Syria.

A notorious member of Abu Nidal Organization (ANO), who had participated in an attack on a ship in a Greek harbour in 1988, was traced to Sweden where he had lived under a false identity. A large weapons depot was found at his house. It was thought the weapons were to be used against a major airport since the ANO member involved had also been the man in charge of an attack on Israeli targets at an airport in Rome in 1985.[5]

The PKK, *Al-Gamaa al-Islamiya*, GIA, *Mujahedin e-Khalk* (MEK), Hamas and Hizb'allah all have had some presence in Sweden over the last twenty years. Never many in number and not coordinating their aims, these groups were mainly concerned with propaganda, fund-raising and to some extent forging passports. Their presence was never seen as a threat to the Swedish state. Also, given that Sweden generally is not considered the hub of the world, none of these organizations placed their main 'offices' in the country. Generally speaking, Sweden, with a well-organized system of control, may be

---

2   SOU (State Official Report) 1989:104, p. 64; Prop (Governmental proposition to Parliament) 1973:37,
     p. 39.
3   SOU 1989:104, p. 65.
4   Björn Kumm, *Terrorismens historia* (Lund: Historiska Media, 1998), pp. 207-215.
5   Kumm, *Terrorismens historia*, pp. 124-128.

considered a country where it is difficult to perform an attack and then disappear. Additionally, as Secret Service members have pointed out in their regular crime-prevention talks with people suspected of links with terrorist organizations, attacking targets in Sweden would mean immediate loss of sanctuary. And that might imply very harsh treatment for activists and their families upon their forced return to their home countries.[6]

The murder of Olof Palme, Swedish Prime Minister and leader of the Social Democratic Party, on 28 February 1986 shocked Sweden. The case has remained unsolved. Over the years, a number of leads have been followed (PKK, Palestinian activists, foreign agents, right-wing activists, etc.) but the case is still open. A lone actor was charged and sentenced in 1989 but acquitted at higher instance.

In 1998 a key figure within the Swedish GIA branch was arrested in Belgium. After finishing his sentence he was expelled to Sweden. There he became a driving force in an increasingly global Islamist movement connected with the Islamic Front for Jihad and Crusaders (today called al-Qaeda).[7] His name also came up in connection with the American 'war on terrorism' in 2001. Some twenty activists living in Sweden today have visited Islamist camps in Afghanistan and Pakistan. They are experienced in warfare or trained in bomb-making. Swedish passports have also been used within the wider al-Qaeda network. The Swedish Security Service claims to have tied a number of Swedish residents to al-Qaeda, some with very close ties to central figures within the network. According to the Security Service, a new generation of extreme Islamists have grown up in Sweden. Generally well integrated into Swedish society, some have Swedish citizenship. They also, however, have Koran studies in Yemen or Saudi Arabia on their CVs.[8] One Swedish citizen has been detained in the American prison camp in Guantanamo Bay.

Over the last decade, Hizb'allah members have been expelled from Sweden due to alleged connections with terrorist attacks or planning of such. A few members of this organization still live in Sweden, although they have kept a low profile since the expulsions in 1995. The Swedish Security Service has maintained an eye on them, between 1999 and 2000 due to alleged connections with the Security Apparatus run by Imad Mughniye.[9] The EU did not include Hizb'allah or the Security Apparatus on its list of terrorists, which might explain why there is no mentioning of the need to monitor them continuously in the Security Service's *Report* for 2001.

As a consequence of Swedish participation in international cooperation against terrorism, three Swedish citizens of Somali origins had their assets frozen in November 2001 due to alleged links with financing terrorism. The UN's Counter-Terrorism Committee produces the list with individuals and organizations linked to terrorism, on the basis of material primarily provided by the US. However, the Swedish Security Service claimed that the evidence provided as background to the allegation against the three Swedes was not sufficient to prosecute them in a Swedish court. The fate of the three led to an increasingly fierce public debate. Various support groups challenged the sanctions

---

6   SÄPO [*Säkerhetspolisen* or Swedish Security Police], *Verksamhetsåret 1998*, p. 29.
7   SÄPO, *Verksamhetsåret 1998*, p. 28.
8   SÄPO, *Verksamhetsåret 2001*.
9   SÄPO, *Verksamhetsåret 1999* and *Verksamhetsåret 2000*.

by donating money for their upkeep. At the end of January 2002, the Swedish Government was the first to demand changes in the present sanctions list, and called for a public set of criteria for groups and individuals to be listed. In August 2002, two of the three suspects were taken off the American list, after which they could be cleared from the UN and EU lists as well.[10]

Domestic Groups and Networks

THE EXTREME RIGHT

In the mid-1990s a number of smaller groups influenced by extreme right-wing, racist ideologies attracted growing attention in Sweden. With the far-right-wing book *The Turner Diaries* as their Bible, these groups legitimized violence and romanticized terror. Revolutionary music, concerts and magazines promoting the ideas of White Supremacy and White Power have long been the magnets attracting believers. For a number of years these groups, in cooperation or in competition, controlled a vast global business in producing and selling this music. Sweden, together with the UK and the US, had a leading position in this production. According to the Swedish Security Service, the music was the driving force within the movement. Without it the 1990s' growth would not have been possible.[11] Consequently, the Swedish Security Service and other law enforcement agencies have over recent years focused specifically on obstructing this business.

The National Socialist Front (*National Socialistisk Front*, NSF), established in 1994 and based in the south of Sweden, became the leading group within the White Power movement and today has about twenty local groupings. The Front advocates the repatriation of immigrants, national self-sufficiency and governmental race control. Over recent years, the Front, similar to radical Islamic activists, has shifted its focus from national to global perspectives, although still based on the idea of a world run by ZOG (Zionist Occupation Government) and still xenophobic and racist in essence. Despite this, NSF proclaimed itself a political party in 1999. The party programme defined as its goal to 'abolish democracy using democratic means'. In 1998 a member of NSF was arrested trying to smuggle explosives when flying from Stockholm to a local group in the south of Sweden.[12]

Another influential grouping in the White Power environment is the Swedish Resistance Movement (*Svenska Motståndsrörelsen*, SMR/NU). It is racist and preaches violence. Although SMR/NU is mainly concerned with propaganda and recruitment, one of its members participated in the political assassination in 1999 of the syndicalist Björn Söderberg, a vocal critic of the group and the ideology of the White Power movement.[13] In 1999, in connection with the investigations on the above-mentioned murder, a database with photos and addresses of 1,300 persons was found. This database was intended to help White Power followers identify future targets.

---

10 'Två av tre utpekade slipper terroriststämpel', *Dagens Nyheter*, 2002-08-22.
11 SÄPO, *Verksamhetsåret 1995/1996*, introduction by the Head of the Security Service. SÄPO, *Verksamhetsåret 1999*, p. 31.
12 SÄPO, *Verksamhetsåret 1997, 1998*, and *1999*.
13 SÄPO, *Verksamhetsåret 1999*, p. 29.

Intensified and targeted action against these groups since the mid 1990s did not prevent car bomb attacks in 1999 on a journalist and his son and on a policeman; the victims were seriously injured. Two policemen were murdered in a pursuit of bank robbers connected to the White Power movement. During late 1999, leading Swedish newspapers in a joint action published the names and photographs of people belonging to the White Power movement.[14]

The prison organization Aryan Brotherhood (*Ariska Brödraskapet*, AB) was an important feature in the White Power movement in the mid 1990s. AB was a small, violent organization. Membership was granted only to members who had been sentenced to imprisonment for heinous crimes with a political dimension (murder, homicide or arson). Its members called themselves prisoners of war, and in 1997 members took responsibility for sending a letter bomb[15] to Minister of Justice Laila Freivalds.[16]

Many of the members left the movement after the press published their names. Yet new recruits were attracted precisely because of the media attention, so AB's membership remained the same. These movements are not illegal per se according to Swedish Law. However, it is illegal to express or use racist or nazi sympathies or symbols.

THE EXTREME LEFT

The counterpart to the White Supremacy movement is the so-called Autonomous Network. This is a typically 'post-modern' movement: it is a loosely knit network of groupings formed under principles and ideas rather than a strict political agenda. Most of these groupings perform their extra-parliamentary struggle within the law. But within this larger network, individuals and cells can hide a more violent agenda. Ideologically, they gather under ideas of anarchism and syndicalism. All forms of hierarchies are defined as oppression and the state is seen as the primary target. Secondary targets are opponents that are seen as maintaining oppressive structures. Groups or parts of the Autonomous Network have taken part in large-scale destruction of property over the last decade. Over the last couple of years, however, they seem to have gone through a normative shift. They have increasingly armed themselves and have been known to target individuals openly.

An increasingly militant animal rights movement has gained 'prominence' through various extra-parliamentary actions: releasing animals, harassing owners and veterinarians, etc. The release of 20,000 minks in 1998 was the most extensive of its kind and gained world-wide attention.[17] In 1999 four activists were arrested after throwing corrosive acid at the sentry outside a research institute for infectious disease.[18] The animal rights activists, although not necessarily damaging people physically, have created an environment where people have left veterinary positions or given up business due to harassment and threats. The activities in defence of animal rights have decreased considerably over the last years, mainly due to activists changing their focus towards anti-globalism.

---

14   This goes against the Swedish media tradition where names and photographs are not published until after a sentence has been passed.
15   The bomb was not adapted but came with a letter signed from the neo-Nazi movement 'Combat 18'.
16   SÄPO, *Verksamhetsåret 1997*, p. 26.
17   SÄPO, *Verksamhetsåret 1998*, p. 33.
18   SÄPO, *Verksamhetsåret 1999*, p. 33.

AFA AND GOTHENBURG 2001

Perhaps the most influential grouping within the Autonomous Network is Anti-Fascist Action (*Anti-Fascistisk Aktion*, AFA). In 2000 and 2001, the movement changed its focus from confronting the right-wing White Power movement to the struggle against capitalism and the European Union, and specifically prepared for the EU Summit in Gothenburg in June 2001. AFA was seen as the driving force behind the violent events of the large demonstrations that took place in connection with the Summit and the visit of the American President George Bush. Despite long and intense planning and preparation for this action it became clear that the police were not able to handle the large demonstrations nor the well-coordinated actions of the violent cells linked to the larger network.[19]

After hacking into the police communication system, the activists could listen to police communications and disturb and even disinform the police in the field. They coordinated their activities with the help of portable computers and SMS, and could obviously redirect their activities in a much more flexible way than the police. On 14 June 2001, the threat from these groups was perceived to be large enough to justify the use of the National Task Force, which raided a school where foreign activists were suspected to be hiding. This Force had been created in 1991 as an elite police force to be used in cases of hijackings or occupation of houses by terrorists. Critics have suggested that the activities by the police at the time were intended to prevent demonstrations anywhere close to the visiting American president. During the days following 14 June, enormous material damage was caused and a large number of police officers and activists were injured in the rapidly escalating spiral of excessive violence on both sides.

On the evening of 15 June 2001 three demonstrators were shot by the police, something so far unheard of in the context of similar demonstrations that had previously taken place in Seattle, Prague and Sydney. It also came as a shock to most Swedes. Demonstrators in Sweden had not been fired at since soldiers shot political demonstrators in Ådalen in 1931.

If the goal of the violent anti-EU demonstrations was to demoralize rather than to defeat their opponents, they arguably succeeded.

PUBLIC REACTION AND DEBATE TO THE GOTHENBURG EVENTS

Even though law enforcement services had prepared themselves for the EU Summit for over a year and were provided with risk and threat assessments based on previous experiences (both in Sweden and abroad), the lasting impression in Gothenburg still became one of chaos, lack of communication and excessive violence on all sides. It seems that developments in Gothenburg became an unfortunate example of intra-agency competition rather than intra-agency cooperation and open communication with the public.[20] It can also be seen as a striking example of blurred responsibilities due to lack of experience, training, equipment, information and communication (ironically enough a drawback from the low levels of terrorism and political violence that Sweden generally

---

19   Jan Flyghed, 'Policing Protests: Gothenburg June 2001. Have the Police Learnt Lessons, or Will There be a Stronger Response Next Time?', *Statewatch*, vol. 11, no. 6, November-December 2001, pp. 18-20.

20   Erik Magnusson, 'Polischefer i praktgräl innan EU-mötet', *Sydsvenskan*, A7, 21 December 2001.

has).[21] But thirdly, the media played a damaging role by drumming up fear and expectations of violence on all sides.

Until summer 2001 and the riots in Gothenburg, it was generally accepted in Sweden that there is no military solution to counter politically motivated violence. As a direct reaction of what happened in Gothenburg, however, some demands for change were put forward. More police officers and joint task forces of police and military from a number of EU states would be the solution, claimed one prominent journalist and researcher.[22] Another journalist, after reading handbooks of activism produced or spread by the Autonomous Network, exclaimed in an editorial that Sweden now had political terrorism.[23] This alarmist trend was naturally enforced by the horrific attacks in the United States less than three months after the Gothenburg riots. At a seminar at the Stockholm International Peace Research Institute (SIPRI), it was suggested that Sweden needed to look at new forms of organization such as the *Guardia Civil* in Spain or *Carabinieri* in Italy, in order to find models of cooperation between military and law enforcement.[24] Also, the parliamentary inquiry established after the Gothenburg Summit was directed to look, inter alia, into the possibility of using reservist civilians trained for deployment as police in periods of *international* crisis.[25]

On the other hand, activists and an increasing number of academics, journalists and parents reacted strongly to the harsh sentences given after the demonstrations. In appeals, they branded the sentences as political. By consequence, the prisoners were political prisoners as well, they argued. A parents' organization supporting the activists demanded a commission to investigate law enforcement actions taken before, during and especially after the Gothenburg summit.[26] The Swedish High Court ruling in April 2002 that part of the violence was a reaction to police methods rather than a planned strategy of activists, further intensified this debate, especially since the High Court also changed the sentence from twenty months to four months imprisonment. Erik Wijk, journalist and author, has looked into 15 sentences given for violent resistance in connection with the demonstrations at the EU summit in Gothenburg, and concluded that the defendants' political affiliation has been part of the discussion in the passed sentences.[27] Wijk claims that these political affiliations also inspired substantially longer sentences than would have been the case previously. This implied a breach with previous norms.

LESSONS TO BE LEARNED FROM THE GOTHENBURG EVENTS AND THEIR EFFECTS

(1) In Gothenburg, part of the problem has been that accurate threat assessments and intelligence reports provided by the Swedish Security Service were disregarded in the operative planning of the local police.

21　*Kaos: Göteborgs operationen, juni 2001*; and *Utvärdering av EU-kommenderingen i Göteborg, år 2001*.
22　Anders Mellbourn, 'Militär bevakning måste övervägas', *Dagens Nyheter Debatt*, 24 June 2001.
23　Hans Bergstöm, 'Sverige har fått politisk terrorism', *Dagens Nyheter*, 12 August 2001.
24　Stockholm International Peace Resarch Institute, Seminar Report, 23 October 2001.
25　Committee Directive 2001:60, p. 2.
26　Erik Wijk, 'Vart tog vår rätt vägen?', *Aftonbladet Debatt*, 22 December 2001, A-infos (sv) Motkraft, http://www.ainfo.ca/sv/ainfos00317.html. For a full discussion of the subject, see Erik Wijk, *Göteborgs-kravallerna och Processerna* (Stockhom: Manifest 2002).
27　Wijk, Erik, 'Den som bryr sig straffas hårdare', Aftonbladet, 23 March 2002.

(2) From a policing perspective, success is often described as 'getting the bad guys behind bars'. In Sweden this was obtained by the targeted campaign against right-wing activists. In 1993 the entire leadership of White Aryan Resistance was put in jail, but during their stay in prison they organized themselves and improved their IT skills. In jail the earlier-mentioned Aryan Brotherhood was created. With the long sentences for some of the activists in Gothenburg, a similar counter-productive effect might have been created.

(3) The political impact of the large anti-EU or anti-globalization demonstrations has been considerable. It has therefore been suggested that the severity of sentences pronounced in first instance in the case of the Gothenburg riots mark a shift in application of Swedish law that has been caused by explicit or implicit urges put forward by powers within the EU. This suggestion has been strongly rejected by a high official of the Swedish Security Service.[28] It has also been suggested that the sentences could have been the consequence of a collective moral panic among policy makers and local judiciary.[29] The Gothenburg defendants were in any case given less severe sentences in higher instance.

(4) The mere suspicion that the Swedish judiciary could be influenced by current political trends would undermine the very notion of an independent judiciary. The sentences given have (mainly by activists) been described as political, and following this logic the prisoners as political.

Professional Current Threat Assessments and Risk Analysis

The Swedish Security Service is responsible for providing the Swedish government with threat and risk analyses on political violence and terrorism. The Service publishes an annual strategic assessment and provides regular operative assessments to the Swedish Ministry of Justice, the Ministry of Foreign Affairs and the Board of National Police. In order to obtain relevant analysis, the Service increasingly cooperates with agencies and departments nationally and internationally.

In the early 1990s the Swedish Security Service began publishing an *Annual Report* on its activities. This and a yearly report on criminal offences related to Sweden's internal security (i.e. ideologically motivated crimes performed in Sweden) are the open written forums of the agency to describe proactively its perceptions and policies. The Service has become increasingly involved in informing the public and the media, but setting up a public information agency or appointing a spokesperson for the Service seems a distant goal. Media issues are to a large extent dealt with by the head of the Service.

This is understandable in an organization with long traditions of secrecy and that deals with highly classified information. But it has created a situation where the sometimes more moderate threat and risk analyses of the Swedish Security Service are

---

28   Arne Andersson, Deputy Head of the Counter-terrorism Department, SÄPO, in an interview with the
      author on 22 March 2002.
29   Jan Flyghed, 'Rättsakerhet på glid', editorial in *Arbetaren*, no. 47/2001/23/1129/11. For a full discussion
      on moral panic, see Flyghed, *Brottsbekämpning*.

not communicated to the public. This information vacuum is easily filled by 'experts', some of them with little or no relevant knowledge. This was a prevailing feature both during the riots in Gothenburg and immediately after the attacks on 11 September 2001.

It is not in itself a bad thing if journalists, politicians, academics or other researchers formulate threat perceptions. It is, however, important to keep in mind that these groups may also have their own agendas. Thus, with the expected increase in research grants focused on terrorism, the number of terrorism experts in Sweden increased notably directly after the attacks in the United States. Public research on terrorism has been performed by agencies linked to the Swedish Ministry of Defence (Swedish Defence Research Agency (FOI) and National Defence College (*Försvarshögskolan*)) rather than by research departments connected to the police or crime prevention.

As it is sometimes difficult for researchers 'on the outside' to assess actors'/activists' motivations and moreover actual capabilities, and actors 'on the inside' have tended to be vague and unclear on the actual risks, inflated risk scenarios have been circulated at times. Using worst-case scenarios – all-inclusive definitions and experiences taken from completely different contexts – does not provide policy-makers and concerned public with relevant information. It might lead to a waste of resources, rather than to relevant policy changes.

As Sweden also has limited experiences of terrorism, there has been a tendency to analyse risks from the angle of consequences rather than capability and motivation. This is particularly true when it comes to the perceived threat posed by NBC terrorism (terrorism perpetrated with the aid of nuclear, biological or chemical devices).[30]

Legal changes should ideally be based upon thorough and relevant long-term threat and risk analyses, assessments of the effectiveness of existing countermeasures and a safeguarding of the liberties of individuals, i.e. the notion of a democratic state. Only if there is a de facto threat, if current legislation is ineffective and the restrictions on liberties are deemed acceptable, should new legislation be considered. Without a threat or an expected effective countermeasure, changes ought not to be considered.[31]

According to the Swedish Security Service, the democratic values and the Constitution are no more threatened today than one year ago. Nor is the risk of terrorist attacks on Swedish targets higher today than before. The number of international targets with intensified levels of threats (i.e. American, British and Israeli) in Sweden must be described as limited and relatively easy to distinguish and protect. Despite the growing realization that today also Islamists born in Sweden sympathize with the goals and aspirations of Osama bin Laden and his network, the general level of threat from international terrorism is low. Consequently the Swedish Security Service disclaims solid threats against Swedish or other targets in the country in 2001.[32]

---

30 A threat of terrorism is a combined set of features that by themselves do not constitute a risk or a threat. When assessing risks and threats from terrorism or other forms of politically or religiously motivated violence, one initially has to search for actors with *intent*. If these actors are also perceived as having a *capability*, the probability for an act of terrorism of course increases, i.e. there is a *threat*. If there is also some sort of *vulnerability* one can talk of a *probability*, a probability that in combination with negative *consequences* constitutes a *risk*. If there are no (negative) consequences then there is no real risk. More on this subject at http://www.algonet.se/~psand/risk.html.

31 Jan Flyghed, 'Maktens dilemma: Hur reagera lagom?', in Jan Flyghed (ed.), *Brottsbekämpning: mellan effektivitet och integritet* (Lund: Studentlitteratur, 2000), pp. 58-63.

32 SÄPO, *Verksamhetsåret 2001*.

If these threat assessments are valid, one might wonder why there has been such a rush to accept or adhere to legislation that could arguably be seen as undermining the ultimate (and fundamental) goal of countering violent extremism and terrorism?

Legal Framework

The Swedish response to terrorism and other forms of ideologically motivated violence has been based on the criminal justice model. Terrorism has been regarded as a crime and the aim has been to arrest and penalize rather than to eliminate the activists involved. The responsibilities of counter-terrorism rest with law enforcement and the Ministry of Justice rather than with the military and the Ministry of Defence.[33] Swedish law has not known any references to specific criminal offences for terrorist acts or a definition of terrorism. This may rapidly change, however, since in May 2002 the Swedish Parliament passed the EU's Framework on Terrorism, which includes an attempt to define terrorism and to stimulate the harmonization of relevant legislation.

Sweden has a long tradition of participation in international cooperation against terrorism. It has signed and ratified all relevant treaties and conventions but two: the International Convention for the Suppression of the Financing of Terrorism (signed in October 2001 and in the process of being implemented); and the Convention on the Marking of Plastic Explosives for the Purpose of Detection.[34]

Acts that constitute offences within the scope of international criminal law conventions for the suppression of terrorism are classed as crimes in Sweden, and are punishable by up to life imprisonment. By the Swedish Penal Code, preparation or conspiracy to commit any crimes enumerated in the conventions are also – with some limitations – punishable with imprisonment. Persons not regarded as actual perpetrators might still be sentenced for aiding and abetting or inducing crimes within the realm of these international conventions. It is also unlawful to recruit people for military service without the authority of the Swedish government, a legal restriction that would apply to recruitment for terrorism. The Swedish legislation on arms is considered stricter than in most other countries.[35] The legislation in preparation primarily focuses on terms of punishment and is planned to come into effect by the end of 2002.

The above applies to Swedish citizens and requires evidence of a crime being planned or executed. For non-Swedish residents the situation is slightly different. Non-Swedes can become subjected to the Aliens Act or the Act Concerning Special Control with Respect to Aliens (referred to as the Terrorist Law) from 1991.[36] The Aliens Act allows expulsion of a person who has committed crimes and been a resident in the country for less than two years, if it can be expected that he/she will commit terrorist acts

---

33 For a fuller discussion on theoretical models of counter-terrorism, see Ami Pedahzur and Magnus Ranstorp, 'A Tertiary Model for Countering Terrorism in Liberal Democracies: The Case of Israel', *Terrorism and Political Violence*, vol. 13, no. 2, summer 2001, pp. 1-26.
34 *Report by Sweden to the UN to the Counter-Terrorism Committee*, ref. S/2001/1233, 20 December 2001.
35 *Report by Sweden to the UN to the Counter-Terrorism Committee*, ref. S/2001/1233, 20 December 2001.
36 *Utlänningslag* (1989:529) and *Lag om Särskild utlänningskontroll* (1991: 572), respectively. These regulations are not specifically defined to counter-terorrism but apply to, for example, espionage and sabotage as well.

or other forms of serious crime. Local police authorities or the authority in charge of immigration decide on expulsion according to the Aliens Act and these decisions can be appealed, even if the reason for expulsion is terrorism. If it concerns an expulsion based on arguments of state security, the Swedish government decides.

When these rules do not apply, the Act concerning Special Control with Respect to Aliens does. This law regulates the expulsion of a non-Swedish citizen *suspected* of planning crimes that include violence, threat of violence or force for political purposes in Sweden *or elsewhere*. In other words, it can be used for preventive purposes. Its conditions ruling surveillance are also less restricted than those concerning a Swedish citizen, and can be used for preventive purposes. Application of this law does not require membership of an illegal (terrorist) organization. Each case is based on an individual risk assessment made by the Swedish Security Service.[37] Decision on expulsion based on the 'Terrorist Law' is taken by the Swedish government, and a decision to expel a person based on this Law cannot be appealed. Both laws became subject to revision, partly to meet criticisms raised.

With the application of the EU-framework against terrorism, the discrepancy in legal standing between Swedes and non-Swedes has been adjusted. Charges and definitions of terrorism now apply regardless of nationality. Critics consider this an ironical advantage of legislative changes they otherwise wholeheartedly oppose.

Sweden does not as a rule expel a person if there is a risk that this person will suffer physical punishment, torture, persecution or threat to his/her life. In cases where expulsion cannot take place due to the above, the person in question could be ordered to report on a regular basis. In these cases the Swedish Security Service can also obtain permission to monitor the suspect with the help of surveillance (renewed on a monthly basis if suspicion remains and the crime is punishable for more than two years).

The 'Terrorist Law' has been criticized for violating conventions on human rights, discriminating against foreigners. Moreover, given that the investigations behind application of the Law's regulations are classified and there is no possibility to appeal, the regulations have also been criticized for lack of parliamentary transparency.[38] Without a comprehensive analysis it is impossible to say whether suggestions that the law is subject to political considerations and selective application are valid. However, it is remarkable that this critique is similar to the one regarding a number of political and legal developments in the wake of the attacks in September 2001.

In this context it should be noticed that the Swedish report to the UN Counter-terrorism Committee on 20 December 2001 underlined that '[P]ersons who risk capital punishment or torture or other inhuman or degrading treatment or punishment may never be returned to their country of origin or another country where they would be exposed to such a risk'.[39] Yet also in December 2001 two Islamists were expelled from Sweden to their country of origin, Egypt, where they were alleged to be members of terrorist organizations. Egypt, of course, adheres to the death penalty as a legal punishment and

---

37   Antonia Ribbing, 'Sveriges terroristbestämmelser: Brottsprevention och demokratiska rättsideal', in Flyghed, *Brottsbekämpning*, pp. 114-146.
38   Ribbing, 'Sveriges terroristbestämmelser', pp. 114-146.
39   *Report by Sweden to the UN to the Counter-Terrorism Committee*, ref. S/2001/1233, 20 December 2001.

Egypt has previously complained that political dissidents are given asylum in Sweden, from where they are able to continue to spread their ideological message.

The expulsion, which was criticized by Amnesty International, could be seen as a consequence of Swedish participation in the global alliance to fight terrorism, an alliance that also includes states not primarily recognized for their allegiance to democracy and rule of law. Part of the shift in Swedish policies concerning acceptable means to counter extremism and terrorism has its origins outside Swedish borders. The formulation of counter-terrorism policies has increasingly been transferred from the national to the international level, and Sweden, being a member of the EU and the UN, would have a difficult time pursuing an independent policy.

Questions have, however, been raised over the long-term consequences of this development, particularly regarding the speed with which new legislation has been introduced. The Secretary General of the Swedish Law Association, Ann Ramberg, has repeatedly warned that some of the new regulations might be unconstitutional and pointed to the fact that Sweden has left it to the EU to define the needed changes with respect to fulfilment of UN resolutions – a strange policy since the European Union is not a member of the UN. The Swedish Law Association is also critical of the wide definition of terrorism used by the EU, fearing that it could lead to increases in outlawing organizations and groups. Decisions taken in May 2002 to expand the EU's terrorist list justify this fear. Through the European arrest warrant, where the country asking for extradition also has the right to define the crime, and bearing in mind different legal and political cultures prevailing among EU countries, activities that are not considered a crime in Sweden could be the basis for expulsion to another EU member state. Furthermore, Sweden would lose its right to try the evidence before responding to demands[40] (similar to the UN regulation regarding freezing of assets in line with UN Resolution 1373).

Other leading specialists in the field of crime prevention or law have voiced similar concerns. Erik Östberg, a former prosecutor at the War Crimes Tribunal for former Yugoslavia in The Hague, suggested that the Swedish government should have attempted to slow down the process in order to guarantee a rule of law,[41] while a scholar in the field of criminology warned that basic civil rights would be consumed by spreading moral panic.[42]

A former Swedish Prime Minister has argued that the attacks against the US should be seen as a consequence of unequal power relations in the world today and that more work most go into peaceful struggle against the roots of terrorism. In the same article it was also stressed that the issue of guilt should be tried in an international criminal court.[43] Other former officials have, in their critique of the support for the American right to self-defence and military strategy against terrorism, gone as far as to argue that Sweden with

---

40   Anne Ramberg, *Dagens Nyheter Debatt*, 16 April 2002; and telephone interview with the author on 2 May 2002.
41   Eric Östberg in an interview with Swedish National Radio on 26 January 2002.
42   Jan Flyghed, 'Rättsakerhet på glid', editorial in *Arbetaren*, no. 47/2001/23/1129/11. For a full discussion on moral panic, see Flyghed, *Brottsbekämpning.*
43   Ingvar Carlsson (former Swedish Prime Minister) and Carl Tham (former Minister of Education), *Dagens Nyheter Debatt*, 22 September 2002.

this support must also be regarded as at war.[44] This harsh statement disregarded, there seems to be a widening gap in Sweden between the policy of combating extremism and terrorism internationally and how this work is actually organized on the national level in Sweden.

Organization of Counter-terrorism

Law Enforcement in Sweden is organized under the National Board of Police. Under a formal leadership appointed by the Swedish government, three agencies work: *Säkerhetspolisen* (SÄPO); *Rikskriminalpolisen* (NCID); and *Statens kriminaltekniska laboratorium* (SKL). Twenty-one relatively independent authorities are responsible for police work at the local level. In 1991 the *Nationella Instatsstyrkan* (NI) was created as an elite force to be used in extreme situations. It was argued that with the increase in international terrorism (where hijackings and hostage-taking was modus operandi) and Swedish adherence to international cooperation against terrorism, there was a need for special troops (or other countries would be inclined to send theirs to Swedish territory). However, as there were few instances where the special force could be used, it was eventually argued that its mandate should be expanded to include situations not connected to terrorism, something that the criminologist Jan Flyghed warns is a normalization of the exceptional.[45] After Gothenburg, it was suggested that this force should be put under a central command instead of, as previously, under local police authorities.

The Swedish Security Service has prime responsibility for counter-terrorism and protection of the Constitution. The Service takes orders and guidelines from the Ministry of Justice and its work is regulated in the Police Act of 1984, *Säkerhetsskyddslagen* (1996:627) and *Säkerhetsskyddsförordningen* (1996:633). With a staff of around 800 the Security Service is an independent authority within the Swedish National Police Board. The Security Service mainly focuses on prevention and early detection but it also has executive powers. The Swedish Migration Board and the Aliens Appeals Board can, with the help of assessments from the Security Service, make decisions in asylum matters to hinder potential terrorists from gaining access to or residence in Sweden.

NCID is responsible for liaison with Europol in Sweden. However, it has no mandate to work with counter-terrorism as this rests with the Security Service. Legally, Europol's work in most parts overrides national legislation, but the Security Service argues that it is bound by the National Secrecy Act and therefore cannot share intelligence information. This is a stance with bearing on the Europol Convention, which specifies that a member is not obliged to hand over information if this could harm national integrity or safety of individuals, or jeopardize current investigations.[46] The Service also argues that it cannot hand over operative intelligence information since that would breach the golden rule of intelligence cooperation: no third-party dissemination without the consent of the providing government. Such a breach would threaten the Service's long tradition of

---

44 Ambassador Sverker Åström, 'Ingen bryr sig om att Sverige är i krig', *Dagens Nyheter Debatt*, 14 April 2002.
45 For a full discussion on this subject, see Flyghed, *Brottsbekämpning*.
46 Europol Convention 1995, Title 1, Article 4, para. 5.

bilateral or multilateral cooperation with other security and intelligence services, particularly western and more particularly European. Furthermore, the Service argues that it is difficult to have full cooperation with an 'open' organization such as Europol. So from the perspective of the Security Service, Europol's involvement in counter-terrorism is more a political construction that consumes resources than a practical help in its counter-terrorism work.[47]

There is no indication that suggested changes in legislation will solve this dilemma. Instead, a catch-22 situation continues, where Europol will not receive material to analyse and the Security Service can argue that Europol does not add value to counter-terrorism work.

So far, despite the realization that the threat has changed considerably, no genuine changes towards 'more effective inter-agency approaches' can be seen in Sweden. A merger between the Swedish Security Service and the Swedish NCID has been suggested in order to meet tomorrow's threat, but this suggestion (lacking purpose, means and consequence analysis) was eventually changed into the two agencies finding methods to cooperate more intensely.

The budget of both the Swedish Security Service and the 'ordinary' police has recently grown compared with previous years. The real increase will, however, be limited by a number of factors. The year 2001, with the summit in Gothenburg and the attacks on 11 September, badly strained resources. Increased international cooperation in the wake of 11 September also means that two-thirds of the manpower of the Department of Counter-terrorism today has to be focused on answering queries from other countries, Europol and the UN rather than proactively investigating and analysing current and potential risks and threats.

Meanwhile, the role for the Swedish military has changed profoundly since the end of the Cold War. As stated earlier, there has been solid opposition against using the military in or for police work. However, a slow shift has been taking place over the last decade. There is no longer a risk of military invention so the military has been restructured and is focusing more on the protection of civilians and infrastructure than on actual warfare. The Swedish defence forces have also had their mandate slightly enlarged due to these changes. A new agency has been created under the Ministry of Defence specifically to coordinate crisis management and contingency planning in times of emergencies (for example, caused by terrorist attacks).[48] Executive powers, however, still rest with the law enforcement and have been strictly regulated by law where help from the military is to be used.[49]

The committee in charge of preparing Swedish defence policies (*Försvarsberedningen*) suggested in 2001 in a report that the necessary changes in formulations and regulations be undertaken so that defence resources could also be used to protect Swedish society in peacetime.[50] With a wider definition of national security, however, and as the Swedish defence forces send soldiers to areas of conflict as international peace-keeping forces, there will increasingly be a need for intelligence

---

47   Author's interview with Arne Andersson, Deputy Head of Counter-terrorism Department, SÄPO, 22 March 2002.
48   Comittee for contingency planning, Ministry of Defence (F2001:04).
49   For a full overview on these regulations, see SOU 2001:98, *Stöd från Försvarsmakten*.
50   *Försvarsberedningen*, Ds 2001: p. 21.

reports going from the Swedish Security Service to the military, something that would challenge the strict division between police and the military regarding terrorism and extremism.

One way to overcome the barrier between police and the military was the creation of a national forum for coordination of intelligence (*Regeringskansliets samordnings-sekretariat för säkerhetspolitiska underrättelsefrågor*, SUND). As this new organization, which works directly for the Swedish government's office but is placed organizationally under the Swedish Ministry of Defence, gains more influence and weight it will affect the work of the Swedish Security Service.

It seems increasingly evident that new forms of organizational cooperation are needed, both between different law enforcement agencies and between these agencies and the Swedish armed forces. However, given the comparatively low threat that politically motivated violence still poses in the Swedish context, it is hard to see why such radical methods as forming paramilitary policing units should be needed. It has, rather, been argued that creating a defence for society by giving priority to identifying and minimizing vulnerabilities would be a more effective role for the Swedish armed forces than a higher degree of military deterrent.[51]

Networks and How (Not) to Deal with Them: Swedish Experiences and Possible Lessons to Learn

Networks: New Challenges from New Structures

While limited in experiences of terrorism, Sweden – with a rather flat sociopolitical society and early promotion of IT skills – has already for some time seen the dark side of the cherished corporate model of networking. Extremist activists in Sweden have on the whole become more networked in structure – whether in small and closed, or open and loosely knit structures. Their ideologies are less clear-cut than they used to be. Their party programmes and agendas of the 1970s and 1980s have given way to gathering under an umbrella of principles (or a least common denominators) and general consensus rather than a predefined political agenda. Most of them have fewer (or no) obvious leaders and membership is more flexible and floating. There is also a higher degree of cooperation among different networks so that expert knowledge in one can be used by another. The networks or interconnected nodes[52] often communicate and carry references from a global arena, be that of various Islamist, racist or anti-capitalist origins.

With the use of information technology (internet, encrypted email, SMS, etc.), terrorists and extremists today have gained global strengths previously held only by structures with large assets. They communicate world-wide and can at low cost exchange experiences, coordinate actions or attacks, spread ideas, recruit new members and in real-time adapt to changes in their environment. As Manuel Castells has aptly noted, 'as long

---

51 Bengt Sundelius, Professor in Political Science and leader of the Centre for Crisis Management Studies at the Swedish National Defence College, *Dagens Nyheter Debatt*, 20 July 2001.
52 For a full discussion on what constitutes and caracterizes a network, see Manuel Castells, *The Rise of the Network Society* (Oxford: Blackwell, 1999), pp. 470 ff.

as they share the same communication codes (for example, values or performance goals)' they are able to expand without limits.[53] Actors today do not have to meet physically in order to be used as an asset for the network. A feature that is seen is the increasing use of 'experts' utilized for special assignments, be these bomb-making or hacking into police communication systems.

To a large extent, extremists in Sweden, be they nationally or internationally rooted, seem to fit many of the characteristics of Netwar as put forward by Arquilla, Ronfeldt and Zanini,[54] who conclude that he who masters the network model first and best will gain major advantages.[55] They sum up as follows:

- Hierarchies have a difficult time fighting networks;
- It takes networks to fight networks;
- Whoever masters the network form first and best will gain major advantages;
- Therefore it will take more effective inter-agency approaches in more networked structures to fight radical or extremist networks.[56]

It is important to emphasize that Netwar in this definition can be performed by activists that reject violence as part of their struggle, so inclusion of, for example, anti-globalist movements in this chapter does not mean to say that they are or should be defined as terrorists. They are included in this discussion since they exemplify a trend with consequences, also for countries facing serious threats from terrorism.

These changes do not constitute an increased threat because groups are becoming more fanatical and ruthless. Nor are they related to their *motivation* for the use of violent struggle. Instead, the primary change among extreme movements in Sweden relates to their *organizational* structure becoming more networked and less hierarchical in structure.

The emergence of the networking model has put new demands on law enforcement, in analysis, in organization and in cooperation. The Swedish context might therefore also serve as an illustration of the difficulties that hierarchical, competitive, albeit competent law enforcement agencies face when trying to counter violence from actors organized in this way. These difficulties were noticed early in Sweden, but also seem to exist for law enforcement agencies facing much graver threats than their Swedish colleagues.

New Environment, New Maps: Need for New Analysis?

Rather than further expanded countermeasures and the use of the military or more advanced surveillance equipment, it is perhaps new analytical methods that are needed. Analysing these network structures is different from analysing hierarchical, small, defined and more static structures. It is not necessarily a priority in a network to identify

---

53 Castells, *The Rise of the Network Society*, p. 470.
54 John Arquilla, David Ronfeldt and Michele Zanini, 'Networks, Netwar, and Information Age Terrorism', in Ian Lesser *et al.*, *Countering the New Terrorism* (Santa Monica CA: RAND, 1999), pp. 39-84.
55 Arquilla, Ronfeldt and Zanini, 'Networks, Netwar, and Information Age Terrorism', p. 55.
56 Arquilla, Ronfeldt and Zanini, 'Networks, Netwar, and Information Age Terrorism', pp. 55-56.

and isolate the leader, but more important to identify the actors or nodes that are absolutely *crucial* in maintaining and driving the network further. It is also important to recognize that key figures at one time are not necessarily the most important for the network in a longer perspective.[57] For example the activists charged with constructing the central communication command for activists in Gothenburg did not function as key actors in the movement despite being vital for the actions taken at the time. So locking them up does not necessarily affect the ability of the network to continue its activities.

If a network has loose ties and decentralized leadership, it is often considered to be weak. Yet this is only half-true. For where a centralized, tight network is strong in trust, loyalty and continuity, it also seems to lose out on motivation, creativity and innovation. In order to identify triggers for change within these networks, especially when it comes to the use of violence, it is important to look at the norms within the network. How is the need for violence legitimized? What may make a movement accept more violence in the struggle? Finally, what methods of sanctions are used against participants breaching the norms? And, of course, since a network is dependent upon communication, it is important to appraise its complexity, i.e. the grade of intensity and quality of the contacts and communication of the network.[58]

Instead of network analysis, the tendency seems to have been – in Sweden as elsewhere – to 'hierarchify' the organizational structures of ideologically motivated violent actors. In order to make them fit previous notions (and the organization of law enforcement or the military), mirror images of hierarchy are applied to these networks: a cognitive process where triangular-shaped blocks are pressed into circular holes. Law enforcement agencies thus run the risk of a) disregarding information that does not fit into the triangular model, b) not being able to identify crucial information, and c) becoming drowned in an information overload. When this is the case it is not relevant how many well-placed informants the agencies have to work with, or how good the techniques for interception or wire tapping are. When the analytical model is outdated, the analysis will be inaccurate.

Conclusions

Sweden's participation in the international community and the EU brings with it that its freedom to choose and define counter-terrorism policies on the basis of national threat perception has been considerably reduced.

The way in which a number of collective measures have been implemented during the last year (enhanced national and international cooperation, a joint EU definition of terrorism, lists of suspected terrorists and resolutions) has shown an amazing flexibility, speed, adaptability and ability to cooperate beyond national boundaries. Reforms and decisions that would normally have taken months and years, this time instead took hours, days and weeks.

---

57 For an extensive discussion on this subjectm, see Live Fyrand, *Sosialt Nettverk* (Oslo: TANO AS, 1998); and Kripos, Okokrim, POT and Oslo politidistrikt, *Et Nettverksprojekt: 'Nettverksperspektivet fra ulike vinkler'*, report from the Norwegian Cooperation Group, December 2000.

58 Kripos, Okokrim, POT and Oslo politidistrikt, *Et Nettverksprojekt*, pp. 9-13 and 25-27.

A positive reading of these developments would be that decision-makers have come to realize that new, flatter forms are needed to counter today's and tomorrow's threats. Unfortunately, little indicates that this is actually the outcome of the 'new' cooperation within the EU and within the global coalition against terror. Instead, it seems that the flexibility and speed are better explained by a wish to be seen to belong to the 'right' side. Unfortunately, reflection and analysis may get lost in the process. Worst of all, the international cooperation seems to be based on a hierarchical competitive system where one party is defining the aim, the threats and the means and those not in agreement with all three are considered against. As has been argued above, this is not the best way to fight networks.

The much-needed reflection over the events in Gothenburg was, especially after the events in the US, overtaken by calls for quick fixes and re-establishment of order and control. It seems that a shift has taken place, not so much based on *actual* increases in national threat levels. Instead, a *perceived* level of threat (based on worst-case scenarios and mirror-imaging of contexts such as that of the US) has cleared the way for the acceptance of methods previously unacceptable in a Swedish notion of effective counter-terrorism.

This development might have caused democratic values to be smothered in expanded legislation, slacker criteria for evidence, and selective application of the law. The current changes evolved in a perceived threat situation. Under different circumstances, they might have been introduced as temporary emergency legislation. This, limited, safeguard has not been used this time. Debate, reflection, and voiced concerns over threats to constitutional values have indeed increased on the national level. They may, however, have come too late, given that parliamentary decisions tend to be hard to reverse.

If citizens see the new measures as too harsh, too wide in scope and too narrow on the liberties and integrity of individuals, there is a possibility that these measures, rather than creating stability and peace, will nourish a counter-reaction. The growing support for people in Sweden who have had their assets frozen and for activists sentenced for activities in relation to the EU Summit, could be interpreted as early (non-threatening!) signs of this.

Taking this argument further still, new regulations and a harder line from prosecutors may incite rather than deter terrorism and extremism. If the new legislation is seen – as current debate in Sweden implies – as undermining or even suspending constitutional safeguards, groups and networks of activists may be created that choose violence less out of a tactical and strategic choice than out of anger.

A better way to approach the issue of effective counter-terrorism would be to improve intelligence analysis (not so much by collecting more and more data, but by interpreting relevant data in an adequate fashion), to demolish impediments to the necessary flows of information between involved agencies, and to sensitize decision-makers to the fact that they need to make use of analysis and intelligence information.

The Swedish experience has shown with chilling clearness that there is a price to be paid for not being able to solve intra- and inter-agency rivalry within law enforcement. Lack of communication among law enforcement agencies, it should be noted, is not unique to Sweden.

Finally, none of these measures reflects the actual roots of terrorism and extremism, so the current road might not be the way best to maintain the fundamental goal of counter-terrorism work, which is to protect democracy and human rights.

11 The EU Counter-Terrorism Wave: Window of Opportunity or Profound Policy Transformation?

Monica den Boer[1]

Introduction

Experiences with terrorism in European countries have traditionally mainly – although not solely – been of the 'domestic' type. As a consequence, governments by and large have approached anti-terrorist policies from a national perspective. Yet in the past decade, the general focus has gradually shifted to international and/or imported terrorism. Developing an EU policy against terrorism has therefore become more relevant. Generally speaking, member states of the European Union are under pressure to achieve a balance between preservation of their own national policies and laws and progress towards a harmonization of laws, politics and policies, and this is particularly true with regard to security issues. It is far from certain that the EU will ever arrive at a fully harmonized horizontal strategy against terrorism.

Analysis of the EU anti-terrorism strategy is focused on three elements. Firstly, EU member states have sought to mobilize their efforts against terrorism despite the heterogeneity of their experiences. Ironically, this has become both a binding and a divisive issue. Secondly, and strongly as a result of the impact of the 11 September 2001 attacks, EU efforts in the struggle against terrorism are no longer isolated from US influence on internal security policy. Thirdly, a gradual but inevitable merging between internal and external security is taking place.

---

1   This chapter was written on a purely personal basis.

M. van Leeuwen (ed.): *Confronting Terrorism*, pp. 185-206
© 2003 Kluwer Law International. Printed in the Netherlands.

After a short history of anti-terrorism efforts within the EU, this chapter will analyse the current EU strategy against terrorism in four respects: issues concerning the definition of terrorism; the mobilization of intra-European and transatlantic coalitions; the pursuance of the legal harmonization agenda; and the rapid expansion of institutional capacity within the EU. The chapter will conclude with an (early) assessment of the EU's potential effectiveness of its anti-terrorism efforts, and its impact on fundamental rights and democratic standards.

Terrorism and Anti-Terrorism in the EU: Experiences, Perceptions and Paradoxes

Overcoming the Heterogeneity of Experience

The EU member states' experiences with terrorism have been strikingly heterogeneous, as is illustrated by the various chapters in this book. Counter-terrorism strategies have also varied in priority-setting, available resources and methodologies. Thus Germany responded to the *Rote Armee Faktion* by staging large-scale data-gathering operations, while Italy attempted to undermine the Red Brigades by extensive anti-terrorist legislation.[2] Moreover, national legislation does not always define terrorism and acts of terrorism: only Spain, France, the United Kingdom and Portugal have adopted a definition in their legislation, and the German and Italian laws merely mention terrorist organizations or groups. Also the scale of punishments, the specific investigation provisions and the courts responsible vary enormously.[3]

The long predominant 'domestic' type of terrorism in Europe, focused on nationalist or ethnic grievances, is still a major problem in a country like Spain. Within the EU, Spain has been pleading for international attention to this phenomenon, which has been defined as 'internal security'. Yet especially with the progress in the Northern Irish 'peace process', domestic terrorism in its pure form has become relatively rare. The same is true of home-grown ideologically inspired terrorism. The Italian Red Brigades have been inactivated, although the recent murder of Biagi may imply a resurgence of the Red Brigades. Similar observations apply, for instance, to the *Rote Armee Faktion* in Germany, and the *Action Directe* in France, which are rarely heard of anymore.[4]

The question now presents itself of whether a new Europe-wide trend is emerging: whether international terrorist organizations or networks of foreign origin are gradually settling or even taking root in European countries. We may think especially of the surfacing of 'Islamic fundamentalism' in France and other countries.[5]

---

2   Bruce Hoffmann and Jennifer Morrison-Taw, 'A Strategic Framework for Countering Terrorism', in Fernando Reinares (ed.), *European Democracies against Terrorism* (London: Ashgate, 2000), pp. 3-29, on p. 16.

3   European Parliament, *Report on the Role of the European Union in Combating Terrorism* (2001/2016(INI)), A5-0273/2001 final, Committee on Citizens' Freedoms and Rights, Justice and Home Affairs, Rapporteur Graham Watson, 12 July 2001.

4   For a concise overview, see also Cyrille Fijnaut, 'De aanslagen van 11 september 2001 en de reactie van de Europese Unie', *Justitiële Verkenningen*, 2002.

5   *Groupe Islamique Armée* (GIA), which performed bomb attacks in the Paris underground.

Although terrorists have not so far targeted EU institutions, at least according to public sources, following the events on 11 September 2001 the protection of EU VIPs and buildings has increased. Fears about terrorism and war clearly rose after 11 September, as 86 per cent of Europeans say that they personally fear terrorism (+12 percentage points compared with a barometer survey a year earlier). Moreover, at the time when the survey was carried out (between 13 and 23 November 2001), one European out of five said that they 'certainly' expected terrorist attacks. Nine Europeans out of ten thought that it was 'essential' or 'necessary' to improve European cooperation between the police and judicial authorities. The results of the survey also show the clear distinction drawn by Europeans between terrorist acts and the Muslim and Arab communities. Over 85 per cent of Europeans agreed that the Arab world could not be judged on the basis of terrorist acts committed by a few individuals.[6]

The History of Anti-Terrorism within the EU (1975 until 11 September 2001)

Anti-terrorism: At the Roots of EU Justice and Home Affairs Cooperation

Terrorism within the European Union has traditionally had to compete for attention with other international security issues such as drug-trafficking, organized crime and illegal immigration.

The concern about *domestic* terrorism brought European Home Affairs Ministers together in 1975. The first EC-wide initiatives in the field of internal security were taken in the context of European Political Cooperation.[7] The European Council created the Trevi group as a framework for internal security cooperation, particularly against terrorism. The scope of the Trevi activities gradually expanded and eventually included football hooliganism, illegal immigration, organized crime, and preparations for the establishment of the area for free movement of people. By the end of the Trevi era, a Europol project team was set up. Activities decided within the Trevi framework were supervised by senior officials from the (then) twelve interior ministries, and by Working Group meetings. A resolution of member governments of 29 June 1976 stated Trevi's objectives as: cooperation in the fight against terrorism; exchange of information about terrorist organizations; and the equipment and training of police organizations, in particular in anti-terrorist tactics.[8] The first Working Group, created in 1977, carried responsibility for anti-terrorism, exchanges of information and intelligence, and the security aspects of air traffic, nuclear installations and cross-border transport. Its mandate was widened in 1985.[9] By creating interdependency in the fight against terrorism, the

---

6   See http://europa.eu.int/comm/dg10/epo/flash/fl114_ip_en.html.
7   Malcolm Anderson, Monica den Boer and Gary Miller, 'European Citizenship and Cooperation in Justice and Home Affairs', in Andrew Duff, John Pinder and Roy Price (eds), *Maastricht and Beyond* (London and New York: Routledge, 1994), pp. 104-122, on p. 113.
8   Monica den Boer and William Wallace, 'Justice and Home Affairs: Integration through Incrementalism?', chapter 18 in Helen Wallace and William Wallace, *Policy-Making in the European Union* (Oxford: Oxford University Press, 2000), pp. 493-518, on p. 494.
9   Den Boer and Wallace, 'Justice and Home Affairs', p. 494.

contours of a nascent European police force were drawn: *'C'est l'euroterrorisme qui sert de justification à la coopération européenne des polices'.*[10]

The Insertion of Anti-terrorism in the EU Treaties

By the time that the Maastricht Treaty was signed, the issue of terrorism had been returned to the back-boiler. The scope of cooperation outlined in Article K.1 of the Maastricht Treaty comprehensive, embracing almost all aspects of national security policy.[11] Terrorism was merely mentioned in the context of Article K.1 (9), concerning 'police cooperation for the purpose of preventing and combating *terrorism*, unlawful drug trafficking and other serious forms of international crime...' [author's emphasis].

The Amsterdam Treaty on European Union, signed on 1 October 1997 and in force on 1 May 1999, raised the visibility of terrorism slightly by declaring – in Title VI, Article 29 – that the objective of the Provisions on Police and Judicial Cooperation in Criminal Matters 'shall be achieved by preventing and combating crime, organized or otherwise, *in particular terrorism*, trafficking in persons and offences against children...' [author's emphasis]. The Nice Treaty on European Union, signed in December 2000 but not yet fully ratified, follows the same line.

Until today, the fight about terrorism has been a 'Third Pillar' issue, which implies that it is subsumed in one of the two intergovernmental areas of cooperation. The artificial distinction between communitarian and intergovernmental cooperation has several administrative drawbacks. The EU response to the events of 11 September 2001 revealed that anti-terrorism is increasingly seen as a 'horizontal' policy issue. As long as anti-terrorism is predominantly an intergovernmental matter, however, neither the European Commission nor the European Parliament have a firm grip on policy-making in this area.

Recent EU Performance on Anti-terrorism Efforts

Ironically, the European Parliament issued recommendations about the EU fight against terrorism only a week prior to the attacks in the US.[12] It regretted the EU's slowness in responding to 'the' terrorist threat. It recommended preventive measures and called on the European Council to adopt a framework decision 'with a view to approximating legislative provisions establishing minimum rules at European level relating to the constituent elements of criminal acts and to penalties in the field of terrorism; a framework decision aimed at legislative harmonization (...) and adopting the principle of mutual recognition of decisions on criminal matters, including pre-judgment decisions,

---

10 Daniel Hermant and Didier Bigo, 'Les Politiques de Lutte contre le Terrorisme: Enjeux Français', in Fernando Reinares (ed.), *European Democracies against Terrorism* (London: Ashgate, 2000), pp. 73-118, on p. 93.
11 Anderson, den Boer and Miller, 'European Citizenship and Cooperation in Justice and Home Affairs', p. 115.
12 *European Parliament Recommendation on the Role of the European Union in Combating Terrorism* (2001/2016(INI)).

relating to terrorist offences; a framework decision establishing measures governing and guaranteeing the implementation of a "European search and arrest warrant" with a view to combating terrorism in the context of action against crime (...); and to adopt the appropriate legal instruments for the approximation of national legislation concerning the compensation of victims of terrorist crimes'.

The visibility and implementation of legal instruments in the fight against terrorism have thus far been limited, as the two EU extradition conventions of 1995 and 1996[13] have not been ratified,[14] a fate shared with most intergovernmental legal instruments adopted by the EU's Justice and Home Affairs Council and an impediment to effective implementation.

Anti-terrorism Efforts within the EU after 'Nine-Eleven'

Some characterize the weeks between 20 September 2001 and 19 October 2001 as the 'month of transformation'.[15] The events on 11 September 2001 have accelerated decision-making about terrorism in particular and justice and home affairs (JHA) in general beyond belief. Within one month of the terrorist attacks in the United States, several EU meetings were convened, including an Extraordinary Council on 21 September 2001. Several groups and institutions saw their mandate widened: the Task Force of Chiefs of Police, for instance, was charged with building a US liaison contact; Europol had to be linked to the Police Chiefs and a team of counter-terrorist officers was to be established within Europol without delay. The acceleration of the legislation process may entail that badly drafted *ad hoc* decisions made in the context of the Third Pillar 'feed out' into the EU (see table 1 for a chronology of decision-making).

As a prominent advocate of the EU's effort against terrorism, the Spanish Presidency of the EU (from 1 January-30 June 2002) took a dominant lead in implementing the EU's anti-terrorism agenda. Its priority programme[16] put 'combating terrorism in an area of freedom, security and justice' first in a list of six, before the introduction of the euro, EU enlargement and other important matters. The programme's introduction called the EU's future fragile '...with the emergence of new transnational challenges and dangers such as terrorism and organized crime...'. The only answer to this, the Spanish Presidency maintained, was 'wholehearted multilateral cooperation and adjustment of the cooperation mechanisms of international organizations, including the European Union itself.' Moreover, the Spanish Presidency wished to reinforce the external security dimension of the fight against terrorism, and re-emphasized the importance of the Atlantic alliance.

---

13 These were ratified by only nine and eight member states respectively.
14 The Justice and Home Affairs (JHA) Council, in its *Conclusions* of 20 September 2001, even urged EU member states to take all the necessary steps for the two conventions on extradition to enter into force on 1 January 2002 (SN 3926/6/01 REV 6).
15 Elspeth Guild and Didier Bigo, CEPS-JHA conference, Brussels 7-8 December 2001, mimeo.
16 See http://www.ue2002.es/principal.asp?idioma=ingles.

Table 1 *Chronology of salient decision-making moments within the EU after
11 September 2001*

Date	Meeting/Forum	Decision(s)
20 September 2001	JHA Council	General anti-terrorism plan in Council *Conclusions*,[17] consisting of several measures including the creation of a special anti-terrorist unit at Europol; request to member states to reinforce their external border controls[18]
20 September 2001	Solana	Joint EU-US statement on terrorism
21 September 2001	EU Extraordinary Council[19]	EU-wide search and arrest warrant to be adopted; new extradition procedures; agreement on data-sharing; more prominent role for Europol and Eurojust
26/27 September 2001	JHA Council	Anti-terrorism roadmap[20]
4 October 2001	European Parliament	Vote on European Council of 21 September 2001: 431 votes in favour; 45 against; 24 abstentions
16 October 2001	JHA/ECOFIN Council	Political agreement about the revised EU Money Laundering Directive
17 October 2001	General Affairs Council and European Commission	*Conclusions*; General description of EU action after the events on 11 September 2001 and evaluation of their possible economic impact[21]
19 October 2001	European Council	Declaration[22]
16 November 2001	JHA Council	Political agreement about list of offences appended to European arrest warrant, with the exception of the Italian delegation[23]
6 and 7 December 2001	JHA Council[24]	Momentum for adoption of the Framework Decision on the European Arrest Warrant and Framework Decision on Terrorism; adoption of anti-terrorism road map[25]

17 JHA Council Conclusions, SN 3926/6/01, REV 6.
18 Objective 41, doc. 12759/01; JHA Council *Conclusions* of 20 September 2001, SN 3926/6/01 REV 6.
19 See http://europa.eu.int/comm/external_relations/cfsp/doc/concl_21_09_01.htm.
20 SN 4019/01, revised SN 4019/1/01 on 2 October 2001. The overall plan was brought together as 'Coordination of Implementation of the Plan of Action to Combat Terrorism', first as 12579/01 (12 October 2001), then as 12800/01 (16 October 2001) and 12800/1/01 REV (17 October 2001). Also see Tony Bunyan, *Statewatch: Analysis Reports on Post-11 September*, no. 7.
21 COM(2001) 611 final, Brussels, 17 October 2001.
22 SN 4296/2/01.
23 Alternative proposal lodged by Italian delegation: 14559/01 COPEN 78 CATS 43; proposal of the Belgian Presidency: 1 January 2004; see Article 26 of the Draft Framework Decision (provision concerning transition), 14867/1/01 REV, 10 December 2001.
24 14581/01 (Presse 444), provisional version.
25 No. 14925/01 (7 December 2001; POLGEN 35); 14919/1/01 (13 December 2001; POLGEN 34).

Encapsulating anti-terrorism measures in the EU's foreign policy agenda

The overall tenor of EU strategies is predominantly repressive, proactive and aimed at undermining terrorist organizations. Thus far, the preventive approach to terrorism has hardly been considered. In its intensification of the fight against terrorism, the EU has been active on four different dimensions, namely: 1) the construction of a uniform conception of terrorism as a dominant security threat, building on the merging process between internal and external security; 2) encapsulating the anti-terrorism agenda in the EU's foreign policy agenda and the reinforcement of transatlantic relationships; 3) the active and accelerated pursuit of legal harmonization; and 4) the rapid expansion and reinforcement of institutional capacity within the EU.

Semantic Transformation: Shaping Uniformity in Threat Perceptions

The EU's discourse on terrorism seems to be moving from state-based terrorism to globally dispersed terrorism, from organized terrorist groups/movements to 'terrorist networks', and from anti-terrorism to the 'war against terrorism'. In the security discourse, the use of these terms and concepts, strongly invigorated after the 11 September 2001 attacks, may lead to a harmonization of threat perceptions and an intensified search for a consensus definition of terrorism as a phenomenon. This is certainly not a trivial exercise, given the continued emphasis on terrorism as a territorially and ethnically driven issue.

The establishment of a uniform definition of terrorism would arguably be a great help in the drive to harmonize national policies. There has never been a EU definition of terrorism as such. States have, until now, preferred to declare certain specific acts as terrorist crimes, such as hijacking, hostage-taking and bomb attacks.[26] EU efforts had been limited for a long time to trying to reach agreement on details and parts of a definition. The Belgian Presidency of the EU was working on a possible difference between specific terrorist offences (such as membership of a terrorist group) and offences that are usually/often committed in the context of terrorism (such as murder or kidnapping). This was also relevant in view of the European arrest warrant, which was going to state specific offences in its list at the instigation of the (then) Belgian Presidency of the EU. The subject has obviously been very controversial: the sensitivity of the subject even forced the relevant Working Group on Terrorism to adopt different lists of terrorist organizations and suspects.[27] Spain, for instance, was in favour of adding

---

26   COM(2001) 743 final.
27   These lists have been controversial and confusing, and have been subject to frequent amendments. In an information letter to the Dutch Parliament, three lists were brought to the fore, namely the UN list, the Bush list (8 October 2001) and the Treasury list (12 October 2001). By inclusion of these lists in the EU's Council Regulation on Specific Restrictive Measures Directed Against Certain Persons and Entities with a View to Combating Terrorism (OJ C 75 E 303), assets belonging to persons and organizations can be 'frozen'. On 2 October 2001, the European Commission added a completely new draft regulation with an open appendix that allows insertion of groups and people whose assets should be frozen in accordance with the terrorist danger they present. This draft regulation allows the EU member states to implement the financial paragraphs of UN Security Council Resolution no. 1373. The European Parliament had an emergency procedure on 4 October 2001 to give its advice about the draft regulation. [Cont.]

Herri Batasuna to the list.[28] With the United States, the EU is to carry out an immediate assessment of terrorist threats, including in particular the identification of terrorist organizations, which suggests that input from the US may influence the proposed EU list of proscribed organizations.

The basic issue here is whether harmonization is to be based on a wide or a narrow definition of terrorism. Human rights organizations, for instance, fear that a common and wider definition of terrorism will undermine human rights, and that legislative harmonization will evolve into the direction of the most repressive legal regimes within the EU.[29]

When the compilation of the list of terrorist offences was first announced, the then President of the EU Task Force of Chiefs of Police, Mr Fransen (head of the Belgian Federal Police), explained that such a list has already been established for some time and is updated on a biannual basis and then reported to the Justice and Home Affairs Council. In this context, a crowded policy space like the EU should avoid repetitions and lack of operationalization of lists, inventories and definitions.

The introduction of a mutual evaluation system, in which member states evaluate each other's ability to exercise legislative, administrative and technical measures against terrorism,[30] suggests that best practices and the exchange of information[31] may also contribute to the convergence of various concepts of terrorism.

Formulating a uniform definition of terrorism is dependent upon a rather fundamental transformation in international politics, namely the merging of internal and external security. This process was set in motion by the fall of the Berlin Wall, which eroded traditional and security conceptions. Illegal migration, cross-border crime and the public's alarm caused by the recent terrorist attacks may well feature much more strongly in people's fears than war.[32]

Some argue that public safety has become the subject of international cooperation over a whole range of policies, including the use of armed forces. The declaration of

---

Swift adoption of this directive was emphasized at the European Council on 20 October 2001 (see Doc. 12759/01). The Council adopted a decision by written procedure on the updated list concerning the fight against terrorism. The acts adopted concerned a common position updating common position 2001/931/CFSP on the application of specific measures to combat terrorism, and an implementing decision establishing the list provided for in Article 2(3) of the Regulation (EC) No 2580/2001 on specific restrictive measures directed against certain persons and entities (this decision repeals Decision 2001/927/EC adopted on 27 December 2001). The acts adopted extend the list of persons, groups and entities involved in terrorist acts whose assets are frozen and/or which are subject to judicial and police cooperation among member states. The Council of the European Union adopted a new decision by written procedure on 3 May 2002 (8549/02 (presse 121) – *Fight against Terrorism: Updated List*), which included the PKK.

28 Cees Zoon, *De Volkskrant*, 7 November 2001.
29 See, for example, statements of representatives from Amnesty International, in *Newsletter from the European Parliament*, issued on 6 November 2001.
30 Objective 37, doc. 12759/01.
31 Brussels, 17 September 2001, 10524/5/01 REV 5 LIMITE ENFOPOL 69.
32 Heather Grabbe, 'Breaking New Ground in Internal Security', chapter from *Europe after September 11th* (London: Centre for European Reform, November 2001); see www.cer.org.uk.

NATO partners to regard the terrorist attacks in the US as an act of war against a NATO partner contributed to a further identification of internal and external security.[33]

In sum, traditional internal threats are being reconceptualized: non-European, transnational components of political terrorism have gained greater relevance in public opinion and political discourse, in spite of the persistence of various forms of terrorism in several European countries. At the substantial-political level, the fundamental issue is represented by the coexistence of different security models or security cultures, whereas at the institutional level, the key question concerns the most efficient and transparent methods to avoid overlapping, competition and contradiction between the 'pillars' (cross-pillar coordination).

The Mobilization of Intra-European and Transatlantic Coalitions

The reinforcement of transatlantic cooperation against terrorism had been preceded by earlier initiatives. In June 1995, December 1995 and July 1996, US President Bill Clinton initiated some high-level conferences about anti-terrorism in cooperation with France, the United Kingdom, Germany and Italy. But none of these conferences were officially referred to in the definition of an EU anti-terrorism policy.[34]

The new strategy pursued by the EU after 11 September 2001 consisted of mobilization and the formulation of a horizontal (cross-pillar) EU anti-terrorism policy. The first strategy mainly consisted of rallying key figures in European politics, and by consolidating political union.

Despite the self-acclaimed independence of its Common Foreign and Security Policy (CFSP) and European Security and Defence Policy (ESDP), the EU went out of its way to support the United States and explicitly labelled the 11 September 2001 attacks

> 'an assault on our open, democratic, tolerant and multicultural societies. ... The European Union will cooperate with the United States in bringing to justice and punishing the perpetrators, sponsors and accomplices of such barbaric acts. On the basis of [UN] Security Council Resolution 1368, a riposte by the US is legitimate. The Member States are prepared to undertake such actions, each according to its means.'[35]

The attacks stimulated the reinforcement of ties with US authorities.[36] The latter had long since sought access to the EU Justice and Home Affairs bureaucracy, but until then with limited success only. Traditionally, the US had requested (and generally received) assistance from the EU in police and judicial cooperation, in particular regarding

---

33 Ferruccio Pastore, 'Reconciling the Prince's Two "Arms": Internal-External Security Policy Coordination in the European Union', paper published as *Occasional Paper* no. 30 (Paris: Institute for Security Studies, Western European Union (ISS/WEU), September 2001).

34 Fijnaut, 'De aanslagen van 11 september 2001 en de reactie van de Europese Unie', 2002 forthcoming.

35 *Conclusions and Plan of Action of the Extraordinary Council Meeting on 21 September 2001*, Press Release 140/01.

36 European Parliament Committee on Foreign Affairs, Human Rights, Common Security and Defence Policy, Rapporteur James E.M. Elles, *Report on the Commission Communication to the Council on Reinforcing the Transatlantic Relationship: Focusing on Strategy and Delivering Results*, 25 April 2002, A5-0148/2002.

regulations on extradition and police surveillance,[37] notwithstanding different ideological views about repressive law enforcement action against terrorism.[38] But the road has now been opened for more institutionalized ties: in addition to reinforced cooperation with Europol and Eurojust (see below), the US has also demonstrated interest in more direct access to the Schengen Information System (SIS), which is operational in thirteen EU member states (except the United Kingdom and Ireland), Norway and Iceland.[39] Moreover, as a consequence of 11 September 2001, data exchange regimes have been relaxed. For instance, the EU's anti-terrorism roadmap suggests that access to the SIS may be extended to police, immigration and customs officials in the context of counter-terrorism. It may, moreover, refer to the planned access to national vehicle licensing by the security and intelligence agencies.[40] On a European bureaucratic level, reports from COTER (the counter-terrorism groups under CFSP) and the JHA Working Party on Terrorism Troikas will be fed into 'high-level Transatlantic Dialogue Meetings'.[41]

Furthermore, a cooperation agreement was signed on 16 November 2001 between the US and Europol, which provides for an exchange of liaison officers between Europol and US agencies that are active in the policing sector.[42] The anti-terrorism roadmap[43] announced a visit of the heads of police, prosecution, Europol, Eurojust and the European Commission to Washington on 18 October 2001. Moreover, a secret agreement between the EU and the US seemed to be in the making on criminal matters, investigative procedures and joint investigation teams.[44]

On 26 April 2002, EU Justice and Home Affairs Ministers approved conditions to negotiate judicial and extradition cooperation agreements with the US. The agreements are specially designed to promote cooperation in counter-terrorism matters, provided that the US respects the human rights of suspected terrorists extradited to the United States. In a commentary, it is said that it remains to be seen whether the US will be able to meet EU conditions, such as concerning the guarantees that persons extradited would not be subject to the death penalty, life imprisonment, or trial by special tribunals. Another potential problem is that some EU member states want to prohibit judicial and mutual

---

37   Peter van Ham, 'Politics as Unusual: NATO and the EU after 9-11', in: Peter van Ham, Kees Homan, Marianne van Leeuwen, Dick Leurdijk, Frans Osinga, *Terrorism and Counterterrorism. Insights and perspectives after September 11* (The Hague, Clingendael, 2001) p. 53.
38   See the concerns expressed in the European Parliament's *Resolution on EU Judicial Cooperation with the United States in Combating Terrorism*, 13 December 2001, B5-0813/2001.
39   The Council accepted a fundamental modification of the nature of the Schengen Information System, to the extent that in the near future the data in SIS II may be used for objectives other than the original ones introduced into the system. The renewal of this finality is related to the maintenance of public order (read: anti-globalization protests), and particularly also terrorism. It is also proposed that access to SIS should be extended, notably to security and intelligence services; and perhaps also to civil services and the military services; Document of the Presidency, SIS 100, COMIX 742, 14091/01, Brussels, 21 November 2001.
40   Bunyan, *Statewatch: Analysis Reports on Post-11 September*, no. 7.
41   SN 3926/6/01 REV 6.
42   JHA Council *Conclusions*, 20 September 2001, SN 3926/6/01 REV 6. Note here that data protection regimes differ considerably. In view of increased penal cooperation on terrorism with the US, it has been noted that certain states within the USA still operate the death penalty. The EU Charter on Fundamental Rights excludes all extradition of people to a state that still exercises the death penalty, but this Charter is not binding.
43   12759/01.
44   *Statewatch Bulletin*, March-April 2002 (www.statewatch.org).

assistance in capital cases, and Germany has called for strong guarantees to ensure data protection.[45]

The merging of the EU's agenda against terrorism into the foreign policy agenda materialized during a visit of the EU troika to Pakistan, Iran, Saudi Arabia, Egypt and Syria, 'as part of an effort by the Union to strengthen the international coalition against terrorism'. Moreover, at the Ghent European Council of 18 October 2001, EU member states expressed the need for more dialogue with the Arab and Islamic worlds, to rekindle the Middle East peace process, and 'to reinforce the comatose Barcelona process'.[46]

Legal Harmonization

The accelerated pursuance of legal harmonization emerges as the EU's third strategy against terrorism. It proves to be difficult, notably within a context of intergovernmental decision-making. National preoccupations still prevail throughout the negotiation process. A shared system of norms and values, however, is a precondition for a successful and efficient system of cooperation. There are different schools of thought about the desirability and usefulness of legal harmonization. The European Commission not only pleads for legal harmonization within the EU but also for activation of existing legal frameworks at the UN level (notably the UN Convention for the Suppression of the Financing of Terrorism), which is in line with the more global approach to regulation and legislation.[47] Some believe that the creation of uniformity between all criminal law systems in the European Union will not be a solution at all.

More concretely, legal harmonization is being shaped through the adoption of various instruments.[48] The most contentious of those has been the Framework Decision on the European Arrest Warrant.[49] The 'Euro-warrant' had already been on the shelves,[50] but the coordinated fight against terrorism provided a window of opportunity for political decision-making on this instrument. Political agreement about the Framework Decision

---

45   Bruce Zagaris, 'European Union Agrees to Cooperate with the US', *International Law Enforcement Reporter*, vol. 18, issue 6, June 2002, p. 242.

46   Van Ham, 'Politics as Unusual', p. 53.

47   COM(2001) 611 final, 17.10.2001; SN 3926/6/01 REV 6.

48   See also: *Council Common Position of 27 December 2001 on Combating Terrorism*, OJ L 344/90 (2001/930/CFSP); *Council Common Position of 27 December 2001 on the Application of Specific Measures to Combat Terrorism* (OJ L 344/93; 2001/931/CFSP); *Council Regulation (EC) No 2580/2001 of 27 December 2001 on Specific Measures Directed Against Certain Persons and Entities with a View to Combating Terrorism* (OJ L 344/70, 28.12.2001).

49   There is no publication in the *Official Journal*, and discussions are based on the latest version of Doc. 14867/1/01 REV 1, 10 December 2001.

50   Proposed *Framework Decision on a European Arrest Warrant from the Commission*, COM (2001) 522, 19 September 2001. Graham Watson, MEP and rapporteur of the European Parliament's report on terrorism, said that the Parliament adopted calls for a European arrest warrant and clearer definitions of terrorist crimes and penalties on 5 September 2001, just days before the terrorist attacks on New York and Washington. 'Without those attacks', said Mr Watson, 'the report's recommendations could have taken months or years to be considered by EU governments'. As it was, new anti-terrorism measures were approved by the EU within three months, with final endorsement due on 28 February 2002. From: www.theepc.be/documents/, 21 February 2001; see also *Sixth Report of the Select Committee on the European Union 'Counter Terrorism: The European Arrest Warrant*, UK House of Lords, http://www.parliament.the-stationary-office.co.uk/.

was not obtained unanimously, however, as Italy initially raised objections against the inclusion of corruption and money-laundering in the appendix; it withdrew its objections before the Laeken European Council of 14 and 15 December 2001.[51] A few days earlier, the Netherlands had submitted reservations concerning the reach of the Framework Decision, and issued criteria for refusing to extradite in case of offences committed within its own territory that are not necessarily considered punishable according to national Dutch law, such as euthanasia and abortion.

The most salient aspects of the (conditional)[52] compromise that was achieved at the JHA Council of 6 and 7 December 2001 concerned: a) a wide field of application to 32 offences including terrorism onto which the 'double criminality[53] control' will not be exercised, under the condition that these offences are punishable in the extraditing country with a prison sentence of minimally three years; b) moreover, a clause concerning territoriality makes execution of the arrest warrant facultative for offences committed in the country of execution, or for offences that took place in a third country but that are not recognized in the country where the warrant is carried out; c) a retroactive clause that offers the possibility for a member state to treat the introduced demands before the adoption of the Framework Decision according to existing instruments in the field of extradition.[54]

The 'Euro-warrant' will replace already existing extradition agreements. The explanatory memorandum to the European arrest warrant states that the principle of double criminality will be removed at the expense of states with the most lenient legislation. Various states lodged reservations against the removal of the double criminality principle. This boils down to a negative list, which allows member states choosing to decriminalize certain aspects to exclude these from the warrant.

Another contentious issue at the JHA Council of 6 and 7 December 2001 proved to be that the European arrest warrant covers various crimes besides terrorist offences. The decision-making concerning the European arrest warrant has been notably hasty, partly due to the use of the procedure of urgency within the European Parliament, which also applies to the decision-making procedure concerning the instrument (to be discussed next).[55]

The European arrest warrant may raise constitutional issues for some member states in regard to the possible extradition of their own nationals,[56] and the binding nature of this instrument raises questions as to whether member states are prepared to revise their national extradition regimes. Article 37 of the (draft) Framework Decision on the European Arrest Warrant was inspired by the Portuguese declaration annotated to the extradition convention of 1996, namely to request the guarantee, if a person is sentenced

---

51   14581/01 (Presse 444 – G). Italy decided to accept the list of offences and therewith also the Framework Decision. According to the Italian Prime Minister Berlusconi, the Italian Constitution would have to be changed and it would remain to be seen whether the Italian Parliament would adopt it; see Willem Beusekamp, *De Volkskrant*, 12 December 2001.
52   Parliamentary scrutiny reservations submitted by Denmark, the Netherlands, Sweden, the United Kingdom and Ireland. The Belgian Presidency noted that the draft Framework Decision would have to be presented to the European Parliament for advice for a second time.
53   This means that the offence for which extradition is sought is recognized and penalized in both states.
54   14581/01 (Presse 444 – G).
55   12759/01.
56   Bunyan, *Statewatch: Analysis Reports on Post-11 September*, no. 6.

to life imprisonment, that the penalty shall ultimately not be executed. The European arrest warrant is generally regarded as a first step towards a European Judicial Area, despite the absence of uniform definitions of terrorism and other offences, and despite the absence of a binding framework of fundamental rights for citizens.

Another important legal instrument supposed to infuse further the process of legal harmonization is the (draft) Framework Decision on Terrorism.[57] It was adopted at the JHA Council of 6 and 7 December 2001, but three parliamentary reserves had been submitted. The instrument uses the key concept of terrorist offences, and as such, it establishes minimum rules relating to the constituent elements of criminal acts and compiles a common list of offences.[58] As far as the penal sanctions are concerned, the JHA Council chose a maximum penalty with a limit of fifteen years of imprisonment for leading a terrorist organization, and eight years for other offences in relation to a terrorist group, which are specifically foreseen in the Framework Decision. In principle the Council decides who is to be inserted on the list. It is unclear whether an appeal can be raised against insertion on the list, although it seems that – as with all intergovernmental legislation in the EU – complaints would have to be addressed first of all through one of the national judges within the EU member state's court systems.

A third legal instrument, the Framework Decision on the Freezing of Assets of Suspects, had also been underway for a while.[59] The proposal on the mutual recognition and execution of orders to freeze the assets and evidence of suspects by all member states was made in November 2000. Originally it was supposed to be part of the mutual recognition programme and it covered drug trafficking, EC budget fraud, money-laundering, counterfeiting of the euro, corruption and trafficking in human beings, but it was presumably amended to include terrorism.[60] The mechanism proposed in February 2001 provides for the automatic execution in one state of orders to freeze assets or evidence from another. From the perspective of mutual recognition, member states are expected to treat these orders as if they would be requested by their own national authorities to freeze assets. Shortly after the events on 11 September 2001, the European Commission introduced emergency legislation to freeze more than 100 million euros worth of assets of people suspected of terrorism.[61]

This draft seems to be overtaken by Council Regulation (EC) No 2580/2001 of 27 December 2001, which is referred to in the Council Decision on Specific Measures directed against Certain Persons and Entities with a View to Combating Terrorism and in

---

57 Proposed *Framework Decision on Terrorism from the Commission*, COM (2001) 521, 19 September 2001.
58 Bunyan, *Statewatch: Analysis Reports on Post-11 September*, no. 6. The proposed *Framework Decision on Terrorism from the Commission* included a possible broadening of the concept of terrorism to cover protests at international summits and international violence. However, the JHA Council Conclusions of 6 and 7 December 2001 argue in favour of a balance between suppressing terrorist offences and guaranteeing fundamental rights in order to ensure that legitimate activities – such as trade union activities or the anti-globalist movements – do not in any case fall under the application of the definition of terrorism (14581/01 (Presse 444-G)).
59 Proposed in November 2000 as part of the mutual recognition programme; Proposal by France, Sweden and Belgium on the execution of orders, assets and evidence, 13986/00, 30 October 2000; 5126/01, 2 February 2001; principle agreement reached by JHA Council on 28 February 2002; see *De Volkskrant*, 1 March 2002.
60 Bunyan, *Statewatch: Analysis Reports on Post-11 September*, no. 6.
61 Bunyan, *Statewatch: Analysis Reports on Post-11 September*, no. 6.

the Council Common Position on the Application of Specific Measures to Combat Terrorism.[62] These instruments contain no information on who precisely decides on listing these organizations (except 'the Council'), nor do they outline how these organizations can appeal against that decision.

Other avenues towards legal harmonization include: the ratification of existing conventions, including the 1995[63] and 1996[64] EU Conventions on Extradition[65] and the 2000 Mutual Legal Assistance Convention;[66] EU-wide standards introduced by the Commission to improve security for air travellers, and measures to reinforce security measures of the common visa;[67] investigations by the Commission into how EU legislation on asylum and financial markets can be made 'terrorism proof';[68] and tackling illegally obtained profits that are exploited for the benefit of sponsoring terrorist activities, under the 1985 EC Directive on Money-Laundering.

New EU instruments are binding upon domestic legislation. For instance, Dutch criminal law has no explicit articles on punishable terrorist offences. To date, suspects in the Netherlands can merely be prosecuted for criminal offences committed in relation to terrorism, such as kidnapping, breach of domestic peace, manslaughter or murder. Also, Article 140 of the Dutch Code on Criminal Procedure offers the possibility to prosecute a group of people for membership of a criminal organization. Proposals have been submitted to adapt existing legislation to EU prescriptions.

In this era of increased global regulation, there is a danger of proliferation of international agreements and a lack of mutual legal consistency between them. For instance, UN Resolution 1372 demands the freezing of assets of terrorist organizations, and the content of this Resolution has to be interpreted and executed by Working Groups within the EU. Lists of terrorist organizations are being assembled within the 'Third Pillar', and parts of these lists are used within the 'First Pillar' as a basis for legal intervention in the freezing of terrorist assets. The coordination with UN regulations is always assured in the preambles of these instruments.

---

62   OJ L 116/33, 3 May 2002; and OJ L 116/75, 3 May 2002, which repealed former decisions.
63   In October 2001, this Convention still had to be ratified by France, the UK, Ireland, Italy and Belgium (Doc. 12759/01).
64   In October 2001, this Convention still had to be ratified by France, the UK, Ireland and Italy (Doc. 12759/01).
65   *Convention on Simplified Extradition Procedures between the Member States of the EU*, signed 10 March 1995; *Convention on Extradition between the Member States of the EU*, signed 27 September 1996.
66   See *Conclusions of the JHA Council 20 September 2001* (SN 3926/6/01 REV 6); and *Convention on Mutual Assistance in Criminal Matters between the Member States of the EU* (OJ 2000 C 197/1). Eurojust is given a role in seeking a practical solution if one member state refuses to cooperate with a request for legal or police assistance from another. The protocol will have to be ratified by national parliaments in the member states. See Bunyan, *Statewatch: Analysis Reports on Post-11 September*, no. 6; doc. 12759/01.
67   Within the EU, there is discussion about a uniform model document for visas in case the travel document of the traveller is not officially recognized (use of biometrics and in the future digitalized versions of the photographs). Moreover, work is carried out concerning the standardization of residence permits for non-EU citizens; see *Brief Tweede Kamer*, 27 October 2001.
68   Van Ham, 'Politics as Unusual' p. 53.

The Expansion and Reinforcement of Institutional Capacity

The creation of new forums and reinforcement of inter-institutional relationships is significant (for example, greater cooperation between security bodies of the EU member states).

The widening of the Europol mandate to cover all forms of serious crime (per 1 January 2002)[69] is one of these relevant developments. According to its Senior Deputy Director,[70] this will 'not necessarily increase the number of tasks of Europol but will allow greater flexibility in using data relevant to organized crime groups'. A draft legal instrument is currently under discussion, containing possible amendments to the Europol Convention.

Furthermore, Europol established a team of counter-terrorist specialists, with – in principle – two liaison officers from each EU member state, one from the police and one from the intelligence service.[71] This team has been set up for a renewable period of six months, and was due to report to the Council in March 2002 for the first time.[72] The remit of the team is to collect all relevant information and intelligence concerning the current threat; to analyse the collected information and undertake the necessary operational and strategic analysis; and to draft a threat assessment document based on information received (this study will in particular list targets, damage, possible modi operandi and consequences for the security of the member states) with a description of possible situations. It will identify those areas in which preventive measures must be taken (air traffic, official buildings, VIP protection,[73] etc.).[74] The team is requested to collaborate directly with American counterparts.[75]

An added task of Europol has become to open and expand 'analysis files' on terrorism based on information and intelligence provided by national police forces and intelligence services. At the JHA Council of 6 and 7 December 2001, Europol's Director presented a detailed overview of the activities of the al-Qaeda network within EU territory, which was mainly based on the first activities of the counter-terrorism team. Europol was also charged with the establishment of an agreement concerning information exchange with the US. The Director of Europol was instructed to conclude an 'informal agreement', pending a formal one, to be concluded by 16 November 2001. The agreement would provide for 'the exchange of liaison officers between Europol and US

---

69 Council Decision of 6 December 2001 extending Europol's mandate to deal with serious forms of international crime listed in the Annex to the Europol Convention, OJ C of 18 December 2001, pp. 1-2.

70 Willy Bruggeman, 'How can Europol Assist in the Effective Organization of Measures against Transnational European Crime?', in College of Europe and EULEC (eds), *Integrated Security in Europe: A Democratic Perspective*, Collegium no, 22 – XII, 2001, pp. 65-72.

71 Guild and Bigo (in CEPS-JHA network conference, 7 December 2001) note that this blurs the distinction between the police and intelligence function at EU level, and that national constitutional settlements are being superseded at the EU level. In practice, not every country seconds two liaison officers to Europol, some only one, and others three.

72 Objective 31, doc. 12759/01.

73 See, for example, the recommendation of the Council concerning the development of a common evaluation scheme to assess risks for VIPs and visitors to the European Union, OJ C 356/1 (2001/C 356/01), 14 December 2001.

74 JHA Council *Conclusions*, 20 September 2001, SN 3926/6/01 REV 6.

75 Objective 48, doc. 12759/01.

agencies that are active in the policing sector'.[76] Moreover, the Director of Europol was to open negotiations with the United States on the conclusion of and agreement that includes the transmission of personal data.[77]

Finally, the JHA Council of 20 September 2001 requested Europol to update the Directory of Specialized Counter-Terrorist Competences, Skills and Expertise provided for by the Joint Action of 15 October 1996.[78]

A second institution sailing with the tide of EU anti-terrorism efforts is Eurojust. Its establishment was decided upon at the Tampere European Council (15 and 16 October 1999), as it was perceived necessary to improve judicial cooperation between the member states and to overcome obstacles thrown up by mutual legal assistance agreements (such as disparate procedural requirements for evidence-gathering). Following a Council Decision of 14 December 2001, the decision to create Eurojust formally was adopted by the JHA Council on 6 and 7 December 2001, but four parliamentary reserves were submitted. On 28 February 2002, the Council adopted the Decision setting up Eurojust with a view to reinforcing the fight against serious crime.[79] Eurojust, which is composed of one national member from each EU member state (prosecutor, judge or police officer), has a wide general competence over all types of crime and the offences on which Europol is also competent, but also computer crime, fraud and corruption, money-laundering, environmental crime, and participation in a criminal organization. Eurojust will be based in The Hague and will pursue close cooperation with Europol.

The provisional Eurojust (Pro-Eurojust) began operating in January 2001, and throughout 2001 it was working on 170 cases. According to the conclusions of the Extraordinary Council on 21 September 2001, Eurojust has to pursue a strengthening of 'cooperation between anti-terrorist magistrates'. The first such meeting was held on 10 October 2001. Eurojust's activities naturally entail the exchange of personal data.[80] Despite a recommendation from the European Parliament that the 1981 Council of Europe Convention and supplementary Recommendation 87(15) should apply, there are no data protection provisions in the draft Council Decision.[81] This deficit is only slightly compensated by a specially appointed Data Protection Officer at Eurojust, who shall be a staff member. The final Council Decision also contains provisions on the handling of personal data, data security and the appointment of an independent joint supervisory body to monitor Eurojust's activities.

---

76 The agreement was officially signed in the margin of the JHA Council of 6 and 7 December 2001, between the Director of Europol, Jürgen Storbeck, and the US Ambassador Rockwell Schnabel, in the presence of the Ministers of Justice and the Interior of the EU Member States and US Secretary of State Colin Powell. The JHA Council Conclusions (14581/01 (Presse 444 – G)) state that the cooperation should be enforced against serious crime and in particular terrorism. The cooperation agreement aims at prevention, detection, suppression and investigation of forms of serious crime, and excludes the transmission of personal data.

77 Objective 52, doc. 12759/01. Heather Grabbe, 'Breaking New Ground in Internal Security', notes that cooperation with the US is already running into difficulties: 'Behind all expressions of solidarity and support, European police forces and the FBI are reluctant to share sensitive information with one another'.

78 SN 3926/6/01 REV 6.

79 OJ L 63/1 (2002/187/JHA), 6 March 2002.

80 Bunyan, *Statewatch: Analysis Reports on Post-11 September*, no. 7.

81 Bunyan, *Statewatch: Analysis Reports on Post-11 September*, no. 6; see *Decision 2000/799/JHA setting up the Provisional Judicial Cooperation Unit (Eurojust)* (OJ 2000 L 324/2); *Draft Council Decision setting up Eurojust*, 11685/2/01, 20 September 2001.

Like Europol, Eurojust was asked to intensify its cooperation with anti-terrorism magistrates in the US.[82] The (then) President of Eurojust assured that the facilitated liaison between EU and US magistrates does not involve the direct exchange of information between them.[83] A Eurojust magistrate was appointed by the US, which implied a more direct operational contact with the US magistrate working in Paris.

Alongside Europol and Eurojust, there is much talk about the Joint Investigation Teams. These teams, consisting of officers and officials from EU member states were to be set up in order to coordinate current investigations into terrorism that are linked in any way. A team will comprise police officers and magistrates who specialize in counter-terrorism, representatives of Eurojust, and Europol officers to the extent that this is allowed by the Europol Convention.[84] The decision to create joint investigation teams partly flows from the Tampere conclusions (October 1999), partly from an early implementation of the (not yet fully ratified) EU Convention on Mutual Legal Assistance. The draft Framework Decision[85] authorizes joint teams to carry out criminal investigations concerning trafficking in drugs and human beings as well as terrorism. EU member states should have the possibility of deciding whether representatives of authorities of non-member states, and in particular the US, can participate. A *procédure d'urgence* was introduced into the European Parliament in order to accelerate decision-making, and the Framework Decision is to be implemented by 1 July 2002.[86]

The Article 36 Committee, which consists of senior civil servants from Justice and Home Affairs ministries, is to ensure the closest possible coordination between Europol, Eurojust and the EU Police Chiefs Operational Task Force. The Committee was also asked to hold a policy debate on strengthening cooperation between police services, including Europol and intelligence services. The JHA Council of 20 September 2001 instructed the Article 36 Committee to work out a speedier version of the evaluation mechanism defined in the Joint Action of 5 December 1997. This Action established a mechanism for evaluating the application and implementation at national level of international undertakings in the fight against organized crime, in order to define a procedure for the peer assessment of national anti-terrorist arrangements, on the basis of considerations of a legislative (such as legislation allowing the interception of telephone communications or to draw up a list of terrorist organizations), administrative or technical nature. The JHA Council wished to receive an evaluation report together with proposals by the end of 2002. The General Secretariat of the Council would accordingly be host to two national experts specializing in counter-terrorism and seconded from police and intelligence services.[87]

---

82 Objective 54, doc. 12759/01.

83 Michèle Konincxs, in an interview with *Agence Europe*, 5 November 2001.

84 For Europol to participate fully, the 1995 Europol Convention must be amended by way of a protocol amended by national parliaments. It appears that Europol has already been participating in de facto joint teams for some time in contravention of Article 4(2) of the 1995 Convention; see Bunyan, *Statewatch: Analysis Reports on Post-11 September*, no. 6.

85 Proposed *Framework Decision by Belgium, Spain, France and the UK on Joint Investigation Teams*, 11990/01, 19 September 2001.

86 In addition, the Council adopted a Council Recommendation for the establishment of multinational *ad hoc* teams for gathering and exchanging information on terrorists (25-26 April 2002, 5715/6/02 ENFOPOL 19 REV 6).

87 SN 3926/6/01 REV 6.

The Police Chiefs Operational Task Force (PCOTF) was charged with organizing high-level meetings between the heads of EU counter-terrorist units. In cooperation with the Council Working Group on Terrorism, the PCOTF is to compile an inventory of national measures and alert plans. Moreover, it was charged with preparing measures to strengthen controls at external borders, and had to report to the JHA Council on 6 and 7 December 2001.

The Heads of Security and Intelligence Services[88] are to meet on a frequent basis, and they were expected to include internal security agencies (such as MI5 in the UK) and external intelligence agencies (such as MI6 and GCHQ in the UK). Bunyan argues that it is 'likely that assessments compiled by Europol concerning threats emanating from outside the EU will pass straight to this new *ad hoc* group'.[89] The group will stand alongside the PCOTF, but in practice 'it will be the senior group'. Data between Europol and this group are likely to be passed on a 'need-to-know' basis. This new group, as Bunyan puts it concisely, 'has no legal standing, no provision for data protection, and no mechanism for parliamentary scrutiny or accountability'. A first meeting was held on 11 and 12 October 2001, while the Heads of EU counter-terrorist units met on 15 October 2001.[90] The latter meeting was held in order to improve operational cooperation between member states and third countries, to coordinate measures implemented in the Member States to guarantee a high level of security, including in the field of air safety, and to consider the missions to be entrusted to the team of counter-specialists within Europol.[91]

Other inter-institutional relationships include joint meetings between COTER (the CFSP's counter-terrorism group) and the JHA Working Party on Terrorism Troikas, which will be held four times a year. They will report to high-level transatlantic meetings. Other fora to be reinforced included the Forum of Magistrates, the Financial Action Task Force (FATF),[92] and the European Coordinator of Civil Protection (biological and chemical weapons).[93]

The (Potential) Effectiveness of EU Anti-Terrorism Efforts

It is justified to ask whether the EU's anti-terrorism efforts can be considered effective and successful. In search of an answer, we should begin with an assessment of the national security services and evaluate whether the national and international exchange of intelligence has become more structured. The Action Plan on Organized Crime, adopted under the Dutch EU Presidency in spring 1997, recommended the central coordination of

---

88 Working on an inventory of legal competences of the secret intelligence services in the field of anti-terrorism. The anti-terrorism directors of the fifteen national secret intelligence services met towards the end of the year 2001.
89 Bunyan, *Statewatch: Analysis Reports on Post-11 September*, no. 7.
90 See objective 25, doc. 12759/01.
91 JHA Council *Conclusions*, 20 September 2001, SN 3926/6/01 REV 6.
92 FATF is an independent body under the OECD and consists of 29 states (including all EU member states). It organized an extraordinary meeting in Washington DC on 29 and 30 October 2001, during which it adopted recommendations and an action plan to combat terrorist financing; see http://www.fatf-gafi.org, from: *Newsletter to the European Parliament*, 6 November 2001.
93 An extraordinary meeting of Civil Protection Directors-General was held in October 2001 in Knokke, Belgium.

intelligence, as it was supposed to ameliorate the concerted fight against organized crime. Implementation of the Action Plan's recommendations is subject to monitoring by the Multidisciplinary Group on Organized Crime. Although most EU member states now have a national facility for the coordination of intelligence, such as the National Criminal Intelligence Service in the UK, structures in the member states are still differentiated.[94] Moreover, criminal intelligence departments still demonstrate significant reluctance to share sensitive information with national intelligence services, which has negative repercussions on the centrally coordinated intelligence-gathering within Europol. The call for better-structured intelligence exchange thus pre-dates the events of 11 September 2001, but the terrorist attacks have had an undeniable impact on calls for a more important role for Europol in the fight against terrorism.

Related is the question of how Europol can function effectively if it suffers from information shortage. An evaluation of the Conclusions of the Tampere European Council reveals that despite providing Europol with the best working conditions, a higher budget and wider competencies, Europol has – with over 250 employees and a budget of 35 million euro – not yet succeeded in providing the member states with finely tuned analyses and information.[95] The Belgian Presidency of the EU concluded that the most important reason for this is the 'exaggerated' reluctance of national police agencies to provide Europol with sensitive information. To this day, no evaluation instrument has been made available to assess the added value of international cooperation compared with purely national efforts. One of the great handicaps of international cooperation is that anti-terrorism strategies are developed, negotiated and implemented within a crowded policy space (internally and externally). Too many actors (Europol, Eurojust, Interpol, OLAF, FATF, the OSCE and Council of Europe) are involved with overlapping competences, and proper inter-institutional arrangements are absent. Moreover, unbridled proliferation and even fragmentation of international legislation can be an obstacle for effective cooperation against terrorism.[96]

Under Pressure: Privacy, Human Rights, Transparency and Accountability

Human rights organizations have been particularly dismayed about the speed at which the Council has agreed to various measures (notably the European arrest warrant).[97] They feel that the agenda is 'already unbalanced in favour of facilitating the free movement of investigations and prosecutions ahead of the need to guarantee the fundamental rights of suspects and defendants'.[98] Concerning the encouragement of mutual recognition and the freezing of assets, criminal lawyers and human rights organizations are concerned that

---

94 Monica den Boer (ed.), *Organized Crime: A Catalyst in the Europeanization of National Police and Prosecution Agencies?* (Maastricht: European Institute of Public Administration, 2002).
95 Council of the European Union, 13416/2/01 REV 2 (Limite, JAI 133), *Note from the Presidency*, Brussels, 14 November 2001.
96 Graham Watson MEP, http://www.theepc.be/.
97 Professor Vermeulen argued that the incoherence in the EU's existing anti-terrorism *acquis* was being neglected in the rush to secure the formulation and adoption of the European arrest warrant; conference report by Peter Cullen, ERA, Trier, 24-25 November 2001.
98 Bunyan, *Statewatch: Analysis Reports on Post-11 September*, no. 6.

the presumption of innocence is gradually being suspended, as suspects are required to prove to authorities in another country that their assets were required lawfully. The pressure group Fair Trials Abroad has proposed a system of 'Euro-bail' to allow provisional liberty to suspects arrested under the EU warrant, and the introduction of civil rights at EU level ('Euro-rights') that would protect citizens in any country.[99]

From the perspective of civil rights organizations, it is mandatory to monitor the discursive link between terrorism and asylum/immigration. For instance, in the JHA Council *Conclusions* of 20 September 2001, the European Commission was invited to examine 'urgently the relationship between safeguarding internal security and complying with international protection obligations and instruments'.[100] Moreover, the EU anti-terrorism roadmap urged intensified cooperation with the US concerning illegal immigration, visas and forged documents.[101] The UNHCR notes that under the (proposed) Council Framework Decision on the European Arrest Warrant and the surrender procedures between member states,[102] a refugee could be transferred from one EU member state (which has recognized the person as a refugee) to another member state for prosecution.[103]

Moreover, the situation of asylum-seekers requires particular attention. The UNHCR's suggestion is that if an asylum-seeker is transferred from one EU member state to another pursuant to the Decision, the asylum procedure in the first state should be suspended. Then, after the resolution of the prosecution, whether by acquittal or conviction and sentence, the asylum-seeker should be returned to the state responsible for determining the asylum claim, and consideration of the case resumed to its final conclusion. This is to prevent refugees and asylum-seekers from losing their status. The UNHCR also pleads in favour of inclusion of reference to the European Convention for the Protection of Human Rights and Fundamental Freedom in the Framework Decision itself, and submits that EU member states should be able to apply the political offence exemption clause.[104] Concerning the EU Framework Decision on Combating Terrorism[105], the UNHCR emphasizes that the exclusion clauses of the refugee definition 'should make it impossible for terrorists to benefit from the protection of the 1951

---

99   Grabbe, 'Breaking New Ground in Internal Security'.
100 See Commission Working Document, COM(2001) 743 final, Brussels, 05 December 2001. The paper analyses the existing legal mechanisms for excluding 'those persons from international protection who do not deserve such protection, focusing in particular on those suspected of terrorist acts'. At the same time, the document argues that bona fide refugees and asylum-seekers should not become victims of the events on and after 11 September 2001. In taking this stance, the Commission argues that it 'fully endorses the line taken and expressed by the UNHCR.'
101 Objective 55, Doc. 12759/01.
102 Referring to COM(2001) 522 final – 2001/0215 (CNS).
103 'As long as the crime for which the refugee is tried and, if convicted, punished is not of the nature or severity to invoke Article 33(2) of the 1951 Convention, the refugee protection of the person should not be affected by the transfer and prosecution. This means, *inter alia*, that the protection against expulsion and *refoulement* contained in Articles 32 and 33 of the 1951 Convention continue to apply. Appropriate safeguards would therefore have to be built into the Decision which would ensure that the protection of refugees is not undermined by its operation.'
104 UNHCR Geneva, October 2001.
105 COM (2001) 521 final 2001/0217 (CNS).

Convention'.[106] However, the UNHCR pleads in favour of an examination of the individual circumstances of each case, as well as the gravity of the excludable act.

Already in June 2001, the Council decided to provide the European Parliament with an annual report entitled *TE-SAT (Terrorism Situation and Trends)*, outlining the terrorist situation in the European Union over the last twelve months and analysing the trends established.[107] In view of the European arrest warrant, the European Parliament adopted several amendments to strengthen the right of the accused, to assure that minor offences should be excluded from the application of the arrest warrant, and pledged that the person in question will not be extradited to a third country that applies the death penalty.[108]

Conclusions

In many ways, the reinforced efforts of the EU against terrorism imply a revival of the grand old Trevi days. The explosion of initiatives after the events of 11 September 2001 has created a crowded policy space in which too many actors are contributing to what they perceive as a joint EU strategy. It must be deplored, however, that these developments have turned the tide of previous positive developments concerning the consolidation of democratic control and improving transparency and accountability.[109] Also to be criticized is the mounting pressure on citizens' rights concerning personal privacy and fair trial.

Paradoxically, however, the emergence of a no-nonsense strategy against terrorism is accompanied by a simultaneous process of consolidation and institution-building. New institutions such as Eurojust are able to enjoy the benefit of renewed attention for international judicial cooperation in criminal matters. If one development within the EU has been dominant, it is that the terrorist attacks have provided a window of opportunity for outstanding JHA business, and may have contributed to the acceleration of a convergence among national anti-terrorism laws.

After years of seeking access to the EU's Justice and Home Affairs cooperation arena, US authorities are no longer circumvented by Europe. The terrorist attacks in the US inspired a transatlantic axis of police and judicial cooperation, even to the extent that the US seeks to exercise active influence on the EU's internal security agenda, which is

---

106 UNHCR, Geneva, November 2001.

107 SN 3926/6/01 REV 6, with a reference to 8466/2/01 ENFOPOL 41 REV 2.

108 No. 12 of the explanatory memorandum of the draft Framework Decision (14867/1/01 REV 1 COPEN 79 CATS 50, Brussels, 10 December 2001) submits that the fundamental rights are being obeyed, and that nothing in the Framework Decision prevents refusal to extradite a person against whom an arrest warrant has been issued if there are objective reasons to assume that the arrest warrant has been issued with a view to prosecution or sentencing of that person on the basis of his sex, race, religion, ethnical origin, nationality, language, political conviction or sexual identity, or that the position of that person can be harmed because of one of those reasons. Moreover, the draft Framework Decision allows application by the EU member states of their constitutional principles concerning fair trial, freedom of association, freedom of press and freedom of expression in other media; *Newsletter of the European Parliament*, 3 December 2001.

109 Bunyan, *Statewatch: Analysis Reports on Post-11 September*, no. 7, argues that accountability, data protection or recourse to courts for individuals are not mentioned to the European Parliament or national parliaments. Moreover, arrangements may become permanent, leaving a layer of EU inter-agency informal groups, information and intelligence exchanges and operational practices that are 'quite unaccountable'.

not necessarily welcomed by all EU member states. In a letter from President Bush to European Commission President Prodi, it became clear that the kind of cooperation desired by the US goes further than anti-terrorism, and should include visa policy, passport and border control. Hence, not only the link between internal and foreign policy has been reinforced, also the (already ongoing) merging process between internal and external security has been given a significant impulse.

Chronologically, however, there is no cause-and-effect relationship between the terrorist attacks and the tightening of visa regimes, as the latter was already on the agenda before the terrorist attacks in the United States. US authorities, however, have sought to exploit the momentum that was opened up through terrorism, mainly to expand their influence on internal security in the EU. Meanwhile however, the anti-terrorism momentum already seems overshadowed by another of the EU's prime security concerns: illegal immigration.

12 The United Nations: Towards a Comprehensive Convention on Combating Terrorism

Bibi T. van Ginkel

Introduction

The interest shown by the international community on the subject of combating terrorism immediately after the attacks of 11 September 2001 was overwhelming.[1] It was, however, not a new subject on the United Nations' agenda. Over the last thirty years, the international community has shown an unmistakable interest in combating terrorism. The last five years in particular clearly show an increase in the number of Conventions in this field.[2] A reason for this is fear of all new kinds of terrorist threats, for example with nuclear, chemical or biological weapons, or even acts of cyber-terrorism. But most interesting was India's proposal in the 1996 UN General Assembly (GA) for a draft

---

1   More than 160 representatives spoke on the subject of terrorism during the plenary session of the UN's General Assembly. Never in the history of the General Assembly had so many representatives made a statement on a topic in the General Assembly's plenary session; see Press Release GA/9929, 5 October 2001, on the Fifty-sixth General Assembly Plenary, 22nd Meeting. See also Press Releases GA/DIS/3219, 6 November 2001; GA/SHC/3667, 19 November 2001; SOC/CP/237, 16 November 2001; GA/EF/2952, 1 October 2001; GA/SHC/3632, 12 October 2001; SG/SM/8067-HR/4575-OBV/255, 5 December 2001, as examples of the fact that the subject was also discussed in several other committees.

2   Namely the International Convention for the Suppression of Terrorist Bombings, adopted by the UN General Assembly on 15 December 1997, Doc. A/Res/52/164, and entered into force on 23 May 2001; the International Convention for the Suppression of the Financing of Terrorism, adopted by the UN General Assembly on 9 December 1999, Doc. A/Res/54/109, and entered into force on 10 April 2002; and the Draft International Convention for the Suppression of Nuclear Terrorism, document A/C.6/53/L.4, Annexe I.

M. van Leeuwen (ed.): *Confronting Terrorism*, pp. 207-225
© 2003 Kluwer Law International. Printed in the Netherlands.

Comprehensive Convention on the Suppression of Terrorism.[3] The international community has, up until now, not been able to conclude such a treaty, one reason being the absence of a general definition of terrorism that would define the scope of such a Convention. However, since the international community could not possibly ignore the need for repressive action against life-threatening forms of terrorism, international Conventions have been concluded in the field of specific forms of terrorism, for example hijacking and the taking of hostages.[4]

The negative aspect of this piecemeal approach to combating terrorism is that new forms of terrorist attacks will continue to occur (such as cyber-terrorism), and these new forms might not fall under the scope of existing Conventions. The piecemeal manner of combating terrorism can therefore never be as effective as a Comprehensive Convention on the subject.

This chapter gives some insights in the developments within the United Nations with regard to combating terrorism, with a special focus on the input of the European states. Since formulating a definition of terrorism – particularly with regard to the delimitation of terrorism from the legitimate use of force in the struggle for self-determination – caused and is still causing many difficulties in drafting a Comprehensive Convention, it is first necessary to survey these definitional problems. An overview will then be given of the issue-specific Conventions on Terrorism that have been concluded, and the developments towards the draft proposal of the Comprehensive Convention will then be discussed. Finally, the content of this Comprehensive Convention and the last hurdles that have to be taken will be elaborated upon. A question that arises in this context is whether the events of 11 September 2001 forced a breakthrough in the decision-making process.

Definitional Obstacles: One Man's Terrorist is Another Man's Freedom-fighter

Until now, the international community has not been able to agree on a definition of terrorism, as most Third World states hold on to their conviction that a definition of terrorism should explicitly exclude the use of force in the struggle for self-determination. Western states, on the other hand, are reluctant to agree to a definition that suggests a legitimization of the use of force in the struggle for self-determination.

The phrase 'one man's terrorist is another man's freedom-fighter' is frequently used to illustrate the difficulties that exist with regard to formulating a definition of terrorism. Those states supporting a definition that explicitly excludes the fight for self-determination, base their position on several international legal documents. Depending on the situation, international law 'legitimizes' the use of force in a struggle for self-

---

3   See document A/C.6/51/6, 11 November 1996.
4   The 1963 Tokyo Convention on Offences and Certain Other Acts committed on Board Aircraft (UKTS 126, 1969, Cmnd. 4230); the 1970 Hague Convention for the Suppression of Unlawful Seizure of Aircraft (UKTS 39, 1972, Cmnd. 4965); the 1971 Montreal Convention for the Suppression of Unlawful Acts Against the Safety of Civil Aviation (UKTS 10, 1971, Cmnd. 5524); and its 1988 Protocol for the Suppression of Unlawful Acts of Violence at Airports Serving International Civil Aviation; the 1979 UN Convention Against the Taking of Hostages (18 ILM 1456, 1979).

determination.[5] But even though the use of force may be legitimate in some cases, the way that force is used can, of course, still amount to an act of terrorism, or to an illegal act of warfare.

The following overview of the development of the principle of self-determination may illustrate why and how attempts to define terrorism have to date met with major difficulties.

At an international level, the principle of self-determination was proclaimed for the first time by Russia in 1917.[6] It was intended to apply both to nationalities in Europe (for example those under the Austro-Hungarian monarchy) and to colonial peoples.[7] In the same period, the American President Woodrow Wilson also proclaimed the principle of self-determination. However, his understanding of the principle was slightly different. Although self-determination should apply to Europe and colonial peoples, Wilson believed that it should also take account of the interests of colonial powers.[8]

In the period between the two World Wars, the principle of self-determination was indeed implemented in Europe, in the sense that some new European states claimed their sovereignty and right to self-government. Its application to colonies was, however, minimized by the establishment of the mandate system as laid down in the Covenant of the League of Nations,[9] and when the principle was laid down in the Charter of the United Nations, it became an international legal concept.[10] Initially, the Charter's drafters merely meant to lay down the equal rights of states to protect their own population from foreign interference (also called the right to self-government). In the late 1950s – the period of decolonization – the notion of self-determination evolved into a universal principle with a direct impact on international reality. This happened mainly under the influence of socialist states, supported by an increasing number of Third World countries.[11] This modification in meaning was laid down in several General Assembly resolutions, such as the Declaration on the Granting of Independence to Colonial Countries and Peoples.[12]

In 1966 the *principle* was upgraded to a *right* to self-determination, by virtue of which all peoples had the right to freely determine their political status, and to freely pursue their economic, social and cultural development.[13]

The textual basis of the problems with regard to the delimitation between acts of terrorism and the legitimate use of force in the struggle for self-determination can be found in the 1970 Declaration on Principles of International Law concerning Friendly Relations and Cooperation among States in accordance with the Charter of the United

---

5   A. Cassese, *Self-determination of Peoples: A Legal Reappraisal* (Cambridge: Cambridge University Press, 1995), p. 153.
6   Lenin's *Fourth Letter from Afar*, 25 March 1917, which was a reiteration of Lenin's *Theses on the Socialist Revolution and the Right of Nations to Self-Determination*, January-February 1916.
7   A. Cassese, *International Law in a Divided World* (Oxford: Clarendon Press, 1986), p. 131.
8   Cassese, *International Law in a Divided World*, p. 132.
9   Cassese, *International Law in a Divided World*, p. 132.
10 See Article 1, para. 2, and Article 55 of the United Nations Charter.
11 Cassese, *International Law in a Divided World*, p. 133.
12 GA Resolution 1514 (XV) of 14 December 1960.
13 See Article 1 of both the International Covenant on Civil and Political Rights, and the International Covenant on Economic, Social and Cultural Rights.

Nations.[14] According to the text of this Declaration, the right to self-determination means that a people has the right to 'freely determine, without external interference, their political status and to pursue their economic, social and cultural development', and that states have a duty

'to respect this right in accordance with the provisions of the Charter ... The establishment of a sovereign and independent State, the free association or integration with an independent State or the emergence into any other political status freely determined by a people constitute modes of implementing the right to self-determination by that people.'

However, it also states that

'[n]othing in the foregoing paragraphs shall be construed as authorizing or encouraging any action which would dismember or impair, totally or in part, the territorial integrity or political unity of sovereign and independent States conducting themselves in compliance with the principle of equal rights and self-determination of peoples as described above and *thus possessed of a government representing the whole people belonging to the territory without distinction as to race, creed or colour* [emphasis added].'

It seems to be generally accepted that peoples under a colonial, foreign or racist power have the right to seek independence, something that is also called the right to *external* self-determination. But most questions regard the way in which the so-called *internal* right to self-determination is implemented. What kind of measures will still be acceptable when a people that is not under a colonial, foreign or racist power tries to exercise its right to self-determination by demanding to be represented in the government? According to the wording of the Friendly Relations Declaration, they cannot go as far as to endanger the territorial integrity of a state. But what if that state does not conduct itself in compliance with the principle of equal rights and self-determination, and does not possess a government that represents the whole people? Does such a case legitimize as an *ultimum remedium* the use of force in a struggle for independence? The latter interpretation is especially favoured by national liberation movements, but it is supported, albeit in more moderate terms, by some well-established authors on international law.[15]

Article 7 of the '1974 Definition of Aggression'[16] – which in general prohibits the use of force and aggression – provides yet another argument for this interpretation. It reads:

'Nothing in this Definition ... could in any way prejudice the right to self-determination, freedom and independence, as derived from the [United Nations] Charter, of peoples forcibly deprived of that right and referred to in the Declaration on Principles of International Law concerning Friendly Relations and Cooperation among States in accordance with the Charter of the United Nations, particularly peoples under colonial and racist regimes or other forms of alien domination; nor the right of these peoples to struggle to that end and to seek and receive

---

14   GA Resolution 2625 (XXV) of 24 October 1970, which was adopted without a vote.
15   See, for example, O. Schachter, *International Law in Theory and Practice* (The Hague: Kluwer Law International, 1995), p. 119; Cassese, *Self-determination of Peoples*, p. 153.
16   GA Resolution 3314, UNGAOR 29th Session, Supp. No 31, at 142, UN Doc A/9631 (1974).

support, in accordance with the principles of the Charter and in conformity with the above-mentioned Declaration.'

Socialist states and Third World countries in particular favoured this broader interpretation.[17] Nevertheless, they did distinguish between insurgents and freedom-fighters: only the latter have a legitimate right to use force. Western states, on the other hand, have always contradicted this broad interpretation. On many occasions they have strongly emphasized that only peaceful means should be used to obtain this right.[18]

These differences of opinion on the distinction between terrorism and the legitimate use of force in the struggle for self-determination still exist. They are still an impediment in the process of drafting a Comprehensive Convention on Combating Terrorism.

The Issue-Specific Approach to Combating Terrorism: A Temporary Solution?

The first major multilateral attempt to adopt an international instrument addressing the problem of international terrorism was the 1937 Convention for the Prevention and Punishment of Terrorism drafted under the auspices of the League of Nations.[19] The murders of King Alexander III of Yugoslavia and the French Minister of Foreign Affairs in Marseille in 1934 initiated the preparation of this draft. Italy refused to surrender the alleged murderers to France by stating that the acts committed were political offences, which would amount to an exception to their obligation to surrender the alleged criminals based on the extradition treaty between France and Italy. France therefore called for international measures on a universal level.

The League of Nation's Convention for the Prevention and Punishment of Terrorism was concluded at the same time as the League of Nation's Convention for the Creation of an International Criminal Court. The latter could only be signed and ratified by states after they had signed and ratified the Convention for the Prevention and Punishment of Terrorism. Although twenty European and non-European states signed the first Convention and ten European states signed the second, as of 1941 only India had ratified the prior. Consequently, neither Convention entered into force.[20] After the Second World War, the differences between East and West with regard to issues such as decolonization and self-determination prevented these Conventions from becoming operable. Moreover, many states started to doubt the necessity and the desirability of such a Comprehensive Convention.

Terrorism, however, did not cease to exist. And the international community needed to cooperate in order to respond to the threats and terrorist attacks committed. Therefore, the prevention and suppression of specific terrorist acts have been the subject of a number

---

17   *Yearbook of the United Nations*, 1974, pp. 845-846.

18   See GAOR, XXIXth Session of the Sixth Committee, in which *inter alia* Canada, Belgium, the United States, United Kingdom, the Netherlands and Israel clarified their points of view.

19   Hudson, M.O. (ed.), *International Legislation*, Vol. 7, No. 499, at p. 862; *League of Nations Official Journal*, Vol. 62, Jan. 1938, p. 23. (the first title is a collection of the texts of multipartite international instruments of general interest: beginning with the Covenant of the League of Nation).

20   E. Chadwick, *Self-determination, Terrorism and the International Humanitarian Law of Armed Conflict* (The Hague: Martinus Nijhoff, 1996), p. 97.

of multilateral legal instruments adopted within the framework of the United Nations and three of its specialized or related agencies – the International Civil Aviation Organization (ICAO), International Maritime Organization (IMO), and the International Atomic Energy Agency (IAEA).

There are currently nineteen global or regional treaties pertaining to the subject of international terrorism.[21] Terrorist acts whose prevention or suppression is the subject matter of international instruments adopted under the auspices of the UN system may be categorized as follows: (1) acts against certain means of transport or specific facilities; (2) acts against specific categories of persons; (3) hostage-taking; and (4) use of certain substances or devices for terrorist purposes.[22]

The majority of those instruments focus on the question of individual criminal responsibility of the terrorists and are based on the principle of *aut dedere aut judicare*. In that respect, the provisions of those Conventions are quite similar. State parties are required to make the crimes defined in the relevant instruments punishable under their national laws. The state in the territory of which an alleged offender is found has the duty either to extradite that person to the state that is claiming jurisdiction or to submit the case to its competent authorities for the purpose of prosecution. States must take all necessary measures to establish, when appropriate, their jurisdiction over the crimes in question. While all Conventions recognize the principle of territoriality as a basis for

---

21 The 1963 Tokyo Convention on Offences and Certain Other Acts committed on Board Aircraft, UKTS 126 (1969), Cmnd. 4230, entered into force on 4 December 1969; the 1970 Hague Convention for the Suppression of Unlawful Seizure of Aircraft, UKTS 39 (1972), Cmnd. 4965; (1971) ILM 133, entered into force on 14 October 1971; the 1971 Montreal Convention for the Suppression of Unlawful Acts Against the Safety of Civil Aviation, UKTS 10 (1971), Cmnd. 5524, entered into force on 26 January 1973; and its 1988 Protocol for the Suppression of Unlawful Acts of Violence at Airports Serving International Civil Aviation, 27 ILM 627 (1988); the 1973 UN Convention on the Prevention and Punishment of Crimes Against Internationally Protected Persons, Including Diplomatic Agents, Misc. 19 (1975), Cmnd. 6176, entered into force on 20 February 1977; the 1979 UN Convention Against the Taking of Hostages, (1979) 18 ILM 1456, entered into force on 4 June 1983; the 1980 IAEA Convention on the Physical Protection of Nuclear Material, Misc. 27 (1980); (1979) 18 ILM 1419, entered into force on 8 February 1987; the 1988 IMO International Convention for the Suppression of Unlawful Acts Against the Safety of Maritime Navigation and its Protocol on the Suppression of Unlawful Acts Against the Safety of Fixed Platforms Located on the Continental Shelf, (1988) 3 IJECL 317; the Convention on the Marking of Plastic Explosives for the Purpose of Detection, on 1 March 1991, entered into force on 21 June 1998, UN Doc. S/22393, Annexe; the International Convention for the Suppression of Terrorist Bombings, adopted by the General Assembly of the United Nations on 15 December 1997, Doc. A/Res/52/164, entered into force on 23 May 2001; the International Convention for the Suppression of the Financing of Terrorism, adopted by the General Assembly of the United Nations on 9 December 1999, Doc. A/Res/54/109, entered into force on 10 April 2002. At the regional level: the 1971 OAS Convention to Prevent and Punish Acts of Terrorism Taking the Form of Crimes Against Persons and Related Extortion that are of International Significance, 10 ILM 225,1971, entered into force on 16 October 1973; the 1977 European Convention on the Suppression of Terrorism, ETS no. 90; UKTS 93 (1977), entered into force on 4 August 1978; the SAARC (South Asian Association for Regional Cooperation) Regional Convention on the Suppression of Terrorism, signed at Kathmandu on 4 November 1987, entered into force on 22 August 1988; Treaty on Cooperation among State Members of the Commonwealth of Independent States in Combating Terrorism, on 4 June 1999 (Minsk); Arab Convention on the Suppression of Terrorism, on 22 April 1998 (Cairo); Convention of the Organization of the Islamic Conference on Combating International Terrorism, on 1 July 1999 (Ouagadougou); OAU Convention on the Prevention and Combating of Terrorism, on 14 July 1999 (Algiers).

22 Categorization follows from the Report of the UN Secretary-General of 6 September 1996, document A/51/336.

primary jurisdiction, they vary as to the degree of recognition of other bases for primary jurisdiction, for example nationality, the place where the act is committed, or the landing status or status of registration of the aircraft. They must cooperate not only on matters of judicial assistance, but also in the prevention of relevant crimes.

Most of these Conventions were, sadly enough, drafted after specific terrorist attacks had occurred, and can therefore be characterized as repressive instruments. The most recent (draft) Conventions, namely on the suppression of financing of terrorism and on the suppression of nuclear terrorism,[23] are, however, of a more preventive character. Nevertheless, each of them is only applicable to a specific act of terrorism. By maintaining this approach, the international community will always risk not being in time to draft a new Convention for yet another kind of terrorist act.

The Dragging Process towards a Draft Proposal for a Comprehensive Convention

After the fiasco of the first attempt of 1937, the subject of combating terrorism was replaced on the agenda of the UN's General Assembly at the request of the Secretary-General in 1972.[24] The Organization of American States had made an attempt to draft a Convention on Combating Terrorism in 1971, in which it tried to formulate a general definition of terrorism. This attempt failed, but apparently the United States felt it necessary to continue the discussion on this topic. In 1972 it proposed a draft Convention for the Prevention and Punishment of Certain Acts of International Terrorism to the Sixth Committee.[25] Although it was not possible at that time to take action on the draft Convention, on 18 December 1972 the General Assembly decided by Resolution 3034(XXVII) to establish an *Ad Hoc* Committee on International Terrorism to examine the question in all its aspects. One should also keep in mind that in the 1960s and early 1970s many kidnapping and hijacking incidents occurred. This, of course, also enhanced the pressure on the United Nations to reconsider the subject.

The *Ad Hoc* Committee of thirty-five members did not produce a definition of terrorism in its reports of 1973 and 1979. Or rather, an attempt to define terrorism was avoided. 'If the West was nervous that a definition of terrorism could be used to include "state terrorism", the Third World was nervous that any definition which emphasized non-State actors would fail to differentiate between terrorism properly so called, and the struggle for national liberation.'[26]

From the *Ad Hoc* Committee's Report of 1973 it became clear that although all nations wanted to outlaw terrorism, many states interpreted international terrorism differently. Each state wanted to outlaw those acts that it considered terrorism, but did not

---

23 The International Convention for the Suppression of the Financing of Terrorism, adopted by the General Assembly of the United Nations on 9 December 1999, Doc. A/Res/54/109, entered into force on 10 April 2002; the Draft International Convention for the Suppression of Nuclear Terrorism, document A/C.6/53/L.4, Annexe I.

24 Report of the UN Secretary-General of 2 November 1972 on Res. 3034 XXVII.

25 United States working paper, transmitting text of the draft Convention for the Prevention and Punishment of Certain Acts of International Terrorism (document A/C.6/L.850).

26 R. Higgins, 'The General International Law of Terrorism', in Rosalyn Higgins and Maurice Flory (eds), *Terrorism and International law* (London: Routledge, 1997), p. 16.

want to outlaw those acts that would impinge upon its national sovereignty. Moreover, the discussion on the exclusion of wars of national liberation from the scope of the definition prevented any further rapprochement on the topic. These differences of opinion led to a variety of proposals on the definition of terrorism, each written to encompass, and exclude, specific actualities and potentialities.

The results of the meetings of the *Ad Hoc* Committee leading up to the 1979 *Report* were no improvement over those of 1973. The problems relating to the delimitation between terrorism and the struggle for self-determination remained insuperable. Some delegations made it clear that the liberation struggle should be strictly distinguished from terrorist acts. Since, in their opinion, a liberation struggle was a legitimate war against the terror of occupation or colonialism, it should be placed in the same category as armed conflicts and fall within the provisions of the Geneva Conventions of 1949 and their Additional Protocols.[27] The political debate and the legal discussion with regard to the status of the al-Qaeda and Taliban prisoners kept by the United States at Guantanamo Bay show the importance of such a qualification. Other delegations made it clear that although they respected the right of all peoples to self-determination, as recognized in several UN documents and resolutions,[28] certain acts, even if intended to further a good cause, were so heinous that they merited international condemnation. It was stressed that the liberation movements must adapt their conduct so that they could not be associated with criminal or terrorist groups, which tried to link themselves with such movements to improve their image.[29]

The General Assembly did, however, follow the recommendations of the *Ad Hoc* Committee by adopting a resolution stating that 'all States [should] fulfil their obligations under international law to refrain from organizing, instigating, assisting or participating in acts of civil strife or terrorist acts in another State, or acquiescing in organized activities within their territory directed towards the commission of such acts'.[30] It also invited all states to harmonize their domestic legislation with international Conventions and to implement assumed international obligations.[31]

Almost ten years passed before another serious attempt at defining terrorism was made within the UN. In 1985, the General Assembly adopted Resolution 40/61 in which, for the first time, terrorist offences were criminalized, irrespective of their motivation. Also in this Resolution, the UN Secretary-General was requested to collect information submitted to him by states, in order to get an overview of the measures that states had taken to suppress and prevent terrorism.

In 1987, the Syrian Arab Republic requested the inclusion of a supplementary item to the provisional agenda of the Sixth Committee of the item entitled: 'Measures to prevent international terrorism which endangers or takes innocent human lives or jeopardizes fundamental freedoms and study of the underlying causes of those forms of terrorism and acts of violence which lie in misery, frustration, grievance and despair and which cause some people to sacrifice human lives, including their own, in an attempt to effect radical

---

27   See paragraph 30 of the Ad Hoc Committee's Report of 1979 (document A/34/37 of 17 April 1979).
28   Such as, for example, the Charter of the United Nations and the Declaration on Principles of International Law concerning Friendly Relations and Cooperation among States.
29   See paragraph 31 of the *Ad Hoc Committee's Report of 1979* (document A/34/37 of 17 April 1979).
30   GA Resolution 34/145, 105th plenary meeting, 17 December 1979, para. 7.
31   GA Resolution 34/145, 105th plenary meeting, 17 December 1979, para. 9.

changes'. The title of the supplementary item that Syria proposed read: 'Convening, under the auspices of the United Nations, of an international conference to define terrorism and to differentiate it from the struggle of peoples for national liberation'.[32] The proposal was supported by Democratic Yemen, Algeria and Kuwait (on behalf of the Group of Arab States).

The UN General Assembly adopted this proposal in Resolution 42/159, with the sole opposition of Israel and the United States. Moreover, the UN Secretary-General was asked to report to the General Assembly on the possibility of convening an international conference 'to define terrorism and to differentiate it from the struggle of peoples for national liberation'.[33] He should therefore seek the views of member states in all its aspects and on ways and means of combating it.

In the preamble of the same Resolution another 'revolutionary' point was made by '[r]ecognizing that the *effectiveness* of the struggle against terrorism could be enhanced by the establishment of a generally agreed definition of international terrorism' [emphasis added]. Although the discussions with regard to the need and desirability of a definition were far from being over, a majority of states did at least agree on including this phrase in the preamble of the General Assembly Resolution. Indeed, the Secretary-General in his *Report* in 1989 made it clear that the problems about defining terrorism had not disappeared with the improved relationship between the East and the West. It is remarkable to note that one of the remaining obstacles, according to his *Report*, is the question of the usefulness of one comprehensive definition. Apparently, some states still felt that an issue-specific approach of combating terrorism would be more effective then a comprehensive approach. The discussion was further hampered by the continuing controversy on whether there should be an explicit exclusion of a legitimate struggle for the right to self-determination from the definition of terrorism.[34]

In the Secretary-General's *Reports* that followed, several states more or less explicitly supported the attempts to define terrorism and to convene a conference.[35] Some states were still hesitant, such as Malta,[36] Poland,[37] Turkey[38] and Argentina. They argued that convening an international conference would not be worth the effort until there was a prior basic agreement on the part of governments on such fundamental matters as whether international terrorism should be defined according to its underlying causes or motivation or according to the methods used.[39] Other states were very outspoken with regard to their opposition to the proposals to define terrorism, such as Israel, the (then) European Community, and the United States. Spain, on behalf of the twelve member states of the European Community, made clear that it would favour an approach that

---

32   *Report of the Sixth Committee* of 3 December 1987 (document A/42/832).
33   See para. 12 of GA Resolution 42/159, 7 December 1987.
34   *Report of the Secretary-General, 1989*, (document A/44/456), 25 August 1989.
35   Namely Mexico, Mongolia, Saudi Arabia, and the Ukrainian SSR (1989). *Report of the Secretary-General*, document A/48/267, 5 August 1993: in favour of convening an international conference: Bolivia, Cyprus, Ecuador, Guyana, Iraq, Libyan Arab Jamahiriya, Qatar, Syrian Arab Republic and Venezuela. *Report of the Secretary-General*, document A/49/257, 25 July 1994: Belarus, Cuba, Ecuador, Tunisia, Brunei Darussalam.
36   *Report of the Secretary-General*, document A/48/267, 5 August 1993.
37   *Report of the Secretary-General*, document A/49/257, 25 July 1994.
38   *Report of the Secretary-General*, document A/49/257, 25 July 1994.
39   *Report of the Secretary-General*, document A/49/257, 25 July 1994.

avoids generalities and focuses on specific acts of terrorism. This approach, Spain argued, had been followed with success within universal organizations by the conclusion of a number of Conventions. The convening of an international conference to define terrorism and to differentiate it from the struggle of peoples for national liberation would depart from this approach and serve no useful purpose. Indeed, it would only perpetuate the false idea, which the (then) twelve European Community members had always opposed, that there is a link between terrorism and the exercise of the rights to self-determination.[40] In 1994, Greece, on behalf of the European Union, more or less renewed the point of view that had been made by Spain on behalf of the European Community.[41]

In 1994, Algeria – which had suffered many terrorist attacks by the *Front Islamique du Salut* (FIS) since 1992 when this party was declared illegal – argued strongly for a more comprehensive approach towards the struggle against terrorism. It stated that the Conventions concerning various aspects of the problem of international terrorism all had the great disadvantage of covering only certain acts of international terrorism, taken individually and in isolation. Algeria argued that since terrorism had taken on a multitude of other characteristics not covered by international law, there was need for wider codification in order to place it in a global perspective, regardless of terrorism's forms, methods and practices. The future Convention should provide the appropriate framework for strengthening international legal cooperation and mutual assistance between states, for example by fostering exchanges of information on efforts to combat and prevent terrorism and by promoting multilateral, regional and bilateral agreements on legal cooperation and extradition.

Algeria proposed that for the purpose of a Comprehensive Convention, a definition of terrorism should concentrate on the material and practical manifestations of terrorism, on which a consensus could be reached, rather than on the conceptual aspects of the phenomenon. The government of Algeria proposed that the principle of 'prosecute or extradite' on the basis of individual criminal responsibility should be one of the core obligations of states. In addition, it argued that such a Convention should also codify a general obligation that had been solemnly reiterated for many years in the General Assembly, namely, that states shall 'refrain from organizing, instigating, assisting or participating in terrorist acts in other States, or acquiescing in or encouraging activities within their territory directed towards the commission of such acts'.[42]

Although it might be possible to achieve consensus on this proposal, the question remains of whether this would amount to a definition that could be used effectively. By using such an approach, it will hardly be possible to surpass the model used by the Council of Europe in its Convention on Combating Terrorism.[43] In this model, terrorism was defined by listing offences already criminalized in other Conventions. It also included a vaguely worded rest category. Would this really be a step forward? The approach proposed by Algeria is, however, the first serious attempt to come forward with a comprehensive legal instrument in a political climate that is changing very slowly.

---

40   See paragraph 6 and 8 of the *Report of the Secretary-General*, document A/44/456, 25 August 1989.
41   *Report of the Secretary-General*, document A/49/257, 25 July 1994.
42   *Report of the Secretary-General*, document A/49/257, 25 July 1994.
43   The 1977 European Convention on the Suppression of Terrorism, ETS no. 90; UKTS 93 (1977), entered into force on 4 August 1978.

India, which had suffered a great deal from terrorist attacks by Kashmiri extremists, strongly supported Algeria's proposal. Like Algeria, it called for an umbrella Convention, which should be a comprehensive, binding international legal instrument establishing universal jurisdiction over and criminality of terrorist activities and offenders.[44] In November 1996 India again stated in the Sixth Committee that attempts to suppress international terrorism on a selective geographical basis had little hope of lasting success. Piecemeal efforts could not be a substitute for a comprehensive international effort. Although it had welcomed the measures addressing specific aspects of the problem, it had now prepared a draft Comprehensive Convention on the Suppression of Terrorism for presentation to all members, which it presented to the Sixth Committee.[45] During the same session of the Sixth Committee, only Cameroon and Ethiopia explicitly made it clear that they endorsed such a global approach.

Although the General Assembly, for the first time, made reference to the possibility of considering in the future the elaboration of a Comprehensive Convention on the Suppression of Terrorism in the preamble of Resolution 51/210 of 17 December 1996,[46] it took indeed until the year 2000 before the subject was seriously discussed. Meanwhile, the General Assembly decided to establish an *Ad Hoc* Committee to elaborate an International Convention for the Suppression of Terrorist Bombings and, subsequently, an International Convention for the Suppression of Acts of Nuclear Terrorism. In 1999, the elaboration on an International Convention on Prevention of the Financing of Terrorism was added to the 'to-do list' of the *Ad Hoc* Committee.

At first, India's proposal was not greeted warmly. During the meeting of the Sixth Committee in November 1997, only Sudan referred to the draft proposal for a Comprehensive Convention on the Suppression of Terrorism, which it supported. No other states made any comment or reference to it at all.[47] However, possibly due to the terrorist attacks on the US embassies in Nairobi and Dar es Salaam in 1998, more states endorsed India's proposal for a Comprehensive Convention on the Suppression of Terrorism during the debates held in the Sixth Committee in 1998[48] and 1999.[49] In 1999,

---

44   *Report of the Secretary-General*, document A/49/257, 25 July 1994.
45   Press Release GA/L/3013, 1 November 1996.
46   *Report of the Sixth Committee of 1998* (document A/53/636, 27 November 1998) once more recommends the General Assembly to consider the elaboration of a Comprehensive Convention. However, this time it adds the intention to consider it 'on a priority basis'. The General Assembly indeed adopts this recommendation in its Resolution A/RES/53/108, 26 January 1999.
47   Press Release GA/L/3063, 14 November 1997.
48   Namely: United Republic of Tanzania (Press Release GA/L/3093, 11 November 1998), Turkey, Bangladesh, South Africa (Press Release GA/L/3094, 11 November 1998), Croatia, Cuba, Uganda (Press Release GA/L/3095, 12 November 1998), Syria and Mongolia (Press Release GA/L/3096, 12 November 1998).
49   Namely: Japan (Press Release GA/L/3134, 12 November 1999); Slovakia, Algeria, Iran, Mongolia, Qatar, Turkey, Cuba (Press Release, GA/L/3135, 15 November 1999); China, South Africa, Kuwait, Malawi, Malaysia, Lebanon, Bahrain (Press Release GA/L/3136, 15 November 1999); Costa Rica (on behalf of the sub-regional group of Costa Rica, El Salvador, Guatemala, Honduras, Nicaragua, Dominican Republic and Panama), Brazil, Angola, former Yugoslav Republic of Macedonia, Indonesia, Democratic Republic of the Congo, Ghana, Liechtenstein (Press Release GA/L/3137, 16 November 1999); Vietnam, and Ethiopia (Press Release GA/L/3138, 18 November 1999).

Canada was the first western state to give its support to India's proposal,[50] although it did warn of the difficulties in drafting such a Convention.

Taking Up the Challenge: A Comprehensive Convention or Actually a Complementary One?

The 27-Article draft text on a Comprehensive Convention on International Terrorism, [51] prepared by India, expresses deep concern about the world-wide escalation of acts of terrorism, as they endanger or take innocent lives, jeopardize fundamental freedoms and seriously impair the dignity of human beings. The text also expresses the conviction that the suppression of terrorist acts is an essential element both in the maintenance of international peace and security and in the sovereignty and territorial integrity of states. It does not, however, make any reference to the legitimate struggle for self-determination, neither in its preamble, nor in its articles. The text seeks to define terrorism within the context of the Convention, and reads as follows:

> 'Any person commits an offence within the meaning of this Convention if that person, by any means, unlawfully and intentionally, does an act intended to cause:
> (a) Death or serious bodily injury to any person; or
> (b) Serious damage to a State or government facility, a public transportation system, communication system or infrastructure facility with the intent to cause extensive destruction of such a place, facility or system, or where such destruction results or is likely to result in major economic loss;
> when the purpose of such act, by its nature or context, is to intimidate a population, or to compel a Government or an international organization to do or to abstain from doing any act.'[52]

Article 3 of the draft Convention states that the Convention is not applicable when an offence is committed within a single state, and when the offender is a national of that state and is present in the territory of that state. The text also urges domestic legislation and the establishment of jurisdiction, and ensures that state parties do not grant asylum to any person involved in a terrorist act. The text also addresses questions of liability, extradition and custody, stating, among other provisions, that state parties should offer the greatest measure of assistance in connection with investigations or criminal or extradition proceedings, including assistance in obtaining evidence. Clearly, this proposal surpasses the ambitions of Algeria (see previous section), since India does propose a conceptual definition. The specification 'within the meaning of this Convention' does, however, limit its applicability. It will nonetheless be included in this draft version until clarity is created on the relationship of this draft Convention to existing Conventions (see below).

---

50   Press Release, GA/L/3137, 16 November 1999.
51   The text of the original proposal can be found in document A/C.6/51/6, 11 November 1996. The original proposal was revised by India in 2000, see document A/C.6/55/1, 28 August 2000.
52   Article 2, para. 1 of the draft Comprehensive Convention on International Terrorism, see document A/C.6/55/L.2.

Prior to 11 September 2001

Before the meeting of the Sixth Committee in November 2000 on measures to eliminate international terrorism, a Working Group of the Committee elaborated on the draft Comprehensive Convention on International Terrorism in October 2000. Introducing the report of the Working Group, Rohan Perera, its Chairman, said that the group had identified most of the key issues it needed in its future work. Among them was the question of the scope of the draft Convention and whether actions by occupying armed forces should be included. Another important issue concerned the relationship of this draft to existing Conventions dealing with specific aspects of international terrorism. The issue of the definition of terrorism in the context of a comprehensive approach to international terrorism was also raised (and therefore the question of whether a definition should distinguish between legitimate acts of people attempting to exercise their right to self-determination and terrorist acts).[53] These key issues will be discussed below.

By 2000, most states appeared to be fairly positive about the Indian initiative. It received the explicit support of the Movement of Non-Aligned countries, as well as that of the Group of Eight's Ministers for Foreign Affairs at their meeting in Miyazaki, Japan, in July 2000.[54] But France too, declared on behalf of the European Union in November 2000 that it should be possible to conclude work on the draft Comprehensive Convention against Terrorism.[55] This is quite remarkable, since the European Union had previously taken the position that it preferred an approach that would focus on specific acts of terrorism. However, in 1998 the European Union started to change its position when it adopted the Action Plan of the Council and the Commission on how best to implement the provisions of the Treaty of Amsterdam on an 'area of freedom, security and justice'.[56] But although most states supported India's proposal, differences remained, as indicated above.

On the question of the relationship between the draft Comprehensive Convention on International Terrorism and the earlier specific Conventions, it was observed that, generally speaking, three different concepts of the purpose of the draft Convention had emerged. The first one's main focus was that the draft Convention should be truly comprehensive in nature, i.e. that it should be an 'umbrella' Convention covering all aspects of terrorism, including aspects already governed by existing Conventions and areas not yet covered, and thereby superseding existing Conventions. The second concept propagated that the draft Convention should provide a framework to cover existing and future activity not already covered in the existing Conventions, and that it should complement the existing Conventions by filling in the gaps with regard to offences not already defined in those Conventions, including new types of offences that might be committed in the future. And the third concept only focused on the filling of gaps in existing Conventions, for example, by extending to the earlier Conventions the ancillary offences and cooperation provisions found in the most recent Conventions (such as the

53　See Press Release GA/L/3167, 13 November 2000.
54　Report of the Working Group, *Measures to Eliminate International Terrorism*, document A/C.6/55/L.2, 19 October 2000, para. 9, p. 42.
55　Press Release GA/L/3167, 13 November 2000.
56　See Article 29 of the Treaty of the European Union; and OJ C 19, 23 January 1999, p. 1.

International Convention for the Suppression of Terrorist Bombings and the International Convention for the Suppression of the Financing of Terrorism).[57]

Western states, including the European states, particularly seem to favour a Convention with a more complementary character. They underscore the importance of preserving the specific Conventions, and stress that the Comprehensive Convention should be used only to fill the legal lacunae. Legal overlaps should be avoided.

On behalf of the European Union, Sweden stated the Union's continued belief that the existing international Conventions on terrorism, as a whole, were considerable achievements. The European Union held that any Comprehensive Convention should therefore avoid creating legal overlaps with the existing body of counter-terrorism Conventions, and represent an added value.[58] In this respect, the Netherlands submitted a proposal, stating that '[t]he provisions of this Convention do not apply if the act described in paragraph 1 constitutes an offence within the scope of a previous or future more specific Convention relating to acts of terrorism'.[59] The United Kingdom also submitted a proposal of a similar character, stating that 'the provisions of the Convention shall not affect the rights and obligations of State Parties under treaties adopted before this Convention', and that 'State Parties are not precluded from adopting treaties which confirm, supplement, extend or amplify the provisions of this Convention'.[60]

Other states, on the other hand, expressed their support for the view that in cases of conflict the Comprehensive Convention would prevail. It was also suggested that for the draft Convention under consideration to be truly 'comprehensive', it would have to be structured in the form of an 'umbrella' or framework Convention.[61]

An issue that is closely linked to the discussion on the relationship of the draft Comprehensive Convention to the existing Conventions, is that of the definition of terrorism. Failure to address that important issue in the draft Comprehensive Convention on International Terrorism would bring into question the utility of the exercise.[62] Some delegations – clearly more ambitious than India – stressed the importance of including a definition of terrorism in the Convention as a necessary condition for the usefulness and applicability of the Convention. The point was made that agreement on more contentious issues would be facilitated if common legal notions of terrorism were first defined.[63] In that connection, Malaysia, on behalf of the Organization of the Islamic Conference (hereafter OIC), called for the inclusion of the terms 'terrorism' and 'terrorist crime' as laid down in the Convention of the OIC on Combating International Terrorism.[64] Malaysia indicated that those essential definitions were based on General Assembly Resolution 46/51 of 9 December 1991. The definition of terrorism given in the Convention of the OIC on Combating International Terrorism reads as follows:

---

57   See document A/C.6/55/L.2, para. 19, p. 45.
58   See Press Release L/2917, 12 February 2001, on the 19th meeting of the fifth session of the *Ad Hoc* Committee on Terrorism.
59   Proposal for a new paragraph 4 to Article 2, document A/C.6/55/WG.1/CRP.7.
60   See document A/C.6/55/WG.1/CRP.16.
61   See, for example, the proposal by Guatemala, document A/C.6/56/WG.1/CRP.1 and Corr.1.
62   See document A/C.6/55/L.2, para. 12, p. 43.
63   Informal summary of the general exchange of views, prepared by the Chairman in the *Report of the Ad Hoc Committee established by General Assembly resolution 51/210 of 17 December 1996, fifth session (12-23 February 2001)*, A/56/37.
64   See document A/C.6/55/WG.1/CRP.30.

'[T]errorism means any act of violence or threat thereof notwithstanding its motives or intentions perpetrated to carry out an individual or collective criminal plan with the aim of terrorizing people or threatening to harm them or imperilling their lives, honour, freedoms, security or rights or exposing the environment or any facility or public or private property to hazards or occupying or seizing them, or endangering a national resource, or international facilities, or threatening the stability, territorial integrity, political unity or sovereignty of independent States.

Terrorist crime means any crime executed, started or participated in to realize a terrorist objective in any of the Contracting States or against its nationals, assets or interests or foreign facilities and nationals residing in its territory punishable by its internal law.'[65]

Malaysia, along with some other states, also stressed that the definition of terrorism must clearly differentiate between terrorism and the legitimate struggle in the exercise of the right to self-determination and independence of all peoples under foreign occupation.[66] In Article 2, paragraph (a) of the above-mentioned Convention, this delimitation had been formulated as follows:

'Peoples' struggle including armed struggle against foreign occupation, aggression, colonialism, and hegemony, aimed at liberation and self-determination in accordance with the principles of international law shall not be considered a terrorist crime.'

It is probably because of this Article 2 that it became possible to formulate a comprehensive definition of terrorism within the framework of the OIC. After all, the use of force in the struggle for self-determination could otherwise easily be characterized as a terrorist act in the meaning of Article 1, especially because it states that *its motives or intentions* are of no relevance.

However, other delegations in the Working Group, among them the delegations of the European Union, expressed their reluctance to accept Malaysia's proposal. According to those delegations, a definition of terrorism was not required, as Article 2 already provided an operational definition, especially in the phrase 'within the meaning of this Convention'. This way of defining the scope of a Convention had been successfully used in the specific anti-terrorism Conventions. Discussion of the definition issue also involved a proposal for the recognition of the existence of state terrorism. However, the point was made that the term 'terrorism' was inapplicable to the conduct of states that were governed by other rules, specifically those relating to the use of force – for example, Article 2, paragraph 4, and Article 39 of the Charter of the United Nations – and that this proposal should therefore not be discussed in this context.[67]

---

65 Article 1, para. 2 of the Convention of the Organization of the Islamic Conference on Combating International Terrorism, adopted at Ouagadougou on 1 July 1999, deposited with the Secretary-General of the Organization of the Islamic Conference; see also http://www.oic.un.org/26icfm/c.html.

66 See once more the proposal of Malaysia (document A/C.6/55/WG.1/CRP.30) on the definition of terrorism and additional paragraphs to Article 2. Similar proposals were made by Lebanon, Pakistan and Côte d'Ivoire.

67 See document A/C.6/55/L.2, para. 12, p. 43.

After 11 September 2001

Days after the attacks of 11 September 2001 the UN Security Council (SC) and the General Assembly each placed the subject of combating terrorism on their agendas.[68] SC Resolution 1373[69] in particular placed a number of far-reaching obligations concerning the financing of terrorism upon the member states of the United Nations. This was remarkable, since this Resolution applies not only to the terrorist acts of 11 September 2001, but also to any future terrorist act. It was especially remarkable in the light of the fact that this Resolution does not provide a definition of a terrorist act. One might therefore wonder how the Counter-Terrorism Committee, which was established by the Security Council in the same Resolution to monitor its implementation, will verify whether or not states live up to their obligations as laid down in this Resolution.

Several times after the September 2001 attacks, the Security Council's Sanction Committee for Afghanistan[70] amended the lists of individuals and entities associated with terrorism whose assets should be frozen.[71] On 8 October 2001, for example, the so-called Bush list[72] was integrated in the Committee's list. Although, in accordance with paragraph 8 (c) and 16 (b) of SC Resolution 1333 (2000), the Committee has the competence to maintain an updated list based on information provided by states and regional organizations, the Resolution explicitly states that those persons or entities should be designated as being associated with Osama bin Laden, al-Qaeda or the Taliban. Nevertheless, some of the names and entities added to the list did not show any clear connection to any of them.[73] Another aspect of concern is the arbitrary way in which names of persons or entities are placed on the list.[74] Although the Committee is a political organ, it functions as a quasi-judicial organ, but without offering the possibility of appealing against its decisions.

Notwithstanding these critical remarks, the number of statements made and actions taken by many members of the international community in the days following the September 2001 attacks indicated the eagerness of the international community to make significant progress in the struggle against terrorism. Moreover, the statements made in

---

68   See GA Resolution 56/1 of 18 September 2001; S/Res/1368 (2001) of 12 September 2001.
69   S/Res/1373 (2001) of 28 September 2001.
70   Established by SC Resolution 1267 (1999) of 15 October 1999.
71   Addenda to the list were issued on 8 October 2001 (SC/7166), 19 October 2001 (SC/7180 and SC/7181), and 9 November 2001 (AFG/163-SC/7206).
72   Annexe to the Executive Order on Terrorist Financing Blocking Property and Prohibiting Transactions With Persons Who Commit, Threaten to Commit, or support Terrorism, 24 September 2001.
73   For example the *Groupe Islamique Armé* (GIA), especially active in Algeria, and the Abu Sayyaf Group, active in the Philippines.
74   See, for example, the case of three Swedish citizens of Somalian origin, namely Abdirisak, Ahmed Aliyusus and Abdulaziz Ali, whose names have been placed on the list because they are allegedly members of the Al Barakaat organization with connections to al-Qaeda. Only after a lot of political pressure did the Swedish government receive the 29 pages of the FBI file, which, according to the three's lawyer, Leif Silbersky, did not provide sufficient evidence. The three have also started an annulment procedure before the European Court of Justice, Case T-306/01 of 10 December 2001, against Commission Regulation no. 2199/2001 of 12 November 2001 and Council Regulation no. 467/2001 of 6 March 2001, which implement SC Resolution 1267 and SC Resolution 1333.

the plenary session of the General Assembly[75] showed that many states call for a speedy conclusion of a Comprehensive Convention against Terrorism. However, it also became clear that many representatives still strongly insist that a definition of terrorism should explicitly exclude from its scope the Palestinians' struggle for independence, or in more general terms exclude the struggle for rights to self-determination. In addition, some states also call for the criminalization of state (or state-sponsored) terrorism in the proposed Comprehensive Convention, thereby referring to the violence used by Israel in the conflict with the Palestinians.[76]

The Working Group underlined the urgency of adopting a Comprehensive Convention on International Terrorism, and stated that they aimed to conclude their work on the Comprehensive Convention during their session from 15 to 26 October 2001 in order to make it possible for the text of the Convention to be adopted before the end of the plenary session of the General Assembly in 2001.[77]

Clearly, this did not happen. The tragic events of 11 September 2001 did not change the positions of UN members to such an extent that obstacles to the conclusion of the Comprehensive Convention were overcome. The main differences in the definitional debate and in the debate concerning the relationship with the specific Conventions apparently remained the same. The Sixth Committee, consequently, decided that the *Ad Hoc* Committee on Terrorism should meet in the week of 28 January to 1 February 2002 to continue its negotiations. During these negotiations the Coordinator of the negotiations and the member states of the Organization of the Islamic Conference both proposed a savings clause and exclusion from the scope of the Convention in paragraphs 2 and 3 of article 18.[78] The Coordinator's proposal reads as follows:

'2. The activities of the armed forces during an armed conflict, as those terms are understood under international humanitarian law, which are governed by that law, are not governed by this Convention.
3. The activities undertaken by the military forces of a State in the exercise of their official duties, inasmuch as they are governed by other rules of international law, are not governed by this Convention.'

The proposal of the member states of the Organization of the Islamic Conference differs by referring in paragraph 2 to 'the Parties' instead of to 'the armed forces', and by inserting the words 'including in situations of foreign occupation'. In paragraph 3, the member states of the Organization of the Islamic Conference propose the words 'in

---

75 See Press Releases GA/9921 of 1 October 2001, GA/9922 of 2 October 2001, GA/9923 of 2 October 2001, GA/9924 of 3 October 2001, GA/9925 of 3 October 2001, GA/9926 of 4 October 2001, GA/9927 of 4 October 2001, GA/9928 of 5 October 2001 and GA/9929 of 5 October 2001.
76 During the plenary meeting of the General Assembly, the following states put forward that they would oppose to a definition that would not on the one hand exclude the struggle for self-determination from the scope of the definition, or would on the other hand criminalize state terrorism: Malaysia, Pakistan, Libya (speaking on behalf of the Arabic Group), Qatar, Bahrain, Iraq, Kuwait, United Arab Emirates, Guyana, Albania, Namibia, Sierra Leone, Zimbabwe, Saudi Arabia, Iran, Oman, Egypt, Yemen, Sudan, Congo and Syria.
77 See document A/C.6/56/L.9, Annexe IV, Informal Summary of the general discussion in the Working, Group, prepared by the Chairman.
78 See document A/57/37, *Report of the Sixth Session of the Ad Hoc Committee established by General Assembly Resolution 51/210 of 17 December 1996*, 28 January-1 February 2002.

conformity with international law' instead of the words 'inasmuch as they are governed by other rules of international law'. Although both proposals seem to have overcome a lot of earlier differences, no consensus has yet been achieved. At the time of writing, the next attempt was set for October 2002.

One remarkable aspect with regard to the counter-terrorism measures developed within the EU in the aftermath of the September 2001 attacks is, however, worth mentioning here. Due to many discussions on the scope of the definition of terrorism in the draft Framework Decision on Combating Terrorism,[79] a non-binding Declaration was added to this document, which reads as follows:

> 'The Council declares that the framework decision on the fight against terrorism covers acts which are considered by all member States of the European Union as serious infringements of their criminal laws committed by individuals whose objectives constitute a threat to their democratic societies respecting the rule of law and the civilization upon which these societies are founded. It has to be understood in this sense and *cannot be construed so as to argue that the conduct of those who have acted in the interest of preserving or restoring these democratic values, as was notably the case in some Member States during the Second World War, could now be considered as 'terrorist' acts. Nor can it be construed so as to incriminate on terrorist grounds persons exercising their legitimate rights to manifest their opinions, even if in the course of the exercise of such right they commit offences* [emphasis added].'[80]

This statement would appear to recognize a distinction between 'terrorism' and liberation struggles and, second, to recognize that people can 'manifest their opinions' without being terrorists. Although this is a non-binding declaration, it does clarify in a way the sudden possibility of rapprochements in the two main camps with regard to the negotiations on the UN's Comprehensive Convention.

Conclusions

Through the years many discussions have taken place on the formulation of a definition of terrorism. The main problem, which has continually formed an impediment to the formulation of this definition, has been the delimitation between terrorism and the legitimate struggle for the right to self-determination by peoples. Third World and Arab states in particular favour a definition that would explicitly exclude from its scope this struggle for self-determination. On the other hand, western states favour a definition that will not mention this right to self-determination at all.

Moreover, states did not agree on the question of whether a selective approach or a comprehensive approach would be the best way of combating terrorism. For a long time the only solution possible seemed to be the drafting of issue-specific Conventions.

Through the years, some futile attempts were made to place the drafting of a Comprehensive Convention on the UN's agenda. However, the strong opposition by the European states in particular frustrated the discussions on this topic. Finally, in 1996

---

79 Proposal for a Council Framework Decision on Combating Terrorism, COM (2001) 521 final, 19 September 2001.
80 Council of the European Union, *Outcome of Proceedings*, 14845/1/01, Rev. 1, 7 December 2001, p. 15.

India managed to propose a draft text for a Comprehensive Convention on the Suppression of Terrorism.

Negotiations on the draft text of the Comprehensive Convention started in 2000. An inventory of the problems was prepared, and, not surprisingly, the formulation of the definition of terrorism was still one of the main obstacles to overcome. However, the relationship of the Comprehensive Convention with other existing anti-terrorism Conventions posed yet another problem that needed to be dealt with. Once more, it appeared that two different approaches were propagated: on the one hand, the approach that emphasized the Convention's comprehensiveness; and on the other hand, the approach that favoured a more complementary role for the Convention. The European states clearly favoured the latter approach.

The September 2001 attacks at first sight seemed to accelerate the process of consensus-building. The Working Group of the *Ad Hoc* Committee on Combating Terrorism declared that it was hoping for a speedy conclusion of the negotiations in order for the General Assembly to adopt the text of the Comprehensive Convention before the end of its plenary session. However, the problems identified earlier appear to be fundamental and, consequently, no agreement has yet been achieved.

The quantity of measures that are currently adopted within the European Union will have their influence on the position that the European Union will take in further UN negotiations. The Declaration attached to the draft Framework Decision on Combating Terrorism might be an opportunity for rapprochements of positions between Arab states and European States on the point of terrorism's definition, but it is, however, no guarantee.

13 Democracy versus Terrorism: Balancing Security and Fundamental Rights

Marianne van Leeuwen

Experts in this book have analysed the ways in which nine European countries have confronted terrorism of various kinds in the recent past and how these countries have reacted to the attacks of 11 September 2001 against targets in the United States. Moreover, they have analysed trends within the European Union and the United Nations in dealing with terrorism. Building on the analyses and conclusions of these authors, I now endeavour to present some conclusions of my own as well.

Past Experiences

All of the European countries featured in this book have suffered terrorist attacks on their territories and/or against their citizens abroad.[1] Their experiences, however, have varied greatly in many respects: in the background and motivations inspiring acts of terrorism, the nationality of the attackers, the severity of attacks, the recurrence of attacks by a particular terrorist organization or particular terrorist organizations, the selection of targets, and the impact of terrorism on public and political life.

At the heaviest tip of the scale, in Spain and in the United Kingdom (especially in Northern Ireland) terrorism has been largely domestic and mainly driven by separatist nationalistic motives. It has been murderous in practice, it has been a persistent problem over a long period of time, and it has had a serious impact on public life. Both in Spain and in the UK, specific anti-terrorism policies and legislation have been installed. In both

---

1   The chapters by Bossis, Cettina, De Lutiis, Malthaner and Waldmann, Muller, Reinares, Rembe, Walker and Walsh provide concise surveys and suggestions for further reading.

M. van Leeuwen (ed.): *Confronting Terrorism*, pp. 227-233
© 2003 Kluwer Law International. Printed in the Netherlands.

countries, major efforts have also been undertaken to alleviate or end problems with (semi-) indigenous terrorism through various kinds of political action, with varying levels of success.

The Republic of Ireland's experience with terrorism has been associated almost entirely with the Northern Irish problem. While the number of victims has been significantly lower than in the UK, the problems in Ireland have been as persistent and effects on public life and politics have been serious.

In the past, France, Italy and Germany have had to cope with vicious terrorism from various quarters – mainly domestic but also international – and they introduced specific legislation and other measures to tackle the problem. In recent years, however, they have enjoyed relative quiet on the terrorist front.

In Greece, domestic terrorism has been endemic over the past twenty-five years. Successive Greek governments have been strikingly unsuccessful in catching the perpetrators. Yet the Greek public at large has not, it is argued in the country chapter, felt particularly threatened. Many victims of Greek terrorists were, in fact, Americans residing in the country.

At the lightest end of the scale, in Sweden and the Netherlands, terrorist attacks (of diverse backgrounds) have in comparison been few and far between, although some of them have been quite severe. Until September 2001, the Swedes and the Dutch had not deemed terrorism a major threat for any considerable period of time, nor had their governments considered specific legislation useful or a range of special policy measures necessary in confronting it.

Current Threat Perceptions and Policy Trends

Against this highly variegated backdrop, the attacks on the United States of 11 September 2001 made a major impact on threat perceptions of citizens and governments in Europe. In particular, they equalized threat perceptions among citizens of EU member states, while governments tried to harmonize their threat and risk assessment methods. Many governments professed that the attacks on the United States were in fact an attack on western democratic values and that democratic states should unite to confront this common danger. European states that had suffered few terrorist problems in the past, such as the Netherlands and Sweden, were roughly shaken out of their innocence – or indifference. While in many European countries accustomed to severe terrorism the shock and indignation were great, the surprise was less and thus fear did not appear to rise so steeply. One important exception was the United Kingdom, where concerns did increase, probably because the British government became the main military ally of the United States in the war on the Taliban and al-Qaeda fighters in Afghanistan. As months passed without major terrorist incidents in Europe, however, and as the United States and their allies managed to inflict major military defeats on the Taliban much more rapidly than many had expected, concern about catastrophic radical Islamic terrorism striking in European countries abated among the general public, even in the UK.[2]

---

2   It would probably take 'just' one major attack by radical Islamic terrorists in a European country to change this mood again, however.

This relative decline of the general fear for a terrorist attack among the public did not prevent governments from planning and implementing new anti-terrorism measures. Their energy was closely linked to developments in Brussels, where the process of decision-making on counter-terrorist measures in the European Union was accelerated after 11 September 2001.

Cooperation with the United States intensified in comparison with the pre-11 September period, when Brussels had tended to react rather reservedly towards proposals from across the ocean for closer transatlantic working relations on combating terrorism and international crime. Now, as a result of threat perceptions or at a minimum an urge on the European side to demonstrate solidarity with the stricken superpower, principled and practical concerns that harsher anti-terrorist measures might produce detrimental effects on society were by and large dismissed or overruled. In the early months after the September 2001 attacks, hardly any criticism was voiced about this development. By the beginning of 2002, however, doubts were beginning to be publicly expressed from various quarters.

Concerns and Remedies

Regarding concerns about terrorism and finding effective remedies to counter the threat, two main themes emerge from the contributions in this book: how can democracies develop additional legal means and how can they improve the role of intelligence and security services in preventing terrorism, while maintaining fundamental rights at the same time?

Legislative Approaches: Problematic Solutions

After September 2001, European governments accelerated decision-making concerning existing plans on harmonizing instruments in the fight against crime in general and terrorism in particular. They also initiated new measures. They did so partially at the purely national level, for instance by improving disaster management scenarios. More-over, they committed themselves to adapting national legislation and policies to new framework legislation agreed upon by the EU Justice and Home Affairs Council and to incorporate United Nations agreements into national legislation and policy in general.[3] Consultations with US officials on these issues became a regular feature.

One specific fundamental change speeded up by the September 2001 attacks has been the introduction of the European Arrest Warrant, intended to harmonize international cooperation within the European Union in bringing felons to justice. Member states of the European Union are now also cooperating in implementing sanctions connected to the EU's list of terrorists and terrorist organizations.[4] They are also committed to implementing the measures associated with the UN's list of terrorists and terrorist organizations. These lists are interrelated and subject to periodic updates.

---

3   Details are found in the chapters by den Boer and van Ginkel, respectively.
4   More details in the chapter by den Boer, including footnote 27.

Until September 2001, countries like the Netherlands and Sweden had maintained that ordinary criminal law sufficed in bringing terrorists to justice. Now they in particular faced the task of addressing what politicians and policy-makers had come to consider as unacceptable lacunae in law. Following policy directions agreed upon by the EU member states, the introduction of specific articles in the penal code dealing with terrorist crimes was proposed, making support for terrorism a punishable act and prescribing severe punishments in cases of terrorist crimes. Even in countries like France, Italy and the United Kingdom, where specific anti-terrorism laws had been in existence for a long time, amendments were made. This was particularly striking in the case of the UK, as the UK Parliament had only enacted a new Anti-Terrorist Law early in 2001. Its ink had hardly dried when the September 2001 attacks inspired the UK Parliament to update anti-terrorism legislation once again.

One particularly difficult problem in introducing legislation dealing specifically with terrorist crimes is the continuing absence of a precise, value-free, universally and legally effective definition of the concept of terrorism. In my introductory chapter I have argued that trying to formulate such a definition is like chasing a pink elephant. The United Nations in any case has failed until now to come up with 'the' definition, and the EU's version first formulated in December 2001 is very broad and thus liable to lead to controversial interpretations. Critics have pointed out that previously acceptable expressions of political dissent such as demonstrations may conceivably come to fall under the EU's new formula for terrorism, with all possible consequences for the alleged offenders and, in final and worst-case analysis, the freedom of speech and expression.

Legally defining terrorist crimes and the supporting, aiding and abetting of such crimes as penal offences is a workable alternative. It is imperfect, however, because terrorists, like ordinary criminals, may be very inventive in developing new techniques and methods. This will mean that legislators will have to continue to adapt the law in order to respond to new terrorist modes of working.[5]

Checks and Balances

The need for strengthening legislative tools against terrorism is widely recognized and accepted by governments and parliaments in the EU member states, as well as a large part of the general public. Still, it is of great importance that the consequences of these changes are carefully supervised, as the sweeping measures recently adopted to increase the security of people may affect fundamental rights if they are not accompanied by strengthened checks and balances. The experiences of European countries with a history of working with specific anti-terrorist legislation are worth considering in this context.[6] The chapter on France analyses criticisms of radical measures, but by and large shows confidence that these measures will contribute to security without adversely affecting the rule of law.[7] The chapters on the United Kingdom and Ireland are less sanguine, arguing that there is a need to heed against the 'migration' of particularly heavy measures against

---

5   See van Ginkel's chapter.
6   See the chapters by Walker, Walsh, Cettina, Malthaner and Waldmann, and Reinares.
7   See the chapter by Cettina.

terrorism into ordinary criminal law. In order to protect democratic standards, it is advisable to stay as close to ordinary criminal law as possible in the prosecution of persons or organizations suspected of terrorist crimes or the aiding and abetting of such crimes. Then, as noted above, there is the danger that non-violent political protest may come to fall under broadly interpreted definitions of terrorist crimes, which could amount to weakening the fundamental right of the freedom of speech. Experience also highlights the risk that the rights of suspects to defend themselves properly may be undermined, which may lead to miscarriages of justice. Finally, the experiences of at least some countries with specific anti-terrorism legislation suggest that an expansion of police powers without sufficient independent checks may conflict with the fundamental rights of individuals. If that occurs, it may undermine the authority and legitimacy of the state.

The implementation of sanctions by member states based on the EU's and UN's lists of people or organizations associated with terrorism may illustrate the risks of developing and strengthening anti-terrorist measures on an international scale, however sensible these measures may be. For those who find themselves listed, the consequences (the freezing of financial assets) are potentially quite serious. This can be considered as perfectly legitimate, as long as it can be proven in court on the basis of sound legal evidence that these individuals or organizations have played an active role in the (financial) support of terrorist activities. The difficulty is, however, that the current procedures of decision-making on listing must be characterized as opaque.[8] In the context of the listings, transparency and proper procedure are lacking. Under the circumstances, there is a risk of misapplications. Such misapplications have indeed already been reported.[9] Well-defined and public criteria for listing will form an impediment against possible arbitrariness. With such criteria, erroneous listings will become less likely and easier to redress if they still occur. Equally important, an independent, accessible and institutionalized procedure of appeal is needed. At present, it does not exist.

The Preventive Role of Intelligence and Security Services: Opportunities and Risks

If the best way to confront terrorism is to prevent it, this automatically highlights the importance of early detection and apprehension of terrorists. And this points above all else to the importance of the work of intelligence and security services and criminal investigation departments, both nationally and internationally. The effectiveness of intelligence services has been criticized both before and after September 2001. Concerns have been voiced about intelligence services' reluctance to coordinate with sister organizations, their reportedly old-fashioned hierarchical and bureaucratic structures, and perhaps most fundamental of all, their lack of analytical capabilities. Most of the criticisms were aimed at US services – they should have prevented the September 2001 attacks, it was claimed – but they rubbed off on services elsewhere as well.

After the September 2001 attacks, both on national levels and within the EU, efforts were made to intensify coordination and cooperation between intelligence services. The

---

8   Details in the chapters by den Boer and van Ginkel.
9   See Rembe and van Ginkel on the controversial case of three Somali residents of Sweden who were listed and then, at least two of them, unlisted again without proper explanation.

United States also urged closer cooperation. The international modus operandi of radical Islamic terrorist activists in particular suggests that the only way to try and deny success to these networking terrorists is for intelligence specialists and criminal investigators to organize their efforts on an international scale as well.[10]

Concomitantly, steps were considered to broaden the competence of services with regard to obtaining information. Such steps, however, are controversial. Human rights organizations and parliamentarians warn against encroachments upon the privacy of citizens. The strengthening of investigative bodies' competences and the facilitation of data exchange between such bodies, while logical and needed on the one hand, does carry risks at the same time, particularly in an international context (not just within the EU but also between the EU and privileged third parties, in particular the United States). Security services may make mistakes, however genuinely they may be committed to protecting democracy and civilians. They or their political superiors may disagree on the evaluation of a particular case, and so on. Innocent and uninformed people may become the victim of errors or differences in interpretation. Again, the crux of the matter is that at present, effective checks and balances are substandard. While a relevant level of democratic control may be realized on a national scale, for instance through regular evaluations by specialized parliamentary committees and proper appeal procedures, similar measures will be much more difficult to institutionalize and implement on an international level. The governments and parliaments of EU member states and the European Parliament should ensure that the extension of the competences of intelligence and security services and criminal investigators be matched with an increase in effective democratic control.

One of the criticisms voiced against intelligence services has been focused on an alleged lack of analytical capability. There may be truth to this accusation, although its relevance may vary from service to service. It is, in any case, only just to point out that intelligence services by the nature of their work will not as a rule boast their successes in the prevention of crime or political violence. Their failures, by contrast, are likely to become glaringly public. Another problem adversely influencing the reputation of intelligence services' smartness may have been that in some cases policy-makers have not acted effectively enough upon substantially correct intelligence reports. It should be noted that many European services have already for some years been expressing concern about suspect activities by (visiting) Islamic radicals in their countries.[11]

Be this as it may, several contributors to this book have remarked that intelligence officials might profit from incidental or perhaps even structural closer cooperation with academic specialists in a whole variety of fields, ranging from history, religious studies and languages to cultural anthropology, psychology and computer sciences. Arguably, even if such academics are no specialists on terrorism, they may still add valuable perspectives to the services' own analyses.

It is not only cooperation with academia that may be useful. The same is arguably true of participation in the public debate and collecting 'open source' intelligence. In recent history, some major successes in apprehending terrorists have been made possible by the alertness of citizens.[12] Public support will materialize under two conditions only:

---

10   More on this subject is found in the chapter by Rembe.
11   See, for example, the chapters by De Lutiis and Muller.
12   See examples concerning the *Rote Armee Faktion* in the chapter by Malthaner and Waldmann.

that citizens recognize serious security threats, and that they feel confident that the officials they entrust with their observations will deal with these in a legal and responsible manner. If intelligence or police services have a history of association with a repressive regime, violent treatment of suspects (innocent or otherwise) or wide and arbitrary undercover surveillance of the general public through tapping or infiltration, this is likely to prevent citizens from coming forward with relevant data.[13]

One major impediment in the creation of trust between citizens and intelligence and security services is the incontrovertible fact that such services, in order to be effective, have to perform a substantial part of their work away from public scrutiny. Yet pursuing the argument about the potential usefulness of cooperation between the public and academics on the one hand and intelligence services on the other, it stands to reason that services will gain by being as open as their responsibilities allow. Services in several countries have now taken to publishing annual reports containing substantially argued threat analyses, explaining views on the development of actual or potential threats to society and democracy. Separate analyses of specific security concerns have also been made public. In some instances, such analyses may stimulate public awareness of potentially dangerous trends or developments, although how to achieve public awareness without creating panic or a general atmosphere of distrust is an important and difficult question. In other instances, published analyses may help to place certain public debates on security issues into a more sober, less frightening perspective, and thus contribute to balanced policy-making.[14] Until now, a number of services have been increasingly providing public information at a national level. At a European and a wider international level more openness concerning expert threat analyses, while arguably desirable, will be more difficult to achieve because the services involved will have to agree on the substance of such analyses.

In sum: protecting democracies against terrorists demands determination, intelligence, effective tools, and in many cases international cooperation. At the same time, parliaments and governments should see to it that fundamental rights are not sacrificed in the protection of democracy against these insidious and mortal antagonists. If democracies cut constitutional corners in their fight against terrorism, their challengers will be the ones to benefit and see their aims fulfilled.

---

13   See especially the chapters by Bossis and Reinares on the importance of constitutional behaviour by services in relation to public trust.
14   See, for example, the chapter by Rembe.

About the Authors

Monica den Boer is Doctor of European Laws and Managing Director of the European Institute for Law Enforcement Cooperation (EULEC) in Brussels.

Mary Bossis is Doctor in International Relations and Head of the Foreign Affairs and Defence Committee of the Institute of Strategic and Development Studies in Athens.

Nathalie Cettina is a Doctor in Public Law and author of *L'antiterrorisme en question* (Edition Michalon, 2001) and *Terrorisme: l'histoire de sa mondialisation* (Edition L'Harmattan, 2001).

Bibi T. van Ginkel is a research fellow at the University of Utrecht, the Netherlands. She is currently working on a dissertation on the UN and combating terrorism.

Marianne van Leeuwen is Doctor in Contemporary History and Deputy Director of Studies at the Netherlands Institute of International Relations 'Clingendael' in The Hague.

Giuseppe de Lutiis is a consultant to the Parliamentary Commission of Inquiry concerning the Mitrokhin Dossier and the Activities of the Italian Intelligence Services (*Commissione Parlamentare d'Inchiesta concernente il dossier Mitrokhin e l'attività di intelligence italiana*).

Stefan Malthaner is a political scientist and doctoral assistant to Prof. Peter Waldmann at Augsburg University, Germany.

Erwin Muller is Dean of the Dutch Police Academy, Director of the Institute of Security and Crisis Management and Professor of Conflict Resolution at the University of Leiden, the Netherlands.

Fernando Reinares is Professor and Chair in Political Science at the King Juan Carlos University in Madrid.

Malena Rembe was a Senior Analyst at the Swedish Security Service and is currently working for the International Criminal Tribunal for Former Yugoslavia in The Hague.

Peter Waldmann is Professor of Sociology at Augsburg University, Germany.

Clive Walker is Professor of Criminal Justice Studies and Head of the Department of Law at the University of Leeds.

Dermot Walsh is Professor of Law, Director of the Centre for Criminal Justice and Assistant Dean for Research (Humanities) at the University of Limerick, Ireland.

Clingendael Publications

Books

Kosovo: From Crisis to Crisis, door Dick Leurdijk en Dick Zandee, Ashgate Publishing Limited, 2001, 218 p. Price: € 39,95 ISBN 0 7546 1554 5

Early Warning and Conflict Prevention; Limitations and Possibilities, Klaas van Walraven (ed.), Kluwer Law International, 1998, 204 p. Price: € 47,73
ISBN 90 411 1064 X

The Clausewitzian Dictum and the Future of Western Military Strategy, Gert de Nooy (ed.) Kluwer Law International, 1997, 192 p. Price: € 38,64 ISBN 90 411 0455 0

The Role of European Ground and Air Forces after the Cold War, Gert de Nooy (ed.), Kluwer Law International, 1997, 227 p. Price: € 43,18 ISBN 90 411 0397 X

The United Nations and NATO in Former Yugoslavia, 1991-1996: limits to diplomacy and force, door D.A. Leurdijk, Den Haag: Atlantische Commissie en Instituut Clingendael, 1997, 152 p. Price: € 6,80 ISBN 90 73329 07 8

Clingendael Studies

On Cores and Coalitions in the European Union. The Position of some Smaller Member States, door Alfred Pijpers (ed.), December 2000, 200 p. Price: € 7,50
ISBN 90 5031 079 6

Crying Wolf? Assessing unconventional terrorism, door Marianne van Leeuwen, September 2000, 78 p. Price: € 7,50 ISBN 90 5031 077 X

Peace or Human Rights? The Dilemma of Humanitarian Intervention, door Barend ter Haar, August 2000, 82 p. Price: € 5,- ISBN 90 5031 076 1

The pretence of peace-keeping: ECOMOG, West-Africa and Liberia (1990-1998), door Klaas van Walraven, November 1999, 131 p. Price: € 7,50 ISBN 90 5031 074 5

Building Blocks for Peace. Civil-Military Interaction in Restoring Fractured Societies, door Dick Zandee, September 1998, 79 p. Price: € 5,- ISBN 90 5031 067 2